BOOKS BY STANLEY P. HIRSHSON

Farewell to the Bloody Shirt (1962)

Grenville M. Dodge (1967)

The Lion of the Lord (1969)

The Lion of the Lord

THE LION
OF THE LORD

A BIOGRAPHY OF

Brigham Young

Stanley P. Hirshson

Alfred · A · Knopf / New York

1973

THIS IS A BORZOI BOOK
PUBLISHED BY ALFRED A. KNOPF, INC.

Copyright © 1969 by Stanley P. Hirshson
All rights reserved under International and Pan-American Copyright Conventions.
Published in the United States by Alfred A. Knopf, Inc., New York,
and simultaneously in Canada by Random House of Canada Limited, Toronto.
Distributed by Random House, Inc., New York.
Library of Congress Catalog Card Number: 70-79334
Manufactured in the United States of America
Published September 26, 1969
Second Printing, January 1973

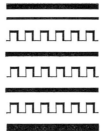

I KNOW THE TWELVE AND THEY KNOW ME. *Their names
are Brigham Young, the lion of the Lord;
Heber C. Kimball, the herald of grace; Parley P. Pratt,
the archer of paradise; Orson Hyde, the olive branch
of Israel; Willard Richards, the keeper of the rolls;
John Taylor, the champion of right; William Smith,
the patriarchal Jacob staff; Wilford Woodruff,
the banner of the gospel; George A. Smith,
the entablature of truth; Orson Pratt, the gauge of
philosophy; John E. Page, the sun dial; and
Lyman Wight, the wild ram of the mountain. And they
are good men; the best the Lord can find; they do the
will of the Lord, and the Saints know it.*

William W. Phelps in 1844.

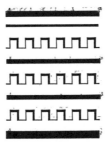

PREFACE

THIS BOOK IS ABOUT A MAN two and a half million people consider a prophet of God. As the author of the first biography of Brigham Young to be written in nearly fifty years and one of the few non-Mormons in this century to deal seriously with Young's religion, I have never allowed myself to forget the esteem in which he is still held. Many times I have wished for the wisdom and powers of a prophet.

To add to my problems, I was told this book could never be written. At the Mormon Church Historian's Office in Salt Lake City, where I received no help or encouragement and was informed that a superficial, uncritical biography of Young published in 1876 had stood up for one century and would last for at least another, several people warned me I would never finish it.

It is my contention and, surprisingly enough, that of several of the Mormon scholars to whom I have talked, that the widely circulated stories of secret materials in the possession of the Mormon church are, if not false, exaggerations. The specialized studies by those who have had free rein in the historian's office—most of them were church officials—support this view, for in my opinion they offer nothing startling. I also believe that those who have previously studied Young have scoured the wrong places. The key to understanding him is not in the Rocky Mountains but in the Midwest and along the Atlantic Coast, not in secret materials but in the rich holdings of Yale University, of the New York Public Library, and of the National Archives, and in such neglected places as the Grenville M. Dodge Papers in Des Moines, the Stephen A. Douglas Papers in the University of Chicago Library, and most especially in the files of the New York *World,* the New York *Tribune,* the New York *Herald, The New York Times,* the Springfield *Republican,* the Philadelphia *Morning Post,* and the other great Eastern newspapers prosperous and wise enough to keep correspondents in Utah, to send their best reporters to Salt Lake City for varying periods of time, and to interview leading Mormons who came east. As the footnotes to this book attest, the amount of material in these journals, most of which I was fortunate enough to use in bound volumes in the New Jersey Historical Society, is astounding, representing a far greater source of information than I expected at the outset. I have found in these newspapers several hundred interviews with Young, his wives, his children, his subordinates, and his enemies, and thousands of articles, both friendly and unfriendly, on the Mormons. Using this material, I have tried as much as feasible to tell the story of Young and his associates in their own words.

In this book I have deviated sharply from most of the previous studies of Mormonism both in interpretation and organization. Every other biography of Young has as much in it about Joseph Smith, Mormonism's founder, as about its subject. These volumes stress the period up to 1844, the year Smith was murdered, and practically ignore Young after he reached Utah. In contrast to my predecessors, I have tried to present Young's early years in perspective and have emphasized his Western experiences, which fully illustrate his powers of leadership. This later period shows that as perhaps no other American of his time Young covered numerous fields: religion, government, exploration, history, business, and sociology. He may not have been the towering giant his church likes to depict, but he was an unusual man nonetheless.

I should like to conclude with a word about the vast hate literature of Mormonism. Several times in this book I have tested the reliability of certain apostates and visitors to Utah by matching their statements with later admissions by Mormon leaders. Those who would summarily discard the writings of all apostates might well compare Catherine Lewis's calmly reasoned and completely neglected *Narrative of Some of the Proceedings of the Mormons* or William Hall's *The Abominations of Mormonism Exposed*, both of which I have used but with extreme caution, with Maria Ward's *Female Life Among the Mormons* and the pamphlets of Maria and Increase M. Van Deusen, which I have rejected as propaganda. It is foolhardy to believe everything an apostate said, but it is equally fatuous to lump the reasonable and unreasonable together and to dump everything written by the enemies of the church into the garbage can. Separating the truth from the untruth is, after all, the primary responsibility of the biographer and his most taxing obligation—to himself, to his readers, and, above all, to his subject.

STANLEY P. HIRSHSON

January 1969

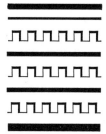

ACKNOWLEDGMENTS

I AM GRATEFUL TO MANY PEOPLE and to many institutions for their aid and encouragement during the writing of this book. I should first like to thank the John Simon Guggenheim Memorial Foundation for a fellowship that enabled me to travel about the United States for a year and study Brigham Young and his religion at leisure. A summer grant from the American Philosophical Society permitted me to complete the manuscript.

For her untiring patience and assistance over a two-year period, I am profoundly indebted to Mrs. Anne Benson Miller, the former librarian of the New Jersey Historical Society, who cheerfully opened to me the vast collection of bound newspapers in that institution. By helping me avoid the use of microfilm she greatly facilitated my work and enabled me to save what little is left of my eyesight. I think it no coincidence that by the time I got through annoying her she decided to retire to her farm in Pennsylvania.

During many months of research in two divisions of the New York Public Library, I was treated with kindness and courtesy. I am especially grateful to Mr. Lewis M. Stark, Mrs. Maud Cole, Mrs. Philomena Houlihan, and Mrs. Sari Shrum of the Rare Book Room and to Mr. Ramon Suarez of the Newspaper Annex.

I am deeply obligated to four good friends who read and criticized the manuscript. Three historians, Professor Arnold S. Rice of Newark State College and two of my colleagues at Queens College, Professors Leonard Tabachnik and Solomon M. Lutnick, undertook this thankless—and gratuitous—task with a cheerfulness characteristic of them. And Professor Mildred W. Weil of Paterson State College applied to the sections on polygamy the insight of the specialist in marriage and family living and many times discussed with me Mormon customs and those of other religious groups.

I also wish to thank Mr. Harmon Walker, now a doctoral candidate at the State University of New York at Stony Brook, who served as my research assistant for a complete year and helped me go through the files of the New York *World*. While pursuing their own researches, Professors Barry Dutka and Edgar J. McManus of Queens College found several valuable references I should otherwise have overlooked. And Mrs. F. L. Stewart, Mrs. Lilia S. Seegmiller, and the late Mr. Stanley S. Ivins talked to me at great length about the history and traditions of the religion they cherish. I hasten to point out that none of the latter is in the slightest connected with any of the interpretations in this book.

Other librarians throughout the country graciously aided me. Among those I am indebted to are: Dr. Everett Cooley and Mrs. Margaret Shepheard of the Utah State Historical Society; Miss Prudence Warner of the King's Daughters Public Library, Palmyra, New York; my very dear friends, Mrs. Lida L. Greene and Mrs. Aloys Gilman of the Iowa State Department of History and Archives, Des Moines; and Mrs. Virginia Hawley and Mr. Anthony Phelps of the Western Reserve Historical Society, Cleveland. I also wish to mention the librarians of the Manuscript Division of the New York Public Library, the Bancroft Library of the University of California at Berkeley, the Special Collections Division of the Stanford University Library, the Manuscripts Division of the University of Chicago Library, and the National Archives. I am also grateful to the librarians and History Department of Yale University for allowing me to cite and to quote from the priceless materials in Beinicke Library.

Finally, I should like to thank Professor David Donald of the

Johns Hopkins University, Professors Herman Ausubel and William E. Leuchtenburg of Columbia University, and Professor Ari A. Hoogenboom of Brooklyn College for kindnesses to me during the writing of this book; Mr. Jack Large, the associate director of the Western Reserve Historical Society, for getting up at five o'clock on three consecutive summer mornings and driving me to the Chardon, Ohio, courthouse; and Mr. Ashbel Green, the Managing Editor of Alfred A. Knopf, for suggesting many ways of improving this volume and for the courtesy and kindness with which he has unfailingly treated me.

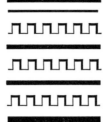

CONTENTS

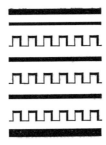

LIST OF ILLUSTRATIONS

follows page 168

Young kept the original of this painting in his office.

Young in later life

Cover of William Jarman's anti-Mormon tract,
    Uncle Sam's Abscess, *1884*

Sketch of Bridger by Frederick Remington for
    Outing *magazine, 1887*

From Uncle Sam's Abscess

Young's most famous son and namesake

Cartoon from humor magazine Puck *which*
    appeared after Young's death

The Lion of the Lord

I

Of Youngs, Kimballs, and Smiths

I

FROM THE CORNERS OF THE EARTH great and famous men journeyed to Salt Lake City to view him. Generals like Ulysses S. Grant and William T. Sherman; statesmen like William H. Seward and Schuyler Colfax; journalists and literary figures like Ralph Waldo Emerson, Horace Greeley, Mark Twain, and Samuel Bowles; explorers and adventurers like Richard F. Burton and Grenville M. Dodge; and showmen like P. T. Barnum came to see and talk to him. For Brigham Young was a marvel of his age: the husband of seventy wives, the father of fifty-six children, the colonizer of vast areas of the West, the Yankee prophet of God, the Moses of the modern children of Israel, the religious imperialist bent upon conquering the world.

Gentiles, or non-Mormons, labeled him a fraud, a dictator, and a murderer. His followers revered him, obeyed his every command, and believed he alone would determine whether they spent eternity in heaven or hell. Among his people his battles with the devil, who needed only the air around him to survive and subvert souls, became legendary and inspirational.

Everyone enjoyed talking about him. In the mid-1860's the Mormons of Salt Lake City told of a woman who asked the prophet for advice. After giving it, Young, wishing to record the incident, said diplomatically: "Let me see, sister, I forget your name." "My name!" the woman retorted. "Why I am your wife." Young asked when they had been married, consulted an account book, slapped his knee, and cried: "Well, I believe you are right. I knew your face was familiar!"[1]

Even in death he remained to Gentiles a symbol of evil. Thousands of readers still remember the title of the story that in 1887, ten years after Young died, introduced to the world the great detective Sherlock Holmes and his companion Dr. Watson. But few people recall that Young was the villain of this novel, *A Study in Scarlet*, which tells of the attempts of two unhappy Mormons, John Ferrier and his daughter, to escape from Utah. The father is murdered, and the heartbroken girl is forced to marry a leading Mormon. Soon she too dies.

In the book's most dramatic scene Young warns Ferrier that the "Sacred Council of the Holy Four" has given his daughter a month to choose between two prominent churchmen. Hearing these words, "John Ferrier groaned internally." Referring to Mormonism's founder, Young adds: "What is the thirteenth rule in the code of the sainted Joseph Smith? 'Let every maiden of the true faith marry one of the elect; for if she wed a Gentile, she commits a grievous sin.' This being so, it is impossible that you, who profess the holy creed, should suffer your daughter to violate it."

Young begins to leave. "He was passing through the door, when he turned, with flushed face and flashing eyes. 'It were better for you, John Ferrier,' he thundered, 'that you and she were now lying blanched skeletons upon the Sierra Blanco than that you should put your weak wills against the orders of the Holy Four!'"[2]

II

YOUNG'S ANCESTORS PROBABLY never suspected the family would someday contain a prophet of God. His great-grandfather, William Young, a shoemaker, first lived in New Hampshire and then moved to Hopkinton, Massachusetts, where he prospered and left ten thousand dollars when he died in 1747.[3] William's son, Joseph, a surgeon, served in the army during the French and Indian War but was killed in 1769 by a falling pole.[4]

Joseph's son, John, was born in Hopkinton on March 7, 1763. From childhood John, a Methodist, was, according to his children, "very circumspect, exemplary and religious." At sixteen he enlisted in the Revolutionary army and six years later married Nabby Howe, a nineteen-year-old girl with blue eyes and yellowish-brown hair. Nabby's family had come to America in 1640, and her relatives included Elias Howe, Jr., the inventor of the sewing machine, and Samuel Gridley Howe, the reformer.

Nabby and John had six sons and five daughters. The fourth boy and ninth child was born on June 1, 1801, five months after the family moved to Whitingham, Vermont. His parents named him Brigham.[5]

Living in an age of backwoods revivals—replete with tales of devils and evil spirits—John and Nabby passed on to their children a deep religious feeling. "Of my mother—she that bore me —I can say, no better woman ever lived in the world than she was," Brigham once said. ". . . My mother, while she lived, taught her children all the time to honor the name of the Father and Son, and reverence the Holy Book. She advised, 'Read it, observe its precepts and apply them to your lives as far as you can. Do everything that is good; do nothing that is evil; and if you see any person in distress, administer to their wants; never suffer anger to rise in your bosoms, for if you do, you may be overcome by evil!' "[6]

John strictly observed the Sabbath. He prohibited the members of his family from taking Sunday walks of over a half hour, and these were to be for exercise, not pleasure. His children, however, told of one Sunday stroll he and a neighbor took. The walkers heard barking, investigated, and saw that their dogs had treed a large black bear. John suggested that the neighbor stay with the bear while he ran home for a rifle, but the friend said he would get the rifle. While waiting, Young feared the bear might try to come down, so he cut a hickory sapling, sharpened one end, and prepared to probe if the animal moved. It soon did. The stick proved inadequate, and the bear reached the ground. Luckily a faithful dog caught the enraged beast by the end of the nose. When the bear opened its mouth, Young thrust the sharp stick down its throat. The neighbor, meanwhile, walked home and ate dinner before returning with a rifle. By then the bear was ready for roasting.[7]

John was better at killing bears than at politics. In 1804 he supported New York in a boundary dispute with Vermont and was dispossessed when his side lost. He moved to Sherburne, in Chenango County, New York, cleared some land, and again farmed.[8]

In 1812 the family moved once more, this time to Pine Grove, now Tyrone, in Schuyler County, New York. "As farmers they were not successful," an acquaintance explained not too fondly. "The father bottomed chairs and exhorted, while the sons did odd jobs for the neighboring farmers, but chiefly employed themselves in hunting and fishing. . . . The characteristics of Brigham's early manhood were idleness and a fondness for recounting stories and dreams."[9]

Nurtured in frontier poverty, Brigham received but eleven days of formal education. "I have been a poor boy and a poor man," he once said, "and my parents were poor. I was poor during my childhood and grew to manhood poor and destitute." Brigham "used to work in the woods logging and driving teams, summer and winter, not half clad, and with insufficient food until my stomach would ache."[10]

Then in 1815 Nabby died. Her children were separated, and Brigham lived with one family after another, working for nothing more than his board. In Auburn, New York, he was apprenticed to a cabinetmaker, painter, and glazier, and he helped build a house later occupied by Governor William H. Seward's father-in-law.[11]

In 1823, while working in Aurelius, three miles west of Auburn, Young met Miriam Works, a seventeen-year-old blonde with blue eyes and wavy hair. A relative called her "gentle and lovable." She and Brigham were married on October 8, 1824.[12]

At this time Young was, according to a neighbor, vigorous, handsome, and "as fine a specimen of young manhood as I have ever known." Unlike his father, who was only five feet three inches tall, he was five feet ten and possessed the Howe family's large frame. His chest, broadened by the rigors of outdoor life, measured forty-four inches, his hair was light, his eyes blue.[13] Throughout much of his life women found him irresistible.

III

IN THE SPRING OF 1829 Brigham moved his wife and three-year-old daughter, Elizabeth, into a log hut in Mendon, New York, the town in which his father and most of his brothers and sisters now lived. Near a little creek he built a sawmill and with lumber felled by his brothers made chairs and baskets that he peddled from door to door.[14]

But by now the Young family was more interested in religion than timber. Three of Brigham's older brothers, Joseph, John, and Phineas, were itinerant preachers for the Methodist Episcopal Reform Church, which Brigham and his wife joined in 1826. The quest for eternal life tortured the brothers. "Brigham," Joseph once said, "there are no Bible Christians upon the face of the earth, and I do not see any possible escape for the human family. According to the writings of the Old and New Testaments, all must go to perdition." For years Joseph refused to smile. And Brigham, flitting from one sect to another, had "more or less a gloom over my feelings from the earliest days of my childhood. I used to go to meetings—was well acquainted with the Episcopalians, Presbyterians, New Lights, Baptists, Freewill Baptists, Wesleyan and Reform Methodists—lived from my youth where I was acquainted with the Quakers as well as the other denominations, and was more or less acquainted with almost every other religious ism."[15]

In Mendon Brigham met a man destined to be his lifelong associate, Heber Chase Kimball. Like Young, Kimball had been born in Vermont in 1801, but he had spent most of his life in New York. A potter in the summer and blacksmith in the winter, he had operated a shop since coming to Mendon in 1820. Six-feet-one-inch tall, with a strikingly bald head and black piercing eyes that seemed to penetrate one's mind and grasp one's thoughts, Kimball was to prove as faithful a companion as a man ever had.[16]

Through the years Young and Kimball carefully hid their true relationship, for they were more than just friends. In 1853 Lucy Smith, the mother of the original Mormon prophet, first disclosed that Young's sister, Fanny, was the stepmother of Vilate Murray, Kimball's wife.[17] Since then three local historians have pointed out that Vilate's mother "was a sister to Brigham Young,"[18] and the Honeoye Falls *Times*, published in Mendon, reported that "Vilate was a niece of Brigham Young." Young, in fact, named his second daughter, born in 1830, for Vilate.[19]

Kimball, on the other hand, twice acknowledged he was related to the Smiths. "Father Joseph Smith and his brother John Smith were," he once noted, "acquainted with the Kimballs: the families were connected by marriage." "My father's father and his brothers intermixed by marriage with the Smiths," he recalled another time. ". . . they mixed up in marriage, and in that way the names became changed."[20] Early Mormonism was a family affair.

IV

SHORTLY BEFORE DYING Kimball told how "when nine years old I laid in my bed and in a vision saw those things that I have since passed through."[21] This parade of events might have made even a grown man shudder, for Kimball's life was almost as eventful as Young's. On the night of September 22, 1827, for example, Kimball, Vilate, John P. Greene, a traveling Reformed Methodist preacher, Father Young, and two of Brigham's sisters, Rhoda, Greene's wife, and Fanny, saw remarkable visions in the sky. "It was so clear," Kimball revealed, "that you could see to pick up a pin. We looked to the eastern horizon and beheld a white smoke arise towards the heavens, and as it ascended it formed itself into a belt, and made a noise like the rushing of a mighty wind, and continued southwest, forming a regular bow dipping in the western horizon. After the bow had formed it began to widen out and grow clear and transparent of a blueish cast; it grew wide enough to contain twelve men abreast. In this bow an army marched from east to west. "We could see distinctly the muskets, bayonets, and knapsacks of the men, who wore caps and feathers like those used by the American soldiers in the last war with Britain; also their officers with their swords and equipage, and heard the clashing and jingling of their instruments of war and could discover the form and features of the men. The most profound order existed throughout the entire army, when the foremost man stepped, every man stepped at the same time: I could hear the step. When the front rank reached the western horizon a battle ensued, as we could distinctly hear the report of the arms and the rush. No man could judge my feelings when I beheld that army of men, as plainly as I ever saw armies of men in the flesh; it seemed as though every hair of my head was alive. . . . Subsequently," Kimball observed, "I learned this took place the same evening that Joseph Smith received the records of the Book of Mormon from the Angel Moroni."[22]

Then in April 1830 Phineas Young was visiting a friend in Lima, New York, when a young man entered the room, walked over to him, held out a volume, and said: "There is a book, sir, I wish you to read." Asked what it was, the stranger answered: "The Book of Mormon, or, as it is called by some, the Golden Bible." "Ah, sir," remarked Phineas, "then it purports to be a revelation." "Yes," the man replied, "it is a revelation from God. If you will read this book with a prayerful heart, and ask God to give you a witness, you will know the truth of this work." The stranger was Samuel H. Smith. "I know the book to be a revelation from God," he continued, "translated by the gift and power of the Holy Ghost, and that my brother Joseph Smith, jun., is a Prophet, Seer and Revelator." Phineas took the book home and read it twice, expecting to expose its errors, but instead he found a new faith.[23]

Questionable are the assertions of Phineas and Lucy Smith that this copy of *The Book of Mormon* was carefully read by most of the Young family and carried about by Brigham.[24] At this time Brigham could barely sign his name, let alone read a complex and detailed work. And Kimball, whose education was as meager as Brigham's, left no evidence he ever learned to read and write.[25]

Kimball remained uninfluenced by these events, and in 1831 he became a Baptist. But about three weeks after his conversion five elders of the newly founded Mormon church came to Phineas's home in Victor, five miles from Mendon. Kimball and Brigham now heard more about Joseph Smith, revelations, and the laying on of hands for the reception of the Holy Ghost. The Mormons,

1832

however, ran into difficult days in Mendon and Victor, for skeptics broke up their meetings by throwing stones.[26]

Sometime thereafter Father Young, Brigham, Joseph Young, and Kimball were chopping wood when they began discussing Mormonism. Soon the forests reverberated with shouts and screams. The men were "hardly able to contain ourselves," Brigham reported, "and we did shout aloud 'Hosannah to God and the Lamb.'" Intensely stirred, Miriam, Brigham, Kimball, Phineas, and Phineas's wife took Kimball's sleigh and in January 1832 drove to Columbia, Pennsylvania, where for six days they observed life in a Mormon colony.[27]

Deeply impressed, Brigham left to discuss things with his brother, Joseph, then preaching in Canada. With Father Young they briefly revisited the Columbia colony and decided to convert. Early in April, Joseph and Father Young became Mormons, and on Sunday morning, April 15, Brigham was baptized "in my own little mill stream; I was ordained to the office of an Elder before my clothes were dry upon me. I passed the day in meeting, and one week from that day I had the pleasure of meeting with and preaching to a large congregation. I think there were present on that occasion four experienced Elders, formerly of the Methodist and Baptist persuasions."[28]

Young immediately gave up his other labors, informing Captain George Hickox, for whom he was making furniture: "I can't finish my work for you here, for from now on I have much more important work to do—preaching the gospel."[29]

Before long the entire Young and Kimball families were baptized. Brigham's wife, his sisters Fanny and Rhoda, his brother-in-law John P. Greene, his brothers Lorenzo Dow and Phineas, and Vilate and Heber Kimball became Mormons. While Phineas spread the gospel in Canada, Brigham and Greene spent the summer of 1832 preaching their new religion around Mendon.[30]

Then on September 8, 1832, Miriam died of consumption at the age of twenty-seven. Young and his two daughters moved in with the Kimballs.[31]

Soon after Miriam's death, Young, Kimball, and Joseph Young decided to visit Kirtland, Ohio, where the Mormons, following one of Joseph Smith's cardinal principles, were assembling. On the way they met a Methodist minister, who warned them Smith was a money-digger and a horse thief. "Joseph Smith I never saw," Brigham answered. "He says that he has received revelations from God, and declared that an angel visited him. He has declared that he found plates, and other witnesses have seen and handled them, from which the Book of Mormon was translated. I know nothing about the witnesses, nor do I care. I went to my Father in heaven and asked with regard to the truth of the doctrines taught by Joseph Smith, and I know they will save all that will hearken to them, and that those who do not will miss salvation in the celestial kingdom of God; and though Joseph Smith should steal horses every day, or gamble every night, or deny his Saviour from the crowing of the cock in the morning until sunset in the evening, I know that the doctrine he preaches is the power of God to my salvation, if I live it. I did not make him a revelator; I have no business to dictate to him."[32]

Encountering Smith while he was chopping wood, Young knew from the first that here was God's prophet. His and Smith's spirits mixed, he later said, as completely as two drops of water.[33] After twenty years of religious traveling, Young was home at last.

That evening, when called on to pray, Young babbled in some incomprehensible tongue. Rising from their knees, the Mormons flocked about Smith, who explained that Young had spoken in pure Adamic tongue. "It is of God," Smith reportedly observed, "and the time will come when brother Brigham Young will preside over this Church."[34]

After spending much of 1833 preaching in Canada, Young induced his relatives and friends to migrate to Kirtland that fall. For Young and his brothers the move involved nothing more than piling their household furniture into a wagon, for they owned no property. But Young's father was forced to sell his forty-five-acre farm for $725.13,[35] and Kimball, deeply in debt, disposed of his pottery shop for $100 and his farm for $375, hardly enough to satisfy the creditors who by court order had attached his personal property. The escape to Kirtland saved Kimball from debtor's prison.[36]

Arriving in Kirtland about the beginning of November 1833, Young built a small frame house for Kimball and himself and began "enjoying the society" of his fellow Mormons. He "had the privilege of listening to the teachings of the Prophet" and worked hard "at my former trade."[37] His fortune was now inextricably intertwined with Smith's—and Smith's religion.

I I

"*A Child or a Fool Could Have Done It*"

I

NEAR THE THIRD DECADE of the nineteenth century, after a long sleep, the gods inexplicably awakened and walked the land. They assumed numerous forms but expounded similar doctrines. In 1828 in Salesville, Ohio, Joseph Dylks announced he was the Messiah, could perform miracles, and could disappear at will. He bragged he would never die and promised his followers eternal life. Run out of town by a mob, Dylks disappeared on his way to Philadelphia, where he planned to establish his holy city.

The following year his disciple Thompson revealed in Vermont that Jesus Christ was a woman and inferior to Dylks, God Himself, and predicted the millennium would arrive in 1832. "They got about thirty disciples on the Sabbath," recorded an observer, "and rolled naked on the floor, men and women together, and committed other sins too revolting to mention. Still they found plenty of followers." Thompson was finally tarred and feathered.

There were others. Matthias strode about New York City with a sword and a seven-foot ruler shouting he would redeem the

1 3

world. And a Connecticut man asserted he was Jesus and exhibited the marks of the nails driven into his hands during the
Crucifixion. After being horsewhipped, he fled.[1]

Dylks, Thompson, and Matthias are now merely names. Their
stories amuse more than anything else. But where they failed,
Joseph Smith, Jr., succeeded. No one reveres Dylks, but nearly
two and a half million people still consider Smith God's prophet.
His religion is today one of the world's fastest-growing.

II

NEITHER BRIGHT STARS NOR WISE MEN bearing gifts greeted
Joseph Smith's birth in Vermont in 1805. Both of his parents
came from old but undistinguished New England families. Joseph
Smith, Sr., usually farmed and sometimes ran a village store, but
at each of the nineteen places to which he moved his family in ten
years he was no more successful than at the previous one. Finally
in 1816 Father Smith brought his wife and eight children to Palmyra, New York, fifteen miles from Mendon and ten from
Rochester, in the heart of the "burnt" or "burned-over" district, a
region continually swept by the fires of religious excitement.[2]

Early in 1828 word spread through Palmyra that young Joseph
had uncovered a treasure on a nearby hill. He later testified that
the angel Moroni had appeared in his room as he prayed on the
night of September 21, 1823, and informed him that God had
work for him. The angel spoke of a book written upon gold plates
that could be translated by using two stones, the Urim and Thum-
mim, deposited with them. With the angel's guidance, Smith found
the plates on the Hill Cumorah, near Palmyra, but greed filled his
heart and Moroni stopped him from carrying them home until
September 21, 1827.[3]

Smith translated the plates, and in the first week of July 1829,
after several revelations from God, he finished *The Book of
Mormon.* It told of the journey of two ancient peoples to America,
the promised land. The first, the Jaredites from the tower of Babel,
sailed to the New World about 2500 B.C., bringing with them
horses, swine, cattle, sheep, and other animals that somehow disappeared by Columbus's arrival. The Jaredites quarreled violently

and were nearly all killed. The second people left Jerusalem about 600 B.C. In the wilderness their leader, Lehi, died and was succeeded by his son, Nephi. As might be expected, however, Nephi's older brothers, Laman and Lemuel, disputed his inheritance and after the tribe reached America killed him. For this God cursed them with a red skin. Destined to redeem the country for the Nephites, who had been wiped out in a decisive battle fought near Palmyra in 400 A.D., Smith had dug up the plates written and deposited by Moroni's father, Mormon, the last of the Nephites.

To insure the authenticity of his work Smith took three men into a field and prayed. Suddenly an angel appeared, plates in hand. "He turned over the leaves one by one," Smith reported, "so that we could see them, and discern the engravings thereon distinctly." Oliver Cowdery, David Whitmer, and Martin Harris signed affidavits swearing they had seen the plates.[4]

But few people believed Smith's stories, and he had to pay a Palmyra printer three thousand dollars, guaranteed by a mortgage on Harris's farm, to publish five thousand copies of his book. Smith and his brothers then hawked the work about the countryside.

One evening after an especially trying day Smith arrived in nearby Victor and exchanged a copy of his book for a room in the local inn. With his remaining few cents he got drunk. Following custom, the boys of the village carried him outside and dumped him into a water vat. "Few would have thought," a local historian noted, "that this awkward, drenched, and drunken young man was destined to a world-wide reputation as the originator and leader of a sect numbering thousands of followers."[5]

On April 6, 1830, Smith established with six members what became the Church of Jesus Christ of Latter-day Saints. Within a month he had forty converts, most of them from around Palmyra. From that town came the Smith family, led by Joseph and his brother, Hyrum; from Manchester, Orrin Porter Rockwell; and from Phelps, the Whitmers. Soon Smith received a revelation to move to Zion, near the western boundary of Missouri, where, the Saints believed, the Garden of Eden once existed, and sent Cowdery and Parley P. Pratt, an Ohio convert, there. On the way the two men stopped at Kirtland, Ohio, near Cleveland, and vis-

ited a colony of Alexander Campbell's Disciples of Christ supervised by Pratt's friend, Sidney Rigdon, northern Ohio's most
famous orator. Believing the millennium was imminent, Rigdon,
who had recently quarreled with Campbell, eagerly read and
embraced Smith's book. In a body his one hundred Campbellites
became Mormons. In January 1831 Smith himself moved to Kirtland, and twenty-two months later he greeted the two men who
would become his most famous disciples and save his reputation
and religion, Young and Kimball.[6]

III

IN THE 1830's, MORMONISM, a mixture of superstition and
tradition, appealed, as Saints themselves admitted, to the fearful,
the credulous, and the downtrodden. Members of the sect, called
"brothers" and "sisters" in contrast to non-Mormons, or "Gentiles," believed that for centuries the earth contained no divine
priesthood. Then, according to Young, the Lord came to Smith
and said: "Bye and bye, you are going to organize my church and
establish my kingdom. I am going to have a church on the earth.
All these churches you have inquired about are wrong; they have
truth amongst them, but not the Priesthood. They lack a guide to
direct the affairs of the Kingdom of God on the earth—that is the
keys of the priesthood of the Son of God." Consequently John the
Baptist appointed Smith to the true Hebraic priesthood of Aaron,
allowing him to baptize converts to God's church, and Peter,
James, and John ordained him to the Melchizedek, or higher,
priesthood, giving Smith "the keys of the Kingdom of Heaven"
and "the power to dispense the blessings of the kingdom." Like
Christ, Smith and his anointed could now confirm by laying on
hands for the reception of the Holy Ghost. Smith declared himself
a "Seer, a Translator, a Prophet, an Apostle of Jesus Christ, and
Elder of the Church through the will of God the Father, and the
grace of your Lord Jesus Christ" and created a church hierarchy
that was eventually led by the First Presidency, the prophet and
two hand-picked advisors.[7]

Then as now the Mormons viewed life—and history—as an
endless struggle with the devil. "There are only two churches on

the earth," Young explained, "only two parties. God leads the one, the devil the other." As Orson Pratt, Parley's brother, saw it, "The Devil, through the medium of Apostates, who subverted the whole order of God, by denying immediate revelation and substituting in place thereof, tradition and ancient revelation as a sufficient rule of faith and practice," created the Roman Catholic Church. In the sixteenth century the Protestant Reformation split "Satan's Kingdom," but the true faith rested upon Smith's revelations. Anything the Mormons disliked became the devil's design. Accordingly Kimball blamed his financial troubles in Mendon on Satan's attempts to foil God. Inspired by the devil, five or six creditors sued him, "but to their great disappointment, God opened my way so that I obtained money to pay all my debts and liberate myself from them."[8]

In 1833 Mormonism closely resembled other backwoods religions. Emotionalism reigned, and one observer found himself "in the midst of shoutings, wailing, fallings, contortions, trances, visions, speaking in unknown tongues, and prophesying that require the pen of a Trollope to describe. The timid were frightened, the credulous believed, and we were frequently eye witnesses to scenes of a strange and unnatural conduct of Mormons professedly under the influence of the Spirit, that staggered the disbelief of the most stable and incredulous."[9]

In their meetings the Saints, like other sects, emphasized the gift of tongues. Particularly talented in this area was Eliza R. Snow, later the wife of both Smith and Young, who frequently rushed up to some woman and exclaimed: "Sister, I want to bless you!" Laying hands on the subject's head, she would pour forth a blessing supposedly in an ancient and long-forgotten language.[10]

Mormonism also stressed faith healing. The Saints asserted they miraculously cured hundreds of people afflicted with cancer, palsy, brain fever, crushed skulls, and other maladies caused by evil spirits. Franklin D. Richards once advertised "Bones set through Faith in Christ," and another elder recorded: "While commanding the bones, they came together, making a noise like the crushing of an old basket."[11] Perhaps Young best summarized Mormonism: "You understand who we are; we are of the House of Israel, of the royal seed, of the royal blood."[12]

IV

MORMONISM FLOURISHED because of something besides Smith's ingratiating personality and the power of his book.[13] Both were important and immediately separated him from the other prophets of his day, but alone they did not guarantee success. Equally unsatisfactory is the common Mormon assertion that the faith thrived because it represents truth, which all religions say they possess.

Believing divine intervention preserved the Saints, Young himself disagreed with the personality theory. One day when a friend suggested Smith's revelations would have perished with him had his successor been less talented, Young exclaimed: "You know nothing at all about the revelations of the Church of Jesus Christ of Latter-day Saints. It didn't depend on Brigham Young or any other man to lead the new Israel. A child or a fool could have done it."[14]

Some of Young's contemporaries connected Mormonism's rise with emotionalism. Many clergymen "occupy all their time in quarrels upon the doctrinal points," the New York *Herald* noted in 1858, "and their flocks, becoming disgusted with theological disputes, wander into forbidden fields. Within the Church there is no excitement, no enthusiasm, and there is a certain class of believers who crave this excitement and enthusiasm. These persons wander away to Mormonism, or spiritualism, or Fourierism, or transcendentalism. . . . It was thus that Brigham Young was enabled to establish a State half way between our Atlantic and Pacific coasts."[15] Still, other sects claiming revelations, the power to heal, and the gift of tongues quickly faded away. In themselves miracles led nowhere.

Smith added to emotionalism and *The Book of Mormon* other things. From the beginning he molded Mormonism as the Catholicism of the future. In an age of turmoil he offered bold, exact, positive answers to ancient questions about God and life. Mormonism's dogmatism attracted those who otherwise would have succumbed to the disorder and fears of the pre-Civil War period.

As much as a church, moreover, the Saints created a society. In specially designated communities they gathered and became in every sense a people. Often migrating in groups, they proved a new society following some model could even be moved physically from one part of the world to another.

Mormonism became not just a religion but a way of life. In Occidental society perhaps only Orthodox Jews, who, unlike the Saints, did not seek converts and distrusted the few who voluntarily came to them, demanded so much from a member. Constantly weeding out unbelievers, Mormon generals led into religious battle a superbly organized and disciplined army.

None of these, however, was the most potent Mormon weapon. Asked late in life to explain the power of his church, Young responded: "The people think it is Brigham Young; but it is not—it is his Priesthood." He admitted that if elected President of the United States he would hold the priesthood above his office.

Mormons revered their priesthood as Roman Catholics loved theirs. From Smith and Young down they believed heaven guided it. But in his greatest religious innovation Smith made every loyal adult white man a priest. Uniquely, the church had no laity, each man having the authority to act and speak in God's name. And from the beginning women shared this power and feeling of belonging. Smith thus brought into service not a few dedicated workers called clergy but a limitless, unpaid, ever-increasing aggregate of Saints.

In a favorite story Young described the magical hold of the priesthood. A gentleman who visited the Saints when they had fifteen thousand members asked: "Mr. Smith, what has enabled you to gather this large body of people, and by what power of government do you rule them and keep them thus united?" "Sir," the prophet answered, "I teach them correct principles and they govern themselves." By correct principles, Young explained, the prophet meant: "I have given them all the Priesthood of the eternities, and I have them sealed to me worlds without end."

Neither Young nor Smith nor any other man was better than the priesthood, which Mormons honored not because their leaders held it but because, each man continually assured himself, "I hold it." Beginning a religious ritual, a Saint immediately acknowledged his indebtedness to it: "In the name of the Lord Jesus Christ, and by the authority of the Priesthood which I hold, I lay hands upon your head to ordain you." For the priesthood no sacrifice became too great. Indeed, Saints demanded the privilege of suffering for it. In its name elder competed with elder, bishop with bishop, apostle with apostle, and branch with branch. Thousands and then hundreds of thousands of people were converted, cities and temples erected, and overseas branches established, all, as Mormons still brag, without payment by the church of a penny in salaries.

Few Mormons voluntarily surrendered the priesthood. Throughout the nineteenth century Saints fought with Smith or Young, left the old church, and created new organizations. Without exception, however, these apostates said they headed God's ministry and set up hierarchies identical to that of the Mormons. They quarreled not with the priesthood but with those they accused of misusing it.

From the earliest days of the church, then, Smith opened up with his revelations this new dispensation of the priesthood. In the 1830's whenever six people received a testimony from God and converted, traveling elders organized church branches. If three of the six were men, the elder usually ordained one a priest, another a teacher, and the third a deacon. Young was even luckier, being made an elder on the day he was baptized. Entering the priesthood, each man assumed duties he allowed his wife to share. Everyone was taken care of.

The Mormons, moreover, developed a group of Melchizedek priests as militant as the Jesuits. This Order of the Apostles of the Seventies, later the Council of Seventies, supervised the church's missionaries. During Young's lifetime its membership rose to between five thousand and seven thousand of the foremost men in Mormondom, almost all of them young, vigorous, intelligent, and imbued with the courage and audacity that came from thinking they spoke for God.

Within this matrix Mormonism expanded almost effortlessly. Had Smith not awarded the priesthood with his revelations, his church—and his reputation—might have quickly perished, and he might well be remembered today, if at all, as another spiritualist. But once he organized his church nothing could stop it. The deaths of a hundred worn-out administrators only brought a thousand eager young men of mark up from the Seventies. Never slowing down, Mormonism, the first religion to extend the priesthood to every loyal man, marched relentlessly on.[16]

V

"WHEN I WENT TO KIRTLAND," Young observed, "I had not a coat in the world, for previous to this I had given away everything I possessed, that I might be free to go forth and proclaim the plan of salvation to the inhabitants of the earth. Neither had I a shoe to my feet, and I had to borrow a pair of pants and pair of boots." Once there Smith advised Young to "go to work and aid in building up Kirtland, and never again assist in building up Gentile cities, and gather together something for yourself." Within five years Young, working for a dollar a day in the winter and preaching all summer, accumulated five thousand dollars.[17]

On March 31, 1834, Young remarried. His new bride, Mary Ann Angell, a plump, round-faced woman of thirty from Seneca, New York, "took charge of my children," Young explained, "kept my house, and labored faithfully for the interest of my family and the kingdom."[18]

Serious matters soon ended Young's honeymoon. In Independence, Jackson County, Missouri, twelve hundred Saints were engaged in an undeclared war with the Gentiles. To the chagrin of their neighbors, the Mormons, although unsympathetic to the plight of the Negro, owned no slaves. And they urged the nearby Indian tribes to cooperate rather than annihilate each other. Thus angered, mobs of Gentiles burned Mormon houses, destroyed a Mormon newspaper, and tarred and feathered several Saints.[19]

Although Zion's population exceeded Kirtland's, Smith decided to lead a relief force to Missouri and urged every able-bodied man to join it. Brigham volunteered immediately, but Joseph Young hesitated. Then one day the brothers bumped into Smith, who remarked: "Brother Brigham and brother Joseph, if you will go with me in the camp to Missouri and keep my counsel, I promise you, in the name of the Almighty, that I will lead you there and back again, and not a hair of your heads shall be harmed." The three men clasped hands, confirming the covenant.[20]

On May 5 fewer than two hundred Saints, carrying old muskets, pistols, knives, and resharpened swords, started for Missouri. Averaging forty miles a day, they finally reached their destination, only to be told by Smith, who realized his force was inadequate, that the Lord desired them to return to Kirtland and raise enough money to buy out the Gentiles in Jackson County. In July they started home. But years later Young bragged how, armed with a rifle, a bayonet, and a dirk, he had stormed about Missouri threatening to allot to each of his enemies six feet of land "in the burying yard."[21]

VI

SHORTLY AFTER RETURNING TO KIRTLAND the prophet invited Brigham and Joseph Young to his house. The brothers sang some songs, and Smith settled back and said: "Brethren, I am going to call out Twelve Apostles. I think we will get together, by-and-by, and select Twelve Apostles, and select a Quorum of Seventies from those who have been up to Zion, out of the camp boys." "He had a revelation when we were singing to him," Brigham revealed. "Those who were acquainted with him knew when the Spirit of revelation was upon him, for his countenance wore an expression peculiar to himself while under that influence . . . there was a peculiar clearness and transparency in his face."[22]

Early in 1835 Cowdery, Whitmer, and Harris, the witnesses to *The Book of Mormon*, ordained the Twelve. Young was the second apostle chosen and Kimball the third. The apostles were informed, Kimball remembered, that they "should have the power to heal the sick, cast out devils, raise the dead, give sight to the blind, have the power to remove mountains, and all things should be subject to us through the name of Jesus Christ, and angels should administer unto us, and many more things too numerous to mention."[23]

In March 1836 another joyful event occurred. After years of toil, during which Smith supervised the stonecutters, Rigdon helped the masons, and Young worked as a carpenter and designed the interior woodwork, the Kirtland temple—God's house —was finished. For four days all the men remained inside it, fast-ing, praying, anointing, and washing. During the final service a veil concealed Smith and Cowdery. When it was lifted, Smith announced: "We have seen the Lord. He was standing upon the breastwork of the pulpit, before us, and under His feet was a paved work of pure gold in color like amber. His eyes were as a flame of fire, the hair of His head was white like the pure snow." Smith added that Moses, Elias, and Elijah had also attended the ceremony.[24]

Kimball noticed someone else there. "During the ceremonies of the dedication, an angel appeared and sat near President Joseph Smith, sen., and Frederick G. Williams, so that they had a fair view of his person. He was a very tall personage, black eyes, white hair, and stoop shouldered; his garment was whole, extending to near his ankles; on his feet he had sandals. He was sent as a messenger to accept of the dedication."[25]

VII

YOUNG ALWAYS POSSESSED boundless faith in the prophet. At a meeting in the temple in the fall of 1836, for example, when several of the Twelve, the three witnesses to *The Book of Mormon*, and some other church leaders tried to make Whitmer the head of the church, Young, Father Smith, and Kimball opposed the scheme. "I rose up," Young related, "and in a plain and forcible manner told them that Joseph was a Prophet, and I knew it, and that they might rail and slander him as much as they pleased, they could not destroy the appointment of the Prophet of God, they could only destroy their own authority, cut the thread that bound them to the Prophet and to God, and sink themselves to hell." One of Smith's enemies, Jacob Bump, "an old pugilist," grew infuriated, shouted "How can I keep my hands off that man," and tried to attack Young, but he was held down. "This was a crisis," Young explained, "when earth and hell seemed leagued to overthrow the Prophet and Church of God. The knees of many of the strongest men in the Church faltered."

Convinced the dissenters wanted to kill Smith, then returning from Michigan, Young and the prophet's brother, William, drove out in a horse and buggy and met the stagecoach carrying Joseph home. The brothers exchanged places, and the prophet slipped into Kirtland unnoticed.

Shortly thereafter a man named Hawley arrived in town. While plowing a field in New York State, he had decided to walk barefoot to Ohio and inform Smith the Lord had rejected him. In Kirtland he was hauled before a court of bishops and excommunicated. Undaunted, Hawley marched through the city in the middle of the night crying, "Woe! woe! unto the inhabitants of this place." At that Young grabbed his pants, his shoes, and a cowhide, ran outside, jerked Hawley about, and warned him that unless he let the people sleep he would be sorry, "for we had the Lord's Prophet right here, and we did not want the Devil's Prophet yelling round the streets. The nuisance forthwith abated."[26]

Soon the Mormon leaders faced a far different problem. In Kirtland Smith permitted almost anyone to perform the marriage ceremony. Smith, Cowdery, Rigdon, Williams, Young, and Don Carlos Smith, the prophet's younger brother, calling themselves either justices or elders, conducted the service.[27] When word leaked out, the county grand jury indicted the prophet, Don Carlos, and Father Smith for "solemnizing marriages without license." For the same offense Rigdon was fined a thousand dollars.[28]

Even more damaging were Smith's financial failures. Enticed by the fever of the day, the prophet speculated in land on a grand scale. To further his activities he borrowed ninety thousand dollars in 1836 alone. Then in November 1836 he received a revelation to establish a bank with a capital stock of "not less than four million dollars." Rigdon became president of the Kirtland Safety Society Bank, and the prophet became its cashier.[29]

Unfortunately the venture fell flat before it began. Deeply involved in Ohio politics, Smith in election after election had delivered to the Democratic party the Mormon vote. Late in 1836 the Whigs in the state Senate retaliated by refusing to charter his bank.[30]

Undaunted, the Saints created the Kirtland Safety Society Anti-Banking Company, stamped *anti* before and *ing* after the word "bank" on the notes engraved for the Safety Society, and circulated them. Dozens of prominent Mormons, including Warren Parrish, Smith's secretary, Whitmer, Rigdon, Young, Kimball,

Lorenzo Young, Joseph Young, and John P. Greene publicly signed the incorporation agreement binding "ourselves to each other under the penal sum of one hundred thousand dollars."[31]

As the bank's stock ledger attests, the undertaking was grossly speculative. Offering as security little more than their homes, important Saints subscribed to large numbers of shares at fifty dollars each. Rigdon and Smith each purchased three thousand shares, Smith's wife, Emma, bought twelve hundred, and Joseph Young and Kimball took a thousand each. Depositing his only payment, seven dollars cash, on December 9, 1836, Young purchased two thousand shares.[32]

Once the bank circulated its notes the Whig press moved in for the kill. "During the past two days," the Cleveland *Gazette* announced in mid-January, "an emission of bills from the society of the Mormons has been showered upon us. As far as we can learn there is no property bound for their redemption, no coin on hand to redeem them with, and no responsible individuals whose honor or whose honesty is pledged for their payment. They seem to rest upon a spiritual basis." The Painesville *Telegraph* asked: "Is not the Bank controlled by men who are in the habit of borrowing *ten* dollars for every dollar they lend?"[33]

The notes immediately dropped in value. Within two weeks they were worth twelve and a half cents on the dollar. Then in the spring of 1837 a nationwide panic struck. Reputable banks in New York, Philadelphia, and other cities closed their doors.[34]

The Saints groped for a way out. With disaster imminent Rigdon transferred his property in Kirtland to his daughter, Nancy, and Young gave his father-in-law land worth six hundred dollars.[35]

In desperation Smith sent several of the Twelve to cities in which the bank's notes were still accepted. Luke Johnson passed off an unknown quantity, and John F. Boynton got rid of twenty thousand dollars' worth. During the first three weeks of August 1837, while the prophet toured Canada, Young reportedly disposed of forty thousand dollars in valueless scrip in New York. "It is said," observed William Hall, a Mormon for seven years, "there were writs for him in great plenty, but he returned after his mission was completed."[36]

Soon after returning to Kirtland, Young, Smith, and some other prominent Saints assembled at the prophet's house and for a week lived on rum, brandy, gin, and port wine. During that time, according to the affidavit of one witness, Smith asserted he had founded the bank because God had told him "to *milk the Gentiles*." He also admitted the bank's notes were worthless and said he had signed them only because he had been paid to do so.[37]

Hardly a prominent Saint escaped unharmed. In 1837 and 1838 twenty-eight suits were brought against Reynolds Cahoon, Joseph and Hyrum Smith, and Young, almost every one of them naming at least two Saints as defendants. The plaintiffs received damages totaling $24,438.39 plus, in each case, court costs. Out of court settlements amounted to nearly ten thousand dollars.[38]

In another way the bank fiasco proved expensive. In September three of the Twelve, Luke Johnson, Lyman E. Johnson, and Boynton, denounced Smith and were excommunicated by a church conference. But at the meeting Young, the prophet's staff, defended Smith and urged Boynton to confess his sins.[39]

One Sunday while Smith was in Cleveland, Parrish, Boynton, and their followers, armed with pistols, swords, and bowie knives, stormed into the temple and attempted to drag from the pulpit Father Smith, who was censuring them. When the prophet's brother, William, rushed to his father's aid, Boynton shoved a sword to his chest and shouted: "If you advance one step further, I will run you through." Frightened women and children escaped through the temple windows.[40]

Still not satisfied, Boynton, Luke Johnson, and Orson Hyde, one of Rigdon's original converts, sued Joseph, Hyrum, and Rigdon and were awarded $2,643.45 plus court costs. As late as 1850 Boynton told a friend: "Mormonism is all humbug from first to last."[41]

Another indication that God had momentarily deserted the Saints came in mid-October, when Hyrum's wife grew ill. Young was called in, prayed with her, laid hands on her, and assured Hyrum she would recover. That evening she died. Two months later Hyrum remarried.[42]

The Mormon world at Kirtland soon collapsed completely. To meet the financial judgments against the church, the temple, worth forty thousand dollars, was auctioned off for $150. And the night

before the sheriff was to confiscate the Mormon printing establishment to pay a two thousand dollar judgment against Smith and
Rigdon for issuing illegal currency, the building burned to the
ground.[43]

On the morning of December 22, 1837, Young fled. Although
his church has steadfastly maintained he left "in consequence of
the fury of the mob spirit that prevailed in the apostates,"[44] he
ran off to escape his creditors. In the middle of the night of January 12, 1838, Smith and Rigdon also started for Missouri, pursued for two hundred miles, according to Mormon historians, "by
human blood-hounds, armed and thirsty for their lives."[45]

In February in a letter endorsed by Boynton and Luke Johnson, Parrish reviewed the episode for the nearby Painesville
Republican. He had, he admitted, listened "with feelings of no
ordinary kind" when Smith "declared that the audible voice of
God, instructed him to establish a Banking–Anti Banking institution which like Aaron's rod should swallow up all other Banks,
and grow and flourish and spread from the rivers to the ends of the
earth, and survive when all others should be laid in ruins. I have
been astonished to hear him declare that we had $60,000 at our
command, when we had not to exceed $6,000 and could not
command any more; also that we had but about ten thousand
Dollars of our bills in circulation when he, as Cashier of the institution, knew that there was at least $150,000. Knowing their ex-
treme poverty when they commenced in this speculation, I have
been not a little surprised to hear them assert that they were worth
from three to four hundred thousand Dollars cash, and in less than
ninety days after, became insolvent without any change in their
business affairs. But such has been the audacity of these boasting
blasphemers, that they have assumed the authority to curse, or to
bless, to damn, or to save, not only this Church, but this entire
generation, and that they hold their destinies in this and that
which is to come." By "lying deception and fraud" Smith and
Rigdon "have reduced their followers to wretchedness and want."
To keep the printing press from his enemies Smith ordered it
burned and escaped in the night. "But the most astounding thing
after all is, that men of common sense and common abilities
should be so completely blinded as to dispense entirely with the

evidence of their sense, and tamely submit to be led by such men. . . . However justice seems to be in pursuit of the workers of iniquity; and sooner or later will overtake them; they will reap a just and sure retribution for their folly. This then is the conclusion of the whole matter; they lie by revelation, swindle by revelation, cheat and defraud by revelation, run away by revelation, and if they do not mend their ways, I fear they will at last be damned by revelation."[46]

Striving to be impartial, the *Republican* offered to publish a reply to Parrish's letter "should any be offered with the author's name thereto attached." No defense of Smith, Rigdon, and Young ever came.[47]

III

The Hand of God

I

A MAN MUST LEARN to overcome misfortune. Until now, Young had never prospered, but he had known nothing comparable to the Kirtland disaster, which forced him to sneak out of town on the fastest horse he could find. What would he do now?

Leaving Kirtland, Young headed for Dublin, Indiana, where his brother Lorenzo and some other Saints were wintering. A few weeks after his arrival, the prophet, Rigdon, and George W. Robinson rode in. Having lost his temple, his printing press, his money, and many of his followers, Smith asked about a job sawing logs. "Brother Brigham," he said, "I am destitute of means to pursue my journey, and as you are one of the Twelve Apostles who hold the keys of the kingdom in all the world, I believe I shall throw myself upon you, and look to you for counsel in this case." "If you will take my counsel," answered Young, "it will be that you rest yourself and be assured, brother Joseph, you shall have plenty of money to pursue your journey." Relief came several days later, when a Saint sold his tavern and gave the prophet three hundred dollars.

Proceeding toward Far West, in Caldwell County, Missouri, Smith and Young met John P. Barnard, a Saint who agreed to drive the prophet the rest of the way in his wagon. While crossing a frozen prairie, one of the wagon's axletrees sprung. When Joseph said he could fix it, Barnard replied: "I am a blacksmith and used to work in all kinds of iron, and that axeltree is bent so round that to undertake to straighten it would only break it." Undaunted, Smith pried it into place, and it gave no more trouble. When the travelers reached Far West on March 14, 1838, Barnard vowed never again to contradict a prophet of God.[1]

The trip did wonders for both Smith and his religion. Two months of travel restored his hopefulness and love of life. Soon Missouri contained eight to ten thousand Saints, including a thousand from Kirtland.[2]

Just after reaching the state, Smith led some men to the west fork of the Grand River, about fifty miles north of Jackson County, and located the Valley of God, where, he insisted, Adam had lived following his expulsion from the Garden of Eden, now Independence, and where, he predicted, a great Mormon city, Adam-ondi-Ahman, would rise. "Brethren," Smith called to Young and Kimball, "come along with me, and I will show you something." Smith led them to the ruins of three stone altars and explained: "There is the place where Adam offered up sacrifice after he was cast out of the Garden." Situated on a high bluff, Adam-ondi-Ahman was planned by Young.[3]

II

FOR PEACEFUL PEOPLE no place was worse than Missouri in the 1830's. Within the state raged every imaginable conflict: slaveholder fought abolitionist; Indian battled white man; and Democrat clashed with Whig. To this was added another struggle: Saint versus Gentile. As Young observed, the Missourians in 1838 began "to stir up the old mob spirit, riding from neighborhood to neighborhood making inflammatory speeches, stirring up one another against us. Priests seemed to take the lead in this matter."[4]

In June the Mormons, caught in this bloodthirsty atmosphere, formed a secret society called the Daughters of Zion, the Sons of Dan, or, most commonly, the Danites. Its leader and organizer was Dr. Sampson Avard; its purpose was to drive from the region all anti-Mormons. Every Danite swore unquestioning allegiance to the heads of the church and agreed to forfeit his life if he revealed the society's secrets. In turn, the First Presidency— Joseph, Hyrum, and Rigdon—blessed the members, "declaring," in Avard's words, "that they should be the means, in the hands of God, of bringing forth the millennial kingdom."[5] The prophet once pledged to give the Danites "his head for a foot-ball" if he led them into difficulty.[6]

The society's leaders concocted numerous schemes for battling the enemy. Rigdon and Lyman Wight sent twelve Danites to induce the Indians to join the Mormons in a war against the people of Missouri, and another twelve, the destruction company, were specially trained in burning and wrecking. According to Thomas B. Marsh, then the president of the apostles, Avard once proposed to start a pestilence among the Gentiles "by poisoning their corn, fruit &c., and saying it was the work of the Lord; and said Avard advocated lying for the support of their religion, and said it was no harm to lie for the Lord."[7]

Smith, meanwhile, infused courage into the Danites by telling them stories of the glory and battles to be won. He promised that God would send angels to help them and swore that enemy bullets were powerless against the Danites, two of whom could put to flight ten thousand Gentiles. After listening to such talk, Alexander McRae admitted: "If Joseph should tell me to kill [Martin] Van Buren in his presidential chair, I would immediately start and do my best to assassinate him, let the consequences be as they would."[8]

For decades the embarrassed Mormon hierarchy denied that such a band ever existed. "I have no confidence in the statements about the Danites," John Taylor said after becoming president of the church. "I was at Far West during all these operations and never knew anything about such doings." The *Millennial Star*, the Mormon magazine in England, also insisted that "there never has been in fellowship among the Saints, either a secret or public band called 'Danites,' or by any other name. This is a false and slanderous accusation, originated by Missouri murderers, to justify themselves in butchering men, women, and children."[9]

But such church leaders as William W. Phelps, Marsh, Orson

Hyde, Reed Peck, John Corrill, and Avard himself, all of whom temporarily or permanently apostatized, testified otherwise. Even more damaging were the accounts of men who never left the church. In his diary Oliver B. Huntington, later Young's brother-in-law, often mentioned the Danites, and Albert P. Rockwood, Young's nephew and adopted son, told his parents about the military companies, "called Dan because Prophet Daniel has said the Saints shall take the Kingdom and possess it forever," then drilling in Far West. "Bro. Joseph has unsheathed his sword & in the name of Jesus declares that it shall not be sheathed again until he can go into any country or state in safety and peace."[10] Occasionally called Shenpips, the Danites, whose existence Mormon leaders acknowledged several times in the 1850's, remained for a half century an important Mormon force.

In a fiery Fourth of July address at Far West, Rigdon reflected this militarism. He warned "all men, in the name of Jesus Christ, to come to us no more forever. The man, or set of men, who attempts it, does so at the expense of their lives; and the mob that comes on to disturb us, it shall be between us and them a war of extermination, for we will follow them till the last drop of blood is spilled, or else they will have to exterminate us; for we will carry the seat of war to their own houses and their own families, and one party or the other shall be utterly destroyed. Remember it then, all men!" Years later Young recalled that "Elder Rigdon was the prime cause of our troubles in Missouri, by his Fourth of July oration."[11]

But when Jared Carter, the Captain General of the Danites, protested to the prophet about the sermon, he was tried for criticizing the First Presidency. At the trial Smith declared that if he and Carter had been alone when the complaint was made he would have slit Carter's throat. Avard knew how to deal with dissenters. He would act friendly, "get him a bowl of brandy, and after a while take him by the arm and get him one side in the brush, when I will into his guts in a minute and put him under the sod." Coming within "a finger's point" of surrendering his head, Carter lost his office instead.[12]

In the perspective of time the 1838 conflict between Mormon and Missourian stands as a national disgrace. In August an election day dispute erupted into undeclared war. Prowling the countryside, armed bands of Gentiles burned homes and granaries, stole animals, and whipped Saints. Smith expanded his Danites into the Armies of Israel and conscripted almost every able-bodied Mormon, but he ordered his men not to retaliate. At first he expected a peaceful settlement, but in mid-October he switched to a war policy and sent Apostle David Patten with sixty Danites to rescue some Saints. At Crooked River, Patten, nicknamed "Captain Fearnot," was shot in the abdomen and killed.[13]

Patten's death shocked Smith's followers. "I admit up to this time," confided John D. Lee, "I frankly believed what the Prophet and his apostles had said on the subject. I had considered that I was *bullet proof*, that no Gentile ball could ever harm me, or any Saint, and I had believed that a Danite could not be killed by Gentile hands. I thought that one Danite could chase a thousand Gentiles, and two could put ten thousand to flight. Alas! my dreams of security were over. One of our mighty men had fallen, and that by Gentile hands!"[14]

On October 27 Governor Lilburn Boggs, who for five years had ignored the atrocities against the Mormons, ordered his militia either to drive the Saints from the state or exterminate them. Four days later, to prevent wholesale slaughter, Smith, Rigdon, Parley Pratt, and other leaders surrendered.[15]

III

LATE IN 1838 AND EARLY IN 1839, with Patten dead, Luke Johnson, Lyman Johnson, Boynton, William E. McLellin, and Marsh in apostasy, the prophet's brother, William, close to it, and Rigdon and Joseph Smith in prison, Young, Kimball, and Orson Pratt alone of the Twelve and First Presidency still remained to serve and direct the church. Young visited Liberty jail, comforted the prisoners, and made plans to move to Illinois the helpless and destitute who might fall before Boggs's decree. He asked Bishop Edward Partridge to aid him in this work. "The poor may take care of themselves," Partridge replied, "and I will take care of myself." "Well," Young said, "if you will not help them out, I will." Young circulated among the Saints a mutual aid pact turn-

ing all property over to a special committee. On the first day he
got eighty signatures and on the second three hundred. In February 1839 Young and the reconstituted Twelve headed for Illinois.[16]

Two months later Young, Orson Pratt, Wilford Woodruff, Taylor, and other church dignitaries started back to Missouri to fulfill
Smith's revelation, received on July 8, 1838, that the Twelve
would leave Far West on April 26, 1839. On the way they met
John E. Page, a newly ordained apostle, whose wagon had turned
bottom-side up, upsetting a barrel of soft soap. Page was elbow-
deep in the stuff, scooping it up with his hands, when Young asked
him to come along. Page answered that he had to take care of his
wife and children, but Young assured him they would get along
without him and gave Page five minutes to get ready. The Twelve
helped right the wagon, and Page joined them.

Although warned to keep out, the apostles entered Far West on
the night of April 25. The next day they held a church conference,
excommunicated thirty-one apostates, and visited the place the
prophet had selected for the temple.

On May 2 they arrived back in Quincy, Illinois. The following
day Young saw Joseph and Hyrum Smith, who had escaped from
prison by getting a guard drunk. "It was one of the most joyful
scenes of my life," Young remembered, "to once more strike
hands with the Prophets and behold them free from the hands of
their enemies; Joseph conversed with us like a man who had just
escaped from a thousand oppressions and was now free in the
midst of his children."[17]

IV

SMITH AND YOUNG had in common one trait. Throughout
their lives they had the knack of converting misfortune into
opportunity. Young emerged from the Missouri conflict with
greater power and influence than ever. For months he had led the
Saints. Now, with Patten dead and Marsh in apostasy, he was the
most important of the apostles. Smith too profited from his experiences. A few months before he had narrowly escaped a Missouri
firing squad. But in May 1839, momentarily forgetting his proph-

ecy that Independence, in Jackson County, Missouri, the site of the Garden of Eden, would be his Zion, he started a new city on a tongue of land sticking out of a bend of the Mississippi River just above its first rapids. The prophet named this Illinois town Nauvoo, which meant, he said, "Beautiful Place" in Hebrew. Like Kirtland and Far West, it had neatly laid out square blocks and grew extremely rapidly.[18]

At first Young and his family lived across the river from Nauvoo, sharing with Woodruff's family one room in a military barracks at Montrose, Iowa. Then Young moved his wife and children into their own room. During the summer of 1839 malaria decimated the settlements on both sides of the river. The prophet gave his home to the sick and moved into a tent. On July 22 he prayed for power to heal the sick and almost immediately cured everyone in Nauvoo. Crossing to Montrose, he entered Young's home and, according to Mormon legend, healed Young. Together they went to the house of the dying Elijah Fordham, whom Smith commanded to rise. "Elijah Fordham leaped from his bed," Woodruff recalled, "like a man raised from the dead. A healthy color came to his face, and life was manifested in every act." Fordham lived until 1880.[19]

Even before Young was well, Smith had mapped out for him an important assignment. Unlike many sects, the Saints actively sought converts. In 1837 the prophet had sent Kimball and Hyde to England. In September 1839 he ordered the Twelve to go there.

Young was shocked. Although he subsequently argued that Smith had healed on July 22,[20] he and his family were still sick. For weeks they had not left their beds. Besides, Young and his wife had a ten-day-old baby to care for. "If you will go," Smith promised, "your family shall live, and you shall live, and you shall know that the hand of God is in calling you to go and preach the gospel of life and salvation to a perishing world." Thoroughly convinced, Young explained that "if I had known that every one of them would have been in the grave when I returned, it would not have diverted me from my mission one hour."[21]

Still Young was uneasy. As he prepared to leave, he continually asked Smith how he was to do this or that. "Brother Brigham," the prophet responded, "I want you to understand doctrine as it is.

When you reach England the Lord will teach you what to do, just as He teaches me how to act here."[22]

On September 18 Young and Kimball left Nauvoo with $13.50 in their pockets. That fall and winter they preached in the Midwest and New England. Then, in New York on March 9, 1840, accompanied by Orson Pratt, Parley Pratt, and George A. Smith, the prophet's cousin, they boarded a packet that docked in Liverpool on April 6, their church's tenth anniversary. So emaciated from the long journey that his cousin, Willard Richards, did not recognize him, Young landed with seventy-five cents in his pocket.[23]

The Mormons could not have reached England at a better time. For four years the country's economy had been depressed, and government authorities had recommended migration to America for those able to go. Recently, moreover, the followers of several revivalists, including Johanna Southcote and Edward Irving, had dispersed; disorganized and unchurched, these people sought a new religious home. Finally the Methodists had alienated many members by de-emphasizing fanaticism. The missionaries thus found in Britain a waiting audience.[24]

During their year in Europe the Twelve made Mormonism an international religion. They baptized between eight and nine thousand persons, printed three thousand hymn books and five thousand copies of *The Book of Mormon*, issued over sixty thousand tracts, and established a monthly magazine, the *Millennial Star*. Almost immediately boatloads of converts departed for Nauvoo. All this was accomplished, the Mormons forever bragged, without expense to the brethren in America. "I do not recollect of spending more than one penny, needlessly, while in England," Young said, "and that was for a bunch of grapes while passing through Smithfield market, Manchester. When I took them in my hand I saw women passing through the market who, I knew, were suffering through hunger, and who probably perished and died. I felt that I ought to have given that penny to the poor."[25]

In England Young performed other miracles. Laying hands on Mary Pitt, a cripple for fourteen years, he commanded her in the name of the Lord to arise and walk. "The lameness then left her," recorded Woodruff, "and she never afterwards used a staff or a crutch." The next day, according to the Mormons, she strolled through town.[26]

Satan fought back. In Preston, England, his forces attacked Kimball and Hyde. "Legions of disembodied evil spirits came against me," Kimball recalled with horror, "organized in companies, that they might have more power, but they had not power over me to any great extent, because of the power that was in and sustaining me. I had the Priesthood, and the power of it was upon me."[27]

Returning with Young to Nauvoo on July 1, 1841, Kimball asked Smith about these evil spirits. As they walked alongside the river, the prophet "told me what contests he had with the devil; he told me he had contests with the devil face to face. He also told me how he was handled and afflicted by the devil, and said, he had known circumstances where Elder Rigdon was pulled out of bed three times in one night."[28]

Overjoyed to be home, Young saw in his mission's success "the hand of God." He found his wife and children living in a small, unfurnished log cabin on a piece of swampy land, which he immediately drained and fenced. A week later Smith received a revelation instructing Young to remain at home "and take special care of your family from this time, henceforth, and for ever."[29]

For decades the Mormons proudly pointed to Young's European achievements. By "founding and starting the system of emigration, and gathering thousands upon thousands of people from the old world and placing them in positions to get homes of their own," commented George Smith in 1874, Young had become "the most distinguished and extensive benefactor of his race of any living man within my knowledge."[30]

V

NAUVOO WAS SMITH'S DOMAIN. In all matters he was supreme. Now, thanks to the Twelve, converts streamed into the city, considerably extending Smith's power: 240 arrived in 1840; 1,135 in 1841; 1,614 in 1842; and 769 in 1843. By 1842, Nauvoo, whose three hundred residents made it in 1839 a malaria-ridden dot on the map, had seven thousand people.[31]

Visitors to Nauvoo found Smith physically imposing. Six feet tall, with light blue eyes, graying light-brown hair, a peaked nose, and a large head, he weighed 220 pounds and each year seemed to grow portlier. One visitor, J. M. Sharpe, called him "fond of fun, frolic & brandy," and Charlotte Haven observed: "He talked incessantly about himself, what he had done and could do more than other mortals, and remarked that he was 'a giant, physically and mentally.' In fact, he seemed to forget that he was a man."[32] In reality, the prophet realized he was all too mortal. A bodyguard, a "tall, swarthy, keen-eyed, dark-skinned, daring looking person wearing a red scarf about his neck, and muffled in a black cloak," constantly followed him.[33]

Smith's crudeness struck Edwin de Leon, later the United States Consul General in Egypt. The prophet "spoke very fluently, but ungrammatically," de Leon noted, "like an uneducated man; but he possessed the gift of rough eloquence, and could be most persuasive when he tried." He collected mummies and papyri, and for a quarter his mother showed guests the leg of Pharoah's daughter and specimens of Abraham's and Isaac's handwriting. Smith also devised a baptismal system for the dead, enabling those who perished before God revealed Mormonism to be released from torment when someone received rites for them. On July 4, 1841, one elder was baptized for George Washington and another for General William Henry Harrison, who had just died. Both presidents then became members of the church. "The nation may rejoice," commented the great editor Horace Greeley in his New York *Log Cabin*, "that the illustrious patriots above named are now taken from the possession of the Prince of Darkness, and admitted into the fellowship of the Saints."[34]

At Nauvoo, as at Kirtland, the Saints entered politics. Early in the winter of 1839–40, Smith and Rigdon went to Washington, complained to President Van Buren about their treatment in Missouri, and requested aid. "Help you!" the President shouted. "How can I help you? All Missouri would turn against me." After arguing with his guests for several minutes, Van Buren rose, left the room, and did not return. *"He is not as fit as my dog for the chair of state,"* Smith barked to a reporter, "for my dog will make an effort to protect his abused and insulted master, while the present chief magistrate will not so much as lift his finger to relieve an oppressed and persecuted community of freemen, whose glory it has been that they were citizens of the United States." During the conversation a congressman had entered the room and twitted the president about getting fat. Van Buren replied he was aware of the fact and described in detail how his tailor had to let his clothes out every few days. Smith "hoped he would continue to grow fat, and swell, and before the next election burst!"[35]

During this political disaster help arrived in the form of John C. Bennett, an Ohio physician who became a Mormon late in 1840. Five feet nine inches tall, with black eyes, black hair sprinkled with gray, a dark complexion, and a thin face, Bennett admitted he did not believe Smith's religious pretensions but promised to comply with them. He would even submit to baptism, "a glorious frolic in the clear blue ocean with your worthy friend Brigham Young." With Rigdon ill and Young and Kimball still abroad, Smith eagerly embraced the convert.[36]

Bennett immediately proved his worth. Journeying to Springfield, the Illinois capital, he and Democratic Judge Stephen A. Douglas induced the state legislature to issue three charters. One granted the city of Nauvoo broad powers of self-government, another established the University of the City of Nauvoo, and the third created the Nauvoo Legion, a militia unit of men eighteen to forty-five. Smith became the Legion's lieutenant general, Bennett its major general. A grateful prophet, the nation's highest ranking military officer, now instructed his followers to vote Democratic.[37] In 1842 Smith joyfully bragged to the New York *Herald* that he could "already dictate to the State of Illinois."[38]

VI

AT NAUVOO, when a reporter asked how he prospered, Smith laughed heartily and replied: "None can get ahead of me and few can keep behind me." But here as in Kirtland he engaged in shaky financial ventures. At Nauvoo, he, Young, and the Twelve speculated in land. With a callousness hardly befitting God's prophet Smith displayed slight sympathy for converts. As the newspaperman spoke to Smith, a new arrival came to the door and said: "I wish to buy a piece of land for which I will pay trade of various kinds to the amount of $500, will you sell me some?" "My lands are all good titles," Smith answered, "and I must have the money for them." Like Van Buren at the White House, he turned and left his inferior to reflect.[39]

Smith also ran a general store. Young later revealed how men would say: "Brother Brigham, what do you think? I went down to brother Joseph's store, and I wanted to get a gallon of molasses, eight yards of calico, a little crockery, &c., and I could not have the articles without paying the money down. Do you think that is right?" The grumblers would then go to a Gentile merchant, get what they needed on credit, and bless the storekeeper. "But of Joseph's store it was, 'God Almighty curse you, because you would not allow me to carry off your goods without paying for them.' "[40]

Forced either to give one tenth of their earnings to the church or to spend every tenth day quarrying rock for the temple Smith was building,[41] the Saints circulated stories about the prophet's greed. "Let us not for a moment," urged Young, Kimball, Woodruff, and Taylor in a public letter, "lend an ear to evil and designing men who would subvert the truth, and blacken the character of the servant of the Most High God, by publishing abroad that the prophet is enriching himself on the spoils of his brethren." Smith owned only "his old Charlie horse, given him in Kirtland; two pet deer; two old turkeys, and four young ones; the old cow given him by a brother in Missouri; his old Major, dog; his wife, children, and a little household furniture, and this is the amount of the great possessions of that man whom God has called to lead His people in these last days. . . . Who would be willing to suffer what he has suffered, and labor near twenty years as he has done, for the wealth he is in possession of?"[42]

By 1842 Smith was again penniless. When he and Hyrum defaulted on a note for $5,212.50, several wealthy Mormons offered to pay it.[43] The prophet was a financial failure.

VII

"WHILE WE WERE IN ENGLAND in 1839 and 1840 I think," Young later said, "the Lord manifested to me by vision and his spirit things that I did not then understand. I never opened my mouth to any one concerning them until I returned to Nauvoo." There Smith informed him God wished to revive plural marriage, explaining "that if this principle was not introduced, this Church and Kingdom could not proceed."[44]

No one will ever know when Smith embraced polygamy. Until 1852 the Saints steadfastly denied the practice their opponents denigrated as spiritual wivery and pious Saints still glorify as celestial marriage. In that year Young asserted that polygamy began with a revelation Smith received on July 12, 1843, but, confronted with overwhelming evidence it existed long before then, the church again altered its position and in 1878 announced that God had revealed the system to Smith as early as 1831.[45]

Caught in the mass of conflicting evidence, Smith's church now argues that after 1831 the prophet never denounced polygamy. It explains, for example, that on August 17, 1835, when the General Assembly at Kirtland condemned the practice, Smith was in Michigan.[46]

But on December 16, 1838, from Liberty prison, Smith did exactly what his followers now say he did not do. "Some have reported," he told his people, "that we not only dedicated our property, but likewise our families to the Lord, and Satan taking advantage of this has transfigured it into lasciviousness, a community of wives, which things are an abomination in the sight of God."[47]

By 1841 the prophet spoke far differently. One Sunday morning shortly before the apostles returned from England, he preached on the restoration of ancient ways and said that things would soon be as they had been in the time of Abraham and Jacob. Smith's frankness shocked many of the women present, including his wife, Emma, and Vilate Kimball, and that afternoon he was forced to concede the aforementioned day might be far off.[48]

An even greater furor erupted in 1842, when "J. Smith, Printer" of Nauvoo issued a pamphlet called *The Peace Maker*, a defense of polygamy by Udney Hay Jacob, who identified himself as a Gentile. "It is evident that by the corruption of this holy law of marriage," argued Jacob, "an endless catalogue of crime has been created that otherwise could never have existed: and that does exist at this moment in these States. Husbands forsake their wives, and often brutally abuse them. Fathers forsake their children; young maidens are seduced and abandoned by their deceivers; wives are poisoned and put to death by their husbands; husbands are murdered by their wives; new born babies are cruelly murdered to hide the false shame created by the false, and wicked, and tyrannical law against polygamy: besides the innumerable host of evils created by the destruction of the righteous government of the husband and head of the family. While on the other hand polygamy regulated by the law of God, as illustrated in this book could not possibly produce one crime; neither could it injure any human being. The stupidity of modern Christian nations upon this subject is horribly astonishing."[49] Not a Gentile, Jacob, a sixty-one-year-old carpenter from Massachusetts, was, and to his dying day remained, a Mormon.[50]

Jacob's account created such an uproar that Smith was publicly forced to repudiate it as an "unmeaning rigmarole of nonsense, folly and trash." Meantime, he married many women, including Rhoda Richards, Young's first cousin, Fanny Young Murray, Young's sister, and Helen Mar Kimball, Heber's fifteen-year-old daughter. The prophet now gratefully promised that Kimball's estate in heaven would adjoin Smith's on the north.[51]

Mormon polygamy—or celestial marriage, as Smith and his followers preferred to call it—stressed that the family exists forever and that a man's heavenly glory would be directly related to the number of wives he took. It recognized two degrees of marriage: one bound the husband and wife on earth and the other, performed in a temple, sealed for eternity. A woman might be married to one man for time and to another for eternity, but men might take an unlimited number of women for either time or eternity. Following Smith's teachings, his brothers Hyrum and William, Parley Pratt, Kimball, Lorenzo Snow, Lee, and others soon accepted plural wives.[52]

Instructed to marry again, Young was filled with revulsion. "I was not desirous of shirking from duty," he revealed, "nor of failing in the least to do as I was commanded, but it was the first time in my life that I had desired the grave, and I could hardly get over it for a long time. And when I saw a funeral, I felt to envy the corpse its situation, and to regret that I was not in the coffin, knowing the toil and labor that my body would have to undergo; and I have had to examine myself, from that day to this, and watch my faith, and carefully meditate, lest I should be found desiring the grave more than I ought to do."[53]

During the next two years, however, Young married four women. On June 15, 1842, he took Lucy Decker, the twenty-year-old wife of Isaac Seeley, the Nauvoo physician. Winning Lucy, the mother of two children, would have baffled a man less ingenious than Young. He saw her, fell in love with her, and promised to give her a greater exaltation in heaven than could the ungodly Seeley, whom he sent on a church mission. While Seeley was gone, Young persuaded the stake, or district, high council to annul Lucy's first marriage, leaving her free to accept him. Then on November 2, 1843, Young married Augusta Adams Cobb and Harriet E. Cook, and on May 8, 1844, he added to his list Lucy's fourteen-year-old sister, Clara.[54]

But the girl Young most desired proved elusive. Martha H. Brotherton, a fiery eighteen-year-old convert from Manchester, England, had been in Nauvoo only three weeks when, early in 1842, she agreed to accompany Young and Kimball to Smith's store to buy some goods. "Sister Martha," Kimball asked as they walked along, "are you willing to do all that the Prophet requires you to do?" Martha said she was. "Well," Kimball added, "there are many things revealed in these last days that the world would laugh and scoff at, but unto us is given the mysteries of the kingdom." Kimball escorted the couple to the tithing office above the store and left. Young then extracted from Martha a vow to keep secret what he was about to say and asked if the girl had "an affection for me, that, were it lawful and right, you could accept of me for your husband and companion." He next spoke of Smith's revelation authorizing polygamy: "As it was in the days of Abraham, so it shall be in these last days, and whoever is the first that is willing to take up the cross will receive the greatest blessings; and if you will accept of me I will take you straight to the celestial kingdom; and if you will have me in this world, I will have you in that which is to come, and brother Joseph will marry us here today, and you can go home this evening and your parents will not know anything about it." Young locked the girl in and went after Smith. "Well, Martha," the prophet said upon arriving, "just go ahead and do as Brigham wants you to do—he is the best man in the world except me." Smith would "answer for it before God; I have the keys of the Kingdom, and whatever I bind on earth is bound in Heaven, and whatever I loose on earth is loosed in Heaven—and if you will accept of Brigham, you shall be blessed—God shall bless you, and my blessing shall rest upon you, and if you will be led by him you will do well; for I know Brigham will take care of you, and if he don't do his duty to you, come to me and I will make him—and if you do not like it in a month or two, come to me and I will make you free again; and if he turns you off I will take you on." Martha begged for time to think, and Smith agreed to give it to her but made her swear silence. He then said to Young: "She looks as if she could keep a secret."

The next day, after preaching near Martha's home, Young picked up where he had left off in the tithing store. This time, however, the girl told her parents the whole story. The family packed and moved to St. Louis, where Martha swore out an affidavit that papers throughout the country published.[55]

At the April 1842 conference of the church Joseph and Hyrum denied that Kimball and Young had bolted a girl in a room and "endeavored to induce her to believe in having two wives." The prophet insisted that "no person that is acquainted with our principles would believe such lies."[56] But when Taylor's brother-in-law privately asked about the incident, Smith admitted Martha's account was true. He had heard evil things about her, he said, and was testing her.[57]

Of the apostles, Orson Pratt, later the foremost defender of polygamy, fought hardest against it. Learning the prophet had tried to seduce his wife, his mind, according to Young, "became so darkened" that he rebelled. In vain Young, Kimball, and George Smith argued with Pratt, who was excommunicated and delivered to the buffetings of Satan. Early in 1843, however, he rejoined the church and was restored to the Twelve.[58]

Despite such trouble, Smith undoubtedly enjoyed his wives. With the foolhardiness of youth de Leon asked about the many young girls who marched in and out of the prophet's house. Smith called them his nieces. Becoming friendlier with Smith, de Leon commented "on the curious variety among his nieces, and the want of any family resemblance among them. There was a slight twinkle in the prophetic eye, as he poked me in the ribs with his forefinger, and rebuked me, exclaiming, 'Oh, the carnal mind, the carnal mind!' and I thought it discreet not to press the subject."[59]

VIII

MORMONISM AND CELESTIAL MARRIAGE were not one, for the religion existed years before the practice. Nor did polygamy attract large numbers of people to Mormonism. Although it is difficult to prove, most converts probably sought salvation, not a husband or a harem of beautiful girls.

Like Mormonism itself, polygamy, born of Abraham, the first Hebrew and the father of the faithful, was patriarchal. Considering themselves the heirs of the gospel revealed by God to Abraham and his children, Young and Smith sought to restore these glorious ways, lost to the world for centuries through apostasy. Since Abraham had two wives at one time, Jacob had four, and David and Solomon had many more, the Saints of the modern covenant with God followed their examples. Plural marriage thus sprang from the heart of Mormonism, almost independent of the will of those involved. Once it was introduced, Young and the other Mormon leaders who at first accepted it grudgingly became its slaves, refusing to alter it without instructions from God.

Surprisingly enough, many Mormon women defended polygamy. "If you send our husbands and sons to a state prison for keeping the commandments of God," Phoebe Carter Woodruff, Wilford Woodruff's first wife, once warned the federal government, "make your prisons large enough for us, their wives and mothers, for where they go we will go also."

Like Phoebe, the first women to permit their husbands to take more wives were not Eastern European serfs or refugees from the harems of the Near East. They were daughters of chaste New England families of pure Anglo-Saxon descent. Some had ancestors who migrated from England generations ago. Several could

trace their lines to the Pilgrim fathers. Most were strongly puri-
tanic in character and outlook. The Mormons bragged that perhaps the first plural wife to bear a child was the sister of a United
States senator.

These women, not Smith and Young, established polygamy.
They accepted the seemingly unacceptable because, like Phoebe,
they became convinced their salvation depended upon it. Indeed,
important Saints often conceded that had Smith attempted to
apply plural marriage to the church as a civil contract ending
when death dissolved the earthly union, he would have failed and
raised among these American women a revolt that would have
shaken his church to the ground.

Instead these women were told that this grand order of marriage foreshadowed immortality, an argument that mastered them
and chained them to an institution they despised. Given the choice
of eternal life among the celestials as the plural wife of an elder or
of everlasting damnation as an apostate, a Mormon woman surrendered her pride—and a portion of her husband.

Young contributed immeasurably to this acceptance. In perhaps his most important addition to Mormon theology he asserted
that Adam was God and then applied this to Smith's contention
that since the beginning of time the Lord had given to the earth
seven dispensations, or divine orderings of affairs. The first few
involved the patriarchs Abel, Enoch, Noah, and Melchizedek. The
next included Abraham, Isaac, Jacob, and Jacob's twelve sons,
one of whom was Joseph. After them came Moses, Samuel, Elijah,
David the Beloved, and Solomon the Wise. Jesus Christ, Adam's
dearest son and the world's Redeemer, had spawned the crowning
dispensation of the ancients, that of the meridian of time. The
dispensation of the fullness of times, which would restore ancient
ways, capped them all, however. Given to Smith because about
570 A.D. the Catholic church, "the great whore of the earth," had
corrupted God's word, it began in 1830 and ended 1,260 years in
which the earth had no divine priesthood. It would pave the way
for the second coming of Christ.

As Young saw it, polygamy connected the holders of this final
dispensation with the Creator and with the recipients of the six
earlier ones. Elijah himself had come to earth and empowered

Smith to link the living to the heavenly. But to attain glory man must follow Adam, who had once been human but had grown powerful and exalted. Lorenzo Snow, the brother of a wife of both Smith and Young and later a church president, colorfully summarized this doctrine: "As man is, God once was; and as God is, man may become." Aided by Eve, his first wife, Adam governed heaven, a community of faithful families organized as the Mormon church was on earth. The celestial order of marriage put mortals on the road to godhood and goddesshood and prepared them for the day they would live with Adam, Abraham, and Christ.[60]

IX

IN JUNE 1842 SCANDAL AGAIN ROCKED NAUVOO. After months of quarreling, Smith excommunicated Bennett, his closest adviser for the past year and a half. The two immediately charged one another with licentiousness. In public letters and a book, *The History of the Saints, or An Exposé of Joe Smith and Mormonism*, Bennett spoke of the Martha Brotherton episode, of the prophet's attempts to seduce Sarah M. Pratt and Nancy Rigdon, Rigdon's beautiful nineteen-year-old daughter, and of the Danites and Nauvoo Legion, both of which performed Smith's dirty work.[61]

Retaliating, Smith swore that Bennett, married and the father of several children, had approached "some of the females in the city, who knew nothing of him but as an honorable man, & began to teach them that promiscuous intercourse between the sexes was a doctrine believed in by the Latter-day Saints, and that there was no harm in it."[62] This accusation was undoubtedly true, for Oliver H. Olney, who hated Smith, reported from Nauvoo in July 1842: "Bennett has for months been in clover up to his eyes amongst women that think they have been abused by their husbands."[63]

These episodes failed to stifle Smith's political ambitions. In April 1844 Young sent forth 348 elders to "preach the truth in righteousness, and present before the people 'General Smith's views of the power and policy of the General Government'; and seek diligently to get up electors who will go for him for the

presidency." The Twelve promised to "attend as many confer-
ences as possible."[64]

Young himself vigorously pushed the ticket of Smith for President and General James A. Bennett of New York for Vice-President. But if the July 1, 1844, meeting at the Boston Melodeon was
typical, he accomplished nothing. Catcalls and hoots drowned out
speeches by Young, Lyman Wight, and Hyde. Then a man in the
gallery rose, spoke sentimentally, and sang a love song. When the
police attempted to arrest him, a fight broke out and the audience
fled. The Boston *Mail* called "the whole affair . . . disgraceful."[65]

On the sixteenth of July Young heard the terrible news. On
June 27, while under arrest for arranging the destruction of the
apostate newspaper, the Nauvoo *Expositor,* Joseph and Hyrum
Smith had been murdered in Carthage jail by a mob. "The death
of the modern Mahomet will seal the fate of Mormonism," predicted the New York *Herald.* "They cannot get another Joe
Smith."[66]

I V

"I Know the Twelve"

I

IN A REVEALING ADDRESS he obviously thought Gentiles would never see—only one copy of it exists today—Young conceded that Saints were partially responsible for Joseph Smith's death. "If Joseph Smith, jun., the Prophet, had followed the Spirit of revelation in him he never would have gone to Carthage," Young argued. "Do you understand that? . . . Joseph intended to go West. . . . He said, 'I can see life and liberty and salvation in that course, but if I return to give myself up, it is death and darkness to the full; I am like a lamb led to the slaughter,' and never for one moment did he say that he had one particle of light in him after he started back from Montrose to give himself up in Nauvoo. This he did through the persuasion of others. I want you to understand that."[1]

But what Young uttered for private consumption differed markedly from the doctrine of collective Gentile guilt he tirelessly expounded in public. Gentiles alone had committed the murder and must never be trusted. For decades Young and his lieutenants called every misfortune that befell the United States partial payment for allowing this atrocity.

Young never openly delved into the degree of Mormon responsibility, but he obviously thought about it. When Smith was killed, where were his many bodyguards? Why did none of the numerous wives who asserted they loved him fling herself into his path and stop him from surrendering to the enemy at Carthage? What happened to the four thousand men of the Nauvoo Legion? Why did his followers not accompany him everywhere he went and surround and seal the jail to make sure he would be safe? If this speech is an indication, Young undoubtedly raised these questions in council. But he publicly played up Gentile persecution because such a course won converts and unified his flock.

II

IT IS NOT SURPRISING that the first, and until the assassination of Malcolm X in 1965 the only, American religious leader to be murdered was a Mormon, for the Saints have always inflamed passions. By his own admission Joseph Smith searched for a path out of the religious wilderness, but in doing so he fed the violence to which he succumbed. Smith possessed everything life could give: good looks, charm, fame, youth, thousands of adherents, and dozens of wives, many of them young and lovely. The shots rang out, and in a moment fate took back everything it had given him. The prophet had expected to save mankind but in the process lost himself.

Smith's enemies applauded the action of the mob. "Some of the public journals of the country, we are sorry to see, regret the death of Joe Smith, the Mormon Prophet," Thomas C. Sharp's Warsaw (Illinois) *Signal* observed. "Our deliberate judgment is, that he ought to have been dead ten years ago and that those who at length have deprived him of his life, have done the cause of God, and of the country, good service. Three cheers to the brave company who shot him to pieces!" Sharp and four associates were later tried for instigating the crime and acquitted.[2]

When Smith died, William W. Phelps, John Taylor, and Willard Richards, the sole Mormon leaders in Nauvoo, urged moderation. "Be peaceable, quiet citizens," they advised all Saints, "doing the works of righteousness, and as soon as the 'Twelve' and other authorities can assemble, or a majority of them, the onward course to the great gathering of Israel, and the final consummation of the dispensation of the fulness of times, will be pointed out; ... Rejoice then, that you are found worthy to live and die for God; men may kill the body, but they cannot hurt the soul, and wisdom shall be justified by her children."³

On July 16, when Young, the leading apostle, heard the details of the murders, he first thought not about the victims but about Mormonism's future. Had the prophet, he asked himself, taken the keys of the kingdom of heaven with him? He and Orson Pratt, seated to his left, leaned back in their chairs. Striking his knee with his hand, Young suddenly decided "the keys of the kingdom are right here with the church."⁴

Young, Kimball, and Wight headed toward Nauvoo on July 24. At Albany, Hyde, Orson Pratt, and Woodruff joined them. Journeying day and night, they reached Nauvoo on August 6.⁵

Years afterward Mary Ettie V. Smith, a resident of Nauvoo, described Young's entrance into the city. Learning of Smith's death while in Pittsburgh, Rigdon had rushed back to Nauvoo and was trying to control the church. He hoped to be elected the new prophet before Young returned and succeeded in calling a special convention. In those days, Mary explained, the appearance of a steamboat on the Mississippi River was a special event. One had been expected for several days, and many people hoped it would bring Young. At the convention a number of candidates presented their claims to church leadership. Rigdon, the final speaker, made an especially effective appeal, but as he finished a cry announced a steamboat's approach. Young was aboard. He immediately came to the meeting "and advanced to the stand, with the air of a prophet, and the lofty bearing of one who bore in his person the fortunes of an empire. He was at that time under forty years of age, with a handsome and pleasing face, and an open and frank address; he possessed the rare faculty of inspiring enthusiasm in others, without allowing it to overpower himself." Young's "short and well-timed" address enthralled the crowd, and from that day on, recorded Mary, he governed the church.⁶

This dramatic account hardly stands up in the light of history. True, Rigdon and Young vied for power after Smith's death. And

Rigdon had rushed to Nauvoo from Pittsburgh. A member of the First Presidency, he might naturally have been considered Smith's successor, but over the years the two had drifted apart. During the ordeal in Liberty jail Rigdon had proved a weak reed, spending most of his time sobbing and wailing. In 1842, moreover, he had played the role of offended father when Smith tried to seduce his daughter, Nancy. In 1843 the prophet twice accused Rigdon of allying himself with Bennett, of plotting to betray Smith to the authorities seeking his extradition to Missouri, and of mismanaging the Nauvoo post office. Only pleas to friendship had induced Smith to take Rigdon back. But Smith never again trusted him. Woodruff once heard Smith declare "that elder Rigdon had become like a millstone upon his back—a dead weight—and he had carried him long enough, and must throw him off."[7]

The conference Mary wrote about took place two days after Young reached Nauvoo. On the day following his return Young held a council of war with Taylor, Kimball, the Pratt brothers, Richards, Woodruff, George Smith, and Wight, and attended a general conference of the church. Here, although opposed by nine of the Twelve, Rigdon foolishly chose warfare instead of conciliation. He told of a vision he had received on the day Joseph died commanding him to see that the church was "governed in a proper manner." Young answered that he did not care "who leads the Church," even Ann Lee, the Shaker divine, for the Twelve exercised the real power. "Joseph conferred upon our heads of the keys and powers belonging to the Apostleship which he himself held before he was taken away, and no man or set of men can get between Joseph and the Twelve in this world or in the world to come. How often Joseph said to the Twelve, 'I have laid the foundation and you must build thereon, for upon your shoulders the kingdom rests.' "[8]

The next day at a special meeting of the church Young repeated this theme. "If the people want President Rigdon to lead them they may have him; but I say unto you that the Quorum of the Twelve have the keys of the kingdom of God in all the world. The Twelve are appointed by the finger of God. Here is Brigham, have his knees ever faltered? have his lips ever quivered? Here is Heber and the rest of the Twelve, an independent body, who have the keys of the Priesthood—the keys of the kingdom of God to deliver to all the world: this is true, so help me God. They stand next to Joseph, and are as the First Presidency of the Church. . . . You cannot fill the office of a Prophet, Seer and Revelator: God must do this. You are like children without a father and sheep without a shepherd. You must not appoint any man at our head; if you should, the Twelve must ordain him. You cannot appoint a man at our head; but if you do want any other man or men to lead you, take them and we will go our way to build up the kingdom in all the world." Deeply moved, the congregation unanimously supported the Twelve, who were authorized to complete the temple and select two bishops to act as trustees-in-trust for church property and tithing.[9]

This speech of August 8 became perhaps the most famous in Mormon history. Bishop George Miller, chosen a trustee-in-trust at the meeting, later denounced it as "a long and loud harangue, and as I had always took him [Young] to be a blunderbuss in speaking, and on this occasion to me apparently more so, for the life of me I could not see any point in the course of his remarks, than to overturn Sidney Rigdon's pretensions."[10] But around it the Saints built a legend supported by recollections but no contemporary evidence. The church insisted that at the meeting Joseph Smith occupied Young's person. In 1869 Hyde recalled how, while listening to Young, he asked himself: " 'Am I mistaken, or is it really the voice of Joseph Smith?' This is my testimony; it was not only the voice of Joseph, but there were the features, the gestures and even the *stature* of Joseph before us in the person of Brigham. And though it may be said that President Young is a complete *mimic,* and can mimic anybody, I would like to see the man who can mimic another *in stature* who was about *four or five inches higher than himself*. Every one in the congregation—every one who was inspired by the Spirit of the Lord—felt it. They knew it. They realized it. I sat myself down in the midst of the congregation, with my two wives, whom Joseph had given and sealed to me. When President Young began to speak, one of them said, 'It is the voice of Joseph! It is Joseph Smith!' "[11]

The next step was to get rid of Rigdon altogether. On September 8 the high council of the stake of Nauvoo tried him for illegally ordaining prophets and priests and for palming off on the Saints false revelations. As Young explained at the trial, the struggle pitted Joseph and Hyrum Smith, *The Book of Mormon*, and the Twelve against Rigdon and his followers. Since leaving Missouri, Rigdon had been "whining all the while because of his sufferings." He had, moreover, recently connived with John C. Bennett. If Rigdon were sustained, Bennett, the sponsors of the Nauvoo *Expositor*, and their "murderous clan" would soon control Nauvoo. And Rigdon's revelations were from the devil. Even now Rigdon was feigning illness to avoid appearing at the trial. Completely under Young's control, the council unchurched Rigdon and delivered him to the buffetings of Satan.[12]

The church hierarchy firmly in his hands, Young soon embarked upon a series of power encroachments leading to his eventual designation as prophet, seer, and revelator. By the end of 1844 he was signing his letters not president of the Twelve but "Prest. of the Church of L. D. S."[13] Young, the most forceful and most capable apostle, was ensconced in power.

That Christmas, Phelps, the Mormon poet and journalist, proposed a toast to the victors. "I know the Twelve and they know me. Their names are Brigham Young, the lion of the Lord; Heber C. Kimball, the herald of grace; Parley P. Pratt, the archer of paradise; Orson Hyde, the olive branch of Israel; Willard Richards, the keeper of the rolls; John Taylor, the champion of right; William Smith, the patriarchal Jacob staff; Wilford Woodruff, the banner of the gospel; George A. Smith, the entablature of truth; Orson Pratt, the gauge of philosophy; John E. Page, the sun dial; and Lyman Wight, the wild ram of the mountain. And they are good men; the best the Lord can find; they do the will of the Lord, and the Saints know it."[14]

III

JOSEPH SMITH'S DEATH whetted many appetites. Control of his church offered a man power, fame, and possible wealth. Even after his Nauvoo fiasco, Rigdon retained ambitions. At Pittsburgh his adherents started a magazine, the *Latter Day Saints' Messenger and Advocate*, and condemned the Twelve for "practicing the

doctrine of polygamy, despoiling female virtue and chasity by seducing them, and tyrannizing over those who will not sanction
their work of darkness, and many other like things, for which we
regard them as apostates, and men fallen from the true order of
the church, into a state of wickedness and corruption; therefore,
we hold no fellowship with them, and as a branch of the true
church, standing upon the original platform, and the acknowledged and received doctrine of said church, we do not consider
ourselves identified with them." As the Rigdonites saw it, Young
was a usurper and a liar. In 1844 he had sworn to a Pittsburgh
audience that Smith had at least five more years of life guaranteed
him and would be the next president of the United States. "Verily," commented one Rigdonite, "this is very uncertain trumpeting
to come from Zion."[15]

Late in 1844 Rigdon began a speaking tour that won few converts. "He is a tall, stout, elderly gentlemanly looking man," noted
the New York *Herald*, "apparently about sixty years of age, hollow mouthed, having lost his front teeth. His delivery is rather
indistinct and low, and very rapid; at other times quite as loud,
raising his voice to the highest pitch. He is evidently a person but
of limited education . . . very disjointed in his manner, so as
almost to defy knowing what particular object his subject had
reference to. He used his left hand as if he was pumping violently,
every now and then assisting with the right; and hitting the desk so
violently with one or both as to make every thing on it spring
upwards to a considerable height, and keeping those near him
from napping if inclined."[16]

Early in 1845, after receiving pledges of support from several
important apostates and claiming the priesthood originally given
to Joseph Smith, Rigdon organized his church. His Twelve included Benjamin Winchester and Doctor William E. McLellin, his
First Presidency the great Mormon editor Ebenezer Robinson.
Confident of success, he sent missionaries to spread his gospel
throughout the United States.[17]

In McLellin, one of the original Mormon apostles, Rigdon
temporarily obtained a prize, if peculiar, convert. After leaving
Smith because of the Kirtland bank fiasco, McLellin flitted from
sect to sect, always courted because of his great ability but never

contented. Charles L. Woodward, the New York bookseller and an acute student of Mormonism, characterized him as "a schismatic, erratic, seditious, wrong-headed, foul-weather saint, who has not only been the leader of a schism known as the 'McLellinites,' but has in turn identified himself and quarreled with perhaps every one of the twenty or thirty schisms which have from time to time afflicted the elect people. From the year I, throughout all Mormon literature, we find the Doctor invariably upon the rampage. The old stormy petrel of Mormonism used to favor me with an occasional characteristic letter, but, meeting with no opposition, soon grew tired of the correspondence, and dropped me as he would a cold, and other men a hot, potato."[18]

Soon an apostate far more important than even Rigdon and McLellin emerged. James J. Strang, born in Scipio, New York, in 1813, was at once the most brilliant and most colorful Saint. "I learn from many sources," began his autobiography, "that in childhood I exhibited extraordinary mental imbecility. Indeed if I may audit what is told me on the subject, all who knew me except my parents thought me scarcely more than idiotic." His teachers considered him "too stupid to learn and too dull to feel neglect." As a child, he continually sulked. "Long weary days I sat upon the floor thinking, thinking, thinking; occasionally asking a strange uninfantile question and never getting an answer. My mind wandered over fields that old men shrink from."[19]

Strang studied law and moved to Illinois, where in 1844 he met and was converted by Joseph Smith. Five feet nine inches tall, with a large head, an exceptionally high forehead, a florid complexion, and small light hazel eyes, Strang was extremely nervous, a rapid and loud talker, and a confirmed hypochondriac.[20] He was also an inspiring leader.

Strang's profession to authority rested upon a letter purportedly written by Smith nine days before his death and postmarked in red from Nauvoo on June 19. It authorized Strang to "plant a stake of Zion" in Voree, Wisconsin, and urged all Saints to gather there. For years Young's followers labeled the document a forgery, arguing that the letter, unlike others mailed in Nauvoo, really had a black postmark and that the Nauvoo post office contained no record of it. Incensed by these accusations, some Strangites tried to check the Nauvoo post office records, but they could not find the register and accused Young of stealing it.[21]

Smith's letter to Strang is now owned by Yale University and can be fully analyzed. Even a cursory glance raises suspicions, for, in sharp contrast to the prophet's other letters, this one is printed, not written. Smith's signature, moreover, does not resemble his usual handwriting. The note was written on two different sheets of paper, raising the possibility that the second sheet, the back of which bears Strang's address and the Nauvoo postmark in red, may have been the envelope of a letter actually mailed to Strang on June 19, 1844. After receiving it, Strang could have easily forged the front and back of the first sheet and the front of this second sheet. Two things substantiate this theory: the ink on the second page is much browner than on the first, indicating vast differences in the quality of the two sheets and suggesting that Strang probably found it impossible to match the sheet he added to the one he received, and the address and body of the letter are in different ink. Finally the flowery style closely resembles Strang's, not Smith's, writings. Smith was always direct and matter-of-fact and never composed anything comparable to the portion of the letter that told how "the Almighty came from His throne of rest. He clothed himself with light as with a garment. He appeared & moon & stars went out, the earth dissolved in space. I trod on air & was borne on wings of cherubim. The sweetest strains of heavenly musick thrilled in my ear."[22]

Strang embellished his contentions with stories remarkably similar to the ones Smith told in the 1820's. On June 18, 1844, the day Smith wrote his letter, Strang received visions of a thriving community and saw a vast hall in which he and his counselors were meeting. Upon receiving Smith's letter Strang realized what the dream meant. At 5:30 P.M. on June 27, 1844, the exact hour and day the prophet died, an angel came to Strang, anointed him, and informed him he was to save God's people.[23]

Then in 1845 Strang was instructed to dig up from under a tree on a Wisconsin hill an account of an ancient people, true believers who, like Smith's Nephites, were extinct but were to be revived in the person of the Mormons. Taking several men to the spot, Strang stood far away while they extracted from the earth a clay box holding three plates. The find, the diggers testified, must have been there a long time, for the earth was untouched and the tree's roots had encased the box. Four of the six sides of the plates contained characters in a language only Strang knew. The other two sides had drawings.[24]

Although Young believed Smith's account of the discovery of *The Book of Mormon*, he dismissed Strang's story as nonsense. Since he could not deny that God spoke to men, Young from the time he assumed power to his death labeled all revelations not received by him the work of the devil in disguise. Accordingly he excommunicated Strang.[25]

Still Strang's flock increased. In 1846 the St. Louis *American* estimated that he had 10,000 followers, compared with 15,000 for Young.[26] By ordering to England two talented elders, Page and George J. Adams, to appeal for aid and a treaty of alliance, Young played into Strang's hands. Both men refused to go and joined Strang.[27]

Young also shoved the Smith family towards Voree. Getting rid of Rigdon was simple in comparison with the problem presented by the prophet's eldest son, Joseph III. At Nauvoo Young often promised that the boy, born in 1832, would succeed his father. "I am not the leader of the church, nor the prophet of the church," he told James Whitehead, Joseph Smith's secretary; "we know who that is; it is Joseph, the son of Joseph the Martyr."[28] Lee once heard the prophet's mother beg Young not to rob the boy's birthright. "Don't worry or take any trouble, Mother Smith," Young responded, "by doing so you are only laying the knife to the throat of the child. If it is known that he is the rightful successor of his father, the enemy of the Priesthood will seek his life. He is too young to lead this people now, but when he arrives at mature age he shall have his place. No one shall rob him of it."[29]

But in May 1845 Young alienated William Smith, the prophet's only living brother and the church's patriarch. During a petty power struggle Young had removed Smith from the editorship of the New York *Prophet* and the presidency of the Eastern branch of the church and had refused to publish Smith's complaints in the church organ, the Nauvoo *Neighbor*. Denouncing the *Neighbor* as a "mean little, stinking paper," Smith informed James M. Monroe, who taught Young's children, "that B. Young is not a whit beyond himself or any other of the Twelve. That he is merely President by courtesy. That he has no higher keys, and that the whole Twelve are presidents of the Church and not B. Young and that he does not stand in Joseph's shoes. His words," Monroe thought, "seems to portend a rupture between him and the Twelve, but I hardly know how it will come out. Most probably to his disadvantage, as the authority of the Twelve is too firmly rooted to be broken up very easily."[30]

That summer Smith's position became untenable. Little Joseph was, he wrote from Nauvoo, "his fathers successor although some people would fain make us believe that the Twelve are to be the perpetual heads of this church to the exclusion of the Smith family, but every one who has read the book of Doctrine and Covenants must be aware that Priesthood authority is hereditary and descends from Father to son and therefore Josephs oldest son will take his place when he arrives to the age of maturity. . . . There seems to be a severe influence working against me and the Smith family in this place, which makes our situation very unpleasant and I must say that I have seen more oppression and ingratitude here in one month than in the East in one year."[31]

Smith carefully planned his revenge. In October he published a pamphlet attacking the Twelve, sent a bundle of them to Sharp, and fled to St. Louis, where he began delivering anti-Brighamite lectures. Overjoyed by this rupture in the Mormon ranks, Sharp printed Smith's entire attack, which filled almost two full pages of his newspaper.

"I will state unequivocally at the outset," Smith wrote, "that it is my firm and sincere conviction, that, since the murder of my two brothers, usurpation and anarchy, and spiritual wickedness in high places, have crept into his church, with the cognizance and acquiescence of those whose solemn duty it was to watch guardedly against such a state of things. Under the reign of one whom I may call a Pontius Pilate, under the reign I say of this B. Young, no greater tyranny ever existed since the days of Nero. He has no other justification than ignorance to cover the most *cruel* acts— acts disgraceful to any one bearing the stamp of humanity; and this being has associated around him, men, bound by oaths and covenants, who are reckless enough to commit almost any crime, or fulfill any command that their self-crowned 'head' might give them."

According to Smith, the assassination of Irvine Hodges, who, after publicly proclaiming that Young had hired him to commit murder, was clubbed over the head and stabbed in the side four times within fifty yards of Young's home as Young's bodyguards watched, brought matters to a head. Fearing he would be next, Smith denounced Young and was summoned to a hearing attended by fifty or sixty policemen brandishing bowie knives, hickory clubs, and pistols. At the meeting Smith pleaded for sympathy and described his brother's contributions to Mormonism, but with "boisterous boldness" Young retorted: "I will let William Smith know that he has no right to counsel this Church, for I am the man! I will let William Smith know also, that he shall not counsel the police; furthermore, that where the Smith family goes the Church will not go, nor the Priesthood either! And I will let William Smith know that I am president and head of this Church." In unison the policemen, bishops, and apostles thundered "Amen." Young then declared that Joseph Smith had revealed to him "a mystery concerning the Royal Blood, that none of the rest of his brethren knew anything about." Joseph's son was not and never would be the Mormon prophet. By pushing the boy forward the Smith family was "aiming a dagger at his life blood." Looking over the sixty or so men around him, Smith saw no smiles and heard no consoling words. He became more convinced than ever that his life was in danger.

In his pamphlet Smith accused Young of using church funds to perpetuate polygamy. With mock indignation, Smith, who had six wives, asserted that "it can be proved that B. Young and P. P. Pratt were the first to preach and to practice the 'spiritual wife' doctrine, in the city of Boston and other places, my dissent from any such doctrine of course gave annoyance, as did also my exclaiming against the too common practice among the elders of using profane oaths." In Nauvoo "several houses have been filled up with women who have been *secretly* married to Brigham Young, H. C. Kimball, and Willard Richards—women with little children in their arms, who had no means of support except from the tithing funds." Mormons should refuse to support such evil men.

In "noticing the claims of Brigham Young to superior power and authority," Smith concluded, "I would here observe that I heard my brother Joseph declare before his death, that Brigham Young was a man, whose passions, if unrestrained, were calculated to make him the most licentious man in the world, and should the time ever come, said he, that this man should lead the church, he would certainly lead it to destruction. What, my brethren, I would ask you, are the claims of Brigham Young to the keys of the church, above the rest of the Twelve? They are keys which Joseph never conferred on Brigham Young, nor was power ever given to him to lead the church in his place as his successor. The church is hereby warned against any such pretensions, as little Joseph, the son of Joseph Smith, is the lawful heir to the office, being the oldest son of the deceased prophet. . . . Reflect and you will clearly see that Brigham Young is not lawfully or legally the prophet or head of the church, and that to claim such a right is usurpation and an act of tyranny; it is robbing the innocent—the widow and the fatherless." Delighted with Smith's words, Sharp in an editorial advised the Saints to "Hang the Twelve, the Bishops and the City police, and then scatter."[32]

Faced with other challenges as the years passed, Young and his followers countered with broad declarations of authority. "Those keys and powers were on Joseph Smith when he was in the flesh," said Kimball in 1857, "and before he departed he laid his hands on br. Brigham and br. Heber and others and conferred the keys of salvation upon them."[33] Far truer, however, were the words of Lorenzo Snow: "Brigham Young was never set apart by Joseph Smith as his successor that I am aware of."[34]

IV

ENGULFED BY DISSENSION from within and without, Young established in Nauvoo a police state. When he returned to the town after Smith's death and was served with several writs, he strapped on a pair of six-shooters and vowed he would kill any man who handed him another summons or grabbed hold of him. Until he left Nauvoo, he wore these guns.[35] "Is this the way you have to go armed?" the shocked Boston Saint, Catherine Lewis, asked Young. "Yes," he answered, "and shame to the nation."[36]

In the presence of Joseph Young, Lee, and other important Mormons, Young raised his hand and swore "by the eternal Heavens that I have unsheathed my sword, and I will never return it until the blood of the Prophet Joseph and Hyrum, and those who were slain in Missouri, is avenged. This whole nation is guilty of shedding their blood, by assenting to the deed, and holding its peace. Now, betray me, any of you who dare to do so!"[37]

Substantiating William Smith's charges, Page and other Strangites told how the Nauvoo police, two to three hundred Saints organized as deacons and led by a bishop, stifled all opposition. A common practice was "greasing and swallowing," or tying one end of a rope to the victim and the other to a stone, which was then tossed into the Mississippi River. At a meeting of the high priests in Nauvoo, during which Kimball threatened to take the head off anyone revealing their secrets, some members suggested greasing and swallowing a troublemaker named Madison. The culprit was eventually "whittled" out of town. About twenty men silently surrounded Madison and began slicing shavings off the wooden sticks they held in their left hands so that the points of their long bowie knives ended up against the victim's face. Then they kicked and rolled Madison in the dust for nearly a mile. "Aunt Peggy," or whipping, was also common. "Aunt Peggy was deemed a very severe woman," testified one Strangite, and Young and Kimball habitually warned: "He had better look out. I'll send Aunt Peggy after him."[38]

These charges might be dismissed as enemy propaganda had Taylor not admitted them. Still irritated because the Illinois legislature revoked the charter granted to the Saints, Taylor remarked in 1857: "And that state robbed us of the rights of freemen; and the only chance we had then, when they sent their scamps and rogues among us, was to have a whittling society and whittle them out. We could not get them out according to law, and we had to do it according to justice, and there was no law against whittling, so we whittled the scoundrels out." Taylor recalled that Dr. Charles, a member of the legislature, once complained: "Mr.

Young, I am very much imposed upon by the people around here, there are a lot of boys following me with long knives and they are whittling after me wherever I go, my life is in danger." "I am very sorry you are imposed upon by the people," Young mocked; "we used to have laws here, but you've taken them away from us; we have no laws to protect you. . . . Boys, don't frighten him, *don't*." As Taylor concluded, someone in the audience shouted: "We still have whittling societies." "Yes," acknowledged Taylor, "we still have whittling societies, as br. Kimball says."[39]

At Nauvoo, moreover, the Mormons stole from their neighbors. James M. Adams, a Strangite, testified that he and another Saint slaughtered a huge hog belonging to an apostate. They also took a heifer and a steer and gave the hides and beef to the Twelve as a gift.[40] But Thomas S. Williams made the prize haul. One Sunday he stole the machinery of a small sawmill and sunk it in the Mississippi until the search for it ended.[41] Recalling such outrages, Phelps once declared: *"If the Mormons had behaved like other people, they would never have been driven from Illinois and Missouri; but they stole, robbed and plundered from all their neighbors, and all the time."*[42]

V

WITH THE REPEAL OF THE NAUVOO CHARTER in 1845 Young realized the Mormons would have to leave Illinois. That spring he sent to President James K. Polk and the governors of every state and territory in the Union letters outlining the wrongs done to the Saints. "With these facts before you, Sir," Young appealed, "will you write to us without delay, as a father and friend, and advise us what to do? We are, many of us, citizens of your state, and all members of the same great confederacy. Our fathers, nay, some of us, have fought and bled for our country, and we love our constitution dearly. . . . Will it be too much for us to ask you to convene a special session of your State Legislature, and furnish us an asylum, where we can enjoy our rights of conscience and religion unmolested? . . . Or, will you express your views concerning what is called the 'Great Western Measure' of colonizing the Latter Day Saints in Oregon, the North Western Territory, or some location remote from the States, where the hand of oppression shall not crush every noble principle, and extinguish every patriotic feeling."[43]

The Mormons themselves disagreed about the response they received. George Smith subsequently argued that the only reply came from the governor of Arkansas, who advised the Saints to migrate to Oregon.[44] Young, on the other hand, said he received five answers, all rejecting the plea.[45]

Already bad, the Mormon situation worsened considerably in September 1845. On the evening of the ninth several Mormon-haters barely escaped injury when unknown persons fired into a schoolhouse near Warsaw. The next night Gentiles retaliated by burning some Mormon homes.[46] Then on the sixteenth Franklin A. Worrell, the lieutenant of the anti-Mormon military unit, the Carthage Greys, and reputedly a plotter in the assassinations of Joseph and Hyrum Smith, was ambushed while riding to the camp of the burners.[47]

For years Gentiles charged the murder to Orrin Porter Rockwell, the Danite leader, who before his death attained a reputation comparable to that of Billy the Kid and other Western bad men. But with Rockwell, as with Billy, it is often impossible to separate fact from fiction. In 1870 Fitz Hugh Ludlow, the journalist, attributed to Rockwell over forty murders, but Ludlow was afraid to face him after making the charge. Rockwell's appearance was enough to frighten to death most men. Of medium height, exceptionally strong and broad-shouldered, he possessed steely, searching blue eyes, a chest as broad as a barrel, hands as hairy and powerful as bear paws, and a heavy mane of braided hair he refused to cut after Smith told him it would render him, like Samson, unconquerable. Accused in 1842 of the attempted assassination of Smith's enemy, former Governor Lilburn Boggs of Missouri, Rockwell had changed his name and hid along the New Jersey shore.[48]

Even Mormons admitted Rockwell had murdered Worrell. Like almost every other pious Saint in Nauvoo, Hosea Stout was sure he had. The *Millennial Star* also conceded Rockwell had committed the crime but justified it by pointing to Worrell's misdeeds.[49] In 1846 Rockwell was arrested for the murder, but no one would testify against him and he was released.[50]

Incensed by Worrell's death, the burners intensified their activities. By October 1 they had destroyed 150 Mormon houses. Left with no other choice, the Twelve agreed to remove five to six thousand Saints during the coming spring. They immediately offered for sale hundreds of farms and two thousand homes.[51]

Like many Americans, the New York *Herald* saw tragedy in these events. "No intelligent patriot can regard these outbreaks of popular violence in this country without the deepest sorrow," it commented. "They are eagerly seized upon by the monarchists of Europe, and by the enemies of republican government everywhere, and made the foundation of arguments against the safety and practicability of free institutions."[52]

VI

EVEN IN THE FACE OF DISASTER Young imbued men with hope. Lee remembered building a hall in Nauvoo for the Seventies, the high priests who supervised the church's missionary activities. Both the work and the fund-raising proved difficult, and one night when nearly two stories were finished a tornado ripped down the wall, causing several thousand dollars worth of damage. "I was inclined to be down in the lip," Lee recalled, "but Brigham Young laughed at me, and said it was the best omen in the world." It showed, Young said, the fury of the devil, who quaked in his boots at the mere mention of the Seventies. When building the ark, Noah was mobbed three times, but he stuck to his work. "Just so with you," Young advised; "double your diligence and put her up again. If you do not you will lose many a blessing." Within two months the hall was in use.[53]

Mobs were driving the Saints from Nauvoo, but Young urged his people to finish the temple, needed for religious rites. During the first six weeks of 1846 the structure was sufficiently completed for Young to be sealed to thirty-four of the thirty-five brides he took in Nauvoo after Smith's martyrdom. Among these were eight of Smith's widows, for the Mormon leaders had decided to care for them so that in the next world Joseph might claim them and bless the apostles for their good work. The widows included Rhoda Richards, Young's first cousin;[54] Olive Grey Frost, who went mad and died shortly after marrying Young;[55] Emily Dow

Partridge, one of two sisters sealed to the prophet;[56] Maria Lawrence, who, like Emily, also had a sister married to Smith;[57] and Eliza R. Snow, the Mormon poetess.[58]

Young's marriage to Zina D. Huntington, another of Smith's brides, constituted a saga in itself. Zina was still the wife of Henry B. Jacobs and was seven months' pregnant with his child when she and Smith were secretly married in 1841. Touring Illinois with Jacobs at the time, Lee remembered: "Jacobs was bragging about his wife, what a true, virtuous, lovely woman she was. He also worshipped her. But little did he think that, in his absence, she was sealed to the Prophet Joseph, and was his wife."[59]

In 1846 Young demanded Zina. Before hundreds of people, including Hall, he ordered men walking in other's shoes to step out of them. "Brother Jacobs," Young declared, "the woman you claim for a wife does not belong to you. She is the spiritual wife of brother Joseph, sealed up to him. I am his proxy, and she, in this behalf, with her children, are my property. You can go where you please, and get another, but be sure to get one of your own kindred spirit." Jacobs meekly submitted and departed for England. The following year he returned with two other wives.[60]

On the mission that precipitated this episode Lee converted Emmeline Free, long Young's favorite wife. Both Emmeline and her sister, Louisa, subsequently became engaged to Lee. "One day," Lee recorded, "Brigham Young saw Emmeline and fell in love with her. He asked me to resign my claims in his favor, which I did, though it caused a great struggle in my mind to do so, for I loved her dearly. I made known to Emmeline Brigham's wish, and even went to her father's house several times and used my influence with him to induce her to become a member of Brigham's family. The two girls did not want to separate from each other; however, they both met at my house at an appointed time and Emmeline was sealed to Brigham, and Louisa was sealed to me." But plural marriage, indulged in only by the Mormon elite, was still a secret, and Young lived only with Mary Ann Angell. "Many a night," Lee added, "have I gone with him, arm in arm, and guarded him while he spent an hour or two with his young brides, then guarded him home and guarded his house until one o'clock, when I was relieved. He used to meet his beloved Emmeline at my house."[61]

About this time the details of the most unusual Nauvoo romance began to leak out. Even today church historians almost completely ignore Augusta Adams Cobb and hastily pass over her story. But in 1848 Catherine Lewis told how Augusta abandoned a beautiful home, a high social position, and many children for Mormonism. In a divorce suit Henry Cobb revealed more details. He and Augusta, a stately, attractive woman, had been married for twenty-one years when Young came to Boston in 1843 to preach. Enticed by the apostle's vigorous good looks and his stories of rewards for the faithful in the heavenly kingdom, Augusta fled toward Nauvoo with her two smallest children, one of whom died en route. Reaching Illinois, she married Young without bothering to divorce Cobb. When Augusta briefly returned to Boston in 1844, she met George J. Adams, who warned her that spiritual wivery would lead her to the devil, but Augusta proudly answered that she was ready to go there or anywhere else with Young.[62] Eventually three Cobb women would be brides of Young, and a fourth would marry his son.

Unlike Augusta, Catherine, who lived with Kimball's family for twelve weeks, found plural marriage revolting. After the Twelve began taking Smith's wives, she heard Kimball might be sealed to his own daughter, Helen, the prophet's youngest widow. But in Catherine's presence Helen, who was only fifteen years old when she was married to Smith, boldly told her mother: "I will never be sealed to my Father, and I would never have been sealed to Joseph, had I known it was any thing more than ceremony. I was young, and they deceived me, by saying the salvation of our whole family depended on it. I say again, I will never be sealed to my Father; no, I will sooner be damned and go to hell, if I must. Neither will I be sealed to Brigham Young."[63] In 1874, twenty-six years after Catherine revealed Helen had been married to Smith, the Mormon church, which ignores the testimony of apostates, conceded the wedding had taken place.[64]

Kimball too married dozens of women. Hall "saw twelve in one seat." He considered Kimball "a very mean, low character. Among the vulgar, he was the most vulgar; among the mean men, he was the meanest. He had seduced a beautiful girl by the name of Golden. . . . I saw her with the other spiritual wives in his tent, all clothed alike. My heart grieved for her."[65] Thirty-six years after Hall wrote, Kimball's family acknowledged the marriage in Nauvoo to Christeen Golden.[66]

The Saints, meanwhile, publicly assailed polygamy. In 1845 Parley Pratt warned all Mormons to "beware of seducing spirits, and doctrines of devils, as first introduced by John C. Bennett, under the name of the 'Spiritual Wife' doctrine; and still agitated by the Pittsburg Seer, and his followers under the same title. It is but another name for whoredom, wicked and unlawful connexion, and every kind of confusion, corruption, and abomination. . . . 'The Spiritual Wife Doctrine,' of J. C. Bennett, and numerous other apostates, is as foreign from the real principles of the church as the devil is from God, or as sectarianism is from christianity."[67] When Pratt made this statement, he had six living wives.[68]

VII

LATE IN DECEMBER 1845 the Saints received more bad news. A Circuit Court indicted Young, Richards, Taylor, Parley Pratt, Hyde, and Theodore Turley for counterfeiting. "From the testimony before the Grand Jury," the Illinois District Attorney reported, "it appeared that counterfeiting coin has been largely carried on at their place for some years. The defendants evade the service of process."[69]

One day while in his room at the temple Young learned that a posse, led by a federal marshal, lurked about. He knelt and prayed for guidance. Rising, Young noticed George D. Grant, his driver, and William Miller in the hall. He threw his cloak about Miller and told Grant: "George, you step into the carriage and look towards brother Miller, and say to him, as though you were addressing me, 'Are you ready to ride?'" Falling for the ruse, the marshal arrested Miller, took him to Carthage, locked him in a guarded room, and bragged to everyone in town that he had captured Young. An apostate finally informed the officer he had the wrong man. "What in hell is the reason you did not tell me your name?" the marshal asked Miller. "You did not ask me my name," replied the Saint.[70]

Preparing to leave Nauvoo, the Mormons practically gave away their property. Mary Smith's mother sold a house and lot worth eight hundred dollars for four pounds of pork, and Lee accepted $12.50 for a house costing eight thousand dollars.[71]

Young also took enormous losses. "I believe for some four pretty nice brick houses and a nice large barn, timber land and so on, I got one span of little horses and a carriage worth about a hundred dollars, the horses were worth about sixty dollars apiece, the harness about twenty. I think that was everything I got for my property."[72]

Early in February 1846 about two thousand Mormons began crossing the river to Iowa. As Young departed from Nauvoo, Franklin D. Richards gazed at the temple and sighed: "What a pity it is that we have to leave such a beautiful edifice." "Yes," responded Young, "it is beautiful, but we have the satisfaction of taking the substance with us, leaving behind us only the shadow."[73]

But perhaps Catherine Lewis provided the final footnote to the Nauvoo story. "In the year 1844 I heard Brigham Young say, 'it will not be more than five years before the Gentiles will come bowing and bending down to us; but if the people of this nation knew what men we are, and our power, they would tremble.' I have heard them say," Catherine added, "they would be back within three years from 1846."[74]

V

$\mathcal{T}o$ the $\mathcal{W}$hite Horse

of $\mathcal{S}$afety

I

WHEN WILLIAM SMITH heard Young and the Twelve planned to lead a migration to Oregon or some other God-forsaken spot in the West, he warned his fellow Mormons not to go along. "Mark me, many an honest Saint will bitterly rue they ever followed the advice of such counselors, and the more especially should they wander with such men into the wilds of the forest, and there become, as they assuredly would, slaves, yea even more, a prey to the beastly passions of tyrants, deprived altogether of the sweets of liberty and the freedom of speech. I heard Brigham Young say not long since, and the remark made my blood run cold, that, the man that did not comply with the measures established by them in that land his head should come off, or at all events none should return to tell their tales. These men will tell you stories of peace and plenty, but I warn you to believe them not; they will tell you of a land of liberty, and call it the 'land of the free, and the home of the brave,' they will talk of raising a standard of freedom for the oppressed, and tell you, you will enjoy liberty, sweet liberty; they will tell you all these things and much more, till once they get you within their grasp. Then, my brethren and sisters you will be rob-bed by them of all that is virtuous and good; also of your property, and if need be, even of your lives."[1]

Smith's message deterred few readers. The Saints formed com-panies of one hundred families, established a wagon shop for each fifty, cut and boiled in brine green timber—the only kind avail-able in the forests—and constructed wagons. With their remaining money they bought in the towns along the upper Mississippi what-ever iron they needed.[2]

On February 6 the first migrants crossed the river on flatboats, but within a few days the temperature dropped to twenty degrees below zero and the ice became thick enough to support the thou-sand wagons and two thousand persons in the Mormon caravan. Viewing the migration, the New York *Herald* commented: "This is an incident in religious history that will, undoubtedly, be as remarkable a one as is the Hegira with the Mahometans."[3]

As the first Mormons reached Iowa, papers like the *Herald* and the St. Louis *American* predicted the migrants would go all the way to the Pacific Coast. But as word of the size of the exodus drifted east, most observers realized a mass movement across the plains would be foolhardy. The Saints would undoubtedly halt in Iowa or Nebraska Territory before going on.[4]

The first stop was Sugar Creek, seven miles west of the Missis-sippi, where two thousand people with three thousand wagons and thirty thousand head of cattle eventually congregated. Although acknowledging that the Mormons were suffering from the bitter cold and heavy snows, Sharp's Warsaw *Signal* nonetheless con-sidered this phase of the journey pleasurable. The Mormons "had a good band of music, plenty of young girls, and passed the time very agreeably. Every one who was heard to complain or murmur was immediately sent back to Nauvoo and informed that they should not go to the Land of Promise, until they could learn to put up with hardships without grumbling. . . . The Saints who started in this expedition provided themselves well with young females. Indeed a gentleman who recently visited Nauvoo informs us that many men left their wives in Nauvoo and took with them young girls."[5]

At this point a noted Mormon miracle occurred. To feed his

starving people God sent into their camps flocks of quail. "They came into the tents," Orson Hyde gratefully recalled, "flew into the wagons, rested on the wagon wheels, ox yokes and wagon tongues, and our little children could catch them, and there was an abundant supply of meat for the time being."[6]

When the migrants pushed on, they elected Young, who had left Nauvoo on February 15, president of the "camp of Israel." By March 25 his party was a hundred miles west of Nauvoo, and a month later it reached Garden Grove, at the headwaters of the Grand River about halfway across Iowa. There the Mormons established a settlement, planted two thousand acres of corn, and selected one hundred men to fell trees and build fences.[7]

So reduced by hunger that the tight-fitting coat in which he left Nauvoo lapped over twelve inches, Young led between three thousand and four thousand people in a thousand wagons forward on May 11. At Mount Pisgah, where eight hundred graves still remind visitors of the sufferings of the pioneers, he set up another way station. Then on June 14 the Mormons reached the Missouri River at a spot just south of present-day Council Bluffs. Covering three hundred miles had required five months.

Leaving Hyde to create a colony along the fertile bottomland on the Iowa side of the Missouri, Young built and launched a ferry and on June 29 crossed to Nebraska, then an unorganized territory. Five miles north of where Omaha would rise—it was not founded until 1854—he established Winter Quarters, now Florence.[8]

Meanwhile, the twelve thousand migrants spread between Nauvoo and Winter Quarters suffered intensely. In the spring the Nauvoo *Hancock Eagle* noted the deplorable condition of those clustered along the Iowa bank of the Mississippi. Women and children were exposed to all kinds of weather and frequently fell before starvation or disease. Comparing his people to the victims of the recent European potato famine, one Saint observed: "The sufferings of the starving Irish cannot exceed that which we have in our own land, for the Irish have a roof to die under."[9]

In Nauvoo itself three Mormon trustees, Almon W. Babbitt, John S. Fullmer, and Joseph L. Heywood, offered buyers the concert hall, the Masonic hall, twenty thousand acres of farm land,

and two hundred houses. The Mormons were even willing to sell their temple, which had cost a million dollars, for two hundred thousand. Thus far they had received no bids.[10]

THE SMITH FAMILY refused to follow Young from Nauvoo. Late in 1845, in fact, Emma Smith, Joseph's first wife, publicly denounced "the *tyrants* who have seized on the government of the Mormon church." Like her brother-in-law William she shuddered at the thought of Young dragging the Saints to the Pacific Coast, where they would be forced to obey the Twelve's every whim.[11]

Strang gleefully read Emma's words. "I have never forgotten the kindness shown me by yourself and your husband (now gone home to God) on my visit to Nauvoo two years since," he flattered Emma early in 1846, "and hope the time may come when I shall be able to return all your kindness with interest." Strang endorsed her condemnation of "those who usurp authority in the Church" and lashed out at the "men who not only teach the abominable things now taught and practiced in Nauvoo but are all so ready to rob and plunder the widows and orphans of their benefactors—the men from whom they got all they have, and are. Of those are not we, your brethren of the faith in Voree. Can we ever be useful to you we shall never be found forgetful of the great who have done us good, nor refuse them their reward. . . . Now sister I do not know your intentions, nor feel disposed to be inquisitive in your affairs, but if you intend to remain in Nauvoo, you cannot well imagine how much I should rejoice in your full and hearty cooperation in my efforts for the regulation and salvation of the city. Will you not write me, and communicate your ideas on this subject?"[12]

Meantime, Babbitt, Heywood, and Fullmer further alienated the Smiths by offering the prophet's mother two hundred dollars a year and "a comfortable house" in Nauvoo on condition she prohibit William from denouncing the Twelve in her home. Lucy angrily rejected the offer. "You would have me forsake my children in order that you may give me a living. . . . As to William he is my son and he has rights. As to the Twelve you say they have rights, but who shall decide between them. Are you the judge. The Twelve speak against William & William speaks in his own defence. You say he slanders them, he says, they have slandered him and robbed him of his rights, but I shall leave these things with one who is a just God and will measure to all men their just deserts in the day of accounts. As to the merits of my children none are more worthy to have an inheritance in the city of Joseph and you are now living on the labour of their hands."[13]

Upon this scene arrived John C. Bennett, since 1842 "Professor of Mid-Wifery, and the Diseases peculiar to Women and Children" at the Cincinnati "University of the Literary and Botanico-Medical College." In March 1846 he resigned that post and informed Strang he was "ready to do battle for you *forever* as your 'General-in-Chief.' . . . Can I depend upon my *old* place? I have confidence that you will accord it to me, in justice to all concerned."[14]

Bennett blamed his split with Joseph Smith on meddlers. "*Joseph* and *I* were only severed by the corruptions of Willard Richards, Brigham Young and John Tailor. Their counsel was *damnable*—they *wished* the *death of Joseph that they might rule. I could* and *would at all times* have saved Joseph and the church had I been applied to; and I should have been applied to but for Willard Richards. All I ever said against any member of the church was in self-defence. . . . *I have loved the church for many years; I love it now.*"[15]

Bennett advised Strang to appoint Page and Samuel V. Searles of Cincinnati "permanent Apostles, without an *if* or a *but*. I shall see William E. McLellin at Pittsburg, on my way east; and, if possible, shall induce him to go for you. He is a splendid man. *Sidney Rigdon will not*, in my opinion, go for you; but *if he will*, make him one of your *Councillors*, instead of *me;* but, *by all means, make George J. Adams* the other Councillor. I am not selfish—I do not desire place to the exclusion of *able men*: but I do want you to have an able and strong government. *Rigdon* and *Adams* would make you able Councillors; Adams *will* accept, and I *wish* that Rigdon would but *if he will not, I should like the place. Having once occupied the place*, I would not like to be degraded. . . . I advise you to publish a small pamphlet, setting forth your claims, Joseph's letter, the discovery of the plates, and *every important matter*: the exact situation of Voree, its advantages, etc., etc. This would do incalculable benefit."[16]

Above all, Strang must woo the Smiths. "I would advise you to write, or send a messenger, to our beloved brother William Smith, at Nauvoo, inviting him to the patriarchal see, at Voree; to take with him *his mother*, with the *mummies* and *papyrus*—the bodies of *Joseph* and *Hyrum*—etc., etc., as all these things would have an astonishing effect in congregating the people at Voree. Make a desperate effort *now*, for it is highly important."[17]

In mid-summer of 1846 the alliance was formed. William and his mother announced that Joseph had a vision shortly before his death telling him the church would go to Voree. William had heard Joseph say "that should the time ever come that Brigham Young and Heber C. Kimball would lead this church, that they would lead it to hell. This was said in the hearing of Sister Emma Smith. The whole Smith family of the Joseph stock join in sustaining J.J. Strang."[18]

William promised to leave for Voree in the spring of 1847, "say about the first of April. To remove us," he told Strang, "will require 7 teams and one extra carriage for Mother Smith to ride in. She is quite feeble and I feel anxious that she may be removed to Voree and see the Prophet before she is gathered to the Land of her fathers. The mummies and records are with us and will be of benefit to the Church, if we can get them to Voree. Mother also has the history of her life written and prepared for the Press."[19]

Strang even temporarily won over an important Saint commissioned to battle him. Before crossing the Mississippi, Young authorized Reuben Miller to hunt down and excommunicate all Strangites in Nauvoo. But once Young was out of sight, Miller wrote Strang a friendly letter. "Many have land they cannot sell. Is it best for them to sacrifice their property or not. They want you to write to them as soon as this comes to hand giving your views in full and what they had better do. If you could come down now you could do much good for the way is open for you to have a hearing. The Saints are very anxious to see you here."[20]

Miller visited, and was converted by, his supposedly mortal foe. In mid-1846 he topped off his apostasy by publishing a pamphlet whose title obviously shocked Young: *A Defence of the Claims of James J. Strang to the Authority Now Usurped by the Twelve; and Shewing Him to Be the True Successor of Joseph Smith as First President of the High Priesthood.*[21]

Throughout 1846 Strang, Adams, and other powerful speakers toured the country and established church branches in New York, Chicago, Philadelphia, Cincinnati, Washington, and Dayton.[22] As Young's weary, starving, and weather-beaten Saints, strewn over Illinois and Iowa, limped toward Winter Quarters, Strang's power and influence reached their apogee.

III

MORMON HISTORIANS STILL LOVE TO TALK about an incident that occurred on the ferry carrying Young from Council Bluffs to Nebraska. A federal officer jumped aboard and began smashing the four kegs of malt whiskey the Saints needed to purify their water. Facing disaster, Young immediately drew his pistol, pointed it at the intruder's head, and shouted: "Stay your hand! If you touch that keg, you die by the living God!" The scoundrel quickly withdrew.[23]

About then Young met another officer, Captain James Allen, who had been sent from Fort Leavenworth, Kansas, to raise a Mormon battalion for service in the Mexican War, which had just broken out. "There cannot be a more damnable, dastardly order issued than was issued by the Administration to this people while they were in an Indian country, in 1846," Young subsequently argued. "Before we left Nauvoo, not less than two United States senators came to receive a pledge from us that we would leave the United States; and then, while we were doing our best to leave their borders, the poor, low, degraded curses sent a requisition for five hundred of our men to go and fight their battles! That was President Polk; and he is now weltering in hell."[24]

In reality, the Mormons passed and sent to Polk a resolution thanking him "for his friendly offer of transferring 500 of our brethren, to the land of their destination under command of Col. Allen." Young asked another favor of the President, in whom he had the "fullest confidence." The Mormons had heard "that the friends of Ex-Gov. Boggs are endeavoring to make him governor of California." Polk must veto this appointment.[25]

In a letter to English Saints, Taylor also praised Polk. Since the recruits would be discharged in California and allowed to keep their arms and implements, "and as there is no prospect of any opposition, it amounts to the same as paying them for going to the place where they were destined to go without. They also had the privilege of choosing their own leaders."[26]

Far from opposing Allen's request, Young rode from camp to camp recruiting the battalion, which soon left for Leavenworth. "They stayed there a while," observed Ursulia B. Hascall, a devout Saint, "received their money, sent home to their families considerable of it. They do not need of it at present and they put it into President Youngs hands for the benefit of the Church. He sent one thousand dollars to St. Louis to buy goods of all kinds."[27]

The Saints, meanwhile, constructed a town. Located on a fifty-foot plateau overlooking the Missouri, Winter Quarters, which ran along the river for a mile and a half, had seven hundred houses within three months and a thousand within a year. The city was divided into twenty-two wards, each ruled by a bishop appointed by Young, but like other Mormon communities it was governed by a twelve-man high council appointed by and subject to the will of the apostles.[28]

Squatters on land reserved for the Omahas, the Mormons met with the Indians just after reaching Nebraska. When Young described his people's sufferings, Big Elk, the Omaha chief, said: "My son, thou hast spoken well. . . . I hope we shall be friends. You may stay on these lands two years or more. Our young men shall watch your cattle. We would be glad to have you trade with us. We will warn you of danger from other Indians." Unwilling to accept a verbal promise, Young drew up a lease, which Big Elk signed.[29]

Armed with this guarantee, Young decided to build a mill and asked Lee to ride to Santa Fe to get money for it from the members of the Mormon battalion. Lee hesitated, for his many wives and children needed care, but Young promised to provide for them and in September 1846 the messenger departed. Returning in November, Lee found his family in a snow-covered tent, while the other Saints rested snugly in log cabins. "I took my life in my hands," he muttered to Young, "and went into that Indian country, on that perilous trip, a distance of two thousand two hundred miles, through savage foes, to carry out your orders. I have found things as I feared they would be. When I started I asked you to care for my family, and you promised all that I asked of you. Now I see all my family exposed to the storm; they, of all the camp, are without houses. My best cattle have been butchered and eaten, but not by my family. The choice beef has been given to your favorites, and the refuse to my wives and children."

"Brother John," Young apologized, "I am ashamed of the conduct of this people. I have mentioned the situation of your family several times, but the brethren did not feel like building houses for others until they had their own houses completed. I was intending this very day to call a meeting and have the brethren turn out and build houses for your family. Do not blame me, Brother John, for I have done the best that I could. Come, cheer up," Young counseled, extending his arm about Lee's shoulder, "and you shall have $100 of the money for your services, and you can make a thousand of it." "But this, like all his other promises, fell to the ground," Lee grumbled, "for I never got a cent of the money."[30]

In all, Young received from the Mormon battalion over fifty thousand dollars. "Very much depressed in spirit" because much of it went to stock the store Young, Albert Rockwood, and William Clayton ran in Winter Quarters, Lee complained about this too. Young explained that the store's profits would be used "to liquidate the debt of building the mill" and swore to repay twenty dollars a day once the mill began operating.[31]

Hearing the Twelve had taken about forty thousand dollars sent by battalion members to their dependents, George Miller, the bishop of Nauvoo, openly denounced the men who starved women and children. Young came to see Miller and said such talk had caused Joseph's death. "I told him," Miller boasted, "not to presume to place himself on a parallel with Joseph—the contrast was as disproportioned as between the ox and toad." Equally incensed because Young's store swindled these families, Miller apostatized.[32]

Later Young offered his version of the mill episode. "I had not five dollars in money to start with; but I went to work and built a mill, which I knew we should want only for a few months that cost 3,600 dollars. . . . How did I do that? By faith."[33]

I V

YOUNG SOON FACED MORE TROUBLE. At first the Saints and Omahas got along well. The Mormons gave the Indians maize and protected them from their enemy, the Sioux, but in building Winter Quarters the Saints destroyed the forests and drove the game away. The Omahas had no choice but to order the guests out.[34]

Then Thomas Harvey, the Superintendent of Indian Affairs, protested because the Mormons had settled on land reserved for the Indians. Young answered that Allen had authorized the Saints to stay in Omaha country as a reward for raising the Mormon battalion, but Harvey insisted Allen had overstepped his authority. The Superintendent allowed the ten thousand Mormons to winter where they were but cautioned them to preserve the timber. "I am at a loss in forming an opinion in relation to the future movements of this, to say the least in reference to the masses, deluded people," he informed his superior in December 1846. "They say their intention is to cross the Mountains. If so, I cannot see any satisfactory reasons for their making on the Missouri such substantial improvements."[35]

Long before this, however, the migrants had decided to move west. As early as July 1842 Joseph Smith talked of sending an expedition to the Rocky Mountains to seek among the Indians a permanent home for his oppressed people.[36] In the spring of 1843 Smith predicted his followers would establish beyond the Rockies a community he called the White Horse of Safety. There the Saints would fine refuge, but, he dolefully prophesied, "I shall never go there."[37]

Reacting to an anti-Mormon convention in Carthage, Smith established in March 1844 the earthly Kingdom of God, the organization destined to plan and control the westward migration. Distinct from the church itself, the Kingdom was to prepare the world for the coming of God. Ordained "King on earth," the prophet appointed fifty-three princes to assist him.

Unlike the Twelve and the Seventies, the Council of Fifty was an independent organization and theoretically had nothing to do with the Mormon hierarchy. In practice, however, it touched every phase of Mormon life, and its leaders invariably controlled the church. Soon after its formation, the Council mapped out Smith's presidential campaign. It later completed the Nauvoo temple.[38]

Shortly before Smith's death the Council considered several migration schemes, including the creation of a Mormon buffer state between Mexico and the Republic of Texas. Preliminary discussions proved so successful that the Fifty authorized three commissioners, among them George Miller, to draw up a treaty between Texas and the Kingdom. After the prophet's murder, Miller urged the Council to continue the negotiations, but Young refused. A group of Saints led by Wight actually moved to Texas but met hardship and dispersed.[39]

In later years Young frequently said the Mormons had no idea where they were going when they left Nauvoo. One day he considered California, the next Vancouver Island, the third Oregon.[40] In reality, the Council decided in September 1845 to send fifteen hundred men to the Great Salt Lake, recently explored by Lieutenant John C. Frémont. That December Parley Pratt read to Young and Kimball Frémont's journal, which described the fertility of the Salt Lake Valley, and the following March the Fifty chose twenty-five captains, each of whom was to prepare one hundred families for the trip across the plains. These captains of hundreds were authorized to select captains of fifties, captains of tens, and clerks.[41]

Then in the fall of 1846 Father Pierre Jean de Smet, the Jesuit adventurer, rode into Winter Quarters. For a month, he later recalled, Young and his lieutenants "asked me a thousand questions about the regions I had explored." The priest's glowing account of the Salt Lake Valley "pleased them greatly."[42]

Colonel Thomas L. Kane, one of Young's closest friends, knew exactly where the Saints were headed. Kane's relations with the Saints was a story in itself. A small, nervous hypochondriac, he came from a distinguished Philadelphia family: his brother, Elisha Kent Kane, was the famed Arctic explorer, and his father, John K. Kane, was an elder statesman of the Democratic party. One day while strolling about Philadelphia, Kane stumbled into a Mormon meeting being conducted by Jesse C. Little, the head of the church's Eastern mission. Completely sympathetic to the Saints— his enemies declared he had been secretly baptized—he went to Winter Quarters and saw their plight first-hand. During an epidemic that took six hundred lives, Kane fell ill and was nursed back to health by the Mormons. For a decade thereafter he was Young's most devoted and effective lobbyist and fund raiser.[43]

After his recovery, Kane freely discussed the Mormon plan. "The destination of this body," he wrote Secretary of State William L. Marcy in April 1847, "is the Bear River Valley or some portion of the Utah Country, where they purpose to fix their residence."[44]

Early that year the Saints obtained two sextants, two barometers, telescopes, thermometers, and other needed equipment. And on January 14, 1847, Young received his only existing revelation, "The Word and Will of the Lord Concerning the Camp of Israel in Their Journeyings to the West," instructing his people to start west that spring. Comparing Young's and Smith's communications from God, Thomas B. H. Stenhouse, the famed apostate, noted: "The Lord's style of revelation to Brigham is a great improvement upon the Lord's style of revelation to Joseph. It is just as much better English in Brigham's case than in that of Joseph, as Willard Richards's literary education was superior to that of William Clayton!"[45]

Not all Saints accepted the news joyfully. Within the Twelve itself the thought of crossing a thousand miles of barren plain and high mountains created dissension, and Young openly attacked Orson Pratt and others who withheld animals for their wives' carriages. "I have turned out every horse and mule that I have that is fit to go and would do it again if my wife had to ride on a bob sled, . . ." he insisted. "This Kingdom I am determined to bear off in spite of devils or wicked men."[46]

Young's farewell address to his people offered a glimpse into life at Winter Quarters. He denounced some Saints as "damnable and when the Twelve goes away you will see sights. Those characters will steal old spavin horses, waggon wheels, quilts, &c. Let such men go down to hell and if you do not understand what this means, cut their infernal throats. Never steal till the Lord tells you, and never steal that that should not be stolen. And when you hear of Brigham Young stealing you may know that it should be stolen. . . . Be contented with your lot and station and stop your whining and babbling about the 12, saying that Brigham oppresses the poor and lives off their earnings and that you can't see why you can't have some of his good living, and so on. Did Brigham Young ever get anything from you, did you ever help him to any of his fine living, you poor curses, or was it through Brigham's influence that thousands of the poor have been fed? You poor stinking curses, for you are cursed and the hand of the Lord shall be upon you and you shall go down to hell for murmuring and bickering. This people means to tie my hands continually as they did last year so that we can't go to the place of our destination. They are already coming to me saying can't you take me along? Don't leave me here, if you do I am afraid I shall die, this is such a sickly place. Well I say to them, die, who cares. If you have not faith to live here you will die over the mountains. This people will be subject to sickness and disease and death until they learn to be passive and let council dictate their course; without this their efforts are vain. I shall be glad when the time comes that this people will unanimously hearken to and be governed by council."[47]

V

ON APRIL 14, 1847, 148 Saints in seventy-three wagons headed toward the White Horse of Safety. The caravan included three women—one of Kimball's wives, a bride of Lorenzo Dow Young, and Clara Decker, known ever after as Brigham's "pioneer wife" —two children, eighty-nine horses, sixty-six oxen, fifty-two mules, nineteen cows, seventeen dogs, some chickens, and a few cats. Several men with instruments provided music. The Mormons had tried to get a map from Frémont or anyone else who knew the route to the Great Salt Lake but had failed.[48]

The travelers lived like an army. At five A.M. the blast of a horn awakened the Saints, who rose, tended their animals, and break-fasted. At seven o'clock the camp moved forward; at noon it stopped an hour for lunch. When the Mormons halted for the day, usually after covering at least twenty miles, they formed with their wagons a circle, placing their livestock within it and their tents outside it. At eight-thirty P.M. a horn ordered each man to his wagon for prayers, and by nine everyone was asleep. As the expedition pushed from the Missouri into the unknown, Young insisted that each man keep his weapons handy.[49]

Following the north bank of the Platte River, the pioneers at first found level but dry and sandy ground. They rafted across the Elkhorn River, twenty-three miles from the Missouri, and continued on to the fork of the Platte and Loup Rivers, eighty miles from Winter Quarters, which they forded, "not, however," recorded Orson Pratt, "without danger, in consequence of the quick sands." On May 1 the Saints reached what is now Grand Island, Nebraska, sixty miles further west.[50]

Three days later, while ahead of the main party, Pratt met a Frenchman who described the immense herds of buffalo the travelers would soon hit. Riding on, Pratt peered through his field glasses and saw animals several of his men identified as antelope. Now buffalo and antelope were everywhere. "I think I may safely say," Pratt wrote on May 6, "that I have seen 10,000 buffalo during the day."[51]

On May 14, when the Mormons arrived at the juncture of the North and South Platte Rivers, Pratt observed from a hill breathtaking beauty. To his north a broken succession of hills and ravines resembled "the tumultuous confusion of ocean waves, when rolling and tumbling all directions by violent and contrary winds." On the east a background of blue clouds accentuated the valley containing the Platte's two forks, and on the south a chain of bluffs stretched for forty miles beyond the South Platte's "glistening waters." On the west the muddy, yellow North Platte streamed over quicksand that yielded to and richly contrasted with grassy bottoms. Here and there small herds of buffalo grazed, "and all seemed to conspire to render the scenery interesting and delightful."[52]

The Saints headed up the North Platte and on June 1 reached Fort Platte, 227 miles above the juncture of the North and South Platte, only to find it vacant and crumbling to the ground. But

Fort Laramie, which the American Fur Company operated a mile to the northwest, contained about eighteen men and their families. Greeted cordially, the pioneers also met some Saints who had wintered at what is now Pueblo, Colorado, 250 miles to the south. Because of drought—until recently no rain of consequence had fallen in the region for two years—and warlike Crow Indians, the trappers lived on buffalo meat and did not even try to farm.[53]

Even before this, Young had found Indian women attractive. William Hall told how in mid-January of 1847, during a feast the Mormons gave to conciliate the Sioux, "Two squaws, the daughters of different Chiefs, . . . were 'sealed up' to him, and became his spiritual wives." Young dressed "his young Indian ladies" in "elegant costumes. Large gold chains, elegant slippers, and other ornamental apparel, were bestowed on them in abundance." The Indians "were delighted, especially to see the daughters of their chiefs treated with so much honorable distinction by the Mormon King."[54]

At Laramie, Young tried to repeat the episode. "There was an old Frenchman at the fort with a half-breed daughter," remembered John Y. Nelson, Young's scout; "to her Brigham took a great fancy, and he tried hard to get her to join the party. But *le père* would not consent."[55]

Bidding farewell to his lost love, Young led his people forward. Passing through country with few buffalo but hordes of blacktail deer and antelope, the Saints traveled north of the Wyoming Black Hills, which, Pratt noted, "with their broken ragged cliffs and conical peaks form a scenery grand and interesting," and on June 12 arrived at the crossing, 124 miles from Laramie, of the North Platte and the Oregon Trail. The pioneers moved on to the Continental Divide, where with childlike fascination they searched for the point at which the waters running into the Atlantic and Pacific Oceans separated. Here on June 26 they encountered Major Moses ("Black") Harris, a veteran of twenty-five years in the region. "We obtained much information from him in relation to the great interior basin of the Salt Lake, the country of our destination," Pratt recorded. "His report, like that of Captain Frémont's, is rather unfavorable to the formation of a colony in this basin, principally on account of the scarcity of timber. He said he had travelled the whole circumference of the lake, and that there was no outlet to it."[56]

Two days later the Saints came upon Jim Bridger, the dis-coverer of the Great Salt Lake and the most famous of the mountain men. "He encamped with us during the night," Pratt noted, "and being a man of extensive acquaintance with this interior country, we made many inquiries of him in relation to the great basin and the country south. His information was rather more favorable than that of Major Harris."[57]

Spurred on by this report, the Saints reached Fort Bridger in the southwest corner of present-day Wyoming on July 7 and headed southwest toward the lake. Five days later Young fell ill with mountain fever. To make things more comfortable for him the party slowed down.[58]

Then on July 21 Pratt and Erastus Snow saw from a hill "a broad open valley, about twenty miles wide and 30 long, . . . at the north end of which the broad waters of the Great Salt Lake glistened in the sunbeams." The next day the first Mormons entered the Valley, and on the twenty-third, obeying Young's orders to turn north, some pioneers halted at what was to become the center of Salt Lake City and began damming a creek of pure cold water. At a quarter to noon on July 24, as the Saints doused five acres of potatoes with water, Young and Kimball arrived.[59]

During the journey Young often talked about how he had seen the Promised Land. "I will show you when we come to it," he explained. True to his word, he reportedly said upon emerging from the mountains: "This is the place where I, in vision, saw the ark of the Lord resting; this is the place whereon we will plant the soles of our feet, and where the Lord will place his name amongst his people." To parties about to scour the area for timber, water, and grass, Young remarked: "You will find many excellent places for settlement. On every hand in these mountains are locations where the people of God may dwell, but when you return from the south, west and north to this place, you will say with me, 'this is the place which the Lord has chosen for us to commence our settlements, and from this place we shall spread abroad and possess the land.' "[60]

VI

CEASELESSLY ASSERTING THAT THEY made a desert bloom, Mormon leaders have perpetuated several stories about the barrenness of the Salt Lake Valley. Bridger, for example, was supposed to have warned: "Mr. Young, I would give a thousand dollars if I knew an ear of corn could be ripened in the Great Basin." "Wait eighteen months," Young replied, "and I will show you many of them."[61]

Similarly, during the westward movement Elder Sam Brannan of California urged Young to push on to the Pacific Coast. "For heaven's sake," Brannan exclaimed, "don't stop in this God forsaken land. Nobody on earth wants it. Come on to California, to a land of sunshine and flowers." "Brannan," answered Young, "if there is a place on this earth that nobody else wants, that's the place I am hunting for."[62]

But as Young indicated to those about to search for water, grass, and timber, he realized the Salt Lake Valley, then Mexican territory, was one of the choicest regions available. To produce crops it needed water, but dozens of mountain streams stood ready for that purpose. In the Valley the pioneers found anything but a desert. Frémont spoke of its magnificent grazing land, and Pratt called its soil "of a most excellent quality." For miles around the spring at which Young and his party camped and slaked their thirst the grass towered above a horse's girth and the animals rolled in it and grew fat on it. Farther south, sagebrush, greasewood, and rabbit brush abounded, but wherever the plough turned the soil and water laved it Mother Earth responded bountifully. Young knew where he was going and aimed for the richest possession in the North American interior.[63]

One week after reaching the Valley, the pioneers laid out Great Salt Lake City. Its streets, 132 feet wide, formed square blocks of ten acres that were divided into eight lots, each destined to hold one house. Every other block was to have four houses on its east and west sides but none facing north and south. On the alternate blocks four houses would run north and south but none east and west. Thus houses on opposite sides of the street would never front one another. Those on the same side would be 132 feet apart, with gardens extending 330 feet to the center of the block. Every house was to be at least twenty feet from the street. On August 1, with one block reserved for a temple and other church buildings and fifty-three acres of corn, beans, and garden seed already planted, each apostle present selected a block for his personal use.[64]

Using lumber from the nearby canyons, the Saints then constructed a fort and homes. Young's house rested against the east side of the fort and contained one room eighteen feet square. Its floors were made of puncheon logs split down the middle and rounded underneath. Its roof of willows and earth was but slightly inclined, for the pioneers believed there would be no rain in the Valley. The house had an adobe chimney, a corner fireplace with a clay hearth, and wooden windows that could be taken out during the day and nailed in at night.[65]

On August 2 Young sent to the brethren along the Missouri the first letter written in the Great Basin. Overjoyed "that every soul who left Winter Quarters with us is alive, and almost every one enjoying good health," he advised: "Let all the brethren and sisters cheer up their hearts, and know assuredly that God has heard, and answered their prayers and ours, and led us to a goodly land, and our souls are satisfied therewith."[66]

Bidding farewell to the other Saints, Young, Kimball, and nearly seventy others left the Valley on August 26 and headed back toward Winter Quarters. Not far from the lake they came upon another great Mormon caravan plodding westward: 1,553 people, 2,313 cattle, 887 cows, 716 chickens, 358 sheep, 124 horses, and thirty-seven hogs. Continuing their journey, Young and his companions encountered disaster at the South Pass: Sioux stole their best animals. Forced to walk most of the remaining distance to the Missouri, the travelers lived on buffalo meat, but without suitable horses they were able to shoot only bulls whose flesh was barely edible.[67]

Arriving at Winter Quarters on October 31, 1847, Young decided to revive the hierarchy created by Joseph Smith. He would be the church's prophet and Kimball, his nephew by marriage, and Richards, his first cousin, would be his counselors. The three would constitute the First Presidency. On December 27 the Twelve Apostles ratified the proposal, which now needed approval at the church's April conference.[68]

In February 1848 God stepped in. Orson Hyde, destined to

succeed Young as the chief apostle if the plan was accepted, described a meeting of the Twelve at Hyde Park, Iowa: "We were in prayer and council, communing together; and what took place on that occasion? The voice of God came from on high and spoke to the Council. Every latent feeling was aroused, and every heart melted. What did it say unto us? 'Let my servant Brigham step forth and receive the full power of the Presiding Priesthood in my Church and kingdom.' This was the voice of the Almighty unto us. . . . Men, women, and children came running together where we were, and asked us what was the matter. They said that their houses shook, and the ground trembled, and they did not know but that there was an earthquake. We told them that there was nothing the matter—not to be alarmed; the Lord was only whispering to us a little, and that he was probably not very far off." On April 6, 1848, the Saints obeyed the Lord and unanimously elected Young their prophet, seer, and revelator.[69] Joseph Smith's shoes were filled at last.

As the First Presidency planned the return to the Great Basin, Kane, assisted by Senator Theodore Frelinghuysen of New Jersey, Mrs. Polk, Dolly Madison, and other notables, raised funds for the Saints. After hearing of barefoot Mormons, of black canker epidemics that took thousands of lives, and of the Mormon need for food, clothing, medicine, tools, animals, and seed, the New York *Herald* commented: "We hope they may get a mouthful both of food and common sense."[70]

Young, meantime, stirred his followers to fever pitch. One Sunday just before starting west he assailed the country he was leaving. "The martyrs were brought up as also the usage of this people by the United States," wrote Oliver B. Huntington, "and the whole nation were shown to be accessory to those crimes and persecutions often written and spoken upon in this church and the spirit of God rested upon Brigham that he cursed the Nation by the authority and power of God and the Priesthood given him and all the Saints said amen. He was never known to curse so much in his life as on that day. The nation, the land of Missouri, that sickness should not allow any but the righteous to live upon it, and old Colonel Miller, an Indian agent for his meanness and abuse to the Saints. All the Saints said amen."[71]

Like the pioneers, the 1848 migrants formed hundreds, fifties, and tens, and every fifty was allotted a wagonmaker and a blacksmith to handle all emergencies. A committee inspected the wagons to make sure each migrant brought along three hundred pounds of breadstuff, each able-bodied man possessed a good rifle and one hundred rounds of ammunition, and each family had seed grain and agricultural implements. During the trip Saturday afternoons would be used for washing, baking, repairing wagons, and shoeing animals. On Sundays there would be morning and afternoon services. Dances were also planned.[72]

Late in May Young led 1,229 Saints forward. Several days later Kimball and 662 more Saints left Winter Quarters. Retracing the route of the pioneers, these travelers crossed the Elkhorn, rode alongside the North Platte to what is now Scottsbluff, near the western edge of Nebraska, followed the South Pass, the Continental Divide, and the Green River to Fort Bridger, and on September 20, 1848, emerged from the Wasatch Range of the Rockies onto Great Salt Lake City.[73] Home at last, Young would never again go east.

VII

IN IMPORTANT WAYS the Mormon frontier differed sharply from other American outposts. Unlike the settlers of most regions, who were usually only thirty or forty miles beyond the previous frontier, the Saints were a thousand miles from their nearest neighbors —both those to the east and to the west. The Mormons, moreover, moved west in large, well organized caravans, not in small units or as individuals. Most important of all, they migrated not for economic reasons—the desire for land or for furs—but because of their religious beliefs. The westward trek enabled them to worship God as they pleased.

The Saints shared with other frontiersmen the problem of carving a civilization out of the wilderness, but they adopted unique methods. Led by the First Presidency, they discarded individualism and for the general good exhibited a rare degree of unity and cooperation. As early as July 25, 1847, the first Sabbath after reaching the Salt Lake Valley, Young, for example, announced a land policy far different from that Joseph Smith had used in Nauvoo. No migrant to the Great Basin would have to buy land, he said, "but every man should have his land measured out to him for city and farming purposes, what he could till. He might till as he pleased, but must be industrious and take care of it." The church would decide how big a lot each man would receive, and anyone who did not use his share properly would lose it. Nor could land—the gift of God and the property of the community—be sold by its occupant, for the Saints believed that the earth belonged to the Lord and the men who held it were merely His stewards. During much of Young's lifetime a lot cost a Mormon settler only $1.50, a dollar for surveying it and fifty cents to record the deed.[74]

After allotting the acreage in the center of town, Young turned to farm land. The first plots, distributed in October 1848 in five-acre and ten-acre parcels, were in a huge field to be surrounded by a fence on which each farmer would labor in proportion to his holdings. "I would rather fence a block of ten acres, and have a crop," Young advised his people, "than plant a hundred acres for the cattle to destroy."[75] Facing novel conditions, the Saints in the Great Basin were forced in this and other instances to bend and to destroy traditions and to modify the old formula for American living.

V I

Honey in the Carcass

of the Dead Lion

I

OST MEN THRIVE ON INCONSISTENCY. They are guided by no basic principles except self-interest and perhaps some religious beliefs. Their lives resemble patchwork quilts.

But between his return to the Salt Lake Valley in 1848 and his death in 1877 Young was hardly the average man. Time after time he acted predictably. His views on life, government, and religion coincided in every particular with the philosophy of the Kingdom of God formulated and publicized in the late 1840's and early 1850's by Orson and Parley Pratt and John Taylor.

Like much of Mormonism, the Kingdom of God was a product of its times, embodying, among other things, the notion of destiny prevalent in the 1840's when the United States annexed Oregon, Texas, and California. Just as expansionists considered it the destiny of the United States to acquire this territory, the Mormons viewed as inevitable their conquest of the religious world. From this era stems the imperialism still common to Mormonism.

The Saints also shared with contemporaries a reliance on higher law. In the 1840's and 1850's Southerners frequently justified slavery by calling it part of God's order, and Northerners opposed the return of fugitive slaves by emphasizing a law above that of Congress. The Kingdom of God applied to Mormonism this commonly accepted principle.

"The kingdom of God is an order of government established by divine authority," explained Orson Pratt in 1848. "It is the only legal government that can exist in any part of the universe. All other governments are illegal and unauthorized. God, having made all beings and worlds, has the supreme right to govern them by His own laws, and by officers of his own appointment. Any people attempting to govern themselves by laws of their own making, and by officers of their own appointment, are in direct rebellion against the kingdom of God." For the past thousand years no "true and legal government" had existed. "All the emperors, kings, princes, presidents, lords, nobles, and rulers, during that long night of darkness, have acted without authority. Not one of them was called or anointed a king or prince by the God of heaven—not one of them received revelations or laws from him— not one of them has received any communication whatsoever from the rightful sovereign, the Great King."[1]

The Lord's empire, long absent, was now here, Taylor boldly announced. "As God has dealt in former times, so will he in the latter, with this difference, that he will accomplish his purpose in the last days; he will set up his kingdom; he will protect the righteous, *destroy* Satan, and his works, purge the earth from wickedness, and bring in the restitution of all things."[2]

But, Parley Pratt warned, the devil would fight to hold what he had won during the past thousand years. Before God triumphed, "plagues, earthquakes, storms and tempests" would engulf the earth and "devour the wicked." Pratt saw "the wreck of nations; the casting down of thrones; the crash of states, and the winding up of all mere human institutions; while a new dynasty, as a universal Theocracy, shall succeed and stand forever."[3]

God himself would eventually come to battle the Gentiles, "overthrow their armies, assert his own right, rule the nations with a rod of iron, root the wicked out of the earth, and take possession of his own kingdom." Taylor added "that when the Lord does come to exercise judgment upon the ungodly, to make an end of sin, and bring in everlasting righteousness, he will establish his own laws, demand universal obedience, and cause wickedness and misrule to cease. He will issue his commands, and they must be obeyed; and if the nations of the earth observe not his laws, 'they will have no rain.' And they will be taught by more forcible means than moral suasion, that they are dependent upon God; for the Lord will demand obedience, and the Scriptures say, time and again, that the wicked shall be rooted out of the land, and the righteous and meek shall inherit the earth."[4]

Meanwhile, all men should join God's kingdom and "obey strictly all its laws unto the end of their days. To become a legal citizen in the kingdom is of infinite importance; for salvation is only to be obtained in the kingdom of God. All other kingdoms or governments will be broken to pieces and destroyed, while the kingdom of God will endure for ever."[5]

Most frightening of all, the Mormons demanded that each individual subordinate his welfare to the Kingdom's. "After being adopted into the kingdom of God it is necessary that every citizen should cultivate such a character and disposition as shall be most pleasing to their King. Whenever the King shall give advice or counsel upon any subject, they should, without any hesitation, adhere strictly to that advice or counsel. It is a great thing to find out the will of God, but it is still greater to do it. . . . We may not always discern the end or result of doing as we are commanded; but this is no excuse for disobedience. Abraham did not know the useful result the Lord had in view in commanding him to offer up his son Isaac; if he had followed the dictates of his own natural feelings or affections, he never would have attempted to comply with this command. . . . Does a skillful general reveal to his soldiers all his purposes and designs in regard to the enemy?"[6]

Young too was obsessed with the Kingdom of God and its principles: violence, unquestioning obedience, and holy war against the Gentile. "The great object of my life," he asserted in 1866, "is to establish the Kingdom of God upon the earth."[7] His favorite saying became: "The Kingdom of God or nothing."[8]

But Bill Hickman, the Danite, best summarized the doctrine's effect upon the Saints. "The satisfied point and undoubted fact that God had established His kingdom in the mountains, and Brigham was conversant with the Almighty was a settled question. In all candor I say I do not think there was then in Utah one in fifty, or, I might say, one in a hundred, who did not believe it."[9]

II

THE MORMONS VIEWED THE UNITED STATES and its institutions with mixed feelings. On one hand they cherished America as the Promised Land and called the federal Constitution divine, and on the other they scolded the United States for not protecting them in Missouri and Illinois and unyieldingly battled all enemies of the Kingdom. Accordingly, politics became a device for gain, and candidates for office were pawns in a game. To Mormons democracy and freedom of thought were meaningless words.

During the 1848 canvass, for example, Orson Hyde, the leader of the Mormons at Council Bluffs, or Kanesville as the Saints renamed it in honor of their benefactor, sold the ballots of his followers to Colonel Fitz Henry Warren, the treasurer of the Whig national executive committee, for a thousand dollars. "It has seemed good unto me, your brother and companion in tribulation, and counselor in the Church of God," Hyde explained in a letter read to his people on election day, "to advise and request you to cast your votes at the ensuing election in favor of the whig candidates for office. This letter is placed in the hands of Col. F. H. Warren, *who will give you, or cause the same to be done, all necessary information HOW AND WHERE TO ACT*."[10]

After collecting his money in Washington, Hyde went to Cincinnati, where for eight hundred dollars he bought a printing press. He then returned to Kanesville and started a semi-monthly newspaper, the *Frontier Guardian*.[11]

Even Whig journals were shocked. "From a careful observation of the manner in which they have always exercised the right of suffrage, making it purely an element of *traffic* without regard to principle," the St. Louis *New Era* said of the Saints, "we have always taken the ground that their organization was in derogation of the best interests of society, and at war with most if not all the well established principles of morals and good citizenship. These views remain unchanged, and the scenes that are now transpiring in Iowa confirm the bad opinion we have ever entertained towards them. We regret that any portion of our political friends should have anything to do with the Mormons whatever."[12]

Hyde also infuriated a Saint who was a loyal Democrat. After seeing the thousand-dollar check and hearing how Hyde got it, Almon W. Babbitt issued a letter that newspapers throughout the West published. "How much did you tell me, on your return down the river, the draft on the whig committee at Washington city was for?" he asked Hyde. "What did you go to Washington city for? Of whom in the city of Cincinnati did you get the printing press and materials? Where did you get the money to pay for the press? What did you say to me on the subject in a letter dated at Washington, September 15, 1848?" Babbitt dismissed as unacceptable Hyde's recent explanation of the episode in the St. Louis *Missouri Republican*. "I can assure Mr. Hyde that few of his Mormon friends believe his whig apologies. Mr. Hyde has a style peculiar to himself in writing upon these subjects, and turns many nice points with some anecdote in order to divert the mind from the point, which forcibly reminds me of the Ink, or Cuttle Fish, who, when closely pursued, throws out of his mouth so much fog, and offensive matter that he evades pursuit, and in this way makes his escape." Hyde "had never voted but once in his life, knows little or nothing about Federal and State policy, yet he assumes the responsibility of influencing a whole community; and lest he should betray ignorance as their guide, he directs them to a political knave to counsel them 'when and where to act.' . . . Are not the most cherished institutions of our country endangered by the use of such unhallowed means, when the most sacred of all human rights are prostrated at the shrine of religious despots, and men cease to think and act for themselves?"[13]

Babbitt went even further, establishing in Council Bluffs an opposition weekly, the *Western Bugle*.[14] Because of Babbitt's great ability, Young put up with these violations of discipline, but such insubordination could not be tolerated indefinitely.

III

YEARS AFTERWARD while describing the early days in the Great Basin, Young buried his face in his hands, wept, and cried out:

"When I think of all that, I feel full of unspeakable tenderness for my people: when I look about me and see the multitude of children of that band of pilgrims, and their children's children, I feel like him who found honey in the carcass of the dead lion."[15]

Like most Mormons, Young's family lived at first within the fort built by the pioneers. Soon, however, the prophet erected a log and mud plaster L-shaped house with rooms for each of his wives and their children. One room became the family schoolhouse.[16]

During these years food was scarce, for the winter of 1848–49 was severe, the temperature plunging to thirty-three degrees below zero. Spring brought large black crickets that devoured everything edible. In self-defense the Saints dug around their fields ditches two or three feet deep and two feet wide, which they filled with water. The crickets attempted to jump across the ditches, fell in, and were drowned. Flocks of gulls from the lake helped by feeding on the crickets until full, vomiting, and then beginning all over. The Saints, asserting that God had sent the birds to aid His people, fined anyone who killed one twenty-five dollars.[17]

Despite these hardships, the Mormon settlements grew rapidly. By the end of 1848 five thousand Saints lived in the region, and by 1850 there were 11,354. The church divided Salt Lake City into nineteen wards, each nine blocks long and presided over by a bishop appointed by and responsible to the Twelve. For currency the Mormons used the Kirtland Safety Society's notes, thereby fulfilling Young's promise that they would again be valuable. Now, however, the bills were backed by gold brought from California by members of the Mormon battalion.[18]

A New York *Tribune* correspondent who visited Salt Lake City in 1849 saw thousands of one-story houses made of wood or sundried brick. The Saints had cultivated every available inch of land and were growing yellow wheat, Indian corn, potatoes, oats, flax, and garden vegetables. The many shops in the center of town always seemed filled to capacity. In slightly more than a year the Mormons had created a thriving community.[19]

Water was Salt Lake City's lifeblood, and after much experimentation and squabbling the Saints devised a system that guaranteed each resident a fair share. Discarding the Anglo-Saxon principle of riparian rights, which said that the occupant of land bordering on a lake or a stream controlled its water, the Mormons adopted instead the Spanish doctrine of appropriation, according to which water belonged to the community and was to be administered by the proper authorities. The city's supply came from City Creek, directly to the north, entered the town at its center, and flowed along ditches on both sides of the street. A commissioner, assisted by a watermaster for each ward and a deputy for every block, regulated the supply. Upon assuming office each official swore to distribute the water equitably. A lot of one and a quarter acres usually received water for three hours a week, the residents of the block being notified beforehand of the specific hours, perhaps thirty-five minutes one day, twenty-five the next, and forty the day after. A city property tax of one mill on a dollar financed this ingenious system.[20]

Parley Pratt best summarized Mormon life at this time. "How quiet, how still, how peaceful, how happy, how lonesome, how free from excitement we live. . . . A meeting, a dance, a visit, an exploring tour, an arrival of a party of trappers and traders of a Mexican caravan, a party arrived from the Pacific, from the States; from Fort Hall or Fort Bridger, a visit of Indians, or perhaps, a mail from the distant world, once or twice a year, is all that break upon the monotony of our busy and peaceful life."[21]

IV

A HIGH COUNCIL OF TWELVE plus the stake president and his two counselors was Salt Lake City's first governing body. Its earliest ordinances fined drunks up to twenty-five dollars, subjected adulterers to a fine of a thousand dollars and up to thirty-nine lashes on the back, and punished thieves and housebreakers with thirty-nine lashes and a fourfold restitution of property.[22]

But during these years the Council of Fifty held the real power, regulating such things as the distribution of food, the building of an arsenal, the construction of bridges, land policies, and poor relief. Few matters escaped it.[23]

In accord with the philosophy of the Kingdom of God, the Council frequently employed force and threats. Early in 1849, as

John D. Lee recorded in his peculiar spelling, Young spoke of the corn shortage and warned that "if those that have do not sell to those that have not, we will just take it and distribute amoung the Poors, & those that have & will not divide willingly May be thankful that their Heads are not found wallowing in the Snow. There is some of the meanest spirits here amoung the saints that ever graced this footstool. They are too mean to live amoung the gentiles. The gentiles would be ashamed of them."[24]

One weekend the Fifty judged some Saints guilty of undisclosed crimes. According to Lee, Erastus Snow and several others demanded "their blood ought to floow to atone for their crimes. I wont their cursed heads to be cut off that they may atone for their Sins, that mercy may have her claims upon them in the day of redeemption." The Council agreed that Ira E. West "had forfeited his Head, but the difficulty was ho[w] he should be disposed of. Some were of the oppinion that to execut[e] him Publickly, under the traditions of the People would not be safe; but to dispose of him privately would be the most practic[al], & would result in the greatest good. The People would know tha[t] he was gone, in some manner, & that would be all they could suggest, but fear would take hold of them & they wo[uld] tremble for fear it would be thire time next." Young wanted West and Thomas Byrns put in chains and offered for sale "to the highest Bidder. They have both forfeited their h[e]ad[s] & shall loose them; and if this council wants me to shoulder it, I can do it, but to consent to do anything in the dark, I will not."[25]

In its most important move the Council created a territorial government. At the conclusion of the Mexican War the United States annexed what is now the Southwestern United States, including the Great Basin. The Mormon march to escape federal authority had been in vain. Accordingly in December 1848 the Council drew up a constitution for the proposed State of Deseret, named for the honeybee in *The Book of Mormon*. It nominated Young for governor, Richards for secretary, Kimball—whose only experience with the law had been running away from it—for chief justice, Newel K. Whitney and Parley Pratt for associate justices, and Doctor John M. Bernhisel for federal marshal. The Council vowed that if Boggs, Senator Thomas Hart Benton of Missouri, or other anti-Mormons were sent to govern them, "we would send them Cross Lotts to Hell, that dark & dreary Road where no traveler returns." In March 1849 a convention overwhelmingly approved the constitution and sent Babbitt to Washington to seek Deseret's entrance into the Union.[26]

As Stenhouse later pointed out, the Council's proposed boundaries for Deseret were large enough "to hold half of the monarchies of Europe." Embracing one-sixth of the United States, it reached Oregon on the north, the Pacific Ocean and the Sierra Nevada Mountains on the west, the Rockies on the east, and Mexico on the south and contained two fine ports, San Pedro and San Diego.[27] Salt Lake City would be the center of a vast empire fit for God when He arrived.

Expecting their early admission as a state, the Saints had good reason to celebrate on July 24, 1849, the second anniversary of their entrance into the Great Basin. At daybreak a cannon awakened the townspeople and urged them to prepare for the glorious day at hand. Soon brass and military bands marched through the streets, and at seven-thirty A.M. a giant American flag was raised to the top of a tall pole, as six guns barked and the Nauvoo temple bell tolled. An hour later a parade started toward Young's home. It consisted of the church dignitaries who were to escort him to the scene of the day's activities, a marshal on horseback, the two bands, twelve bishops bearing the banners of their wards, twenty-four young men, and twenty-four young women. Each young man wore a white scarf on his right shoulder and a coronet on his head and held a sheathed sword in his left hand and copies of the United States Constitution and the Declaration of Independence in his right. The girls also had white scarves on their right shoulders but wore wreaths of white roses on their heads. Each young lady carried a Bible and a copy of *The Book of Mormon*. The marchers proceeded from Young's home to the Bowery, a shedlike structure holding three thousand persons that veterans of the Mormon battalion built for church services. Upon arriving the paraders were greeted with nine loud shouts of "Hosannah to God and the Lamb," and as Young, escorted by twenty-four gray-haired men, walked down the aisle, he was serenaded by shouts of "Hail to the Governor of Deseret." At noon between six and eight thousand Saints and two hundred Gentiles began devouring a dinner of meats, vegetables, cakes, pies, breads, coffee, tea, milk, and water.[28] Deseret's officers would not always be this proud of the United States.

V

FATE, MEANWHILE, had already decided to pit Strang, William Smith, and other powerful apostates against Deseret. Of those who refused to follow Young west, Rigdon proved least troublesome. Strang appointed him to the Voree First Presidency, but Rigdon neglected his duties and was excommunicated in 1846. Rigdon then moved to Greencastle, Pennsylvania, and began building a cotton factory. He never again troubled either Strang or Young.[29]

In 1846 Reuben Miller, the president of the Voree stake, also left Strang. The prophet's varied descriptions of the way an angel designated him Joseph Smith's successor led to the break. Strang first maintained that the angel "did not touch him, but that he stood before him with uplifted hands, and gave him the *charge*." Later, however, Strang asserted that the heavenly being had anointed his head with oil. Miller thereupon published a pamphlet attacking Strang and rejoined Young's church.[30]

Lost too was McLellin, who had converted after Strang, carrying a letter of introduction from John C. Bennett, visited him in Kirtland in August 1846. But McLellin soon learned that Strang's First Presidency was filled and in his paper, the *Ensign of Liberty*, began ridiculing the prophet he had praised a few months before. After that McLellin went to Missouri, where David and John Whitmer farmed, and to Wisconsin, where Oliver Cowdery practiced law, and tried to interest them in a new church he would lead.[31]

Late in 1847 Strang excommunicated his two most famous converts. As soon as Bennett reached Voree, he caused trouble. After hearing complaints from over a dozen women, the Voree high council tried him for "Polygamy & Concubinage," but Strang finally unchurched him for trying to establish a stake of Zion by falsehood and deception.[32]

William Smith too was accused of adultery. He broke with Strang, however, over a more spiritual episode. During a church ceremony Strang anointed some followers with a queer-smelling substance and put them in a darkened room, where their heads glowed. The Saints rejoiced, but Smith examined the mixture and found it to be phosphorus and oil. Denying all, Strang insisted that Smith's story proved "only that the AUTHOR of it is a scamp and an UNBLUSHING LIAR."[33]

Still Strangism flourished. In Boston, George J. Adams filled a hall with two thousand prospective converts, and a like number listened outside.[34] Here was a force the leaders of the Kingdom of God could not ignore.

Although Young publicly assailed Strang, he privately wooed him. In 1848 and 1849 the prophet sent his brother, Phineas, to Voree, but Strang rejected these overtures and ended the negotiations.[35]

Lobbying in Washington for a church badly split, Babbitt faced a difficult task. "Yesterday our meetings were more interesting than usual," D.R. Whipple, a Strangite, reported on December 28, 1849. "In the morning A.W. Babbitt attended for the first time. After the meeting was closed he came up and told us who he was (not thinking of course that we knew him). He informed us of his being the delegate from the seeking to be State of Deseret. He told us that he was once a member of the Church of the Saints but that now he was not a member of any Church. Yet he felt an attachment to the name Saint. He also spoke about the Church being divided and invited us to call and see him." Babbitt referred to the Salt Lake City Saints "not as Brethren but as his constituents."[36]

Ten days later the guest came back. "Mr. Babbitt appears very anxious that we should not say or do any thing calculated in the least to hinder them in obtaining a State Government or him a Seat in Congress," Whipple informed Strang. "We have no disposition to interfere with them unless they attack you or your calling in your absence."[37]

William Smith, now leading his own church in Covington, Kentucky, was hardly this compassionate. In petitions to President Zachary Taylor and to Congress he likened Deseret to Sodom and Gomorrah and opposed its admission as a state. As he saw it, the Brighamites "entertain treasonable designs against the liberties of American free born sons and daughters. . . . Their intention is to unite church and state, and whilst the political power of the Roman pontiff is passing away, this American by rant is endeavoring to establish a new order of political popery in the recesses of the mountains of America." At Young's insistence fifteen hundred Saints had sworn to "avenge the blood of Joseph Smith on this nation," to "carry out hostilities against the nation, and to keep the same intent a profound secret, now and forever." Young had warned all Saints to "toe the mark, (that is obey him) or they should be circumcised around the throat." He had "mobbed and plundered President William Smith, entered into his house, he took even the last bed, his children's clothing, horses, wagons &c., amounting to some eighteen hundred dollars worth of property." Young had also taken from Smith a printing press in New York and real estate in Ohio, had robbed and oppressed Lucy Smith, and had "swindled" the members of the Mormon battalion "out of their bounty money and spent it in riotous living with harlots."[38]

Although Smith probably influenced no one, Congress ignored Deseret. Instead, on September 9, 1850, President Millard Fillmore, Taylor's successor, signed the Organic Act creating Utah Territory with boundaries roughly equal to present-day Utah and Nevada. The law authorized the President to appoint for a four-year term a governor, who would head the territorial militia and serve as Superintendent of Indian Affairs, and to pick for Utah a secretary, three judges, a district attorney, and a marshal. The residents of the territory could elect a bicameral legislature and a delegate to the federal House of Representatives. Two months later the Saints heard the good news. Fillmore chose Gentiles for most of these posts, but he appointed Young governor of Utah.[39]

To anti-Mormons the decision was a stunning blow. With Young's mounting importance exposures of him and his religion became more frequent and more vehement. Almost every year Maria and Increase M. Van Deusen, two excommunicated Strangites, issued a new edition of their lurid 1847 booklet, *A Dialogue between Adam and Eve, the Lord and the Devil, Called the Endowment*, which compared Mormonism to bacchanalianism. Anti-Youngism became a business and a way of life. "Some of the old residents of New York," Woodward later wrote, "will remember Van Deusen, as he stood selling his pamphlets in City Hall Square."[40]

VI

UTAH WAS YOUNG'S AS WELL AS GOD'S KINGDOM, for the prophet was involved with every phase of Mormon life. For women he designed the Deseret Costume, which had a skirt falling halfway between the ankle and knee. Under it women wore pantalets of the same material as the dress, over it a long, loose sack of antelope skin. The hat was eight inches high with a straight, narrow brim. Mormon women refused to wear the costume, which soon disappeared from sight.[41]

Just after Salt Lake City was founded, Young began settling other parts of Utah. First, he ordered several families to a region. Those selected must either obey the call or leave the church. Reaching the site, the newcomers immediately diverted a nearby stream or river from its course and directed the water into ditches that ran along the town streets and into the fields beyond. They next built a meeting house that also served as a schoolroom and constructed roads and cabins. Within a few years they erected a sawmill and cut the cost of lumber to the cost of hauling it.

A bishop appointed in Salt Lake City governed the settlement. Technically he possessed no civil authority, but in reality he arbitrated disputes between church members, advised all Saints in his community, and collected and administered the tithe, the tenth of his yearly income donated to the church by each member.[42]

Preparing for the Lord's arrival, Young carefully planned Mormon colonization. Although Congress in creating Utah drastically cut Deseret's boundaries, he sent settlers to all sections of the proposed Mormon state: in 1849 and 1850 he erected forts in Wyoming that guarded the eastern entrance to the Great Basin; in 1850 and 1851 to protect the Mormon passage to the Pacific he began a line of settlements from Salt Lake City to San Diego and San Pedro; in 1851 he sent Amasa Lyman, Charles C. Rich, and 520 other Saints to San Bernardino in southern California; and in 1855 he established Las Vegas in New Mexico Territory and Lemhi, now part of Idaho but then in Oregon Territory. In all, Young founded over 325 Western towns.[43]

Even before returning to the Great Basin in 1848, Young paid special attention to another matter. From Winter Quarters on

December 23, 1847, the Twelve, who had closed emigration when leaving Nauvoo, again urged European converts to gather in America. Advised to sail from Liverpool to New Orleans, then to go up the Mississippi to St. Louis, and finally to travel overland to Council Bluffs, Saints were encouraged to bring with them choice seeds, prize beasts and fowls, and tools and machinery. In mid-1848 the Mormons issued a guide describing all places between the Missouri River and Salt Lake City where wood, water, and grass were available and listing other information for travelers.[44]

To Mormon leaders few things exceeded in importance this assembling of Saints. Asked why his people could not live in New York, Liverpool, Stockholm, or London, Woodruff answered: "Because we should be in the midst of sin and wickedness and abomination, and it would be very difficult, while so situated, to keep from being polluted by the evils which reign upon the face of the earth at the present time. And to overcome these evils we have been gathered together, that we may be taught in the principles of truth, virtue and holiness, and be prepared to dwell in the presence of God."[45]

To gain converts and insure this flow of Saints to America the Mormons developed—and still maintain—a unique missionary system. The church kept no medical missionaries in Africa like David Livingstone and Albert Schweitzer. Nor did it send teachers or humanitarians to aid the Australian aborigines. Mormon missionaries displayed neither special fitness nor aptitude, only an undying and unquestioning zeal for their religion. They received no worthwhile training and served two years usually among people who already believed in the divinity of Jesus Christ. But, as Mormon officials continually noted, the missionaries went forth "without purse or scrip," sharply increasing church membership at no cost to the church.

Some Saints volunteered for missionary work but most were selected without regard for their welfare. At any time, but especially at the semi-annual church conference, Young might announce: "Brother William Johnson is nominated for a mission to Russia of two years at his own expense." Johnson, who perhaps had become a Mormon in Nauvoo and had struggled for months across the plains and Rockies to bring his three wives and ten children to Salt Lake City, sat stunned, for he had not left the Great Basin in years. Young would ask all in favor to say "Aye." The congregation, which never opposed him, roared its approval, and the new missionary, who spoke nothing but crude English and could not apostatize because a polygamist had no place to go, was on his way. His wives and children were left to manage without him.[46]

Young used his absolute power of appointment to great advantage. Like the Biblical hero David who deliberately sent to death in battle Uriah because he coveted Uriah's wife Bathsheba, Young ordered his opponents on one difficult mission after another. In Nauvoo he disposed of Lucy Decker's husband, Isaac Seeley, that way. Later he used this device to rid himself of Orson Pratt.

To win converts Mormon missionaries spoke of Joseph Smith's discovery of the plates of *The Book of Mormon*, of revelations, of visits from angels, of such gifts as tongues, and especially of triumphs over the devil. Captain Daniel Jones, the president of the church in Wales, recalled with gusto battling some agents of Satan who had taken possession of the bodies of three Mormon women. These demons screamed, kicked, uttered vile words, and finally bragged that in 1844 they had helped kill the prophet. *"Old Captain,"* they shouted, *"have you come to trouble us? D——d Old Captain, we will hold you a battle."* The spirits "swore they would not depart, *unless old Brigham Young, from America, would come,"* but Jones finally exorcised them by threatening to excommunicate the women.[47] Young later rewarded these efforts by marrying Jones's widow.

Miraculous cures also won many converts. Kimball told how "In England, when not in a situation to go, I have blessed my handkerchief, and asked God to sanctify it and fill it with life and power, and sent it to the sick, and hundreds have been healed by it; in like manner I have sent my cane. Dr. Richards used to lay his old black cane on a person's head, and that person has been healed through its instrumentality, by the power of God. I have known Joseph, hundreds of times, to send his handkerchiefs to the sick, and they have been healed. There are persons in this congregation who have been healed by throwing my old cloak on their beds."[48]

By 1854 such endeavors paid rich dividends, for the church had branches in England, Scotland, Wales, Denmark, Sweden, Norway, Iceland, France, Germany, Italy, Switzerland, Malta, Gibraltar, Australia, the Sandwich Islands, India, Siam, Ceylon, South Africa, and British Guiana. Although the Prussian king expelled them, the Saints usually succeeded in Protestant countries, especially Scandinavia, northern Germany, and Great Britain, but convinced few people in southern Germany, Italy, Ireland, France, Spain, Portugal, and other Catholic countries. Jewish converts were almost nonexistent. Realizing the power of the written word, the Saints translated *The Book of Mormon* into French, German, Italian, Danish, Welsh, and Polynesian.[49]

To help converts reach Utah the church organized on October 6, 1849, the Perpetual Emigrating Fund, incorporating it the following September with Young as president. In 1849, with five thousand dollars contributed to the fund in cash and oxen, Bishop Edward Hunter began bringing migrants to Salt Lake City. "The few thousand [of dollars] we send out by our agent at this time," Young predicted, "is like a grain of mustard seed in the earth. . . . We expect it will grow and flourish, and spread in a few years to cover England, cast its shadow in Europe and in the process of time compass the whole earth."[50]

Transporting each immigrant from Liverpool to Utah for as little as ten pounds, the company spent over $200,000 annually from 1853 to 1855 and in many overseas towns kept elders with whom prospective migrants deposited as much as they could each week until they had saved enough for the trip to America. When a man could not pay, an elder advanced money from the fund in exchange for a note payable in Utah. By 1870 the fund had financed passage for thirty-eight thousand Britons and thirteen thousand other Europeans.[51]

"We have gathered the poorest class of men to be found on the continent of America," Young boasted, "and I was one of them; and we gathered the same class from Europe, for very few indeed of those who have obeyed the Gospel have ever been the possessors of any wealth. We have taken the poor and the ignorant from the dens and caves of the earth and brought them here, and we have labored day and night, week after week, and year after year, to make ourselves comfortable, and to obtain all the knowledge there is in the world, and the knowledge that comes from God, and we shall continue to do so. We shall take the weak and the feeble and bring them up to the standard that God requires."[52]

In Utah the church directed the convert's activities. It inventoried his goods and if he had money told him what to do with it. An impoverished man was sent to a bishop, who gave him up to ten acres of land, seed, a wagon, and a yoke of cattle. The immigrant signed a note for these items plus interest as high as twelve per cent a year. Until this debt was paid, the bishop disposed of the man's harvest: a tenth went to the church as tithe; a portion provided for the laborer's family; some went for seed; the rest paid off the debt.[53] "The first duty of a Saint when he comes to this Valley," Young informed William Hepworth Dixon, "is to learn how to grow a vegetable; after which he must learn how to rear pigs and fowls, to irrigate his land, and to build up his house. The rest will come in time."[54]

A Mormon, no matter how downtrodden, was always obligated to his church. "Should a man be idle thirty days," the Springfield (Massachusetts) *Republican* observed, "the tithing office claims three days from him on the ground that he may do as he pleases with twenty-seven days, but has no right to idle away the three days belonging to the Lord."[55]

For unemployed carpenters, blacksmiths, machinists, and painters, Young created in downtown Salt Lake City a public works program. But wages were very low, and at least one visitor believed these laborers were "in a state of almost hopeless servitude."[56]

If the church dealt firmly with newcomers, it viewed Gentiles with hostility. Some non-Mormons heading for the California gold fields reached Salt Lake City late in 1849 and decided to winter there. The Saints were elated, for most of the travelers were skilled craftsmen willing to work for low wages. But once snow and cold weather trapped the visitors, the Mormons became oppressive. When the Gentiles refused to convert to Mormonism, the church taxed their property two per cent, and at the end of the season Willard Richards, Ezra Taft Benson, and several other apostles refused to give the migrants their wages. Benson even threatened to fine one traveler two dollars for each minute he delayed in paying a judgment levied against him by a Mormon judge. After reaching California, forty of the miners wrote and published a detailed account of their experiences and a warning to Gentiles to avoid Utah.[57]

Young laughed at such things. "It was prophesied by Joseph the Prophet that the bones of those who drove the Church from Missouri, and killed men, women, and children, should bleach upon the Plains. This has been fulfilled. Did they suffer more than the people of God whom they drove from their homes—from the firesides in winter—from their fathers and mothers and friends, and the land of their nativity? Yes, there is scarcely a comparison. Their sufferings in crossing the Plains to the gold regions of California have been greater in crossing the Plains to Utah. These are facts that are present with us. The bones of those who drove the Saints from Independence, from Jackson County, then from Clay and Davis Counties, and last of all from Caldwell County, from whence they fled into Illinois, have been scattered over the Plains —gnawed and broken by wild beasts, and are there bleaching to this day, while the Saints who have died on the Plains have without exception had a decent burial where they had died—have friends to console with and comfort them in their dying moments, and to mourn for a season with their bereaved relatives."[58]

VII

THE TRIALS OF THE GOLD-SEEKERS proved minor compared with what happened to Fillmore's appointees. As the Saints saw it, the battle pitted God's kingdom against secular usurpers. "Here in Great Salt Lake City is the seat of government for the Church and Kingdom of God, . . ." announced Kimball. "This is the place of deposit of all those keys pertaining to the salvation of the human family; and there never will be one soul of those spirits now in prison will come out of that place, except the keys of the Kingdom of God that are now held in Great Salt Lake City open the door and let them out."[59]

Young, not the President or Congress of the United States, must be obeyed. "If brother Brigham tells me to do a thing,"

Kimball preached, "it is the same as though the Lord told me to do it. This is the course for you and every other Saint to take, and by your taking this course, I will tell you, brethren, you are on the top of the heap."[60]

Following this philosophy, the Saints established their own system of justice. As in Smith's time, the church was governed in spiritual matters by the Melchizedek, or higher, priesthood: the First Presidency, the Twelve, the Seventies, traveling preachers and missionaries who collectively possessed the same authority as the Twelve, and the high priests, who also traveled and preached but collectively possessed no power.[61]

Below this came the Aaronic priesthood—bishops, priests, teachers, and deacons with temporal powers over even high priests. In cities the bishop governed a ward; in rural areas a town. With his counselors he cared for the poor and helpless and conducted a court that arbitrated disputes between brethren. When necessary, teachers and deacons could enter a house and question its occupants. Over this system Young exercised direct control, for he appointed and could summarily remove each bishop.[62]

A Saint objecting to the decision of the bishop's court could appeal to the stake high council. As described by the Frenchman Jules Remy, who saw one operate during a visit to Utah in 1855, this body was both remarkable and unique. At trials it split into two groups, one for and one against the defendant. Before the council assembled no one knew which side each of its members would be on. One member for each side then argued the case, and the stake president announced the verdict, which was invariably unanimous. Parties dissatisfied with the judgment could turn to the First Presidency of the church and eventually to the semi-annual church conference, but appeals were rare, for if the case was important Young told the stake president how he wanted it settled.[63]

In addition to this Mormon legal structure, Utah had four civil courts, which Saints used only in cases involving Gentiles. The highest was the Supreme Court, presided over by the territorial Chief Justice appointed by the President of the United States. Next came the three District Courts, administered by the Chief Justice and the two associate Supreme Court Justices. Each county also had a Probate Court, whose judges, chosen by the Mormon-controlled Utah legislature, were usually Saints. Last came the local Justice Court, invariably run by the bishop. Saints, however, rarely used it, preferring to it the bishop's court.[64]

From the beginning the Mormons quarreled with Fillmore's appointees. Satisfactory to them was Justice Zerubbabel Snow, the elder brother of Erastus Snow and one of nine brothers and sisters who had become Mormons, but Justice Perry E. Brocchus, Chief Justice Lemuel G. Brandebury, and Secretary Broughton D. Harris despised, and were in turn despised by, the Saints.

For Harris and his new bride, Sarah, the honeymoon in Salt Lake City proved a nightmare. In Washington Secretary of State Daniel Webster and other officials had assured them that newspaper and magazine stories about polygamy, which the Saints still denied practicing, were untrue, but in Utah the couple learned differently. The prophet once introduced Sarah to several of his wives with the explanation: "You see many strange things in this valley, Mrs. Harris." Heeding warnings not to offend Young, Sarah replied: "Indeed we do, and have already visited a number, among them the hot sulphur springs, and the Salt Lake." The expression on Young's face changed, Sarah remembered fifty years later, "and I was glad there was no further time for conversation."[65]

At a tea Sarah met six of Kimball's young brides, each of whom was the age of Kimball's eldest daughter, Helen, a widow of Joseph Smith. Three of the wives cuddled infants. When Harris arrived, Vilate Kimball escorted him around the room, presenting her husband's wives as Mrs. Mary Kimball, Mrs. Ruth Kimball, and so on. "This," Sarah recalled, "was the end of our social visiting among the Saints."[66]

Equally shocking was Young's domination of Utah. "Claiming and represented to be the Prophet of God, and his sayings as direct revelations from heaven," Young held "thereby unlimited sway over the ignorant and credulous. His opinions were their opinions," the Gentile appointees informed Fillmore, "and his wishes their wishes. He had but to indicate his sympathies or dislikes, and they were made their sympathies or dislikes. In a word, he ruled without a rival or opposition, for no man dared question his authority."

From the beginning Young abused the officials, refusing to see some and subjecting others to violent harangues and fits of temper. Then on July 24, 1851, during the annual celebration of his people's entrance into the Great Basin, Young discussed Taylor's attitude toward the Saints. "But Zachary Taylor is dead," he announced, "and in hell, and I am glad of it." Drawing himself to his full height and stretching his hands skyward, Young predicted "in the name of Jesus Christ, by the power of the Priesthood that's upon me, that any President of the United States who lifts his finger against this people shall die an untimely death, and go to hell." The audience approvingly shouted "Amen!" "Good!" and "Hear!"

Six weeks later with Brocchus on the platform Young told a large gathering of Mormons: "I did say that General Taylor was dead and in hell; *and I know it.*" When someone asked how Young knew it, the governor replied: "Because God told me so." With that Kimball placed his hand on Brocchus's shoulder and said: "Yes, Judge, and you'll know it, too; for you'll see him when *you* get there."

One day after the foolish Brocchus lectured the Saints on patriotism and the degradation of Mormon women, matters came to a head. Young arose, called Brocchus " 'profoundly ignorant or wilfully wicked'; strode the stage madly, assumed various theatrical attitudes, declared 'that he was a greater man than even George Washington'; that 'he knew more than ever George Washington did'; that 'he was the man that could handle the sword'; and 'that if there was any more discussion there would be pulling of hair and cutting of throats.' . . . By this time the passions of the people were lashed into a fury like his own. . . . Those of us present felt the personal danger that surrounded us. If the governor had but pointed his finger toward us as an indication of his wish, we have no doubt we would have been massacred before leaving the house. But he did not point his finger."

Fearing for their lives, Harris, Brocchus, and Brandebury fled late in 1851. Safely in the East, they wrote Fillmore a long letter, several versions of which were published, describing—and embellishing—their experiences. They also talked of other Mormon abuses, including the sentencing of Gentiles to ten years' labor on the public roads with ball and chain on their legs for trivial offenses and Young's numerous, but futile, attempts to procure $24,000 in federal funds entrusted to Harris.[67] Unfortunately, however, they ignored the underlying cause of the dispute: the Kingdom of God.

As Brocchus and Brandebury found out in Utah, the courts, dominated by Young, meted out strange justice. In Snow's First District Court a Mormon jury freed Howard Egan, the admitted murderer of James Monroe, a Gentile who had seduced Egan's wife. Although both Joseph Smith and Young had taken many women from their husbands, George Smith, Egan's lawyer, informed the court: "The principle, the only one that beats and throbs through the heart of the entire inhabitants of this Territory, is simply this: *The man who seduces his neighbor's wife must die, and her nearest relative must kill him!*"[68]

Young also intervened to save a Saint named Hamilton, who shot to death John M. Vaughn, the Gentile lover of Mrs. Hamilton. Although the murder took place in southern Utah, the trial, which lasted less than fifteen minutes, was held in Salt Lake City. All of the witnesses were friends of Hamilton, who had brought them with him to tell a favorable story. Hamilton supplied the horses on which they rode to town and paid their room and board there. On the stand these witnesses were asked a few informal questions, which they answered without being sworn. Young, who had publicly demanded Hamilton's acquittal, attended the trial not, he said, as the Lord's prophet but as Brigham Young. Cheers greeted the acquittal verdict, and the church confiscated Vaughn's entire estate.[69]

VIII

WITH THE DEPARTURE OF BROCCHUS, Brandebury, and Harris, Major Jacob H. Holeman, the tactful and energetic Indian Agent, became the chief Gentile officer in Utah. Fillmore's best appointee, he provided abundant evidence that the Mormon boast of kindness toward the Indians was a myth.

Mormon historians have painted two contradictory portraits of Young the frontiersman. One depicted him as an outstanding colonizer responsible for populating much of the West.[70] The second pictured him as the kindly helper who said: "It is cheaper to feed the Indians than to fight them."[71]

For a good reason both stories cannot be completely true. As the New York *Herald* observed in 1860, nearly every conflict with the red men, beginning with King Philip's War in 1675, stemmed from "unwarrantable aggressions" on Indian land by whites.[72] Like other Caucasians, the Mormons shoved the Indians about, but because the Saints colonized slowly the struggle was less ferocious than usual.

In 1875 General George A. Custer explained in detail why the Saints got along fairly well with the Indians. "One reason is that they do not encroach on their territories as rapidly as we do. They do not require them to be constantly moving. They buy, and are slow to extend their boundaries. The Indians have a strong attachment for the land containing the bones of their ancestors, and dislike to leave it. Love of country is almost a religion with them. It is not the value of land that they consider; but there is a strong local attachment that the white man does not feel, and consequently does not respect."[73]

Numerically the Indians in Utah were no match for the Saints. The most important tribes were the Paiutes West, six thousand strong, the Shoshones, totaling forty-five hundred, the Elk Mountain Utes, two thousand people, and the Paiutes, twenty-two hundred souls. The entire territory possessed about 18,500 red men.[74]

According to Mormon doctrine, the Indians, or Lamanites, were descendants of the Hebrew tribe of Joseph, which had migrated to America six hundred years before Christ while its members were still righteous and powerful. Through disobedience, they forfeited their priesthood, white color, intelligence, and noble physiognomy, but they retained several Hebraic traditions, such as the belief in one great spirit, the division into tribes, and polygamy. "In time—in God's own time," Young told Dixon, "they will be recalled into a state of grace: they will then cease to do evil and learn to do good; they will settle down in cities; they will become white in colour; and they will act as a nation of priests."[75]

To his superiors in Washington, Holeman frequently described the "enroachments of the Mormons" upon the red men. "In the first settlement of this city and the adjoining country by the Mormons," he explained, "they at first conciliated the Indians by kind treatment, but when they got a foothold, they began to *force their way*—the consequence was, a war with the Indians, and in many instances a most brutal butchery—this, the Indians fear will be the result whenever the Mormons make a settlement. The Indians have been driven from their lands and their hunting grounds destroyed, without any compensation therefor—they are in many instances reduced to a state of suffering, bordering on starvation. In this situation some of the most daring and desperate approach the settlements and demand compensation for their lands, where upon the slightest pretexts, they are shot down or driven to the mountains—these scenes frequently occur—but the other day, an Indian was found dead, in the vicinity of the city, shot through the body."[76]

Through his position as Indian Affairs Superintendent, Young fostered this policy. Late in 1851 he visited every Indian camp attempting to buy "the friendship of the chiefs and headman with presents furnished by the Government." The Mormons were, Holeman insisted, "a people who have no sympathy or respect for our Government or its institutions, and who are frequently heard cursing and abusing not only the Government, but all who are Americans."[77]

After talking to Walker, the Ute war chief, and Sowiette, the tribe's civil leader, Subagent Henry R. Day, another Gentile, agreed. Many chiefs had refused to attend a recent peace parley called by Young because "they believed it to be a trap set by the Mormons to kill them. They seem to have but little confidence in anything the Mormon people say to them and decidedly stand in fear of them and from all the information I could gather not without good cause. . . . I can perhaps convey their ideas better by giving you the language of the old Chieftain, Sowiette, who raising himself up to his full height said to me, American—good! Mormon—No good! American—friend. Mormon—Kill—Steal." Each year, complained Sowiette, the Saints shoved his people further away from good soil and timber. With tears in his eyes he begged the "Great Father" in Washington to stop the aggressors before they drove the Indians into the mountains, where starvation was certain.[78]

The Saints ceaselessly harassed the authors of these reports. Late in 1851 Lot Huntington, the interpreter, and E. W. Vanetten, the trader, visited Holeman and told him that Young had hired Vanetten. When they demanded to know how much Vanetten was to be paid, Holeman said he knew nothing about the matter and advised them to see Young. The Saints left but returned in two hours and asked for orders. Again Holeman refused to get involved in the matter. Several days later Vanetten reappeared, handed Holeman a bill, and "in a very presumptuous manner, demanded payment," insisting, Holeman reported, that "he had been *directed to present it to me*, and if I did not pay it, that he must proceed to collect it." About noon of that day Holeman was served with a warrant directing him to appear before Judge Snow at three o'clock. The territorial attorney general, a Mormon, represented Vanetten and secured a judgment against Holeman. To pay the fine the court seized a government carriage, which it sold the next day. Bewildered and dismayed, Holeman forwarded to his superiors the receipt for the carriage.[79]

Day soon resigned, went to Washington, and told the Commissioner about the "unjustifiable conduct of the Mormon authorities of Utah, and their seditious and violent expression with regard to the Government of the United States. . . . I am still of the opinion as expressed in my Report to you, and which I again beg to refer you, that no officer of the Government other than a *Mormon* can reside within that Territory."[80]

VII

The Twin Relic

of Barbarism

I

IN DENIGRATING POLYGAMY the fleeing officials merely followed other influential Gentiles. In 1848, for example, the New York *Herald* scoffed that by advocating free love the Perfectionists "out-Mormon the Mormons in their spiritual wife doctrines."[1]

Many Northerners compared plural marriage to slavery, denouncing each as its section's peculiar institution. At its first national convention in 1856 the Republican party went further, pledging to exterminate both of these "twin relics of barbarism." In that eventful decade the Saints received sympathy only from those Democrats who during the struggle over slavery in Kansas argued that each territory should be permitted to determine its institutions.[2]

No one will ever know when Mormon polygamy began. In 1852, finally admitting they believed in it, the Saints insisted it had begun in 1843; but, confronted with overwhelming evidence that it existed before then, the church reconsidered and in 1878 conceded that "as early as 1831 the rightfulness of the plurality of wives under certain conditions was made known to Joseph Smith."[3]

Before 1852 the Saints perpetually denied they practiced polygamy. In exceptionally strong terms the European conference of 1846 repudiated the doctrine, and two years later the *Millennial Star* called the vengeance of heaven down upon the liars who charged the church with "such odious practices as spiritual wivery and polygamy. In all ages of the Church, the truth has been turned into a lie, and the grace of God converted into lasciviousness, by men who have sought to make 'a gain of godliness,' and feed their lusts on the credulity of the righteous and unsuspicious. Next to the long-hackneyed and bugaboo whispers of polygism is another abomination that sometimes shows its serpentine crests, which we shall call sexual resurrection. The doctrines of corrupt spirits are always in close affinity with each other, whether they consist in spiritual wifeism, sexual resurrection, gross lasciviousness, the unavoidable separation of husbands and wives, or the communism of property."[4]

The most famous denial came in 1850 from John Taylor during a debate with clergymen in Boulogne, France. "We are accused here of polygamy," commented the apostle, who took his first plural wife in 1841 and had ten wives by 1850, "and actions the most indelicate, obscene, and disgusting, such that none but a corrupt and depraved heart could have contrived. These things are too outrageous to admit of belief."[5]

The widely circulated report of the runaways ended such talk. "So universal is the practice," the justices announced, "that very few if any leading men in that community can be found who have not more than one wife each. The prominent men in the church, whose example in all things it is the ambition of the more humble to imitate, have each many wives; some of them, we were credibly informed and believe, as many as twenty or thirty, and Brigham Young, the governor, even a greater number. Only a few days before we left the territory, the governor was seen riding through the streets of the city in an omnibus, with a large company of his wives, more than two-thirds of whom had infants in their arms."[6]

Finally, on August 29, 1852, Young and Orson Pratt openly discussed a revelation given to Joseph Smith on July 12, 1843. As

Young explained, Smith had entrusted the only copy of the revelation to Bishop Newel K. Whitney. Soon, however, Emma Smith heard of it. She twitted her husband until he gave it to her and then scornfully burned it. Luckily, Whitney had made a duplicate, which he showed to Young at Winter Quarters in 1847. Until now Young had kept the revelation locked in his desk.[7]

Young himself accepted plural marriage only after a fierce internal struggle. "When that revelation was first read to me by Joseph Smith," he said, "I plainly saw the great trials and abuse of it that would be made by many of the Elders, and the trouble and persecution that it would bring upon this whole people. But the Lord revealed it, and it was my business to accept it."[8]

In this revelation and in numerous speeches and documents the Saints justified polygamy in several ways. The most imaginative argument involved spirits, the earliest of whom, Orson Pratt pointed out, had been born in heaven when the world began. Like humans, they had mothers and fathers, although Pratt never explained who created the first parents. Spirits could see humans but were invisible to mortals until they entered newborn bodies, or tabernacles. In the spirit world as on earth good and evil spirits battled one another, one third of the spirit world's inhabitants being agents of the devil who had rebelled against Christ and been cast down to earth by God. When the body died, the spirit left it and returned to the spirit world to await the day of resurrection. The spirit of a dead Mormon elder embarked upon a higher mission. It entered the prison containing the spirits of those who had died outside of Mormonism and offered each a chance to convert to the religion of eternal life.[9]

Young embellished this fanciful account with imaginative tales. He once spoke of a clairvoyant Saint who observed the spirit's departure from the body of a dying woman. The spirit left through the woman's head, snapped the umbilical cord holding it to the tabernacle, and, accompanied by another spirit, walked up an inclined plane and disappeared.[10]

Plural marriage and the spirit world went hand in hand, for, Young insisted, God had introduced polygamy not to satisfy man's lust or punish woman but to create for worthy spirits tabernacles of honor. "It is the duty of every righteous man and every woman to prepare tabernacles for all the spirits they can," he announced; "hence if my women leave I will go and search up others who will abide the celestial law, and let all I now have go where they please, though I will send the gospel to them. This is the reason why the doctrine of plurality of wives was revealed, that the noble spirits which were waiting for tabernacles might be brought forth."[11]

Like the Southerners then defending slavery, the Mormons also evolved a Biblical justification for their deeds. Smith's revelation had mentioned Abraham, Moses, David, and Solomon. Then in 1852, Young announced that Adam was God and a polygamist. "When our father Adam came into the Garden of Eden," said Young, "he came into it with a celestial body, and brought Eve, one of his wives with him. He helped to make and organize this world. He is Michael, the Arch-angel, the Ancient of Days! about whom holy men have written and spoken—He is our Father and our God, and the only God with whom we have to do."[12] The Mormon historian, Edward Tullidge, later commented: "When Brigham Young proclaimed to the nations that Adam was our Father and God, and Eve, his partner, the Mother of a world— both in a mortal and a celestial sense—he made the most important revelation ever oracled to the race since the days of Adam himself."[13]

Jesus's mother, the Virgin Mary, was another of Adam's wives. "That very babe that was cradled in the manger," proclaimed Young, "was begotten, not by Joseph, the husband of Mary, but by another Being. Do you inquire by whom? He was begotten by God our heavenly Father."[14] To an audience including Speaker of the United States House of Representatives Schuyler Colfax, Samuel Bowles of the Springfield *Republican*, and Albert D. Richardson of the New York *Tribune*, Young contended that Adam had created Jesus "by the process known to nature—just as men now create children." The Father and the Son looked exactly alike, except that God was older.[15]

Jesus was crucified, explained both Orson Pratt and Jedediah M. Grant, because he had three wives: Mary Magdalene, the repentant woman in Luke, and Mary and Martha, the sisters of Jesus's friend, Lazarus. "I will venture to say," added Hyde, "that if Jesus

Christ were now to pass through the most pious countries in Christendom with a train of women, such as used to follow him, fondling about him, combing his hair, anointing him with precious ointment, washing his feet with tears, and wiping them with the hair of their heads, and unmarried, or even married, he would be mobbed, tarred and feathered, and rode, not on an ass, but on a rail."[16]

In the sermon Colfax's party heard Young argued that in all ages people embraced polygamy. The ancients practiced it until the barbarian Goths and Vandals conquered Rome and abolished it. In modern times both Martin Luther and the Church of England sanctioned it. In present-day England a man wishing to dispose of a wife needed only to "offer her at auction and knock her off for a pot of beer or a shilling, and marry another."[17]

The final defense of polygamy was perhaps the most frequently heard. In every American community but Salt Lake City, Young noted, prostitution flourished. Men formed clubs to "hire and support" women as "you would hire a horse and chaise at a livery stable." Celestial marriage ended all this by guaranteeing each girl a husband. Lowell, Massachusetts, had, for example, fourteen thousand more girls than men. "They live and die in a single state, and are forgotten. Have they filled the measure of their creation, and accomplished the design of heaven in bringing them on earth? No; they have not. Two thousand good, God-fearing men should go there, and take to themselves seven women a-piece."[18]

II

THE SAINTS HATED THE EXPRESSION "spiritual wife system," which Gentiles used to deride Mormon marriage practices, disliked the word "polygamy," which means that either spouse might have more than one mate, and never used the correct term, "polygyny," under which a man might have two or more wives. They often talked about "plural marriage" and "plurality" but preferred the phrase in the title of Smith's revelation: "celestial marriage."[19]

In a Mormon ceremony couples were "sealed," or bound under God's law, for time, for eternity, or for both. A woman might be sealed to one man for time, or until one of the partners died, and to another for eternity, or their lives in the celestial kingdom. With the permission of the priesthood, men might take an unlimited number of women for either time or eternity. By proxy a live person might marry or divorce a dead one.

A woman sealed for the next world only was her husband's "spiritual" wife. Sometimes such women were helpless old ladies with money or property. Influential elders agreed to serve as their financial advisers and married them for eternity only. Other women had husbands incapable of exalting them in heaven, so they were secretly sealed to someone else for eternity.[20]

Such relationships were often casual. "Because I marry a woman it is no sign I am going to live with her," George Smith informed the Cincinnati *Commercial*. "She is sealed to me for eternity. For instance, a lady whom, perhaps, I have never seen before, comes to me with a letter of introduction from some of our Church officers, saying that she is a good, deserving lady, and desires to be united to a man for eternity, why, I should consider it my duty to marry that lady, although I might never see her again in this world." "But," interrupted the reporter, "suppose the lady already has a husband?" "That don't make any difference," Smith answered, "she can be sealed to me just the same; perhaps her husband is a worthless fellow, and in every way unworthy of her."[21]

In Mormonism marriage saved both men and women. A woman entered heaven only when married to someone endowed with the priesthood, and a man arrived at perfection in the next world only with several wives. The more wives and children he had, the higher his station in the celestial kingdom. A virgin's end was annihilation, and to be childless was almost as tragic as being single.[22] "The saints of God practice this principle of polygamy," Woodruff emphasized, "that they may have wives and posterity in the world to come and throughout the endless ages of eternity."[23]

If women accepted celestial marriage to become, in Young's words, "queens in heaven, and rulers to all eternity,"[24] men sometimes embraced it to enhance their standing in this world as well as the next. Captain William Hooper, the rich, talented Saint who for years was Utah's Congressional delegate, never rose higher in the church because he refused to take a second wife. "We look on Hooper," John Taylor joked to William Hepworth Dixon at a dinner, "as only half a Mormon." Even the young girls present snickered at the remark.[25]

"I shall certainly marry again soon," one pushy elder told Dixon; "the fact is, I mean to rise in this church; and you have seen enough to know that no man has a chance in our society unless he has a big household. To have any weight here, you must be known as the husband of three women."[26]

Young considered bachelors imperfect beings incapable of rising into the higher grades of mortals. Having failed to observe God's law, they would spend the next life as angels. Surrounded by their queens and children, Young and Kimball would occupy celestial thrones, while the unmarried ran their errands.[27]

In Mormon ritual Young possessed enormous power. A married man desiring a second bride had to ask his consent. The President then sought a revelation on the subject. If God approved, the man consulted the prospective bride's parents and the girl herself. All had to agree. Finally the groom sought permission from his other wife. To stop her husband from taking a second wife, the first needed a good reason, which she had to state before the President. If she had none, her husband might marry without her consent.

On the wedding day, the groom and his first wife assembled with the bride and her relatives either in a temple or Young's office. Young, Kimball, or the other officiating dignitary ordered the groom, the first wife, and the bride to face him. The wife stood on her husband's left, the bride on her left. The President then asked the wife: "Are you willing to give this woman to your husband to be his lawful and wedded wife for time and for all eternity? If you are, you will manifest it by placing her right hand within the right hand of your husband." The bride and groom joined right hands and the wife took her husband by the left arm, as if walking. The couple exchanged vows and received the presidential blessing.[28] Joseph Smith's revelation was fulfilled.

III

FOR PRACTICAL REASONS Mormon leaders urged men to marry often. A polygamist rarely apostatized, noted Horace Greeley during a Utah stay, for he had no place to go. Greeley heard of only one such escapee: a Saint who fled to California with his three wives, introduced the younger two, girls of nineteen and fourteen, as his daughters, and married them off within six weeks.[29] A bachelor, by contrast, needed only to saddle his horse and ride off, leaving both Mormonism and the territory forever.

Richard F. Burton, the British adventurer who toured the West in 1860, saw in polygamy economic and social implications. "Servants are rare and costly; it is cheaper and more comfortable to marry them. Many converts are attracted by the prospect of being wives, especially from places where, like Clifton, there are sixty-four females to thirty-six males." In Utah the "old maid is, as she ought to be, an unknown entity."[30]

But revenge was by far the most important Mormon motive. Considering themselves the modern children of Israel, the Saints ceaselessly preached the return to Zion, or Jackson County, Missouri, the site of the Garden of Eden, where they would erect their great temple, enjoy celestial marriage, and live as the ancients did. In this scheme of things polygamy served a dual function, drawing the Saints closer to Hebraic ways and immeasurably enhancing their power by increasing the population of God's kingdom. Remy heard Young predict that by 1890 the United States government would collapse and be replaced by the Lord's empire, whose capital would be Jackson County, where "our Father and our God planted the first garden on this earth, and where the New Jerusalem will come to when it comes down from heaven." Remy could "not remember to have ever had a conversation of any length with the Mormons, without having reason to suppose that they were all harbouring the same extravagant designs."[31]

"And mark my words," warned Brigham Young, Jr., in 1869, "we will reach it if it takes forty years, as it did the Israelites before they entered Canaan. Our children are daily taught to look upon the place as their Zion, where we are to build the temple of the New Jerusalem, the corner-stone of which was laid in 1834 by Joseph Smith. And, remember, these children are continually increasing, and soon will number tens of thousands. . . . I, from the early age of four years, when I was driven out with my people, have always kept my eyes on it."[32]

IV

"THE CAT IS OUT OF THE BAG," Kimball said after Smith's revelation was published, "and that is not all—this cat is going to have kittens; and that is not all, those kittens are going to have cats."[33]

Approximating the number of polygamists in Utah soon became an international sport. In the mid-1860's George Smith, the church historian, put the figure at five hundred bishops and elders, who averaged four wives and fifteen children apiece. According to this estimate, plural marriage affected about ten thousand persons, only ten per cent of Utah's population.[34] Four years later Charles Marshall, the British visitor, guessed that one Saint in eight had two wives, one in thirty had three, and one in a hundred had four or more."[35]

Actually, during peak periods nearly twenty per cent of the Mormon families were polygamous. Of 1,784 polygamists in one recent sample, 66.3 per cent had two wives, 21.2 per cent had three, and only 6.7 per cent had four.[36]

Even though Brigham Young, Jr., who had access to the church's census reports, insisted that Utah had four women for every three men, Remy met in the territory many bachelors who could not find wives.[37] Mormon girls evidently preferred part of an unusual man to an entire mediocrity.

In practice celestial marriage hardly resembled the idyllic system Smith and Young depicted. Often shrouding heavenly glory in earthly tragedy, it influenced almost every phase of Mormon life. Dancers invented a double cotillion giving two ladies to each gentleman,[38] and architects designed long, low houses with separate entrances for each compartment. After marrying again, a husband merely added another apartment and door to the building. In this set-up each wife and her children lived separately, and fights between wives were rare. Some rich men avoided domestic troubles by scattering their families all over town, but others, including Young, preferred harem life, keeping most of their wives together but apart from the husband, who had his own quarters nearby.[39]

Mormon officials supposedly made sure a man could support any woman he married, but those incapable of maintaining one wife were sometimes allowed several. Benjamin G. Ferris, who served briefly as territorial secretary, visited "a wretched hut, in a small village on Utah Lake, where the man and his two wives and grown-up daughter lodged in the same room, containing two beds: it was their parlor, kitchen, and bed-room. It was a manifest struggle between poverty and licentiousness, and there was filth enough to manure a garden."[40] "Brother Brigham counsels poor men to take wives, have plenty of faith, and they will acquire means for their comfortable maintenance," Mrs. Ezra Taft Benson, whose husband was one of the Twelve, informed the New York *World*. "In most cases it seems a very long time coming."[41]

Tales such as the pumpkin episode, which *The New York Times*'s Utah correspondent swore was true, illustrated polygamy's vagaries. In Ogden, ninety miles north of Salt Lake City, a husband tired of his English-born wife and sold her to a neighbor for a wagonload of pumpkins deliverable at harvest time. But the crop turned out so well that the buyer cancelled the deal. The embarrassed husband took his wife back.[42]

At best polygamous children possessed half a father. Touring Utah in 1867, Grenville M. Dodge, the great railroad builder, and General John A. Rawlins, Ulysses S. Grant's chief of staff, entered a large two-family house near Salt Lake City and asked for some milk. As they chatted with their hostess, a small boy emerged from an adjoining room and crawled under a bed. "Jimmy," the woman snapped, "what do you want?" "I am after father's slippers," he explained. "Mother says father is to stay with us this week."[43]

The polygamous father became not the constant companion and adviser but a visitor who occasionally appeared. A teacher, suggesting a pupil talk over with his father a matter that had arisen in school, was told: "I can't do it, because papa isn't staying at our house this week."[44]

In this system death was sometimes unusual. Noting the passing of a Saint with twenty wives, the New York *Tribune* asked: "What better argument against polygamy can be wanted than the ineffable absurdity of twenty widows?"[45]

Abuses were especially common south of Salt Lake City, where the immigrants who lived in the isolated communities were subject to the bishop's absolutism. In Provo, sixty miles south of Salt Lake City, a man settled with his beautiful seventeen-year-old daughter.

Many polygamists desired the girl, but the father warded them off. Early in 1857 he died. At the graveside the bishop who conducted the service ordered the girl to marry him. She had no alternative but to become his seventh wife.[46]

About ten per cent of the polygamous men in Utah married at least one set of sisters. Young was sealed to three pairs and Kimball to five. Several Saints were sealed to three sisters: Amasa Lyman married three daughters of Edward Partridge and Lydia Clisbee, and three of the nine wives of Bishop Aaron Johnson of Springville, near Provo, were sisters. John D. Lee took three sisters and then married their mother.[47]

Young advised men to marry sisters—or for that matter any two women—at the same ceremony. Fanny Stenhouse learned why the first time she attended church in Salt Lake City. She "noticed two young women who sat near me: they were dressed alike in green calico sun-bonnets, green calico skirts, and pink calico sacks. On enquiring who they were, I was told that they were the wives of one man and had both been married to him on the same day, so that neither could claim precedence of the other."[48]

Some Utah matches were even more startling. A man named Winchester married his mother,[49] and Young himself sealed a mother and daughter to their cousin, Luman A. Shurtliff.[50] The prophet often allowed his favorites to marry their stepdaughters, sometimes encouraged brothers and sisters to marry, and at least once sealed a half brother to his half sister.[51] He also sealed an elderly man to a fifty-seven-year-old woman and her fourteen-year-old granddaughter.[52]

V

"MAKE HASTE AND GET MARRIED," Remy heard Young preach. "Let me see no boys above sixteen and girls above fourteen unmarried." Fifteen years later, as Dodge's party listened, the prophet said he had married his wives not "for love or lust" but because God commanded that all women, "young and old, should be made mothers in Israel." Men should take one, two, or three dozen wives. Young threatened that "if the young men did not marry the girls, he and the old men would."[53]

With such encouragement Saints married early. Burton noted that the average Englishwoman was married at the age of thirty, compared with sixteen for young Mormon ladies. In 1857 *The New York Times*, reporting the sealings to old men of two girls aged ten and eleven, estimated that most girls married before they were fourteen.[54]

For practical reasons many of the prettiest Mormon girls accepted elderly men. A girl began looking about when she was thirteen or fourteen and usually concluded that if she accepted a young man she would be the first of several wives. She therefore tried to win a rich bishop, a powerful elder, or someone else who could adequately provide for her and perhaps make her his favorite.[55]

All this appalled Gentiles like Joseph Troskolawsski, the United States Deputy Surveyor for Utah. Troskolawsski knew one bishop who was sealed to four of his nieces, the youngest thirteen years old, and planned to marry a fifth when she became a little older. Unfortunately his opposition to polygamy almost cost him his life. On August 1, 1856, he put on the stagecoach for Ohio twelve-year-old Emma Wheat, who was being forced into a marriage she detested. On the following evening in the Salt Lake City store run by Hooper and Thomas S. Williams he met and spoke briefly to Bill Hickman, the famed Danite, or Shenpip. When Troskolawsski stepped outside, three other Danites sneaked behind him and knocked him down. While one beat him about the head with the butt of a whip, the others stamped and kicked him. "Kill the d—d son of a b—h," Hickman screamed joining in, "kill him quick, I'll stand the consequences." Hooper and Williams eventually rescued Troskolawsski, who by then was choking on his own blood. Hickman and his friends, screaming like Indians, jumped on their horses and rode off unmolested.

The next day David H. Burr, the Surveyor General, burst into Young's office and asked if the prophet was going to tolerate such crimes. Young sent for Hickman, then bragging about his feat all over town, and talked to him for two hours. The following day he got Hickman out of town by sending him with presents for the Indians at Green River. Young charged the government three thousand dollars for the gifts, but, Troskolawsski informed the

New York *Herald*, "I was afterwards told by the Indians them-selves that they had not received anything but one sorry blanket."

From the pulpit that Sunday, President Jedediah M. Grant raged about the incident. "I am sick," he said, "of this sympathizing spirit which you, as individuals, have with the Gentiles and apostate Mormons. I abhor this sympathetic feeling you have towards the wretches who would cut our throats, and of whom I can say, as I have said of Martin Van Buren, that they should be winked at by blind men, they should be kicked across lots by cripples, they should be nibbled to death by young ducks, and be drawn through the key hole to hell by bumble bees. Because a poor d—d scoundrel will come into our streets drunk and fall in a ditch, and some of our 'shenpip' brethren happened to stumble over him, you sympathize with him. I am ashamed of you. We ask no odds of the Gentiles; we care not what they say or do, nor fear what they can do."

Too badly beaten and frightened to work, Troskolawsski resigned his post, went east, and spent months recuperating. Young, meanwhile, punished Williams for his interference by ordering him on a distant mission.[56]

Mormon opponents of celestial marriage fared similarly. In March 1853 Alfred Smith, a follower of Gladden Bishop, who apostatized in Kanesville after learning Young practiced polygamy, attempted to preach in a public square in Salt Lake City. He had just finished a prayer when the town marshal grabbed him by the collar and marched him to jail. The next day he was escorted out of the territory.[57]

The following Sunday Young threatened to kill such men. "I say, rather than that apostates should flourish here, I will unsheath my bowie knife, and conquer or die. . . . Now, you nasty apostates, clear out, or judgment will be put to the line and righteousness to the plummet. . . . DO NOT court persecution. We have known Gladden Bishop for more than twenty years, and know him to be a poor, dirty curse. . . . I say again, you Gladdenites, do not court persecution, or you will get more than you want, and it will come quicker than you want it." All the while the Saints spurred on their prophet with shouts of "Go it, go it."[58]

V I

"WITHOUT THIS REVELATION ON POLYGAMY," Young boasted to Dixon, "we should have lived our religious life, but not so perfectly as we do now."[59] Young's view of grandeur was remarkable, for as practiced by the leading Saints polygamy was hardly beautiful. John Taylor's first wife remarked of her husband: "His eyes are greedier than his belly: he does not attend to the wife he has, and yet he is running after every young lass he can see!"[60]

Orson Pratt, the great public defender of celestial marriage, was no better. By his church's admission he was married to nine women. One day he told his first wife, Sarah, he intended to spend a week with each of his brides. "If you take eight weeks with your other women," she angrily retorted, "you can take the ninth with them also." "If you don't choose to live with me," Pratt said, "I don't know that I'm obliged to support you. You have my permission to go to hell. Stick to it or to starvation." Hated by Young because she still insisted Joseph Smith had tried to seduce her in Nauvoo, Sarah renounced Mormonism.[61]

Parley Pratt resembled his brother. William Hill, who lived in the Great Basin from 1851 to 1856, recalled Pratt's frequent visits to Mrs. Hill. One afternoon Hill came home and found his wife of thirty years gone. In tears he appealed to Young. "If Parley has got your wife," the prophet replied unsympathetically, "you must get another." That Sunday Hill saw her in Pratt's carriage but "the moment I looked to her, a big Danite took me by the shoulder, and said, 'Move on, brother Hill, you can't stand there.'" Mrs. Hill became Pratt's eleventh wife.[62]

Prominent Mormons sometimes purchased girls. Frederick Loba, the Swiss chemist the Saints converted and ordered to Utah to manufacture gunpowder, saw "two young sisters sold by their father to General Horace Eldredge for some groceries."[63] In 1856, according to *The New York Times*, Kimball offered a father a yoke of oxen and a wagon for a sixteen-year-old girl.[64]

Kimball always kept an eye out for romance. "Brethren," he instructed some departing missionaries, "I want you to understand that it is not to be as it has been heretofore. The brother missionaries have been in the habit of picking out the prettiest women for themselves before they get here, and bringing on the ugly ones for us; hereafter you have to bring them all here before taking any of them, and let us all have a fair shake."[65]

Kimball admired women of all nations. "I love the Danes dearly!" he bragged to Ludlow. "I've got a Danish wife." Turning to a rough-looking carpenter working nearby, Kimball asked: "You know Christiny,—eh, Brother Spudge?" "Oh, yes! know her very well!" came the answer. Kimball paused, then added: "The Irish are a dear people. My Irish wife is among the best I've got." He halted again. "I love the Germans! Got a Dutch wife, too! Know Katrine, Brother Spudge? Remember she couldn't scarcely talk a word o' English when she come,—eh, Brother Spudge?"[66]

Such things disgusted apostates and even some Saints. In 1852 John Hardy, an ex-Mormon then living in Boston, called polygamy "licentiousness *run mad*."[67] Five years later an unidentified daughter of Young remarked to *The New York Times*: "If Salt Lake City was only roofed over, it would be the biggest w——e house in the world."[68]

VII

"THE MORMON IDEA OF A WOMAN," observed the New York *Tribune* in 1869, "is not a whit higher than that of the Indian."[69] Young, in fact, tried to improve relations with the red men by inducing Mormon girls to marry chiefs. In 1854, during the troubles with the Ute leader Walker, he informed some elders: "Walker himself has teased me for a white wife; and if any of the sisters will marry him I believe I can close the war forthwith. I am certain that unless men can take better care of their women Walker may supply himself on a liberal scale, and without closing the war either. In conclusion, I will say, if any lady wishes to be Mrs. Walker, if she will report herself to me, I will negotiate the match."[70] Mary Ettie V. Smith heard Young promise one girl immortal glory in the celestial kingdom if she accepted Walker.[71]

Under polygamy as Young molded it, a Mormon woman was in an unenviable position. A marriage band offered her only the prospect of losing her husband to a younger, prettier girl. Even in heaven she was to share him with his other wives.

For several reasons Mormon men looked down on women. "Women will be more easily saved than men," Young told Dixon. "They have not sense enough to go far wrong. Men have more knowledge and more power; therefore they can go more quickly and more certainly to hell."[72] "Women are made to be led, and counseled and directed," Kimball added. "If they are not led, and do not make their cables fast to the power and authority they are connected to, they will be damned."[73]

In 1861 Young outlined a code of behavior for women. "I am almost daily sealing young girls to men of age and experience," he related. "Love your duties, sisters. Are you sealed to a good man? Yes, to a man of God. It is for you to bear fruit and bring forth, to the praise of God, the spirits that are born in yonder heavens and to take tabernacles on the earth. You have the privilege of forming tabernacles for those spirits, instead of their being brought into this wicked world, that God may have a royal Priesthood, a royal people, on the earth. That is what plurality of wives is for, and not to gratify lustful desires. Sisters, do you wish to make yourselves happy? Then what is your duty? It is for you to bear children, in the name of the Lord, that are full of faith and the power of God,—to receive, conceive, bear, and bring forth in the name of Israel's God, that you may have the honor of being mothers of great and good men—of kings, princes, and potentates that shall yet live on the earth and govern and control *the* nations. Do you look forward to that? or are you tormenting yourselves by thinking that your husbands do not love you? I would not care whether they loved a particle or not; but I would cry out, like one of the old, in the joy of my heart, 'I have got a man from the Lord!' 'Hallelujah! I am a mother—I have borne an image of God!'"[74]

On another occasion Young answered the women who complained that "plural marriage is very hard for you to bear. It is no such thing. A man or woman who would not spend his or her life in building up the kingdom of God on the earth, without a companion, and travel and preach, valise in hand, is not worthy of God or his kingdom, and they never will be crowned, and they cannot be crowned; the sacrifice must be complete. If it is the duty of a husband to take a wife, take her. But it is not the privilege of a woman to dictate the husband, and tell who or how many he shall take, or what he shall do with them when he gets them, but it is the duty of the woman to submit cheerfully."[75]

The plight of celestial wives shocked most Easterners. "No where else on the Continent of North America," the New York *Tribune*'s correspondent noted in 1859, "are white women to be seen working like slaves, barefooted, in the field. It is notorious to all here that large numbers of Mormon women are in a state of great want and destitution, and that their husbands do not pretend to provide them even with the necessaries of life."[76]

Mrs. Ezra Taft Benson looked at it a different way. "We do not believe in having any drones in the hive," she told the New York *World*, "and plural wives in the country are expected to do something toward contributing to the support or dress of the family. Some spin, others weave cloth often sufficient to last the entire family through the winter. Some make up the clothing for family use; others again make the butter and cheese, and attend to the cows, pigs, and poultry. All are engaged in some useful occupation by which the whole family will be benefited. Danish wives, who have been used to the occupation in their own country, are placed in the fields during the proper season to plough and harrow the ground, plant the seed, and hoe up the weeds when the time comes. They may also be seen irrigating the crops with water."[77]

Dixon found Mormon women "plainly, not to say poorly, dressed; with no bright colours, no gay flounces and furbelows. They are very quiet and subdued in manner, with what appeared to us an unnatural calm; as if all dash, all sportiveness, all life, had been preached out of them. They seldom smile, except with a wan and wearied look; and though they are all of English race, we have never heard them laugh with the bright merriment of our English girls." Girls invariably called their fathers "Sir" and stood until directed to sit. All women were brought into a roomful of men as children were in England. They entered, curtsied, shook hands, and left. Dixon had "never seen this sort of shyness among grown women, except in a Syrian tent."[78]

Nor did observers find most plural wives attractive. "Handsome girls and women are scarce among the Mormons of Salt Lake— the fewer Gentiles can show many more of them," Bowles reported. "Why is this? Is beauty more esthetic and ascetic? Or, good-looking women being supposed to have more chances for matrimony than their plainer sisters, do they all insist upon having the whole of one man, and leave the Mormon husbands to those whose choice is like Hobson's?"[79]

Richardson saw in Salt Lake City "only two women who could be called comely; . . . and one was a daughter of Brigham Young, recently married. Few, if any, countenances impressed me as vicious. All were plain, many extremely so. As one might expect of humble people gathered from every nation of the earth, they bear the indelible impress of poverty, hard labor and stinted living." Dodge agreed that "not a woman had that cheerful, genial, home-like air of others. They all looked as if some great trouble was weighing them down."[80]

Polygamous wives often collapsed under their burdens. "Lord Jesus has laid a heavy trial upon me," one of them informed Bowles, "but I mean to bear it for His sake, and for the glory He will grant me in His kingdom."[81] When a woman complained that polygamy would kill her, Eliza Snow, the bride of both Young and Joseph Smith, answered: "What if it should? What if it kills the body, then yours is the martyr's crown; such graves are strewn from Nauvoo to this place; it is a martyrdom that has its reward in heaven."[82]

Mormon wives, however, possessed one weapon. A man might get a divorce for adultery, but a woman could get one for neglect, desertion, or cruelty. "The teasers who come all the time after women, and soon get tired of them and want to divorce them," Young said in 1860, "I make pay ten dollars for each divorce." To dissolve marriages for eternity the prophet charged fifty dollars.[83]

Unhappy women sometimes escaped another way. In a remote village Richardson and his friends "dined with a Mormon Elder, whose young wife rarely gave us a glimpse of her black eyes. The driver assured us that she was his *fifth*—that her predecessors all ran away from him. From his cheerful good humor I think he classes them among blessings which brightened when they took their flight."[84]

In Salt Lake City single girls celebrated leap year by inviting men to dances at the Social Hall. At ordinary affairs bids cost five dollars for each couple and a dollar for every additional wife. Retaliating, the girls charged thirty-seven and a half cents for every extra gentleman. "It is all pleasantly enough done," the New York *Herald* observed, "but it is none the less an effective blow."[85]

Children were everywhere. "Babies seem indigenous to Salt Lake," Richardson noted. "Their abundance through all the streets causes wonder till one remembers that they are the only product of the soil which does not require irrigation."[86]

VIII

PERFORMED IN A SPECIAL SALT LAKE CITY HOUSE opened in May 1855, the Endowment depicted for Saints their earthly responsibilities and heavenly rewards. Over the years it changed radically. In Kirtland it was a religious ritual, with such elements as the washing of feet, anointings, blessings, prophesyings, and apparitions of angels. At Nauvoo these things disappeared. Kimball, Young, Taylor, Bennett, Joseph and Hyrum Smith, and several other Master Masons founded a lodge and within six months initiated into it almost every male Mormon, boys included. The order's appalled authorities revoked the lodge's charter.[87]

Undaunted, Joseph Smith altered the Endowment to resemble Masonry. Dramas, oaths, handshakes, grips, and signs replaced the religious rites. "This is *true* Free Masonry," Kimball once argued, "and all you that have been Masons will find how much superior this is to common Free Masonry."[88]

As described by John Hyde, the schoolteacher who apostatized and in 1857 published his memoirs, the Endowment was mystical and frightening but hardly the sex orgy anti-Mormons depicted. One February morning in 1854 Hyde, his wife, and thirty others, following orders, appeared at the Salt Lake City Council House at seven A.M. Kimball examined their tithing office receipts and birth and marriage records and sealed all married couples not previously sealed. Then, leaving their shoes in an outer office, the Saints entered a long room divided by white screens into small compartments. Men were separated from women, and individuals were beckoned into the next room. When called for, Hyde was ordered to undress and lie down in a painted tin bathtub. Each portion of his body was washed in tepid water and blessed: "brain to be strong, ears to be quick to hear the words of God's servants, feet to be swift in the way of righteousness." Parley Pratt then awarded Hyde his celestial name, Enoch, and Taylor and James W. Cummings anointed the celebrant with oil and gave him a long-sleeved muslin or linen dress reaching from neck to ankles, like a child's nightgown. Over this Hyde placed a shirt, a linen robe, and a small, square white linen or silk apron the size and shape of Masonic aprons but with imitation fig leaves painted on it. A cap made of a square yard of linen, socks, and white linen or cotton shoes completed the outfit.

While Hyde dressed, leading Mormons in the next compartment reenacted the Book of Genesis. Grant, as Elohim, counseled Jesus and several others about populating the earth. Depicting the creation of man, Jesus and His associates entered Hyde's compartment, stroked each person there and pretended to form him, and blew at each, giving him life. "The mind," observed Hyde, "was struck with the wild blasphemy of the whole affair."

Soon the wives, who had been through a similar ceremony conducted by Eliza Snow, rejoined their husbands. The men closed their eyes, as if asleep, were commanded to arise, and received their wives. Each couple walked to the next compartment, which with the help of dwarf mountain pines in boxes resembled a garden. There William C. Staines as Adam, Eliza as Eve, and William Phelps as the devil presented the story of the Garden of Eden, emphasizing throughout that only Saints could be saved. The men then promised to touch only women given to them by the officers of the church and were taught a sign, a grip, and a secret word. They were warned that the penalty for violating this first degree of the Aaronic priesthood was death by the cutting of the throat.

Hyde and his companions moved to a room containing Satan's present-day allies: the Catholic Father Boniface, played by George Smith; the Quaker Timothy Broadbrim, depicted by Woodruff; and the Baptist Elder Smooth-Tongue, in reality Phineas Young. Peter, James, and John, portrayed by Parley Pratt, Taylor, and Erastus Snow, entered, with a show of force drove off the devil and his friends, talked loudly about their visits to Joseph Smith and Brigham Young, and explained that Young now held the keys of the Kingdom of God and must be obeyed. The men then practiced more signs, grips, and passwords and were awarded the second degree of the Aaronic priesthood.

For the chosen few the ceremonies continued in a room with an altar. Here the communicants received the first degree of the Melchizedek priesthood, swearing undying allegiance to the church on penalty of having the bowels and navel ripped out.

The second degree of the Melchizedek priesthood was especially ominous. For allowing persecutions of the Saints and not avenging Joseph Smith's murder those present vowed everlasting emnity toward the United States and promised to inspire their children with this spirit.

Hyde then passed through the veil, a thin linen partition. Marks were cut with a scissors on the bosom and front of his shirt, and he entered the Kingdom of God, where Kimball waited to lecture. The subjects retained their holy undergarments, which they were always to wear, dressed, hurriedly ate lunch—it was four P.M.— and returned to the Kingdom to hear the talk, which stressed the seriousness of the affair, repeated the signs, and reviewed the punishments. About six o'clock Hyde returned to the first room, put on his shoes, and escorted his wife home.[89]

Even high Mormons acknowledged that the Endowment contained these horrible oaths, which Young inserted after Smith's death. During an 1889 trial in which the denial of citizenship to an alien who had taken these vows was upheld, Andrew Cahoon, a Saint for forty years and a bishop for eighteen, and Franklin D. Richards, the church historian, both admitted the Endowment preached revenge for the murders of Joseph and Hyrum. Richards further revealed that his arm had been anointed to avenge their blood.[90] Bloodthirsty oaths and polygamy for the masses became Young's legacies to his people.

VIII

.ЛГЛГЛЛЛ

"As Firm in His Seat as the Czar of Russia"

I

I HOPE," REMARKED EMMELINE FREE, long Young's favorite
wife, to the New York *World*'s Utah correspondent in
1869, "that you will give a good report of us to your friends in
the East. There are enough bad reports to make us feel ashamed
of ourselves if they were true." When the journalist suggested
that many of the critics were honest people disgusted with the
attempts of Mormon leaders to fob off on them shoddy doctrines,
Emmeline conceded that some of the stories were true and
added: "I am free to confess that my experience has not always
been a pleasant one, but there is no pleasure without pain, and
we Latter Day Saints have seen more of the trials, troubles, and
vexations of life than its pleasures; but of course we are content
to bear many things for the sake of our religion."[1]

The terrifying oaths of the Endowment were but part of the
bloody and violent atmosphere Young fostered in Utah "for the
sake of our religion." Joseph Smith created Mormonism, but
Young molded it. Unlike most frontier religions, which were par-
ticularistic and individualistic, Mormonism was authoritative,
centralized, regimented, and efficient. In the wilderness these qual-

ities gave it great strength and enabled its followers to survive and prosper. Indeed, as early as 1870 the Saints themselves compared their church to the Prussian army, which had recently swept triumphantly across France.

Mormonism appealed largely to the lower rather than upper classes, to the rural rather than urban dweller, to men rather than women, to the naïve rather than the sophisticated, to the illiterate rather than the educated, to the foreigner rather than the native-born. The most secular of beliefs, it not only invaded but controlled the daily life of its followers. It was the most imperialistic American religion, and the only one with a territorial foundation. The endless stream of missionaries leaving the Great Basin for all parts of the world constituted the soldiers, Young and his hierarchy in their Utah fortress the general staff.[2]

Thanks to polygamy, Young's missionary system, and the principle of the gathering, Utah's population increased rapidly. It grew from five thousand inhabitants at the end of 1848 to almost thirty thousand in 1852. By 1855 the territory had sixty thousand people and Salt Lake City had fifteen thousand.[3]

Overseas the ranks broadened too. By July 1853 Great Britain held 30,690 Saints, who each week loyally bought 25,000 copies of the *Millennial Star*. Several elements besides skillful organization contributed to this success. Conceding nothing and claiming everything, the Saints made extravagant declarations. "Latter Day Saints KNOW that the Lord has spoken in this age," announced the *Millennial Star*. "They KNOW that angels do now converse with men. They KNOW that the gifts of the Holy Ghost are manifested in these days by dreams, visions, revelations, tongues, prophecies, miracles, healings. Latter Day Saints have come to a KNOWLEDGE of the truth."

In an age of working class discontent against the lords of the loom and the soil, Mormon missionaries urged converts to flee to the land of salvation. John Taylor once bragged to a French Communist that the Saints had succeeded where European radicals had failed—in enticing discontented workingmen into their movement. Characteristically, Etienne Cabet, the French socialist who took over Nauvoo after the Mormons left, never made it the thriving community Joseph Smith had.

Finally, the Saints borrowed doctrines from almost every available source. From Masonry came the Endowment, and from the Old Testament came plural marriage, the emphasis upon temples, and the belief in the gathering of all true believers in Zion, not Palestine but a suburb of Kansas City. The New Testament contributed Christ, who emerged from Mormon theology a polygamist, and the Twelve Apostles. And from idolatry the Saints took offerings for the dead and the supposedly magical power of Mormon rites.[4] Here was a religion with something for everybody.

II

THE LONGER YOUNG LIVED the more ambitious he became, both for himself and his church. In Kirtland he desired salvation and considered Joseph Smith's friendship the greatest reward. In Nauvoo he fulfilled the dream of leading his people. In Utah he longed for more wives, additional converts, and greater power. In God's and his church's name he made the Great Basin his private possession.

Every immigrant entering the territory swelled Young's political and religious might, but the Mormon from Scandinavia or Britain differed markedly from other newcomers to America: the German who ran away when the 1848 revolution failed; the starving Irishman escaping from the 1846 potato famine; the Russian Jew who later fled from pogroms. By the 1860's many of the Saints in Utah were immigrants who had passed through the United States as they had crossed the ocean—to reach a place beyond. "The rank and file of the Mormons are for the most part foreigners," the New York *Tribune* noted. "The majority have not even taken the first steps toward naturalization; and they came, as they say, 'not to America, but to Zion.' They despise and contemn the authority of the United States; they deny the right of the Republic to interfere with any form of social, religious, or political order that they may elect; they recognize no government but that of the State of Deseret, no higher law than that of the Church of Latter-day Saints, and hold the seal, arms, and flag of their so-called State (for they ignore the Territory of Utah) above every other symbol of authority in the world."[5]

Young bragged about this unanimity. "Happily for Utah," he

said in 1853, "she has no party politics for her legislature to discuss, she can therefore lend her energies for the benefit of the country, and practicing that industry so worthy of imitation by the people benefit them by example, as well as precept."[6]

But what Young admired Gentiles detested. "Of all things the Mormons least understand," *The New York Times* commented, "one is political principles. Although they all prate about constitutional rights, very few of them know anything about the Constitution of the United States. They have shut themselves up in a contracted circle of illiberal theological views, and outside of that they recognize no point of reason. . . . No political element exists, because Young allows it nothing to feed upon."[7]

The absence of free elections in Utah shocked William Chandless. "The Mormon newspaper always boasts of this as harmony," he wrote, "but it is tyranny, since it's an oligarchy working under and deadening the forms of a democracy. I think this the very worst feature of Mormonism."[8]

Completely isolated, the residents of Utah knew only what Young wanted them to know. Getting news into the territory was almost impossible. Mail arrived irregularly, and Mormon postmasters often refused to accept such popular periodicals as *Harper's*. As one observer noted, the New York *Herald*, the finest daily in America, "like a half beaten army, comes in broken files."[9]

Yearly at a church conference the Saints went through the formality of selecting their leaders, but they always chose Young and his slate. "The election is a mere form," reported George F. Parsons of the San Francisco *Daily Times*, "yet I suppose it soothes the Saints to feel that their President is really only chosen from year to year, and that it would be possible at any time to defeat him. That, however, is not so. He is as firm in his seat as the Czar of Russia on his throne, since no one would dare to nominate another than him. I once asked a Bishop what would be the result of an attempt of this kind, and he regarded me with a look in which horror was blended with amazement. He could not conceive the possibility of so daring an act, and evidently thought the ground ought to open under my feet, for having suggested so blasphemous an idea. In this annual election Brigham has a vote, and always employs it in his own behalf. In this I think he bears out his reputation for shrewdness, for it would show a lack of self-confidence did the Prophet and Leader of the Church hesitate to back himself as the appointed head of the Church. There is a pleasing fiction about the powers and privileges of the Apostles and Counsellors, but so far as I can discover, Brigham has all the power in his own hands, and never loosens his grip upon the reins."[10]

III

THE CREATION OF UTAH did not end Mormon dreams. The State of Deseret, founded in 1849 to foster God's Kingdom, continued as a shadow government. Each year following the adjournment of the territorial legislature Young, as Deseret's governor, convened its legislature, read to it his message, and insisted it was the territory's legitimate governing body. A loyal Saint then proposed the adoption of Utah's laws as Deseret's. The legislature complied, appointed delegates to seek Deseret's admission to the Union, and adjourned until next year.[11]

Especially sensitive to charges of treason, Orson Pratt acknowledged in 1855 the divinity of the federal Constitution. "But there is a nucleus of a government, formed since that of the United States, which is perfect in its nature. It is perfect, having emanated from a Being who is perfect. But some may inquire, is it right, is it lawful for another government to be organized within the United States, of a theocratical nature? Yes, perfectly so. Does not the Constitution of our country guarantee to all religious societies the right of forming any ecclesiastical government they like? Certainly it does, and every intelligent man knows this to be the fact."[12]

"To speak of our rights as citizens of the Kingdom of God," Taylor added, "we then speak of another law, we then move in a more exalted sphere; and it is of these things we have a right to speak. . . . God has established His Kingdom; He has rolled back that cloud that has spread over the moral horizon of the world; He has opened the heavens, revealed the fullness of the everlasting gospel, organized His Kingdom according to the pattern that exists in the heavens; and He has placed certain keys, powers, and oracles in our midst; and we are the people of God, we are His

Government. The Priesthood upon the earth is the only legitimate government of God, whether in the heavens or on the earth. Some people ask, what is the Priesthood? I answer: It is the legitimate rule of God, whether in the heavens or on the earth, and it is the only legitimate power that has a right to rule upon the earth."[13]

In a sermon titled "The Kingdom of God," Young justified disobedience to federal officials. "I say again that the constitution and laws of the United States, and the laws of the different States, as a general thing, are just as good as we want them, provided they were honored. But we find Judges who do not honor the laws, yes, officers of the law dishonor the law. Legislators and law makers are frequently the first violators of the laws they make."[14]

The Saints, on the other hand, never erred. In 1856 Kimball foresaw for the Mormon leaders a great future. "The Church and kingdom to which we belong will become the kingdom of our God and Christ and brother Brigham Young will become President of the United States. . . . And I tell you he will be something more; but we do not want to give him the name; but he is called and ordained to a far greater station than that, and he is foreordained to take that station, and he has got it; and I am Vice-President, and brother Wells is the Secretary of the Interior—yes, and of all the armies in the flesh. You don't believe that; but I can tell you it is one of the smallest things I can think of."[15]

IV

DESPITE THE FREQUENCY OF SUCH PRONOUNCEMENTS, Gentiles ignored them and consequently misunderstood the Saints. Politicians especially heard and learned nothing.

Unfortunately Young's methods reinforced the Gentile belief that the Mormons seriously threatened the federal government. The Saints should, for instance, have revered few non-Mormons more than Jim Bridger, the tall, gaunt, weatherbeaten Virginian who first reached the Great Basin in 1823 and subsequently erected a fort on Black's Fork of the Green River. Coming west in 1847, the Mormons met Bridger and told him such woeful tales of suffering that he gave them provisions, clothes, and cattle. They promised to pay him if they ever prospered and pushed on to the Salt Lake. The following winter, when the Saints ran out of food and ate roots, Bridger responded to their pleas by sending several trains of cattle. After the discovery of gold in California brought visitors—and prosperity—to Utah, the Mormons repaid their benefactor.

For years Young tried to convert Bridger, who knew the Indians and the land better than any other white man, but the mountaineer said he favored no religion over any other. Then in 1849 and 1850 Bridger made Young furious by guiding a group of soldiers into the Salt Lake Valley, for the old pioneer seemed to be encouraging government interference in Mormon affairs. "I believe that Old Bridger is death on us," Young complained, "and if he saw that 400,000 Indians were coming against us, and any man were to let us know, he would cut his throat."

Bridger's ferry across the Green River caused additional trouble. The Mormon-dominated Utah legislature demanded half of his revenues and ordered him to tithe to the church on the rest. In two years Bridger took in $24,000 but ended up with only three thousand.[16]

The end came in the fall of 1853. Young accused Bridger of selling guns, ammunition, and supplies to hostile Indians and sent Hickman, Sheriff James Ferguson, and a large band of men to wreck Bridger's fort. The mountaineer learned of their approach, hid nearby, and watched them devour his supplies. "No ammunition was found," Hickman recalled, "but the whiskey and rum, of which he had a good stock, was destroyed by doses! the sheriff, most of the officers, the doctor and chaplain of the company, all aided in carrying out the orders, and worked so hard day and night that they were exhausted—not being able to stand up. But the privates, poor fellows! were rationed, and did not do so much." After the raiders left, Bridger fled with his wife and children to Missouri.[17]

A year later the church offered Bridger eight thousand dollars for his fort, his buildings, his land, his cattle, and fifteen hundred dollars worth of merchandise. It paid half down and promised him the rest within fifteen months, but Bridger never received the additional money and forever after demanded his fort back.[18]

Bridger's troubles proved minor compared with what hit Captain John W. Gunnison. While surveying near the Sevier River, thirty-five miles from Fillmore, on October 28, 1853, Gunnison and seven members of his party were killed by Indians. Before a rescue party reached the scene, wolves had picked the bodies clean.[19]

But not everyone blamed the murder on Indians. The St. Louis *Missouri Democrat* insisted that Mormons had committed the crime. "Their acts in this State and Illinois show them to be utterly depraved; their morals are infinitely worse than any Indian tribe. We know of no Indians who tolerate adultery and promiscuous intercourse between the sexes. The Mormons not only tolerate these things, but make them a part of their religion. When the morals of a people are thus polluted at the fountain head, there is no depth of depravity into which that people may not sink."[20]

Behind this editorial Young saw his avowed enemy. "It is rumored," he wrote Senator Stephen A. Douglas of Illinois, "that one James Bridger, from Black's fork of Green River, has become the oracle to Congress in all matters pertaining to Utah, not only civil and political, but even historical and geographical, informing them, and the Missouri Democrat of the awfulness of Utah's assessing and collecting taxes, (doubtless unlike any other State or Territory) or in other words having an applicable and well digested revenue law; . . . that the Mormons must have killed Capt. Gunnison because the Pah-van-tes had no guns; that the Mormons are an outrageous set entirely, with no redeeming traits &c. &c.; and rumor further says that all this nonsense was 'confirmation strong as proof from holy writ' for an onslaught upon our character, our institutions, and our boundaries. Now pleasantry aside, is it not a little singular that any person, in any clime (let alone the U.S., and that too in Washington and St. Louis) should have been in the least inclined to listen to Bridger's yarns, more especially if they had eyes, and *could see him*, and still more especially when it is well known that our Delegate is a gentleman of the strictest integrity, and always ready to furnish necessary reliable information." Bridger, "uncivilized" in both "conversation and conduct" and bent on destroying the Saints, had recently sold the Utes one hundred pounds of gunpowder. Listening "to Bridger's statements on any subject, even to Indian trade and trapping," was "perfect folly for any one."[21]

In the spring of 1855 the trial of three Indians charged with the murders provided a strange spectacle. At Young's insistence Babbitt defended the red men. The presiding judge, John F. Kinney, instructed the jury either to acquit or convict of first-degree murder, but instead it found the prisoners guilty of manslaughter. Kinney denounced the verdict and said the evidence pointed to first-degree murder but sentenced the defendants to three years in jail. "I was present during the trial," reported *The New York Times*'s correspondent, "and know that a confidential agent of Brigham was there, acting under secret instructions, and in my presence, it was charged upon one of the Jury that this agent, (one Huntington,) had had access to them and had communicated to them Brigham Young's orders. This charge was not denied. It was even said to the District Attorney, Gen. Hollman, (to whom much praise is due for his exertions in the case,) that 'no matter what amount of testimony had been introduced the verdict would have been the same.' " Shortly after being jailed the prisoners escaped.[22] Sometime later Edmund Ellsworth, Young's son-in-law, publicly remarked: "I think Uncle Sam will get sick of sending officers here, when we serve a few more as we served Gunnison."[23]

v

ASKED ABOUT INDIAN TROUBLES IN UTAH, Young scoffed to Richard Burton that when reporters said twenty men were killed or wounded two or three would be more like it. The prophet boasted that he could do more with several pounds of flour and a few yards of cloth than with all the sabres and rifles in the West.[24] As George Smith once told a correspondent: "Give the Indians over to President Young, and give him $100,000 per year, and he will take care of them, and there will never be any trouble."[25]

In July 1853, however, Young failed to prevent the outbreak of an Indian war. Led by Walker, the red men, incensed by an endless stream of white atrocities, destroyed three hundred houses and uprooted hundreds of families in the Utah, Sanpete, and Juab Valleys. Ignoring Young's advice to settle together and build forts, the victims had spread all over the area. "If the counsel of President Young had been observed," lamented George Smith, "not one of the Saints would have lost his life by an Indian."[26]

"I told you, six years ago, to build a fort that the *Devil could not get into*, unless you were disposed to let him in, and that would keep the Indians out, . . ." Young scolded the Saints. "Let your dwelling house be a perfect fort. From the day I lived where brother Joseph Smith lived, I have been fortified all the time so as to resist twenty men, if they should come to my house in the night, with an intent to molest my family, assault my person or destroy my property; and I have always been in the habit of sleeping with an eye open, and if I cannot sufficiently watch, I will get my wife to help me. Let a hostile band of Indians come round my house, and I am good for quite a number of them. If one hundred should come, I calculate that only fifty would be able to go to the next house and if the Saints there used up the other fifty, the third house would be safe. . . . Let every man, woman, and child, that can handle a butcher knife, be good for one Indian, and you are safe."[27]

Fearing an attack upon Salt Lake City itself, the Saints encased six square miles of the city within a mud wall twelve feet high, six feet wide at the base, and two and a half feet wide at the top. They then stationed armed men around the structure and dug in front of it a wide, deep moat.[28]

Meanwhile, Young wooed Walker. "Instead of being Walker's enemy," he announced, "I have sent him a great pile of tobacco to smoke when he is lonely in the mountains. He is now at war with the only friends he has upon the earth, and I want him to have some tobacco to smoke."[29]

Young personally negotiated the peace with Walker, although Mormon historians needlessly embellish what in truth is an intriguing story. As the Saints tell it, Young and his party one day stumbled onto Walker's camp in Sanpete County. Most of the Mormons wanted to run away, but Young rode right up to Walker's tent. There he found the chief grieving over a papoose for whom the medicine man had predicted an early death. Undaunted by Walker's threat that a white man must accompany the youngster to the happy hunting ground, Young laid hands upon the boy's forehead and in Jesus's name rebuked the disease and death. The child instantly recovered and Walker was forever grateful.[30]

This romanticized version hardly fits the facts, which in themselves illustrate Young's humaneness and ability to handle men. In May 1854 Young and his party, which included Solomon N. Carvalho, Frémont's artist, decided to visit Walker and Kanoshe, the Pauvan chief. When the prophet brought along as gifts sixteen head of cattle, blankets, clothing, trinkets, rifles, and ammunition, Carvalho protested, for the Mormons were supplying and arming the enemy. Young answered that the Indians, whose camp bordered on the immigrant trail, could steal whatever they needed anyway and hoped the weapons would help them obtain food peacefully. During the meeting with the Indians, Walker, Kanoshe, and fifteen other chiefs rose to complain about the white man's brutality. In tears one Sanpete chief told how the whites had murdered his wife and then his son, who was hunting rabbits for food.

That night Young slaughtered an ox and presented fresh meat to everyone in camp. The next morning he assured the Indians he was their friend, loved them like a father, and would always give them food and clothing provided they stopped killing Mormons. He completely won over the Indians by driving the cattle into camp. As the Saints were preparing to leave, Carvalho spied two naked and starving white children whom the Indians had captured. Young bought them and intended to rear them with his own children.[31]

VI

THE TREATY THE PROPHET SIGNED with Walker and Kanoshe illustrated the Mormon hatred for Gentiles. At Young's insistence the Indians, carefully distinguishing between the two, pledged to attack neither "Americans" nor "Mormons."[32]

In 1855 Garland Hurt, the Indian Agent for Utah, complained to his superiors that the Mormon hierarchy deliberately fostered this notion. "At the last semi annual conference of the Latter day Saints a large number of missionaries were nominated to go and preach to the Indians, or Lamanites, as they have been called. Now since my arrival in this Territory I have become satisfied that these Saints have either accidentally or purposely created a distinction in the minds of the Indian tribes of this Territory, between the Mormons and the people of the United States, that cannot act otherwise than prejudicial to the interests of the latter—And what sir may we expect of these missionaries? There is perhaps not a tribe on the continent that will not be visited by one or more of them. I suspect their first object will be to teach these wretched savages that they are the rightful owners of the American soil and that it has been wrongfully taken from them by the whites and that the Great Spirit has sent the Mormons among them to help them recover their rights. The character of many of those who have been nominated is calculated to confirm this view of the case. They embrace a class of rude and lawless young men, such as might be regarded as a curse to any civilized community." But Hurt cautioned his superiors to say and do nothing, for the Saints "always have and ever will thrive by persecution."[33]

The Mormon distinction between Saint and American was but another manifestation of the struggle between the Kingdom of God and the rest of mankind. "We have got a Territorial Government," Young boldly declared, "and I am and will be Governor, *and no power can hinder it, until the Lord Almighty says, 'Brigham, you need not be Governor any longer';* and then I am willing to yield to another Governor. . . . Every man that comes to impose upon this people, no matter by whom he is sent, or who they are that are sent, they lay the axe at the root of the tree to kill themselves; they had better be careful how they come here lest I should bend my finger."[34]

Young showed that he meant what he said when Lieutenant Colonel Edward J. Steptoe arrived in Utah late in 1854 with three hundred troops and orders to survey to California. Suspecting Steptoe had been sent to replace him, Young warned the Saints that the soldiers desired to "creep into your houses, and try to coax your wives and daughters from you. What for? Was it to make them more honorable, to give them a better character in the midst of the inhabitants of the earth, sustain them better, and make them more comfortable, and acknowledge them? No—they wanted to prostitute them, to ruin them, and send them to the grave, or to the devil, when they had done with them." Young knew how to deal with such men: ". . . cut their throats."[35]

VII

YOUNG HAD A PRACTICAL MOTIVE for fighting the Gentiles, for Utah's chief executive was in a position to enrich himself, his church, and his friends. Over the years Young induced the territorial legislature to hand him vast economic privileges. The governor, for example, was empowered to license liquor factories, a source of inestimable wealth and power.[36]

Other juicy plums went directly to Mormon leaders. On December 9, 1850, the legislature gave Apostle Ezra Taft Benson manufacturing and irrigation monopolies in Twin Springs and Rock Springs in the Tooele Valley, just south of the Great Salt Lake. The following month Benson got a timber monopoly in the canyons leading into the Tooele Valley, and on January 5, 1856, Hooper, David Caudland, Kimball's adopted son, and he were awarded herding rights in Lone Rock Valley. As the New York *Tribune* pointed out in 1858, these grants had made Benson "one of the wealthiest men in the Territory. By means of them he has built up a settlement in Tooele Valley called, after the initials of his own name, E.T. City."[37]

Young's brothers were also rewarded. Lorenzo Young got a tract of herding land southeast of the Great Salt Lake, an extremely valuable grant, for in cold weather cattle could not go into the Wasatch Range and had to graze in the valleys. Then in 1855 Phineas Young and Albert P. Rockwood, the prophet's father-in-law and adopted son, received grazing rights on Frémont's Island in the Great Salt Lake, and in 1856 Phineas, Franklin D. Richards, and Lorenzo Snow got a herding monopoly along the northeast shore of the lake. Nor was this all. In 1853 Joseph Young and John Young obtained control for three years of ferries and bridges on the Bear and Malad Rivers.[38] In 1856 Joseph and Brigham Young renewed this latter deed and got permission to charge tolls up to six dollars, a tenth of which would go to the Perpetual Emigrating Fund.[39]

Several grants from the legislature enriched Kimball. In 1851 he received for milling and manufacturing use of the waters of North Mill Creek Canyon and the canyon north of it, and in 1855 two acts gave him and Grant herding and road building monopolies in Parley's Park.[40]

Kimball, who had left Mendon in bankruptcy in 1832, became one of the West's wealthiest men, but his gains did not match the prophet's. Nine acts of the legislature made Young the economic dictator of Utah. On December 9, 1850, for a payment of only five hundred dollars he received control of City Creek and its canyon, the only place to obtain firewood within twenty miles of Salt Lake City. Thereafter he took from everyone who chopped fuel in his canyon every third wagonful. To enforce this edict he built a stone wall across the mouth of the canyon and stationed armed guards there.[41]

Young's demands heavily burdened his people. Chandless called wood the most expensive item in the average family's budget, running to about three hundred dollars a winter. A man with a yoke of oxen worked for two days to chop a load of wood and then had to give Young a third of it.[42]

The prophet also secured exclusive use of Kamas Prairie for herding; with Richards irrigation rights in Mill Creek; with Woodruff and two Danites, James W. Cummings and Hickman, herding and grazing land in Rush Valley; herding and farming monopolies in a portion of Tooele County; and as trustee-in-trust for the Perpetual Emigrating Fund control of Antelope and Stansbury's Islands in the Great Salt Lake.[43]

In parched country control of the waters issuing from the canyons made Young master of the territory. In 1853 he, Kimball, Benson, Grant, Jesse C. Little, and Phineas W. Cook incorporated the Great Salt Lake Water Works Association, a private firm, and sold its shares for a hundred dollars each.[44]

And in Big Cottonwood Canyon the prophet bought the charter issued to his brother, Joseph, formed a company, and by 1856 was operating three sawmills. At each he erected comfortable log houses for workers and their families.[45]

Several observers noted and complained about Young's economic power. "He selects for himself the choicest spots of land in the Territory," Judge John Cradlebaugh commented, "and they yield him their productions, none daring to interfere. . . . The cattle on a thousand hills exhibit his brand. He fixes his pay—he pays himself."[46] Ludlow agreed: "The mountain-stream that irrigates the city, flowing to all the gardens through open ditches on each side of the street, passes through Brigham's inclosure: if the saints needed drought to humble them, he could set back the waters to their source. The road to the only canyon where firewood is attainable runs through the same close, and is barred by a gate of which he holds the sole key. A family-man, wishing to cut fuel, must ask his leave, which is generally granted on condition that every third or fourth load is deposited in the inclosure, for Church purposes. Thus everything vital, save the air he breathes, reaches the Mormon only through Brigham's sieve. What more absolute despotism is conceivable?"[47]

In 1852 Holeman, the Indian Agent, saw other tragic consequences in this policy. Shortly after the legislature granted a ferry and bridge monopoly on the Green River to some prominent Saints, he saw first-hand the Mormon attempts to shove the Indians from the region. Determined to fight this invasion by greedy white men, the braves temporarily forced abandonment of the project. But despite his assertions of friendship for the Indians, Young pushed these encroachments, for the legislature's charter had allotted his tithing office ten per cent of the bridge and ferry tolls, a provision Holeman called "unconstitutional."[48] The church governed Utah, and Young was the church.

IX

ᒐᒐᒐᒐ

Of Danites, Blood
Atonement, and War

I

IN UTAH ENEMIES NEVER SPOKE. Exchanges of ideas and dip-
lomatic gestures were unknown. Because God had made
Young infallible, there was no room for differences of opinion.
Might ruled, but during the late 1850's Young faced for the
first time since reaching the territory a force more powerful
than his.

In the fall of 1855 during a depression Young committed the
first of several blunders by suggesting to Elder Franklin D. Richards in Liverpool a new way of transporting converts to Utah.
"We cannot afford to purchase wagons and teams as in times past.
I am consequently thrown back upon my old plan—to make hand-
carts, and let the emigration foot it." Since most migrants walked
even when they had teams, the march would be no hardship. "If it
is once tried, you will find that it will become the favorite mode of
crossing the plains; they will have nothing to do but come along,
and I should not be surprised if a company of this kind should
make the trip in sixty or seventy days."[1]

In 1856 the church tried the plan. Converts crossed the Atlantic Ocean to New Orleans and then sailed up the Mississippi River

to centers where they bought handcarts like those colored porters used in Eastern railroad terminals. Boxes three or four feet long with sides eight inches high and two wheels, the carts, which weighed four to five hundred pounds when loaded, could be pushed by three or four people walking abreast or pulled by five. Because five persons usually accompanied each handcart, twenty carts constituted a "hundred" and were allotted one wagon and three yokes of oxen.[2]

The Mormons considered the project divine. "The Lord has promised, through His servant Brigham," observed the *Millennial Star*, "that the hand-cart companies shall be blessed with health and strength, and be met part way with teams and provisions from the Valley. And I am not afraid to prophesy, that those who go by the hand-carts, and continue faithful and obedient, will be blessed more than they have ever dreamed of."[3]

Their carts painted all colors and inscribed with such names as "Truth will prevail," "Blessings follow sacrifice," and "Merry Mormons,"[4] three companies of Saints left the Missouri River in the spring of 1856 and reached Utah early that fall. As one of their songs put it:

Oh, our faith goes with the hand-carts,
And they have our hearts' best love;
'Tis a novel mode of traveling,
Devised by the Gods above.

And Brigham's their executive,
He told us the design;
And the Saints are proudly marching on,
Along the hand-cart line.[5]

But tragedy befell the last two groups of migrants. For three weeks five hundred Saints waited near Iowa City for their hand-carts to be finished. Early in July they started west, reaching Florence, Nebraska, formerly Winter Quarters, in August. Near the end of the month the column began the thousand-mile march to Utah. Except for bands of Sioux and Cheyenne, the country was uninhabited. Much of it was dry. Soon the weather turned cold and the winds fierce. Indian war parties and hungry coyotes hovered nearby, and the few oxen in camp died. In mid-September the Mormons arrived at Fort Laramie, where they learned that Young, violating his promise, had failed to send supplies. As the Saints headed towards the Black Hills and Laramie Plains, they cut their daily rations by a quarter. Many handcarts broke, and the starving converts ate axel grease to stay alive.

Then a blizzard swept down from the north. For an hour the Saints tried to walk in it, but they finally gave up and camped. Sixty-seven Mormons died in that storm and more perished before reaching the Great Basin. The final Mormon company suffered even more in this earliest and bitterest winter in years. Frozen corpses marked the route to Utah, but the migrants said only: "It is the will of the Lord."[6]

The residents of Salt Lake City, however, blamed Young for the tragedy. "If any man or woman complains of me or my Counsellors, in regard to the lateness of some of this season's immigration," Young retorted, "let the curse of God be on them and blast their substance with mildew and destruction, until their names are forgotten from the earth. . . . It will cost this people more to bring in those companies from the Plains, than it would to have seasonably brought them from the outfitting point on the Missouri River. I do not believe that the biggest fool in the community could entertain the thought that all this loss of life, time, and means, was through the mismanagement of the First Presidency."[7]

II

IN 1856 THE VISITING Englishman, William Chandless, was shocked by the suffering he saw in Utah. Drought and giant grasshoppers ruined almost the entire crop and killed off much of the livestock. According to Young, God was punishing the Saints for wasting the abundance of 1853, when food was recklessly thrown away.[8]

The prophet answered the discontent brought on by the depression and the handcart fiasco with a policy of repression. "The 'Reformation,' as it has been called, not a change in our religion, nor of the principles revealed through Joseph, but a change in some of the practices and lethargic habits of this people, has begun," Young announced early in 1857, "and its salutary influences are already perceptible."[9]

The originator of the movement was Jedediah M. Grant, the Speaker of the Utah House of Representatives and since 1854 Young's second counselor. Described by *The New York Times* as "a tall, thin, repulsive-looking man, of acute, vigorous intellect, a thorough-paced scoundrel, and the most essential blackguard in the pulpit," Grant well fit his nickname: "Brigham's sledgehammer."[10]

A seemingly unimportant incident during a church conference in Kaysville, twenty-five miles from Salt Lake City, triggered the Reformation. Grant asked several elders to meet him there, and even loaned one a mule. The elders rode exceedingly fast, and when they arrived their beasts were heated and tired. Grant, the final speaker of the day, saw the condition of his mule and burned inwardly, but he remained silent. Suddenly, as he began his address, he grew uncontrollable and denounced the elders for abusing the animals, the bishop of Kaysville for inefficiency, and everyone there for unholiness. He ordered all those present to be rebaptized.[11]

Young himself injected into the Reformation an aura of mystery. At one Salt Lake City meeting he locked the doors, extracted from his pocket a long white paper, and "in the name of Jesus Christ" read thirteen questions: "1. Have you shed innocent blood or assented thereto? 2. Have you committed adultery? 3. Have you betrayed your brother? 4. Have you borne false witness against your neighbor? 5. Do you get drunk? 6. Have you stolen? 7. Have you lied? 8. Have you contracted debts without prospect of paying? 9. Have you labored faithfully for your wages? 10. Have you coveted that which belongs to another? 11. Have you taken the name of the Lord in vain? 12. Do you preside in your family as a servant of God? 13. Have you paid your tithing in all things?"[12]

Grant touched yet another theme. "Do you wash your bodies once in each week, when circumstances will permit? Do you keep your dwellings, outhouses and door yards clean? The first work of the reformation with some should be to clean away the filth about their premises. How would some like to have President Young visit them and go through their buildings, examine their rooms, bedding, &c.? Many houses stink so bad that a clean man could not live in them, nor hardly breathe in them. Some men were raised in stink, and so were their fathers before them. I would not attempt to bless anybody in such places."[13]

During the Reformation two church officials called upon every Mormon family in Utah and asked each Saint questions that were answered under oath. After tallying the results, Young ordered the rebaptism of all Saints and required girls twelve and over to attend lectures by elders on the importance of polygamy and the duties of brides of "God's chosen people." In late 1856 and early 1857 the number of polygamous marriages performed rose sharply.[14]

Blood atonement was the heartbeat of the Reformation. As Lee showed, it went hand in hand with Young's assertions of infallibility. "He claims that the people are answerable to him as their God. That they must obey his beck and call. It matters not what he commands or requests the people to do, it is their duty to hear and obey. To disobey the will of Brigham Young is, in his mind, a sin against the Holy Ghost, and is an unpardonable sin to be wiped out only by blood atonement."[15] "If you do not know what to do, in order to do right," Young advised his people, "come to me at any time and I will give you the word of the Lord on that point."[16]

Every loyal Saint listened to the prophet. Albert Carrington, then the editor of the *Deseret News*, once confessed that if Young directed him to kill his son he would do so unhesitatingly, for he would know God had commanded it.[17]

But a Saint who disobeyed Young had to pay for it. "I say that there are men and women that I would advise to go to the President immediately," advised Grant, "and ask him to appoint a committee to attend to their case; and then let a place be selected, and let the committee shed their blood. We have those amongst us that are full of all manner of abominations, those who need to have their blood shed, for water will not do, their sins are of too deep a dye."[18]

"I could refer you to plenty of instances where men have been righteously slain, in order to atone for their sins," Young joined in. "I have seen scores and hundreds of people for whom there would have been a chance (in the last resurrection there will be) if their lives had been taken and their blood spilled on the ground as a smoking incense to the Almighty, but who are now angels to the devil until our elder brother, Jesus Christ, uses them up—conquers death, hell and the grave. I have known a great many men who have left this church for whom there is no chance whatever for exaltation; but if their blood had been spilled it would have been better for them. The wickedness and ignorance of nations forbid this principle's being in full force, but the time will come when the law of God will be in full force."[19]

The Danites, Young's secret army, enforced this doctrine. First formed in Missouri, these destroying angels, or Shenpips, stirred up such controversy that Mormon officials often denied they existed. "In Utah," wrote President Joseph Fielding Smith, the current church historian, in 1905, "there never were destroying angels or Danites, except in the imagination of bitter anti-Mormons."[20] "Danites are supposed to be a body of men who inflict the penalty of blood atonement," Apostle Charles W. Penrose added. "Let me say here, once and for all, that I know of no such order, never have known of any such order."[21]

Influential Gentiles scoffed at such statements. In 1857 Douglas and Representative Justin Morrill of Vermont both blamed dozens of murders on the Danites, and in 1860 *The New York Times* commented: "However the existence of the Danites or Destroying Angels may be denied, their victims are too many and well known to make the denial of much value."[22]

Leading Saints sometimes admitted these charges were true. In 1856 Grant lashed out at those Saints who sympathized with the brutally beaten Troskolawsski before conceding that "some of our 'shenpip' brethren happened to stumble over him."[23] The next year Young warned: "If men come here and do not behave themselves, they will not only find the Danites, whom they talk so much about, biting the horses heels, but the scoundrels will find something biting their heels. In my plain remarks I merely call things by their right names."[24]

Believing God would reward them in heaven for enforcing His law, the Danites frequently boasted about their exploits. "Rockwell, Hickman, and other members of the Danite band with whom I have been acquainted do not seek to deny their secret occupations but ferociously exult in these things," recorded Caleb Green, a Mormon during the 1850's. "I have heard Rockwell relate some of his hair breath escapes—the Governor Boggs affair included—with as much gusto, and pleasure, as a mountaineer would a hand to hand fight with a bear, in which he had proven himself the victor."[25]

Young alone commanded this bloodthirsty group. "Brigham never tells one of the 'angels' to commit a depredation straight forward," one apostate informed *The New York Times*, "but a wink, a nod, or a 'you know, Porter,' or whoever it may be, will settle the matter as easily as a sermon on the subject."[26]

Aided by this band of enforcers, Young continued his struggle against Utah's federal appointees. "Look at Brocchus, that mean, low curse, who attempted to introduce disaffection among this holy and united people," he boasted to his followers in 1855. "He dared to say in our presence that we had falsely maligned the majesty of the President; but I chastised him—him and all his set—I scourged them till they trembled for their lives; and I assert again, what I asserted to Brocchus, that General Taylor is in hell, for I know he is." Young then turned upon Judge William W. Drummond: "And there is another public officer among us who is a mean, nasty stink. He came here to practise all sorts of evil against this people; and he now goes about the streets with the holy sepulchre in one hand and a bottle of whiskey in the other! . . . It is reported that I have said that whoever the President appoints, I am still Governor. I repeat it, all hell cannot remove me. (Cries of 'Amen.') I am still your Governor. (Cries of 'Glory to God.') I will still rule this people until God himself permits another to take my place. I wish I could say as much for the other officers of the government. The greater part of them are a gambling, drinking, whoring set. They come out here with a little piece of parchment in their pockets, they gallop about our streets with their brass buttons and their fine horses, but they are whited sepulchres. Yes, they are. The first thing they say on coming here is, 'Can't you get me a woman to sleep with to-night?' and they go about the streets seeking whom they may devour. For my part I say to all such, 'If you dare to violate the pure daughters of Utah, d—n you, I'll cut your throats!' (Great excitement, loud shouts of 'Here's one that'll help you,' 'Damn them all,' 'Amen.') Yes; and they go about asking the fair daughters of Utah to go sleigh riding with them: 'Won't you go, my dear?' and 'Oh, we'll have such a sweet time of it'—(Loud laughter)—and then they finger about them, and put their arms round their waists. . . . And these are the men who seek the pap of government. Do you think I'll obey or respect them? No! I'll say as I did the other day, when the flag was hauled down from before the military quarters—'Let them take down the American flag; we can do without it.' (Great applause, stamping of feet and yells.)"[27]

An episode the following year typified the violence of the Reformation. Green, traveling across the plains in a wagon train that included Rockwell and Abraham O. Smoot, was surprised to find at Fort Kearney, 180 miles west of Omaha, Almon W. Babbitt, the outspoken territorial secretary, who explained that Omahas had attacked his party and killed all but three of the white men. Four days out of Kearney, Green saw Babbitt, Thomas Sutherland, and the third survivor ride into camp and leave an hour later in an uncovered light wagon drawn by three pairs of mules. Babbitt expected to cover thirty miles before night and reach Utah in two weeks. That day Green's train made twenty-five miles, bringing it five miles from Babbitt's.

"Rockwell and Smoot left camp at night and returned in the morn," Green noted in his diary. "The next day Smoot left the road with some other men and brought a wagon out of the thicket which skirts the Platte at this point. We suspected that it was Babbitt's," for it had no top. Inside it were three sets of harnesses.

At Fort Laramie, three hundred miles further west, Green learned Babbitt had not yet arrived. Scouts also reported that the only hostile Indians living in the area were in council on the Arkansas River, two hundred miles from where Babbitt and Sutherland had disappeared. "The rumors of Babbitt's death reached Salt Lake," Green added. "The people—always suspicious when Rockwell & his comrades were lurking about—directly attributed his death to the authorities of the church, and much angry and dangerous discussion arose."[28]

Young's denials of responsibility and the assertion of Thomas Twiss, an Indian Agent, that Cheyennes had admitted the murder to him failed to stifle the talk.[29] Babbitt's widow—unquestionably correct—insisted to the New York *Herald* that "Cheyenne savages" had butchered her husband,[30] but Issac Sheehan, Babbitt's brother-in-law, became "fully convinced by the circumstantial evidence that I have had access to, that Mr. Babbitt *was* murdered by the agency of the Danites. . . . They often threatened to make catfish bait of their opponents before they left Nauvoo, and since that time they would threaten to 'salt them down.' "[31] Another denunciation came from Sutherland's cousin, John Hyde, Jr., who, convinced of Young's guilt, produced the decade's most important condemnation of the Saints, *Mormonism, Its Leaders and Designs.*[32]

During the summer of 1862 the prophet supplied a footnote to this episode. "There is no need of any difficulty," he warned Associate Justice Charles B. Waite of the Utah Supreme Court, "and there need be none, if the officers do their duty, and mind their own affairs. If they do not, if they undertake to interfere in affairs that do not concern them, I will not be far off. *There was Almon W. Babbitt. He undertook to quarrel with me, but soon afterwards was killed by Indians.* He lived like a fool, and died like a fool."[33]

III

THE UNREST CONTINUED. Late in 1856 fourteen of the prophet's armed lieutenants, including Hickman, Hiram Clawson, Jesse C. Little, and Brigham Young, Jr., rode into Salt Lake City, intercepted the United States mail carriage, and followed it about. When the carriage headed out of town, the perplexed conductor stopped it and demanded an explanation. The men said that on the way in the train had made needless noise, and they wanted to make sure it made no more. In reality, the band expected to stop several apostates from escaping on the carriage.[34]

Then in January 1857 some Saints broke into the offices of Thomas S. Williams, the merchant and lawyer, and Judge George P. Stiles, took the Supreme Court records, and stripped the federal library of nine hundred volumes of laws furnished by the government. The Mormons were protesting Congress's refusal to admit Deseret to the Union.[35]

That same month three leading Danites—James W. Cummings, the clerk of the United States District Court; Hosea Stout, the acting District Attorney; and Alexander McRae, the territorial marshal—visited David H. Burr, the United States Surveyor General for Utah, and read aloud a letter Burr had recently mailed to Washington charging the Saints with trespassing on federal land and stealing government timber. After Burr admitted he had written the letter, Cummings asked if the Mormons had not earned every stick of timber they took. Burr said he could not judge that but had to report all violations of the law, adding that his men had been ordered from the nearby canyons by Young's guards and had been told to pay for timber they needed for public surveys. Cummings furiously responded that the Saints would have both the country and its timber and warned Burr about writing more letters.[36]

Unfortunately some of Utah's federal appointees deserved such treatment. *"Money is my God,"* Drummond bragged to Remy and Julius Brenchley, "and you may put this down in your journals if you like." Abandoning his wife without support, Drummond brought with him to Utah a prostitute he had picked up in Washington and passed off as his wife. In court she sat beside him.[37]

Continually quarreling with the Mormons over the jurisdiction of his court, Drummond resigned and sent the Attorney General a long letter violently denouncing Young and blaming on the prophet the murders of Gunnison, Babbitt, and the late Judge Leonidas Shaver, who died in 1855 under mysterious circumstances. He also accused Young of tampering with the courts and juries. After Moroni Green, a Saint, was convicted in District Court of assault with intent to kill, Young pardoned him. He also freed Baker, a Mormon who tortured and drowned a dumb boy, and sat alongside him in church the next Sunday. Five or six Gentiles, on the other hand, were serving long prison terms merely for being anti-Mormon.[38]

The *Millennial Star* viewed Drummond's letter with horror. An "infamous scoundrel and dastardly wretch," Drummond was "endeavoring to hide his own filthy, and most heart-sickening crimes, by abusing and slandering the Mormons." En route to Utah this "ignorant, back-woods pettifogger" had "picked up a woman, slept with her during the whole journey, boarded and bedded with her while in the territory, calling her Mrs. Drummond." He was a "beastly criminal," a "horrible monster," a "black-hearted judge" who had ordered his Negro slave to murder a Jewish merchant in Salt Lake City, a "poor wretch," a "lying, adulterous, murderous fiend" who had "escaped from the punishment of his execrable crimes" and now peddled "barefaced, monstrous lies," "a notorious criminal, whose black deeds were publicly exposed many months ago," a "loathsome specimen of humanity," and a "pious whoremaster of a judge who fled from the territory to escape the penalty of the civil law."[39] Forever after the Saints gleefully recorded his every misfortune, including his arrest in Chicago in 1886 for pilfering postage stamps.[40]

Published by papers throughout the United States and Europe, Drummond's letter marked the beginning of the end for Young's opponents. The only remaining federal judge in the territory, Stiles, a Mormon, soon incurred the displeasure of his church by upholding the law, and Williams encountered trouble because he defended Gentiles in court and forced Young's brothers, John and Joseph, to pay him sixty dollars they owed him. Early in April, after Young excommunicated both men, mobs attempted to fire their homes.[41]

Several days later Kimball met Williams on the street and demanded the lawyer's daughter for his son. Williams refused, threatened to kill some leading Mormons, and was jailed. He was freed after his father, a prominent Saint, accompanied by Young's longtime friend, Howard Egan, stormed, gun in hand, into the prophet's office and swore all three men would die on the spot if Williams was not released. But the wedding took place on April 13.[42]

Two days after that Stiles, Burr, Williams, Peter K. Dotson, Utah's new marshal, and Postmaster Hiram F. Morrell of Salt Lake City fled east. On May 29 they arrived at Fort Leavenworth, left their families there, and departed for Washington to urge against the Saints the use of force.[43]

Young countered with character assassination. On July 23,

1857, Charles W. Moeller had published an affidavit in the St. Louis *Missouri Republican* accusing Burr of issuing fraudulent surveying contracts, of hiring unqualified workers, and of padding expense accounts. The following year Moeller admitted that his statement "was extorted from me by fear of personal danger in case I should not sign it." Young, Clawson, Hooper, and Cummings had also made "alterations . . . in the original draft . . . without my consent. I never knew any act or word of Gen. David H. Burr," Moeller now confessed, "which was not entirely upright and honorable."[44]

IV

VIOLENCE, fostered by the pillars of Mormon society, was common in Utah. In the winter of 1849 Lieutenant John Tobin arrived in Salt Lake City with an army surveying team. There he met and fell in love with Young's daughter, Alice, and converted to Mormonism. He went east on business but returned in 1856, again courted Alice, lived for a time with Young's family, and worked with Brigham Young, Jr. Then Tobin apostatized, and Young gave Alice to Clawson as a third wife. When Tobin decided to leave the territory and joined a small group bound for California, Young responded angrily. In the presence of Frederick Loba, the Swiss chemist who became a Saint and was ordered to Utah to make gunpowder, he told his son, Joseph, to take some Danites and stop Tobin. Ambushed in the middle of the night about 375 miles south of Salt Lake City, Tobin and his companions fought off the attackers and finally reached California, but in the battle Tobin was shot in the head and lost an eye. Now Loba feared for his life. In April 1857 he and his pregnant wife walked over snow-covered ground to the camp of friendly Indians on the Snake River.[45]

Then in May 1857 came a murder almost as important as Joseph Smith's. Two years before Parley Pratt had induced Elenor J. McLean, the wife of a San Francisco custom house worker, to desert her husband and three children for him and Mormonism. She became Pratt's twelfth wife and moved to Utah. In 1857, when her children visited her mother in New Orleans, Elenor saw a chance to get them. She went there, took them, and headed for Salt Lake City with Pratt, who had joined her. McLean followed and near Van Buren, Arkansas, overtook Pratt. While both men were still on horseback, McLean twice sunk a heavy bowie knife into the flesh just under the apostle's left armpit. As Pratt lay helpless on the ground, McLean borrowed a derringer and shot him in the neck. Two and a half hours later the apostle died.[46]

In September at Mountain Meadows in southern Utah the Mormons responded. Occurring as rumors placed an invading federal army near the territory, this atrocity is still masked in conflicting testimony. Most Gentiles considered the massacre of 120 Arkansas travelers retaliation for Pratt's death, but many Saints, including Lee, a participant, and Brigham Young, Jr., blamed the crime on Indians. Lee termed the conduct of the victims "scandalous. They swore and boasted openly that they helped shoot the guts out of Joe Smith and Hyrum Smith at Carthage, and that the whole army was coming right behind them, and would kill every G-d d—n Mormon in Utah, and make the women and children slaves. They had two bulls, which they called one 'Heber' and the other 'Brigham,' and whipped 'em thro' every town, yelling and singing, blackguarding and blaspheming oaths that would have made your hair stand on end. At Spanish Fork—it can be proved —one of 'em stood on his wagon-tongue, and swung a pistol, and swore that he helped kill old Joe Smith, and was ready for old Brigham Young, and all sung a blackguard song, 'Oh, we've got the ropes and we'll hang old Brigham before the snow flies,' and all such stuff." Heading north, the Gentiles shot one Indian, crippled another, and poisoned a spring and gave the flesh of an animal that had perished there to some Indians, who ate it and died too. At Mountain Meadows, Lee explained, the Indians overtook and surrounded the party. Three Gentiles sneaked out for help but bumped into some Saints, who recognized them and killed one of them. The other two made it back to camp, but the Mormons now feared exposure and helped the Indians finish the job. Lee, meanwhile, pleaded with his fellow Saints to let the Gentiles go and sent word to Young, who answered: "Spare them, by all means." By then, however, it was too late.[47]

Shortly before his execution for the crime in 1877, Lee offered another version of the massacre. At daybreak on Monday, September 7, the Indians and Mormons attacked the Gentiles, who held out for four days but surrendered after being promised an escort to Cedar City, the nearest settlement. The Saints marched the prisoners a short distance before turning on and butchering all of the men and women and all but seventeen of the children.

After that the murderers sent Lee for Young's advice. Hearing the story, the prophet "wept like a child, walked the floor, wrung his hands in bitter anguish," and said he would ask for divine guidance. "Brother Lee," he reported the next morning, "not a drop of innocent blood has been shed. I have gone to God in prayer. God has shown me it was a just act. The people did right, but were only a little hasty. I have direct evidence from God that the act was a just one, that it was in accord with God's will. I sustain you and the brethren in all that you did. All I fear is treachery on the part of the brethren concerned. Go home and tell the brethren I sustain them. Keep all secret as the grave. Never tell any one, and write me a long letter laying all the blame on the Indians. I will report to the United States government that it was an Indian massacre." Keeping his word, Young forwarded Lee's letter to Washington. He later awarded Lee three more wives and appointed him probate judge of Washington County.[48]

The massacre at Mountain Meadows still stands as Utah's bloodiest episode. Young did not order the butchery, but with fiery speeches he, Kimball, and George Smith, who toured southern Utah just before it, encouraged it. Young would undoubtedly have prevented the murders if he could, but for years he protected the guilty.[49]

On the Sunday before the massacre, for example, Young bitterly denounced Gentiles. "We have borne enough of their oppression and hellish abuse," he fumed, "and we will not bear any more of it; for there is no just law requiring further forbearance on our part." "The thread is cut between them and us," warned Kimball, "and we will never gibe again. No, never, world without end." Inspired by roars of "Amen" from the congregation, Kimball went on: "Do as you are told, and Brigham Young will never leave the Governorship of this Territory from this time henceforth. No, never!"[50]

In 1857 at the Seventies Hall in Salt Lake City the prophet justified the crime. Later, standing before the monument to the slain at Mountain Meadows, he reportedly read the inscription, "Vengeance is mine; I will repay saith the Lord," and added: "Vengeance is mine; I have repaid saith the Lord."[51]

V

As LATE AS 1877 Daniel H. Wells of the First Presidency connected the massacre with the reported entrance into northern Utah of troops under General William S. Harney. "Our previous history," he informed the New York *Herald*, "the condition of our people and their crops at the time, our relations with the Indians and the extraordinary news and rumors which accompanied the simultaneous advance on Utah of Harney's United States Army and the Arkansas emigrants—these things ought to be looked at carefully and examined before a great people are censured and a great Church is prejudiced according to the perjury of a few wicked members. . . . Now, when it was whispered, and it soon began not only to be whispered, but asserted, that these Arkansas emigrants were leagued with the soldiers, and that some of them had been engaged in the murder of Joseph and Hiram Smith at Nauvoo, the air might have seemed almost as heavy over Lower as it certainly was over Northern Utah."[52]

Surprisingly, the invasion took place under a President the Mormons welcomed. Until the mid-1850's the Saints had no party allegiance and usually sold their votes to the highest bidder. Then in 1854 Douglas introduced the Kansas-Nebraska Bill, which permitted the people of those territories to decide whether they wanted slavery. Elated because the extension of this principle meant Utah would be allowed into the Union with polygamy, Young became a Democrat.[53]

The Mormon question figured prominently in the 1856 presidential canvass. Calling plural marriage and slavery the "twin relics of barbarism," Republican orators ceaselessly ridiculed the Saints. In Philadelphia they circulated a handbill in which Young urged all Mormons to vote for James Buchanan, the Democratic nominee, who was tolerant of polygamy. It was a Republican forgery.[54]

Buchanan's election pleased Young. "We believe he will be a friend to the good," the prophet confided to Kane, like Buchanan a Pennsylvania Democrat. "Prest. Fillmore was our friend, but Buchanan will not be a whit behind."[55]

Young wanted Buchanan to give Utah's offices to Mormons. "We of Utah consider that we are entitled to some consideration in regard to having behaved so well for several years past," he innocently proclaimed to Kane. "We desire to have a voice in the selection of our officers. . . . We believe that the interests of the federal government—as well as of the territory—would be promoted by pursuing this course." Gentile appointees were usually good for nothing but stirring up Indians and seducing Mormon girls. "They come here generally without their misses expecting to find the usual accommodations afforded in other parts of the world, and when detected in their endeavors to carry into effect this disgraceful practice they abound in making reports of awful iniquity and treason among the Mormons. How think you we feel towards men who we know if they had the power would cut our throats?"[56]

In analyzing Buchanan's motives for invading Utah, historians have invariably focused attention upon Secretary of War John B. Floyd. Some scholars have charged that on the eve of secession the pro-Southern Secretary tried to bankrupt the federal treasury by a costly expedition to the Great Basin. Others have accused him of concocting the preposterous scheme to aid certain businessmen and contractors.[57]

Far less has been said about the influence of Buchanan's friends. Early in May, acceding to the demands of such Democrats as Benjamin Ferris, who publicly castigated "the unscrupulous set of villains congregated in the valley of the Great Salt Lake," the President decided to go halfway and appoint a new governor for Utah. But as he looked about for someone willing to accept the post, two of his closest Pennsylvania associates, the Reverend Henry Slicer, who would serve in 1860 as chaplain of the Democratic convention in Baltimore, and United States Senator William Bigler, demanded even stronger action. "There is a good deal of honest indignation in the country against the conduct of the Mormons," Bigler wrote the President. *"The universal sentiment seems to demand the assertion & maintenance of the political authority of the General Government over the Territory*, regardless of their peculiar institution. They may convince the world that a man in that country may have more wives than one; but it will be difficult to show that gives him a right to reject the Executive Officer of the law."[58] At once Buchanan alerted fifteen hundred troops for the march to Utah.[59]

For Mormons the harshest blow came on June 12, 1857. Their old friend Douglas joined the attackers. Insisting he had studied the problem for seven years, he denounced nine tenths of the Saints as aliens who spurned American citizenship and refused to swear allegiance to the United States. The Mormons were "bound by horrid oaths and penalties to recognize and maintain the authority of Brigham Young, and the government of which he is the head, as paramount to that of the United States in civil as well as religious affairs. In due time they hope to subvert the government." Young's crimes were unconscionable. He incited the Indians to hostile acts against the government and used his Danites to eliminate dissenters. "Should such a state of things actually exist as we are led to infer from the reports, and such information that comes in an official shape, the knife must be applied to this pestiferous, disgusting cancer which is gnawing into the very vitals of the body politic. It must be cut out by the roots, and seared over by the red hot iron of stern and unflinching law." To bring Mormons "to a sense of their duty" Douglas would repeal the 1850 law establishing Utah "on the ground that they are alien enemies and outlaws, unfit to be citizens of a Territory, much less ever to become citizens of one of the free and independent States of this Confederacy. To protect them further in their treasonable, disgusting, and beastial practices would be a disgrace to the country—a disgrace to humanity—a disgrace to civilization, and a disgrace to the spirit of the age." If, after the territorial government was abolished, Young and his confederates committed a crime, they could be brought to Iowa, Missouri, California, or any other state for trial.[60]

Blaming this address on presidential ambition, Kimball called Douglas "just as big a damned rascal as ever walked. . . . He has taken a course to get into the chair of State, and that is what he is after; he will try to accomplish that if he goes to hell the next day, but he will not get into the chair of State, he will go to hell."[61]

Brigham Young about 1855

Orson Pratt

From Thomas B. H. Stenhouse's The Rocky Mountain Saints

A polygamous family in the Great Salt Lake Valley in the mid-1860's. The man, his wives, and his children all lived in the one-room shack.

Gen. Grenville M. Dodge in 1867, about the time he visited Salt Lake City [OPPOSITE] A Mormon construction crew working on the Union Pacific Railroad under the contract given to Young in 1867. They are blasting a tunnel in Weber Canyon.

[BELOW] A rural town in the 1860's: Coalville in the Weber Valley, sixty-five miles from Salt Lake City, in the midst of the great Utah coal center. The toll road in the picture was owned by an incorporated company.

The Mormon Tabernacle in 1868

[OVERLEAF] *Brigham Young's homes in 1869*

[ABOVE]   *Salt Lake City from the top of the Tabernacle in 1869. The foundation of the great Temple is in the foreground. The house with many windows is Lion House. The mountains are the Wasatch Range of the Rockies.*
[BELOW]   *Young's cotton and woolen factories at the mouth of Parley's Canyon, about three miles from Salt Lake City.*

Heber Kimball   John Taylor

The famed British illustrator Arthur Boyd Houghton drew this sketch for the London Graphic *while listening to Young preach during a visit to Salt Lake City in 1870.*

By Arthur Boyd Houghton for the London Graphic

Two of Young's most famous wives

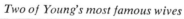

Zina Diantha Huntington   *Eliza Roxey Snow*

[LEFT]   *The Brigham Young monument at the main intersection of down-town Salt Lake City.*   [RIGHT]   *From Thomas B. H. Stenhouse's* The Rocky Mountain Saints

[LEFT]   *Young kept the original of this painting in his office.*
[RIGHT]   *Young in later life*

The cover of William Jarman's anti-Mormon tract, Uncle Sam's Abscess, *written in 1884*

Frederic Remington drew this sketch of Jim Bridger, whom he had never seen, for Outing *magazine in 1887.*

THE LAST IN BED PUT OUT THE LIGHT

From William Jarman's Uncle Sam's Abscess

Young's most famous son and namesake

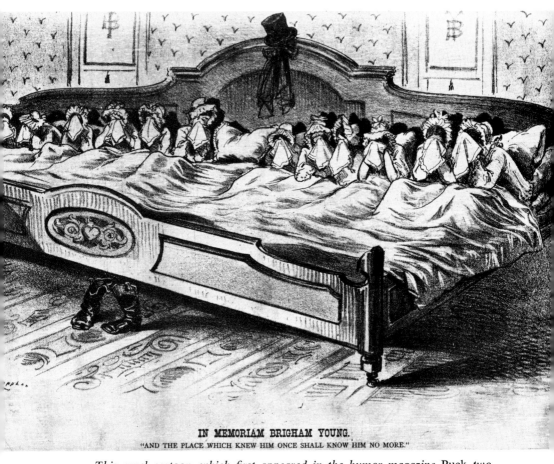

IN MEMORIAM BRIGHAM YOUNG.

"AND THE PLACE WHICH KNEW HIM ONCE SHALL KNOW HIM NO MORE."

This cruel cartoon, which first appeared in the humor magazine Puck *two weeks after Young's death, proved so popular that it was issued separately and for three years was sold at newsstands throughout the United States.*

VI

A LESSER MAN THAN YOUNG would have succumbed to the current of misfortune engulfing him during the winter and spring of 1856-7. While rebaptizing some of the faithful at the height of the Reformation, Grant, only forty years old, developed a chill from too long a stay in a cold stream and died soon after of pneumonia.[62] A few months later *Mormonism, Its Leaders and Designs,* by the apostate John Hyde, Jr., appeared. The decade's most important exposure of Mormonism, it became an immediate best seller. Clearly written and based on the author's long experience as a Saint, it was far more factual than Ferris's superficial *Utah and the Mormons* and Mrs. Ferris's chatty *The Mormons at Home,* both of which were published between 1854 and 1856. Hyde's book could not have appeared at a better time, and even Horace Greeley's New York *Tribune,* which had practically ignored the earlier works, gave it a four-column review.[63]

As the undeclared war began, the church hovered near bankruptcy. In 1856, through an agent, Young had gotten the federal mail contract between Salt Lake City and St. Louis by underbidding the old carriers, John M. Hockaday and W. M. F. Magraw. The church, expecting to transport both passengers and freight, established the Brigham Young Express and Carrying Company and spent nearly $200,000 on stations, teams, equipment, and help. But in June 1857 the government abruptly cancelled the contract, and Buchanan appointed Hockaday the new Utah District Attorney and Magraw the construction superintendent of military wagon roads. Another Magraw, Robert, soon began visiting the White House and courting Harriet Lane, the bachelor President's niece and first lady.[64]

On July 24, 1857, several thousand Mormons were in Big Cottonwood Canyon, east of Salt Lake City, celebrating the tenth anniversary of their arrival in the Great Basin when Rockwell and Smoot rode in with word that an army column was approaching the territory. Young, who had learned of the expedition six weeks before, then recalled that when first entering the region he had said that if the United States would leave the Saints alone for ten years "we will ask no odds of them." Hearing that "priests, politicians, speculators, whoremongers, and every mean, filthy character that could be raked up" were coming to "kill off the Mormons," Young assured his followers: "In the name of Israel's God, we ask no odds of them."[65]

VII

"IT WOULD SWEETEN DEATH TO A MAN," Woodruff advised as troops neared Utah, "to know that he should lay down his life in defense of freedom and the Kingdom of God rather than to longer bow to the cruelty of mobs."[66] Kimball agreed. "The day has come when the Devil is coming with all his combined forces: he has laid siege against the kingdom of God, and it never will cease till this kingdom triumphs." For the United States he predicted chaos. "Let me tell you that ten years will not pass away before God will play with this nation as he did with Pharaoh, only worse."[67] This time Kimball's prophecy proved all too accurate.

Two government appointments in July 1857 incensed the Mormons further. Alfred Cumming's selection as governor created a furor. Learning he was currently the Indian Superintendent at St. Louis, the Saints were sure he had helped drive them from Missouri in 1839. In reality, Cumming, a Georgian, had been nowhere near Missouri then.[68]

A week later the army made Jim Bridger a guide and interpreter. Paid five dollars a day, he would escort the new governor and the new army commander, Colonel Albert Sidney Johnston, whose force was already nearing Fort Laramie, to Salt Lake City.[69]

Journeying the opposite way, Samuel W. Richards, Young's special envoy to Washington, stopped at Fort Kearney late in August and found the troops begging for battle. "Even at Kearney the soldiers were in very high glee at the idea of wintering sumptuously in Utah, where, as the Paddy said, 'the women are as thick as blackberries,' and it was a great wonder to them what Brigham Young would say to see them with his wives parading the streets of Great Salt Lake City. Every dirty, foul-mouthed Dutchman and Irishman, of whom many of the troops were composed, fully expected some 'Mormon' woman would jump into his arms upon his arrival in Utah, and hail him as a heavenly sent messenger to bring deliverance from 'Mormon degradation, wretchedness, and despair.' Who don't wait with almost breathless suspense for the issue?"[70]

On September 8, as Richards arrived in the East, Captain Stewart Van Vliet of Harney's staff reached Salt Lake City for talks with Young and the other Mormon leaders. At their conference Young reviewed for Van Vliet the history of Mormon sufferings, emphasizing the atrocities in Missouri and Illinois. He then accused the government of resuming these persecutions and vowed to keep the federal troops from the basin. Hearing these words, the other Saints present nodded agreeingly.

The Mormons might halt the army approaching Utah, Van Vliet responded, but by next year the government would have so many soldiers in the region that no one could stop them. "We are aware that such will be the case," Young retorted, "but when these troops arrive they will find Utah a desert. Every house will be burned to the ground, every tree cut down, and every field laid waste. We have three years' provisions on hand, which we will cache, and then take to the mountains and bid defiance to all the powers of the government."[71]

Still calling himself Utah's governor, Young informed his people in a proclamation of September 15, 1857: "We are invaded by a hostile force, who are evidently assailing us to accomplish our overthrow and destruction." He promised never to submit, mobilized the Nauvoo Legion, forbade "All armed forces of every description from coming into this Territory, under any pretence whatever," and declared martial law throughout Utah.[72]

Two weeks later along the Green River some Saints swooped down on three government supply trains and destroyed seventy-five wagons. The army commanders decided they could accomplish nothing during the winter and camped near Fort Bridger, which the Legion occupied.[73] In letters to Colonel Edmund Alexander, whose Tenth Infantry Regiment was only thirty miles from Bridger, Young called the soldiers "mere cat's-paws of political jugglers and hucksters, penny a-liners, hungry speculators, and disgraced officials." Rather than remain the tool of evil men, Alexander should pack up and go home.[74]

On November 7, 1857, Young talked ominously to William

Bell, the Salt Lake City merchant. "I say the troops shall never enter this valley," the prophet said, speaking exceptionally slowly and emphasizing the word "never." "We are determined to resist. The Mormon faith will increase and flourish, and the Lord will protect his own. If the troops attempt to enter, we will destroy them."[75]

Meanwhile, the Mormon leaders stirred their flock with fiery speeches. "If this people shall consent to dispossess Brother Brigham Young as our Governor," Kimball preached, "they are just as sure to go to hell as they live, and I know it; for God would forsake them and leave them to themselves, and they would be in worse bondage than the children of Israel were. . . . We shall never leave these valleys till we get ready; no, never; no, never. We will live here till we go back to Jackson County, Missouri."[76]

"Will the President that sits in the Chair of State be ripped from his seat?" Kimball asked. "Yes; he will die an untimely death; and God Almighty will curse him, and He will also curse his successor if he takes the same stand, and He will curse all those who are his coadjutors and all those who sustain him. What for? For coming here to destroy the Kingdom of God and the prophets and apostles and inspired men and women, and God Almighty will curse them in the name of the Lord Jesus Christ."[77]

As Kimball saw it, Buchanan had sent "troops to kill brother Brigham and me; and to take the young women to the States. . . . Those officers out yonder have a good many women with them, and I do not believe there are twenty in the whole camp but what are whores, and they designed to come here to set you a pattern and to moralize this community."[78]

VIII

IF FOR ANYTHING, military tacticians will study the Mormon war of 1857-8 to find out how not to conduct a campaign. Both sides committed unconscionable blunders. Wells, the commander of the Legion, quickly showed he was no Ulysses S. Grant or Robert E. Lee. In 1860 Burton gazed with amazement at the Mormon fortifications at Echo Station. The breastworks were accessible from the rear and so exposed that army sharpshooters might easily have picked off the defenders. Burton heard about two Saints who wanted to see how safe they were. As one mounted the crest of a precipice, the other aimed, fired, and sent a jagerball through his friend's head.[79]

If inexperience constituted the Mormon weakness, politics was the government's. The war soon deteriorated into a dispute between Democrats and Republicans. From Fort Leavenworth late in 1857 and early in 1858 Harney blamed it all on General Winfield Scott, the army commander in chief, who hated all Democrats, Buchanan included. "From the commencement of the Utah Expedition to the present time he has opposed or ignored every useful suggestion I have made to him," Harney told Buchanan, "and his own plans are faulty. I assume very little in predicting a decided failure, should they be attempted to be carried out." Scott, glued to his desk in Washington, had ordered cavalry into the mountains, where horses were useless, and had sent a crack infantry regiment to the plains "to be laughed at by mountain Indians. Has it ever occurred to your Excellency that neither ignorance nor imbecility, but a settled plan to defeat and confuse your administration are the motives of such conduct?" Harney urged Buchanan to assign to Utah eight to ten thousand men. "Whoever you may be pleased to send to Utah, let him throw his reputation and his life upon the die, but give him the sole responsibility of his actions. The campaign to Utah cannot be planned in Washington or New York."[80]

By now the President was dismayed. Late in 1857 Edward de Stoeckel, the Russian minister to Washington, mentioned to Buchanan that newspaper reports said Young planned to lead the Saints either to British Canada or Russian Alaska. When de Stoeckel asked whether the Saints intended to go as conquerors or colonists, the President said he did not care which as long as he got rid of them.[81]

Three prominent apostates offered Buchanan a way out. Now a celebrity, John Hyde, Jr., would go all the way with repression. He would repeal the 1850 act establishing the territory, proclaim martial law there, augment the troops already in Utah with volunteers from California and Oregon, permit all polygamists to leave the country, and offer rewards for the apprehension of Young,

Kimball, Orson Hyde, Wells, Taylor, and Hickman.[82] The next step would be to hang the prophet from one of his own apple trees.

Itching for a share of Young's glory and wealth, John C. Bennett, Joseph Smith's one-time friend and the Legion's former commander, suggested to Douglas another possibility. "That the conflict with Utah will be most sanguinary, there is little doubt. I desire to be in the most bloody and terrible battle. You know my military capacity well. When I commanded the Legion it was the best disciplined body of troops in the Union, so admitted on all hands. I can now select and take against them as formidable a Regiment as America can produce, if President Buchanan will only give me the *authority* to do so. Can I have your influence in procuring such authority? With my knowledge of the Mormons, there is no man living who could do the country better service. Please see the President on the subject, and write me your success."[83]

Another former Saint entertained similar dreams. But James Arlington Bennett, whom the Saints nominated for Vice-President of the United States on Smith's ticket in 1844 only to learn his foreign birth made him ineligible for the office, wrote directly to Buchanan. "By perusing the inclosed letters, which I beg you to keep safe, you will perceive that I am the true heir of Joseph Smith, the Mormon Prophet. That I hold his *seal* (*His head*) and his *Mantle* of Prophetic *Virtue* and could by these matters who no other man can share, not even B. Young the Usurper of my place & power, get a portion if not the whole Mormon people who are filled with superstition to join my Standard. I can rule that people, with or without an army—Your excellency will also perceive that I am the next in Rank to Joseph & would of course claim the Lieutenant Generalship of the Legion. I can do as Napoleon did in Egypt among the Mormons & I trust with more success. Cant I be a turk in profession for I never can be in practice."[84]

Now a salesman for a Brooklyn cemetery, Bennett, a truly fallen prophet, offered the President the sole gift within his power: a three-hundred-foot monument to be erected in the cemetery after Buchanan's death. Bennett sent Buchanan the deed to the lot, but the President returned it with his thanks.[85]

Undaunted by this rebuff, Bennett, with the army bogged down in Utah, again pressed for appointment as Buchanan's envoy. The "strangers" Buchanan might select for the post could accomplish nothing, Bennett wrote from his office in Gravesina, Long Island. "I feel quite sure that no other man than myself can by peaceful & moral suasion bring the Mormons under full subjection to Federal Rule, and were I to go in such capacity I am sure to succeed." Buchanan must send "to the Mormons a General of their own election if not of their own religious creed with a view to persuade them to their duty. . . . It has been done by the Greeks, Romans & other nations with success. I again beg your excellency to pardon me for saying that it is my fixed opinion that there is nothing so likely to affect injuriously one of the best administrations that this Country ever had, as this Mormon War, taking all the circumstances into consideration. Douglas and his adherents are waiting, with hawk eyes, to bring it into political play. The very news papers that are urging on the war against the 'Abominable Polygamists' are making the excitement to serve themselves—May heaven direct your honest efforts to perform your Legitimate duty in your exalted station."[86]

But Buchanan had already authorized someone to go west. Early in December 1857 James C. Van Dyke, the Philadelphia District Attorney, informed his good friend Buchanan of several conversations he had had with Thomas Kane, who believed he could "accomplish an amicable peace" in Utah. "He is willing to make an expedition to Salt Lake this winter even at his own expense, if hostilities have not advanced to such a point as would render useless any efforts on his part. . . . He is full of courage, and if his judgment is correct, he may be able to avert a war of extermination against a poor deluded race."[87]

Returning from a meeting with the President "perfectly charmed," Kane, calling himself "Dr. Osborne," booked passage on a steamer from New York to California. Early in 1858, carrying a letter from Buchanan, he left on the mission he hoped would end the conflict and save the Saints.[88]

IX

IN 1857 AND 1858 the Mormons added to their list of atrocities. One morning while in Salt Lake City on army business, Captain

John I. Ginn learned from his Mormon guide, Joe Hunt, that six Californians with a valuable outfit and eighteen thousand dollars in gold coin had been caught trying to reach the troops. After visiting the captives, Ginn asked what would happen to them. "They will let them start back," Hunt replied, stressing the word "start," but the guide predicted the men would never reach their destination, for "they have too much valuable plunder." A few days later the Aiken party was ambushed at the Sevier River, less than a day's ride north of Fillmore City.[89]

In 1877 Hickman gave the New York *Herald* the rest of the story. Immediately after the massacre took place, he was ordered to Young's office, where the prophet shook hands with him and greeted him as "Brother William." Settling back, Young said: "Some of the boys have made a bad job of trying to put a man out of the way. They have all got drunk and bruised up a fellow, and he got away from them at the Point of the Mountain. He has come back to the city and is telling all that happened. It is making a big stink." Andrew J. ("Honesty") Jones, the escapee, had survived the Aiken massacre. Young wanted Hickman, George Grant, and William Kimball to finish the job. Hickman complied with the request.[90]

Equally notorious was the murder in the fall of 1857 of Richard Yates, the hunter and trader. Shortly after the war began, Yates offered some Indian wares and gunpowder to Wells, who bought the ammunition but refused the trinkets. Infuriated, Yates stormed out of camp and rode to Johnston's headquarters, where he sold the goods and informed the Federals of the enemy's number and position. The Mormons later captured Yates and handed him over to Hickman for delivery to Young in Salt Lake City.

The Saints argued about the remainder of the episode. In 1871 Joseph A. Young, the prophet's son, described to the New York *Tribune* how he met Hickman at the outskirts of the city and urged him to bring Yates in alive. Hickman, however, told the New York *World* a different story. Joseph said Young wanted the prisoner "taken care of," so Hickman waited until Yates was asleep and bashed his brains out with a rock. He and a friend then buried Yates in a trench and scraped the campfire over it to hide the fresh dirt. In Salt Lake City Hickman gave Young a gold watch and six hundred dollars he had taken from Yates's body. He argued that he deserved some of the money, but Young said it would help pay for the war and kept it all. The prophet warned Hickman to keep cool and say nothing about the incident to any-one.[91] Significantly, neither Joseph nor Hickman denied that Mormons had murdered Yates.

The Saints would undoubtedly have given like treatment to any government officials who fell into their hands. Through a released prisoner, Joseph sent a dire warning to Hiram F. Morrell, the hated Salt Lake City postmaster who had fled earlier in the year but had returned with the army: "Tell Morrell, damn him, that we came within one day of catching him, and we'll hang him yet." Morrell considered the threat all too "true."[92]

But in a sense the greatest tragedy of the war was the disruption of Young's colonizing activities. The founder of over 325 Western towns, including San Bernardino and Las Vegas, the prophet or-dered all Saints back to Utah in October 1857. He never again colonized these outposts, preferring later to populate areas nearer Salt Lake City.[93]

X

THROUGHOUT THE WINTER OF 1857-8 almost every important newspaper in the United States carried daily accounts of the Mormon conflict, and the nation's three finest and most influential journals, the New York *Herald*, the New York *Tribune*, and *The New York Times*, had correspondents with the army.[94] Paradox-ically, the war made Young a celebrity.

No one, however, was sure what the prophet would do if troops approached Salt Lake City. To Secretary of State Lewis Cass, Cumming predicted a battle before spring, for the Saints feared the army would soon be reinforced.[95] Far more assuring was Loba, the former Mormon high priest and French army officer, who revealed that the Saints had insufficient ammunition, no gun-powder factory, only one cannon and neither foundries nor ma-chinery for producing more, and few worthy military leaders. He estimated that not one Saint in ten had a serviceable weapon.[96] Another informant told *The Times* that the Mormons lacked the hard coal needed for gunpowder and that they had only the four small, outdated fieldpieces the government had allowed the Mexican War veterans to take for protection en route home.[97]

During the winter both sides suffered. The Grand Jury for the United States District Court indicted Young, Kimball, Wells, Taylor, George Grant, Phineas Young, and others for treason,[98] but the federal troops were starving. Not prepared for the intense cold and heavy snow, the soldiers lived for months on half rations and each day lost fifty to two hundred of their animals.[99]

Reaching Salt Lake City on February 25 in the midst of this chaos, Kane immediately conferred with the Mormon commanders. On March 10 he left for Camp Scott, two miles from Bridger, where he tried to persuade the Federals not to attack the Saints. A "nightmare of misunderstanding," Kane's discussions with Johnston, a newly breveted brigadier general, accomplished nothing. The straight-laced general and the sickly Philadelphian distrusted one another, and Kane finally abandoned the talks. But he still expected to convince Cumming.[100]

Meanwhile, Young and his advisers made an important decision. Between March 10 and 12, 1858, fearing that the army would soon be reinforced, they ordered south all residents of Salt Lake City and the towns north of it. A printed circular called for five hundred teams of animals to aid in the removal and instructed the Saints to allow the troops into the city. Some men would remain in the north to care for property and to plant crops, but they would burn nothing. The Mormons soon began leaving the region, some taking with them the doors and windows of their homes. Spring's balmy breath had induced Young not to fight.

Where would the Saints go? The previous fall newspapers had mentioned Alaska and northern Canada. Rumors now said the Colorado River area, the Mohave Desert, and the valleys of the Sierra Nevada mountains. Cumming believed the migrants would head for Sonora, Mexico.[101] Salt Lake City seemed destined to go the way of Kirtland, Far West, and Nauvoo.

To a special council Young explained the decision to flee. "If Joseph Smith, jun., the Prophet, had followed the Spirit of revelation in him he never would have gone to Carthage." The persuasive words of others doomed him. "I do not know precisely in what manner the Lord will lead me, but were I thrown into the situation Joseph was, I would leave the people and go into the wilderness, and let them do the best they could. Will I run from the sheep? No. Will I forsake the flock? No. But if Joseph had followed the revelations in him he would have been our earthly shepherd to-day, and we would have heard his voice and followed the shepherd instead of the shepherd's following the sheep. When the shepherd follows the sheep it reverses the natural order, for the sheep are to follow the shepherd.

"I want you to understand that if I am your earthly shepherd you must follow me," Young ordered, "or else we shall be separated. As I told the people after Joseph's death, they might cling to the Twelve and receive salvation and be led in the way of truth and holiness, or go to hell if they pleased, for we asked no odds of them. I feel so to-day. . . . I am your leader, Latter Day Saints, and you must follow me; and if you do not follow me you may expect that I shall go my way and you may take yours if you please. I shall do as the Spirit dictates me. . . . Should I take a course to waste life? We are in duty bound to preserve life—to preserve ourselves on the earth—consequently we must use policy and follow in the counsel given us, in order to preserve our lives. Shall we take a course to whip our enemies? or one to let them whip themselves? or shall we go out and slay them? We have been preparing to use up our enemies by fighting them, and if we take that course and shed the blood of our enemies, we will see the time, and that too not far from this very morning, when we will have to flee from our homes and leave the spoils to them. That is as sure as we commence the game. If we open the ball upon them by slaying the United States soldiery, just so sure they would be fired with anger to lavishly expend their means to compass our destruction, and thousands, and millions, if necessary, would furnish means, if the Government was not able, and turn out and drive us from our homes, and kill us if they could."

The Saints were migrating to "a desert region in this Territory larger than any of the Eastern states." Five hundred families would go there immediately and raise corn, potatoes, squash, and beans for the main camp. "Probably there is room in that region for 500,000 persons to live scattered about where there is good grass and water. I am going there, where we should have gone six or seven years ago. Now we are going to see whether the sheep will follow the shepherd. I do not care whether they follow me or not."[102]

For Buchanan, Young held the utmost contempt. "He is becoming a stink in the nostrils of every honorable person throughout the nation, and is so obnoxious to the people that I do not know but that they will kill him. They killed some thirty persons about the time of his inauguration, at the National Hotel in Washington, in trying to kill him; and I do not know but what they will succeed in killing him yet, if the Lord don't let the devil kill him in some other way. He is a disgrace to the Democratic party. Br. George A. Smith was in Washington at the time of the poisoning at the National Hotel, and he says that nearly all then stopping at that hotel were nasty, stinking office seekers, and if so it is a pity that they did not keep on poisoning."[103]

As the Mormons migrated, Kane induced Cumming to enter Salt Lake City. But the governor found there only William Hooper, from whom he received the territorial seal, for two weeks before Young, Kimball, Wells, and George Smith had piled their families and belongings into fifteen wagons and moved to Provo.[104]

Cumming's speech before three to four thousand Saints on April 25 brought forth a scene reminiscent of Brocchus's experience seven years before. Introduced as Utah's governor by Young, who had temporarily returned to the city, Cumming assured his audience: "I have come out here to see that justice is done you— to see that you are protected from the Indians. I have come on my own responsibility, without an escort or guard, or any arms—not even a penknife." To this the Mormons shouted: "It is not true; it is false. You have come supported by 2,000 bayonets," "We won't believe you are our friend until you send these soldiers back," and "You are nothing but an office seeker." The congregation screamed reminders of Joseph Smith's murder, of the service of the Mormon battalion, and of the Mormon sufferings on the plains.[105]

Everywhere Cumming saw roads clogged with fleeing Saints. For years the residents of Salt Lake City recalled how the governor, tears streaming from his eyes, stood on the street and protested that if he followed his feelings he would be going south too, instead of remaining with apostates.[106]

To James L. Orr of South Carolina, the Speaker of the United States House of Representatives, who in turn forwarded the letter to Buchanan, Cumming pointed out that the Mormons had split into peace and war factions. "I esteem it to be the duty and policy of my administration to support the former and break down the latter." Long considered warlike by outsiders, Young really desired peace. "There are in the community other zealots of as old a standing in the church who have great influence among the people in leading them to action, but the spiritual influence of no one in the Territory is equal to his. He is a man earnest, intelligent and of great experience, in addition to all of which he is vested with the authority to announce the terrors awarded to those who sin against the 'Holy Ghost'—the most awful doom to which Mormon humanity can be subjected. There is a division in the ranks, probably; all fear Brigham Young, but many also hate him, in consequence perhaps of the pacific measures attributed to him. However this may be, my chief hope of control, over this extraordinary people is exerted through this man. I believe that I have obtained his confidence and will therefore exercise some ascendancy over his actions. If this be true, it is of importance, especially as connected with a certain degree of personal popularity which I feel that I have acquired with the masses." Cumming dolefully predicted that all-out war, which he hoped to avoid, would last several years, bring death to thousands of innocent people, and extend Mormon influence abroad by spreading over the Saints the mantle of persecution that had already won them numerous converts.[107]

Suddenly the Mormon war ended. In April the President sent two commissioners to offer the Saints, in the words of Buchanan's recent proclamation, "a free pardon" for their "seditions and treasons" if they accepted the federal appointees for Utah and obeyed the nation's laws. In June, after prolonged negotiations, the Saints agreed to allow the army into Salt Lake City, but the troops were not to camp there. On June 26 Johnston entered the city, affirming national supremacy and terminating the conflict.[108]

As the army marched to Camp Floyd in the Cedar Valley, forty miles southwest of Salt Lake City, the correspondents of the *Herald* and *The Times* rushed to Provo, where they found Saints living for miles around in wagons and tents that afforded them slight shelter from the weather. For his wives and children Young had erected in the center of the town a block-long, windowless wooden shed twelve feet wide and eight feet high. Its rooms had walls only six feet high, and an occupant could easily hear what was going on in the adjoining room. Young, however, refused to live in this crowded and noisy building. His office was in a one-story adobe structure across the street, and he slept in Provo's only hotel.[109]

In Provo the *Herald*'s man attended services at the makeshift Bowery, twelve-foot-high beams topped with brush to keep out the sun. "We believed Buchanan's proclamation was incorrect: nevertheless we accepted the pardon," Young informed three thousand Saints who sat on chairs they had brought. "We have no shirt collar dignity to sustain while he has. His character is all he has; that gone he has nothing left. I believe he should have been President twenty-five years ago, when he had good sense if he ever had any."

Later spying the newspaperman, Young, visibly upset, confessed he had not known any correspondents had heard him and asked if the reporter knew shorthand and had taken down the speech. The journalist said he had. Including the "shirt collar dignity" remark? Young asked. Some subordinates began to stare, and Young dropped the subject but afterward sent the correspondent a version of the talk that eliminated the offensive remarks and "greatly modified" Young's "abrupt, rough style." The *Herald*, however, published the original speech.[110]

Fully aware of the power of the Eastern press, Kimball visited and tried to win over *The Times*'s man. "His conversation is a queer admixture of blasphemy, mock piety and vulgar variety," the journalist related. "There is no mistaking the fact that he considers himself a great gun, and nothing pleases him better than to get a crowd about him who will listen to his coarse witticisms, and join in his jolly laugh." After a long conversation, Kimball left the correspondent's room, halted in the courtyard below, assembled an audience, and cursed Douglas for turning on the Saints in the expectation of becoming President. "But I prophesy," he said with extraordinary foresight, "that he will never get into that chair. I say it in the name of Israel's God. And there is old Buch—d—n him—*he* put his foot in it; but he'll never do it again. I prophesy that there will be peace during the remainder of his Administration but after him will come such a time as we have never yet seen, and I know it and intend to prepare for it, laying up stores in the mountains to be ready for that evil time. But the President who puts his heel upon this people will go to hell. Old Buch will go to hell just like Old Tom Benton, who has gone to hell, d—n him, for his persecutions of us. He's gone to hell to follow Old Zach Taylor. The Lord's sent him along quick as he could, lest he should be too late to find Zach after he got there."[111]

When Jacob Forney, the new Superintendent of Indian Affairs, drove to Provo, Kimball advanced and "in the name of Israel's God" blessed him, Kane, and Cumming for aiding the Saints. "I pray also for my enemies," Kimball announced. Forney, a devout Episcopalian, marveled at this display of "Christian spirit," but Kimball suddenly added: "I pray that they may all go to hell."[112]

By July the Saints began returning home, singing, to the tune of Stephen C. Foster's "De Camptown Races," the "Mormon Du Dah":

> Long life, I say to Brigham Young,
>   Du dah, du dah!
> And Heber too, for they are one!
>   Du dah, du dah, day!
> May they and Daniel live to see
>   Du dah, du dah!
> The people gain their liberty
>   Du dah, du dah day!

Then let us be on hand, by Brigham Young to stand
And if our enemies do appear we'll sweep them from the land.[113]

But to Mormons the march was more than a homeward trek. It constituted the first stage of the triumphant advance to Zion. "When we turned back from Provo to re-occupy Salt Lake," Brigham Young, Jr., remarked in 1869, "we entered upon the back track, which is to eventually bring us to Jackson County, Missouri."[114]

X

The Seventy Wives of Brigham Young

I

THE MORMON CONFLICT OF 1857-8 settled nothing and altered nothing. Young remained the leader of his church, Gentiles were still unwelcome in Utah, and polygamy was neither modified nor abolished. One of the wonders of the age, Young continued romancing girls and marrying them.

Strangely enough, any reader of Catherine Lewis's *Narrative of Some of the Proceedings of the Mormons*, published in 1848, would have learned many secrets of polygamy four years before Young publicly read Smith's pronouncement on the subject. Catherine, who boarded with Kimball's family at Nauvoo and was Vilate Kimball's dressmaker, announced that the Saints "professed *immediate* revelation from Heaven, and a *commandment from God to take wives.*" She also disclosed that Young, Kimball, and other apostles had been sealed to Smith's widows, promising to care for them in this world and deliver them to the dead prophet, who would bless these men, in the next. A quarter century before the church acknowledged that Kimball's fifteen-year-old daughter, Helen, had wed Smith in 1843, Catherine reported hearing the girl tell her mother: "I will never be sealed to my Father, and I would never have been sealed to Joseph, had I known it was any thing more than ceremony. I was young, and they deceived me, by saying the salvation of our whole family depended on it. I say again, I will never be sealed to my Father; no, I will sooner be damned and go to hell, if I must. Neither will I be sealed to Brigham Young."[1]

Catherine, a Saint since 1841, also described how plural marriages were performed and explained why the Mormons rushed to finish the Nauvoo temple before leaving Illinois. One day as the girl nursed Kimball's sick child, the apostle entered the room and asked for her opinion of celestial marriage. "I have not, as yet, any evidence that it is right," she answered. "It is all right," Kimball assured her, "and when the Temple is done, my wife will come forward and give you to me, for she likes you." Vowing never to become another Hagar, the Egyptian maid given to Abraham, who desired a son, by his childless first wife, Sarai, Catherine asked for more information, but Kimball only added: "When the Temple is done you will be sent for, and all will be right."

Later, as Catherine sewed a cover for the temple altar, Kimball again approached her. "It is all right," he repeated. "I feel right toward you, and so does my wife; and when this Altar is done, the sealing will commence; my wife will come forward and give you to me, and all will be right, for she likes you, and will choose you for her associate. I shall take you to the West in the first company; you will always abide in my family, which will be a great blessing to you. *I have a number of women,* but do not *lodge* with all; the probability is *I shall with you.*"[2]

By this time Young had radically changed Joseph Smith's marriage system. The first prophet had taught polygamy to a few trusted men, and as late as 1869 Mrs. Ezra Taft Benson remembered "how careful we had to be." Tampering with one of Christendom's fundamental institutions, Smith at first withheld the principle even from his beloved brother, Hyrum. To avoid suspicion Kimball boarded his second wife at the Benson home and visited her either in early morning or in late evening. While he was in the house, Mrs. Benson watched the road from a window and made sure no strangers surprised him. One evening she saw someone approaching and quickly warned Kimball, who jumped out of a rear window and ran into a nearby cornfield. The visitor turned out to be Joseph Smith, and they called Kimball back and had a good laugh. But for a long time only Mrs. Benson, Vilate Kimball, and a few other trusted women knew about polygamy, and they often hid their secret by taking into their homes and passing off as relatives or friends their husbands' celestial wives.[3]

Unlike his predecessor, Young allowed almost any man to take plural wives. During the early months of 1846, when the Nauvoo temple was available for sealings, and the Reformation of 1856 and 1857, the number of such marriages increased sharply, and although the church once estimated that only three per cent of the Saints were polygamists, historians now put the peak figure at nearly twenty per cent.[4]

What had once been unusual became common. In 1858 Loba described Young's courtship of an unidentified wife: "One of my own personal acquaintances, W. C. Staines—one of Brigham's favorite destroying angels and spies—applied to the Prophet for leave to take a third wife. Leave was granted. The next day the lover appeared before Brigham with his betrothed when, greatly to his astonishment, that worthy changed the programme slightly, and married the lady to himself, as he found her a very pretty woman. Poor Staines accepted his cruel bereavement as a trial from the Lord."[5]

No one will ever know how many women Smith, Young, and Kimball married. "Joseph Smith was probably the most married of these men," one scholar noted. "The number of his wives can only be guessed at, but it might have been as high as sixty or more."[6]

Unfortunately such estimates rest upon the work of Fawn M. Brodie, who in her biography of Joseph Smith, published in 1945, added twenty-one wives to the Mormon church's list of twenty-eight. Mrs. Brodie, however, made unconvincing cases for eleven of the women she named. One, Mrs. Edward Blossom, merely slept with Smith. Mrs. Brodie also assumed eight other women were brides of Smith because with twenty-two known wives they were sealed to him in the Nauvoo temple in 1846. As George Smith and other church authorities readily admitted, the Saints often sealed to a dead man women he had never seen, and it is just as logical to assume that these ladies never knew Smith as to assume they did. And although Mrs. Brodie found "no printed or manuscript evidence" linking Smith to Clarissa Reed Hancock, she followed "tradition" and said they were married. Finally, relying on the word of some descendants of Vienna Jacques's neighbors, she included Vienna in her list.[7]

Mrs. Brodie, on the other hand, overlooked at least one of Smith's wives. Fanny Stenhouse told about "a Mrs. Shearer—or as she is familiarly called—'Aunty Shearer.' She is in every respect a unique specimen of womanhood, tall and angular, with cold yet eager grey eyes, a woman of great volubility, and altogether grim-looking and strong-minded. She was an early disciple and is said to have sacrificed everything for Mormonism. She lived in Joseph Smith's family, and, of course, saw and heard a great deal about Polygamy, and so far managed to overcome her feelings as to be married to him for eternity. Like the others, she is called 'Mrs.,' and I suppose there is a *Mr.* Shearer somewhere, but upon that point she is very reticent. Her lonely hut is filled with innumerable curiosities and little nick-nacks which some people are for ever hoarding away in the belief that they will come into use some day. She is a woman that one could not easily forget. She wears a muslin cap with a very wide border flopping in the wind under a comical-looking hood, and is easily recognized by her old yellow marten-fur cape and enormous muff: her dress, which is of her own spinning and weaving, is but just wide enough, and its length could never inconvenience her. Add to these personal ornaments a stout pair of brogues, and you will see before you 'Aunty Shearer,' one of the Prophet's spiritual wives."[8]

Years later Young described the casualness with which Smith took wives. One day Smith and a sister were discussing marriage and heaven. "She told him: 'Now, don't talk to me; when I get into the celestial kingdom, if I ever get there, I shall request the privilege of being a ministering angel; that is the labor I wish to perform. I don't want any companion in that world; and if the Lord will make me a ministering angel, it is all I want.' Joseph said, 'Sister, you talk very foolishly, you do not know what you will want.' He then said to me: 'Here, brother Brigham, you seal this lady to me.' I sealed her to him. This was my own sister according to the flesh."[9] Young performed this ceremony linking

Smith to Fanny Young Murray on November 2, 1843, as two of
his wives, Harriet Cook, who had married him that day, and Mary
Ann Angell, looked on.[10]

Kimball probably had more wives than Smith. At Vilate's funeral he pointed to her coffin and declared, "There lies a woman
who has given me forty-four wives,"[11] but he once said he
"counted them by the scores."[12] One wife admitted she did not
know what number she was or how many women he had taken
before or after her.[13]

At a Salt Lake City dance Kimball introduced five or six of his
brides to Fanny Stenhouse. "Are these all you have got?" Fanny
asked. "Oh dear, no," Kimball responded. "I have a few more at
home, and about fifty scattered over the earth somewhere; but I've
never seen them since they were sealed to me in Nauvoo, and I
hope I never shall again."[14]

Kimball too possessed at least one wife his biographer overlooked. In 1857 the *Police Gazette* mentioned Lucinda Stratton,
an only child who moved with her family from Ohio to Utah. Her
parents died soon afterward, leaving the fifteen-year-old girl,
"beautiful and accomplished much beyond her years," with no
alternative but to marry Kimball, who obviously had more than
forty-five wives.[15]

Like Lucinda, a few of Kimball's wives were beautiful girls.
Christeen Golden's loveliness struck William Hall, who grieved
for her. But in 1869 the New York *World*'s Utah correspondent
noticed Kimball's widows at the theater and commented: "I do
not think that I ever saw a homelier collection of women anywhere." Bowles considered it "rather an imposition on the word
beauty to suggest it in their presence."[16]

Young unquestionably had more wives than either Kimball or
Smith. For a century his church has maintained he had twenty-
seven, but estimates during his lifetime ranged from seventeen[17]
to one hundred.[18] Even in the 1960's, after the noted Mormon
scholar, Stanley S. Ivins, found a list of fifty wives, two historians
still said Young had twenty-seven and twenty-nine.[19]

Like Kimball, Young often joked about his wives. "Tell the
Gentiles," he once observed, "I do not know half of them when I
see them."[20] Later, asked the usual question by a Gentile gover-

nor of Utah, Young answered: *"I don't know myself!* I never refuse to marry any respectable woman who asks me, and it is often the case that I separate from a woman at the marriage altar, never to meet her again to know her. My children I keep track of, however. I have fifty-seven now living, and have lost three."[21] To a lady who wanted to see his wives, Young coldly said: "Madam, they are not on exhibition."[22]

Throughout his long life Young called himself "a great lover of women. In what particular? I love to see them happy, to see them well fed and well clothed, and I love to see them cheerful. I love to see their faces and talk with them, when they talk in righteousness, but as for anything more, I do not care. There are probably few men in the world who care about the private society of women less than I do. I also love children, and delight to make them happy."[23] "From my youth up," he explained, "I never had but one object in taking a wife, and that was to do her good. The first one I had was the poorest girl I could find in the town; and my object with the second, and third, and so on to the last one was to save them."[24]

Believing life was endless and the family stayed together forever, Mormons considered it their duty to have as large a family as possible. "If my wife had borne me all the children that she would bear," Young preached, "the celestial law would teach me to take young women that would have children."[25]

But Young denied carnal desires influenced his selection of brides. Heaven determined such things, he told William Hepworth Dixon, pointing to the "old, plain, uneducated, ill-mannered" women he had married. Other wives were, however, "young, fresh, delicate, and charming," and taking them seemed to Dixon "a call of pleasure."[26]

Perhaps Zina Huntington, the bride of both Smith and Young, best summarized church doctrine on this point. "We believe," she informed the New York *World*, "that Adam will rule over the whole human race, as he was the father of all the living. We believe, also, that Joseph Smith and Brigham Young will have kingdoms of their own, over which they will rule, and thus become gods to their descendants and subjects. The revelation upon celestial marriage was given to the Prophet Joseph for this very pur-

pose, and those who do not obey it will become the servants of
those who do. We also believe that there are three heavens. The
Celestial is the highest, in which dwell the Father and the Son; and
none, except those who have at least three wives, can expect to be
saved therein."[27]

II

OBEYING THIS PRINCIPAL, Young took at least seventy wives.
Once taught polygamy, he never ceased marrying, accepting his
first plural wife in 1842 at the age of forty-one and his last in the
1870's, shortly before his death.

Young's wives follow. The first fifty-three, whose wedding dates
are known, are listed in the order they were married to Young. As
in Mormon theory, if not in Mormon conversation, "sealing"
refers to a ceremony that took place in a temple or Endowment
house.

1. MIRIAM WORKS

Miriam, the daughter of Asa and Abby Works, was born on
June 7, 1806, in Aurelius, New York, and married Young on
October 8, 1824, at the age of eighteen, when both were Meth-
odists. She died on September 8, 1832, shortly after joining the
Mormon church, and was sealed to Young, to whom she bore two
daughters, by proxy in the Nauvoo temple on January 7, 1846.[28]

2. MARY ANN ANGELL

The daughter of James Angell and Phoebe Ann Morton, Mary
Ann, or "Mother Young," was born on June 8, 1803, in Seneca,
New York, and died on June 27, 1882. She married Young on
March 31, 1834, at the age of thirty, and was sealed to him on
January 7, 1846. Called by Catharine V. Waite a "fine-looking,
intelligent woman," Mary Ann was "large, portly, and dignified"
and lived in the beautiful and spacious White House, about a

block east of the homes in which Young's other wives resided. She and Young had three boys, Joseph A., Brigham, Jr., and John W., and three girls, Mary Ann, the twin of Brigham, Jr., Alice, and Luna.[29]

3. LUCY DECKER, the wife of Dr. Isaac Seeley

Lucy was Young's first plural wife and the first of several married women he coveted and took from their husbands. The daughter of Isaac Perry Decker and Harriet Page Wheeler, she was born in Phelps, New York, on May 17, 1822, and was short and stout, with brown eyes and hair as fine as silk.[30]

Lucy was married to Isaac Seeley, the Nauvoo physician, and had two children when Young saw her, fell in love with her, and promised her a greater exaltation in heaven than Seeley could give her. He sent the doctor on a mission, persuaded the stake high council to annul Lucy's marriage, and on June 15, 1842, wed the twenty-year-old girl. On January 14, 1846, they were sealed for time and eternity. Their son, Brigham Heber, born in Nauvoo on June 19, 1845, has often been called the first child of Mormon polygamy. Young and Lucy had six other children. She died on January 24, 1890.[31]

4. HARRIET ELIZABETH COOK

Nicknamed "Harriet the Neglected"[32] and "The Devil of the Household,"[33] Harriet was tall, fair, and slender, with light hair, blue eyes, a long, determined mouth, and a sharp nose. She was born to Archibald Cook, a prominent shipbuilder, and Elizabeth Moshier Campbell in Whitesboro, New York, on November 7, 1824, and died in November 1898.

Harriet later described her early life to her good friend, Joseph Troskolawsski, the Deputy Surveyor for Utah. She was converted to Mormonism while visiting a sister in Michigan and moved to Nauvoo. Soon Joseph Smith told her that God wanted her to marry Young, and on November 2, 1843, at the age of nineteen, she obeyed this revelation. She was sealed to Young for time and eternity in the Nauvoo temple on January 14, 1846.[34]

Unlike most of Young's wives, Harriet was as strong-willed as her husband. "She is a woman of as much intellectual capacity and executive ability as of force and will," the New York *World*'s correspondent noted after interviewing her. "In this she has no equal in all Mormonism; were she on a throne she would govern a nation. Indeed, she said to me, with a marvelous purpose in her words, 'I will yet play Queen Elizabeth to this church!'" The proud girl, a descendant of the ducal house of Argyll, further announced: "I will go through the gates of the kingdom of heaven side by side with Brigham Young or not go with him at all; I will not follow at his back."[35]

No stage—or bedroom—was big enough to hold two such prima donnas, and Young allowed Harriet only one child, a son named Oscar. When Oscar was a boy, Young caught Harriet beating him and demanded she stop immediately. She refused, and Young swore he would give her no more children, a pledge he kept.[36]

In revenge Harriet reared Oscar to hate his father. In later years the son publicly referred to the prophet as "dad," "the old man," "an old humbug," and the like. Young, in turn, denounced Oscar as "that reprobate."[37]

Asked by Troskolawsski why she remained in Utah, Harriet replied: "Where am I to go? There is no place for me but hell. All my womanly character is gone—my family would not acknowledge me—my acquaintances would despise me—I am outcast in the world."[38]

5. AUGUSTA ADAMS COBB, the wife of Henry Cobb and mother of Charlotte Cobb

None of Young's wives had a stranger or more tragic life than Augusta Adams Cobb, who was born in Beverly, Massachusetts, on December 7, 1802. Tall, dignified, and beautiful, with dark hair and gray eyes, she married Henry Cobb, a prosperous Boston merchant, about 1822 and bore seven children.[39]

Augusta lived quietly until Young came east to preach in the summer of 1843. She heard him, converted to Mormonism, and with her two smallest children headed for Nauvoo. In Cincinnati her youngest child died. "She had it put in a tin box," Young noted in his diary, "and took it with her." Accompanied by her daughter Charlotte, Augusta continued on to Nauvoo and on November 2, 1843, without divorcing her first husband married Young. A few months later she briefly returned to Boston, where she saw her other children and told Henry she was leaving him forever.[40]

But one detailed account of Augusta's Nauvoo experiences and Boston visit, and of her motives for entering Mormonism, exists today. In her memoirs Catherine Lewis told how Augusta, an old friend, approached her in Boston and "said she had something to tell me which was *glorious*. She said she would tell me under the injunction of secrecy. I replied, 'I could not promise, before knowing.' After a little pause, she said, 'The plurality of wives is true, &c. I have brought an invitation to you from *one* of the Twelve, and do not refuse; for you know not what you will lose, if you do. If you are not satisfied with *him*, there are *two* others, and you can have your choice of either; they stand higher than he does; and if you take either of these you will be highly exalted, and all your friends, both dead and living, will be benefited thereby.'" After Catherine expressed doubts, Augusta added: "Make it a subject of prayer, and you will receive an evidence; I have an evidence in answer to prayer. . . . Now those two men are on their way here, one of them expects an answer from you. . . . If you tell any one that I have told you these things," Augusta warned, "I will deny it, and throw the lie on you." Catherine laughed but later learned the Saints frequently did this.

Before the men arrived Augusta repeatedly pressed for an answer, but Catherine insisted that "my mind was confused and that I had no evidence it was right." "The reason you are so confused," Augusta advised, "is because you have no head, for the man is the head of the woman."

When the apostles reached Boston, one of them asked Catherine if "Sister Cobb" had told her about the "Plurality of Wives" and requested her views on the subject, but the girl put him off. "I am going to Baltimore," the apostle said, "expect to meet my wife, shall bring her on here, you may see her; when you have talked with her, you will say all is right." Then Joseph and Hyrum Smith were murdered, and the Twelve went back to Nauvoo, postponing a confrontation until Catherine obeyed a call to move there.[41]

Appalled by what she saw in Nauvoo and by Kimball's repeated attempts to make her his celestial wife, Catherine soon decided to apostatize. Hearing the news, Augusta rushed over to see her friend. "I have come with the word of the Lord," Augusta warned, "and do not resist counsel, sister; if you do, you know not what you will lose." Augusta offered the girl Young, Kimball, or any other leading Saint, but Catherine refused them all. "Is there not one you will take?" Augusta pleaded. "No," Catherine answered, "if I cannot be saved without, I will be damned; therefore you need say no more."

Catherine went to St. Louis, but within a month Augusta visited her and begged her to return to Nauvoo. When Augusta again described the glories of polygamy, Catherine shocked her by responding: "In my opinion it is damnable heresy and the doctrine of Devils."[42] Forty years before the Mormon church admitted that Augusta Cobb had married Young—they never acknowledged that she had deserted her husband and children—Catherine revealed both.

Augusta returned to Nauvoo and on February 2, 1846, was sealed to Young for eternity. The following year Henry Cobb, still in Massachusetts, divorced her.[43]

Augusta eventually migrated to Utah and in old age was a cripple. "She was a beautiful woman, even then," remembered an acquaintance. "And proud! Oh, my! How she and Charlotte used to talk about their blue blood. Nothing was too good for them. Every first of the month, when Grandma Cobb received her regular check, Charlotte would cash it and order in the very best steaks and other things like oranges from California and fancy preserves from S.S. Pierce way back in Boston. And, oh, the two of them had lovely clothes. She'd always be wearing a fresh lace cap and a lovely cashmere shawl and a lovely brooch with diamonds in it. Grandma—that's what everyone called her—she couldn't move from her wheel chair and everyone had to run round waiting on her."[44]

After Augusta's death on February 3, 1886, the church newspaper, the *Deseret News*, acknowledged "her sacrifices" for Mormonism. "She left a home of luxury in the city of Boston to dwell in a tent in the wilderness and endured the early privations incident to life in these valleys uncomplainingly and this for her religious faith. . . . She has sown a rich field, full of good works, and has gone where a golden harvest awaits her."[45] This editorial told only part of her story.

6. CLARA DECKER

Clara, Lucy Decker's sister, was born in Phelps, New York, on July 23, 1829, married Young on May 8, 1844, and was sealed to him on January 26, 1846. They had five children. One of three women in the first Mormon party to cross the plains in 1847, Clara was thereafter called the "pioneer wife." Small and slightly sallow, she died in Salt Lake City on January 5, 1889.[46]

7. LOUISA BEAMAN, a widow of Joseph Smith

Often considered Joseph Smith's first plural wife, Louisa, the daughter of Alva and Betsy Beaman, was born on February 7, 1815, in Livonia, New York, and married Smith on April 5, 1841. On January 14, 1846, at the age of thirty, she was sealed to Young, to whom she had been married after Smith's death, for time and to Smith for eternity. Louisa bore Young two sets of twins, but all four children died in infancy. Louisa died of cancer on May 15, 1850, in Salt Lake City.[47]

8. CLARA CHASE ROSS

Derisively dubbed "Clara the Maniac," she was born on June 16, 1814, in Genoa, New York, to William Ross and Phoebe Ogden. Clara, then thirty, married Young on September 10, 1844, and was sealed to him on January 21, 1846. She was medium in height and had dark hair, dark eyes, and a low fore-head. She and Young had two boys, one a graduate of the United States Military Academy at West Point, and two girls. Clara died in Salt Lake City on October 17, 1858, driven insane, according to Salt Lake City gossip picked up by the New York *World*, by her sufferings, "reproaching Brigham as the author of all her sorrows, and doubting the divine authority of polygamy."[48]

9. EMILY DOW PARTRIDGE, a widow of Joseph Smith

A tall, dark, beautiful girl, Emily was born in Painesville, Ohio, on February 28, 1824, to Edward Partridge, the church's first bishop, and Lydia Clisbee, and died on December 8, 1899. On March 4, 1843, she married Smith, in whose home she and her elder sister, Eliza, lived following their father's death in 1840. In September 1844, three months after Smith was murdered, Emily, then twenty, married Young. She was sealed to Smith for eternity and to Young for time on January 14, 1846. She and Young had seven children. Eliza, another of Smith's widows, was one of three Partridge sisters to marry Amasa Lyman.[49]

10. SUSAN SNIVELY

Susan, the daughter of Henry Snively and Mary Havener, was born on October 30, 1815, in Woodstock, Virginia, and died in Salt Lake City on November 20, 1892. On November 2, 1844, at the age of twenty-nine, she married Young and was sealed to him on January 21, 1846. Susan was medium in height and had dark hair, light eyes, and a dark complexion. For years she managed Forest Farm, four miles south of Salt Lake City, which supplied the family's dairy products. She had no children.[50]

II. OLIVE GREY FROST, a widow of Joseph Smith

Olive, the daughter of Aaron Frost and Susan Grey, was born in Bethel, Maine, on July 24, 1816, and married Smith in 1843. Mary Ettie V. Smith reported that when the dead bodies of Joseph and Hyrum Smith reached Nauvoo from Carthage, "Olive Frost went entirely mad." Olive, then twenty-four, married Young in February 1845 and died of pneumonia in Nauvoo on October 6, 1845.[51]

12. EMMELINE FREE

For almost two decades Emmeline, "the Light of the Harem,"[52] blazed as Young's favorite wife. The daughter of Absalom Free and Betsy Strait, she was born on April 28, 1826, in Belleville, Illinois. Tall, graceful, and fair, with large soft blue eyes and light brown hair, she and her sister, Louisa, were converted to Mormonism by John D. Lee, who later described Emmeline's marriage to Young on April 30, 1845, at the age of nineteen. Both girls were "under promise to be sealed to me," Lee recalled. "One day Brigham Young saw Emmeline and fell in love with her. He asked me to resign my claims in his favor, which I did, though it caused me a great struggle in my mind to do so, for I loved her dearly. I made known to Emmeline Brigham's wish, and even went to her father's house several times and used my influence with her to induce her to become a member of Brigham's family. The two girls did not want to separate from each other; however, they both met at my house at an appointed time and Emmeline was sealed to Brigham, and Louisa was sealed to me." Since polygamy was still secret in Nauvoo, Young kept at his house only his first wife. "Many a night have I gone with him, arm in arm, and guarded him while he spent an hour or two with his young brides," Lee continued, "then guarded him home and guarded his house until one o'clock, when I was relieved. He used to meet his beloved Emmeline at my house."[53]

Emmeline was sealed to Young on January 14, 1846, and bore him ten children. In Utah rumor said the prophet built a secret passage to her room so his other wives would not know when he visited her. She had the best quarters, received her company in the grand saloon rather than in her room, and occupied the choicest seat at the table.

Then in 1863 Young married a new favorite, Amelia Folsom. He saw less and less of Emmeline and finally stopped visiting her at all. Emmeline sulked and grew stout and disillusioned with polygamy. "Although it is hard for many to bear," she complained to the New York *World* in 1869, "still we shall reap our reward in the world to come."[54] On July 17, 1875, neglected and forgotten, she departed for that reward.

13. MARGARET PIERCE, the wife of Morris Whitesides

Margaret was born to Robert Pierce and Hannah Harvey on April 19, 1823, in Ashton, Pennsylvania, and on April 5, 1840, became a Saint. On July 23, 1844, she married Morris Whitesides, who died soon after. Margaret then married Young and was sealed to him on January 22, 1846. Their only child, Brigham Morris Young, born on January 18, 1854, was the prophet's fiftieth child. Margaret was average in height and had light hair, blue eyes, and a sharp nose. For some years she faithfully cared for Young's workers and millhands and helped raise silkworms. She died on January 16, 1907.[55]

14. MARGARET MARIA ALLEY

Margaret, the daughter of George Alley and Mary Symonds, was born on December 19, 1825, in Lynn, Masachusetts, and was sealed to Young on January 14, 1846, at the age of twenty. They had two children. Small and fair, Margaret died in Salt Lake City on November 5, 1852.[56]

15. and 16. EMILY HAWS and OLIVE ANDREWS

Young was sealed to both of these girls on January 15, 1846. Emily was born on July 22, 1823, in Malden, Canada, and was twenty-two years old when she was married. She later left Young and married another man.[57] In 1846 Olive, who was born on September 24, 1818, in Livermore, Maine, was sealed to Young for time and to Smith for eternity, but no evidence indicates she married Smith during his lifetime.[58]

17. MARY ELIZABETH ROLLINS, the wife of Adam Lightner and widow of Joseph Smith

Mary's experiences further reveal the vagaries of Mormon marriage. Mary was born on April 9, 1818, in Luna, New York, and in 1835 married a non-Mormon, Adam Lightner, whom she bore ten children. At Nauvoo in February 1842, while still living with Lightner, she married Smith in a ceremony performed by Young. In the Nauvoo temple on January 17, 1846, she was sealed to Smith for eternity and to Young for time. But she remained with Lightner and probably never consummated her marriage to Young. Mary died on December 17, 1913, at the age of ninety-five.[59]

18. ELLEN ACKLAND ROCKWOOD

Ellen, the daughter of Albert P. Rockwood, Young's nephew and adopted son, and Nancy Haven, was born on March 23, 1829, in Holliston, Massachusetts. Tall, slim, and fair, with light brown hair and light brown eyes, she was sealed to Young on January 21, 1846, at the age of sixteen and died childless in Salt Lake City on January 6, 1866.[60]

19. MARTHA BOWKER

A "quiet little body, with dark piercing eyes, and very retiring," Martha, the daughter of Samuel Bowker and Hannah Atkins, was born on January 24, 1822, in Mount Holly, New Jersey, and was sealed to Young on January 21, 1846. She died childless in Salt Lake City on September 26, 1890.[61]

20. MARIA LAWRENCE, the wife of Joseph Smith and Almon W. Babbitt

Maria, the daughter of Edward and Margaret Lawrence, was born on December 18, 1823, in Pickering, Canada. William Law, another Canadian and Smith's second counselor before apostatizing, later told the story of Maria and her sister, Sarah: "Soon after my arrival in Nauvoo the two L—— girls came to the holy city, very young girls, 15 to 17 years of age. They had been converted in Canada, were orphans and worth about $8,000 in English gold. Joseph got to be appointed their guardian, probably with the help of Dr. Bennett. He naturally put the gold in his pocket and had the girls sealed to him."

Early in January 1846 Maria was sealed to Smith for eternity and to Almon W. Babbitt for time. On the twenty-first of that month, however, her marriage to Babbitt was dissolved, and she was sealed to Young for time. Sarah, meanwhile, was sealed to Smith for eternity and to Kimball for time. She divorced Kimball on June 18, 1851, remarried, and went to California.[62]

Maria's later life is shrouded in darkness. Most accounts say she died in Nauvoo, but the scrupulously reliable New York *Tribune* reported in 1871 that Maria and Sarah, the sisters of the wealthy and influential Salt Lake City merchant, Henry W. Lawrence, were still alive and living in Utah.[63]

21. to 23. MARY ANN CLARK; MARY H. PIERCE; and REBECCA GREENLIEF HOLLMAN

Young married these girls in late January of 1846. Mary Ann was born on December 28, 1816, and was sealed to Young on January 21, 1846, when she was twenty-nine years old.[64] Mary, the sister of Margaret Pierce, was born on November 29, 1821, in Mills, Pennsylvania, married Young on January 22, 1846, and died on March 16, 1847.[65] Born on February 20, 1824, in Stafford, New York, Rebecca was sealed to the prophet on January 26, 1846, when twenty-one.[66]

24. and 25. PHOEBE ANN MORTON, the wife of James Angell, and JEMIMA ANGELL, Phoebe's daughter

Young's brides included three members of the Angell family, for Mary Ann Angell was also Phoebe's daughter. Young married both Phoebe and Jemima on January 28, 1846. The mother was born on March 28, 1786, in Guilford, Vermont, and died on November 15, 1854.[67] The daughter was born in Camden, New Jersey, on October 5, 1804, and was forty-one when she was sealed to Young. According to *The New York Times*, the dark-haired girl married the prophet to save from damnation her three children by a previous marriage.[68]

26. and 27. CYNTHIA PORTER WESTON and ABBY WORKS, the wife of Asa Works

On the same day Young wed Phoebe he was sealed to two other old women. Cynthia was born on February 2, 1783, in Redding, Massachusetts, and was sixty-two years old when she married Young.[69] Like Phoebe, Abby was the mother of one of Young's best known brides, for her daughter, Miriam, was Young's first wife. Abby was born on November 6, 1781, in Wilmington, Vermont, married Young at the age of sixty-four, and died on July 14, 1846.[70]

28. and 29. ELIZABETH FAIRCHILD and MARY ELIZA NELSON GREEN

Young accepted these girls on consecutive days. Born on March 6, 1828, in Marion County, Ohio, Elizabeth was sealed to him on January 30, 1846, at the age of seventeen.[71] On January 31 Young took Mary Eliza, who was born on November 24, 1812, in Poughkeepsie, New York, and died in 1855.[72]

30. RHODA RICHARDS, a widow of Joseph Smith and first cousin of Brigham Young

Rhoda, the elder sister of Willard Richards, was born on August 8, 1784, in Hopkinton, Massachusetts. Her first husband died, and she married Smith on June 12, 1843, when she was fifty-eight. On January 31, 1846, at the age of sixty-one, she was sealed to Smith for eternity and to Young for time. Her mother and Young's mother were sisters. Rhoda died at the age of ninety-five.[73]

31. ZINA DIANTHA HUNTINGTON, the wife of Henry B. Jacobs and widow of Joseph Smith

Long deified as one of the great Mormon women, Zina today greatly embarrasses her church. She was born to William Huntington and Zina Baker on January 31, 1821, in Watertown, New York, and became a Saint on August 1, 1835. Tall and well proportioned, with a high forehead and light hair and eyes, she wed Henry B. Jacobs in Nauvoo on March 7, 1841.[74]

On October 27, 1841, seven months' pregnant with Jacobs's child, Zina, without divorcing her husband, married Joseph Smith. Lee recalled touring Illinois that winter. "H.B. Jacobs accompanied me as a fellow companion on the way. Jacobs was bragging about his wife, what a true, virtuous, lovely woman she was. He almost worshipped her. But little did he think that in his absence, she was sealed to the Prophet Joseph, and was his wife."[75]

Jacobs continued to live with Zina, but after Smith's death, Young, within the hearing of many Saints, including William Hall, ordered those walking in other men's shoes to step out of them. "Brother Jacobs," Young declared, "the woman you claim for a wife does not belong to you. She is the spiritual wife of brother Joseph, sealed up to him. I am his proxy, and she is, in this behalf, with her children, my property. You can go where you please, and get another, but be sure to get one of your own kindred spirit."

On February 2, 1846, seven months' pregnant with Jacobs's second child, Zina, then twenty-four years old, was sealed to Smith for eternity and to Young for time. Jacobs stood by helplessly and witnessed the ceremony. According to Hall, he then left for England and in about a year returned with two other wives.[76] In 1869 the New York *World* reported that Jacobs, still a devout Mormon, resided in southern Utah.[77]

Zina gave Young one daughter and reared the children of the dead Clara Chase Ross. The midwife of the Young family, she delivered babies, nursed the sick, and occasionally taught school.[78]

Never Young's favorite, Zina lived with her memories of Smith and her dreams of the celestial kingdom. In 1869, when, in effect, she admitted to the *World* that Hall's account of her was true, she pointed out that she had been a Saint for thirty years, "and I think I shall die, as I have lived, in it. My trials and sorrows have been truly great, but they are the preface to a better life beyond the grave."[79] On August 29, 1901, Zina departed for that life.

32. to 36. JULIA FOSTER; MARY ELLEN
DE LA MONTAGUE; CECILIA
COOPER; ABIGAIL HARBACH;
and MARY ANN TURLEY, later the
wife of John Cook

Young married all of these women on February 3, 1846. Julia
was born on November 18, 1811, in Vienna, Maine, and was
thirty-four when she was sealed to Young, her second husband.[80]
Mary Ellen was born on May 2, 1803, in Philadelphia and was
forty-two when she was married.[81] Cecilia, born on June 30,
1804, in Turnbridge, Massachusetts, was forty-one on her wedding day.[82] Abigail was born on September 20, 1790, in Sutton,
Massachusetts, and died in 1849. Young was her second husband.[83] Far younger than these other women, Mary Ann, the
daughter of Theodore Turley and Frances A. Kimberly, was born
on July 13, 1827, in Toronto, Canada, and married at the age of
eighteen. She subsequently left Young, was sealed to John Cook,
and died in 1904.[84]

37. ELIZA ROXEY SNOW, the widow of
Joseph Smith

The Saints loved no other woman and few men more than
Eliza, "the Sweet Songstress of Zion,"[85] whose poems ceaselessly
extolled her two great loves: her religion and its founder. Eliza
was born on January 21, 1804, in Becket, Massachusetts, to well-
to-do Baptist parents. "In the winter of 1830 and 31," she recorded in a memoir, "Joseph Smith called at my father's, and as he
sat warming himself, I scrutinized his face as closely as I could
without attention, and decided that his was an honest face." In
1835 she became a Saint.[86]

On June 29, 1842, at the age of thirty-eight, Eliza wed Smith
under *"the Celestial Law of Marriage. . . .* This, one of the most
important circumstances of my life, I never have had cause to

regret." Young performed the ceremony. The date of Eliza's sealing to Young for time, probably February 3, 1846, is occasionally given as June 29, 1849, but her autobiography suggests she married him before migrating to Utah.[87]

Physically, Eliza, who died on December 5, 1887, was enticing enough for any man, although Mormons, ignoring rumors she had miscarried Smith's child when Emma caught them embracing and drove Eliza down a flight of stairs and out onto the street, depicted her as their Virgin Queen, untouched by male hands.[88] "She was slight and fragile, and always immaculate in dress," Lucy Decker's daughter observed. "I see her now in her full-skirted, lace-trimmed silk dresses, with her dainty lace caps and a gold chain around her neck, looking for all the world like a piece of Dresden china."[89] "Her head was finely organized," one elder noted, "her forehead classical, but not broad; her nose of the artist type; her mouth elegant and worshipful in its expression, rather than powerful or masculine; her neck swan-like; her hair luxuriant and dark as the raven's plume; her eyebrows and lashes plentiful and soft, and within the eyes which they shaded burned the fire of prophecy."[90]

38. NAAMAH KENDEL JENKINS CARTER, the widow of John Saunders Twiss

Naamah was born in Wilmington, Massachusetts, on March 20, 1821, to Billings Carter and Betsy Law, and became a Saint on April 3, 1842. In Nauvoo on May 30, 1845, she married John Saunders Twiss, who died three months later. Naamah, then twenty-four, was sealed to Twiss for eternity and to Young for time on February 6, 1846. Short and stout, with sandy hair, round features, blue eyes, a low forehead, and freckles, she had no children and until her death on September 26, 1868, ran the Lion House, where most of Young's wives lived.[91]

39. to 41. NANCY CRESSY; CLARISSA BLAKE; and DIORA CHASE

Nancy, Clarissa, and Diora were all sealed to Young on February 6, 1846. Nancy was born on January 20, 1780, in New Brunswick, New Jersey, and was sixty-six when she was sealed to Young for time and to her first husband for eternity. She died in January 1872.[92] Born on October 28, 1796, in Chester, New Hampshire, Clarissa was forty-nine when she was married.[93] Diora was born on July 25, 1827, in Bristol, Vermont, and was eighteen at the time of her marriage.[94]

42. LUCY BIGELOW

An attractive girl of medium height, Lucy had dark brown hair, blue eyes, an aquiline nose, and a pretty mouth. She was born on October 30, 1830, near Charleston, Illinois, to Nahum Bigelow and Mary Gibbs, and died on February 3, 1905. Lucy married Young on March 20, 1847, at the age of sixteen, and was subsequently sealed to him. She lived in Salt Lake City until November 1870, when Young sent her to his home in St. George in southern Utah. She and Young had three lovely daughters.[95]

43. MARY JANE BIGELOW

On the day Young married Lucy Bigelow he also took her older sister, Mary Jane, "a very pretty girl." Mary Jane was born on October 15, 1827, in Lawrence, Illinois, and died on September 25, 1868. "For a time he was very fond of her," reported the Utah correspondent of the Philadelphia *Times*, "and she had a child by him. Suddenly Brigham either did, or pretended to, discover she was untrue to him, and heaped all sorts of abuse on her. She protested her innocence, but Brigham cursed her, and sent her to her parents. The parents received her, but were crushed by the disgrace of their child. The poor girl pined away, and died of a broken heart. Some say she left two children. I have seen a picture of this woman which represents her with two children, a boy and a girl, standing by her knee, but I do not know if the story be true or false."[96]

44. SARAH MALIN

Sarah was born on January 10, 1804, in West Nantmel, Pennsylvania, and was sealed to Young on April 18, 1848, when forty-four years old.[97]

45. ELIZA BURGESS

Born in December 1827 in Stockport, England, Eliza joined the Saints in Nauvoo. When her parents died, she became Young's servant and, according to the New York *Herald*, after seven years asked his permission to marry another man. "Eliza," Young reportedly answered, "you have been in my family so long that I feel I have need of you and cannot part from you. You are of an age when you need a husband, and I will marry you myself. Brother S—— is a very good man, but I can give you a greater exaltation than he can. Come and be my little wife, and I will make you a queen in the first resurrection." Eliza was sealed to Young on October 3, 1850, and on their third anniversary bore a son, Alfales. "In person she is small," added the *Herald*, "with large eyes, dark hair and complexion and a voluptuous bust. She is stout, well built, and of the true English serving-girl type."[98]

46. MARY OLDFIELD, the widow of Eli Kelsey and mother of Eli B. Kelsey

Reporting the excommunication of Eli B. Kelsey, once Young's intimate friend but now the leader of an opposing faction, the

New York *Tribune* noted in 1870 that Kelsey's mother, Mary Oldfield, was "one of Brigham's wives, and the old man is particularly furious that his adopted son should have the presumption to think for himself." Mary was born on June 28, 1791, in Minisich, New York, and died on September 24, 1875. She was sealed to Young on December 6, 1852, obviously as a favor to her son.[99]

47. CATHERINE REESE, the widow of Zepheniah Clawson and mother of Hiram B. Clawson

Young also accepted Catherine to satisfy the bride's son, Hiram B. Clawson. Catherine was born in New York City on January 27, 1804, and was sealed to Young on June 19, 1855, at the age of fifty-one. Hiram, a leading Saint, eventually married two of the prophet's daughters: Alice, whose mother was Mary Ann Angell, and Emily, the child of Emily Partridge.[100]

48. HARRIET EMELINE BARNEY

Tall, slender, and graceful, with hazel eyes and light brown hair, Harriet was, according to Catharine Waite, who hated Mormonism, "indeed a beautiful woman. Her character is as lovely as her face. . . . Her kind and sympathetic nature, and excellent character, place her far above all the other inmates of the Harem." Harriet, the daughter of Royal Barney and Sarah Eastabrook, was born on October 13, 1830, in Amherst, Ohio. After an unhappy first marriage, the twenty-five-year-old girl was sealed to Young on March 14, 1856. She had five children, one by Young. Observed the Philadelphia *Times*: "It does, indeed, seem incredible that such a woman should be led into the hallucinations of Mormonism."[101]

49. HARRIET AMELIA FOLSOM

Amelia, Young's most colorful and most famous wife, was born in Buffalo, New York, on August 23, 1838, and died on December 11, 1910. Her parents, William H. Folsom and Zeruiah Clark, became Saints when Amelia was three years old and later moved to Council Bluffs, a Mormon center, where the tall, fair—the New York *World* termed it "deathly pale"—beautiful teenager emerged as the town belle.[102]

A chance meeting changed Amelia's life—and Young's. Following custom, the prophet rode out of Salt Lake City on October 3, 1860, to greet a party of pilgrims. He spied Amelia and immediately fell in love with her.[103]

But Amelia spurned the suitor. In Council Bluffs she had been engaged to a young Saint named Hills, who followed her to Salt Lake City to be near her. Infuriated, Young threatened to send the lad on a four-year mission unless he left the girl alone. Meanwhile, William Folsom's ambition played into Young's hands. A builder who desired to become church architect, he urged Amelia to accept the prophet. On January 24, 1863, the heartbroken girl was finally pushed into the marriage she loathed.

As the *World* subsequently learned, Folsom soon demanded as additional compensation for the loss of Amelia one of Young's attractive daughters. But the lass Folsom desired loved a young man the prophet greatly admired, so Young gave his new father-in-law a favorite servant girl instead.[104] Forty-four years after the *World* published this story, the Mormon church acknowledged that on December 25, 1863, Folsom took a second wife, Elizabeth Gregory, the twenty-four-year-old English girl listed in the 1860 census as a member of Young's household. Elizabeth and Folsom had seven children.[105] If, however, Folsom had married Young's daughter, he and the prophet would have been each other's father-in-law and son-in-law, and their daughters would have been one another's stepmother and stepdaughter. In polygamy nothing remained simple for long.

Discord soon engulfed Young and Amelia, for the possessive

girl demanded her husband's complete attention. Young's servants told the *World* about an episode that occurred after the prophet had spent the night with another wife. Deciding to breakfast with Amelia, he entered her room but was received with a look foreboding the storm about to burst on him. Quickly seating himself, he said meekly: "Good morning, Amelia. I hope you are well this morning." Not bothering to look up or reply, Amelia continued sewing. For a while Young sat silently but then, seeing no preparations for the meal, announced that he had come for breakfast and asked her when it would be ready. "Go where you staid last night and get your breakfast," Amelia shouted. "You can't have any here." Young coaxed and flattered his wife, trying to calm her, and Amelia finally rang a bell and ordered breakfast. As the icy wife drank her tea, she thawed and spoke to Young, who, believing she had mellowed, began a lecture on the sin of disobedience, pointing out that the angels had fallen because of it and that she would too unless she mended her ways. Amelia rose, kicked over the table, dumping a pitcher of milk and an urn of hot tea onto Young's lap, and flounced out of the room in a rage. The prophet surveyed the damage for several minutes and then went to his room to change his clothes.

Another story involved General Patrick Edward Connor, the army commander in Utah during the mid-1860's, who one day was standing before his Salt Lake City headquarters when Amelia dashed up, told him she had quarreled with Young, and requested sanctuary at Camp Douglas, the nearby army post. From there Amelia expected to go east to some friends. Under the noses of some Mormon policemen, Connor placed Amelia inside a coach and escorted her to the camp. The next day, however, Young's son, Joseph, rode out to Camp Douglas and persuaded Amelia to return home.

However truthful these stories may be, Amelia never masked her scorn for Young. In 1869, when Zina Huntington piously informed the *World* that she knew Joseph Smith was a prophet and Young was his right successor, Amelia, standing nearby, laughed and added: "That is more than I can say, aunt Zina."[106]

50. M A R Y   V A N   C O T T , the wife of James T.
Cobb and daughter-in-law of Augusta Adams Cobb

In strangeness Mary's life approaches her mother-in-law's.
Mormon historians readily relate that Mary was born on February
2, 1844, in Elmira, New York, that she was sealed to Young on
January 8, 1865, and that she died on February 5, 1884. Her
parents, John Van Cott and Lucy Sackett, were devout Saints who
migrated to Utah in 1847.[107]

But for a century the rest of Mary's story has been covered up.
A tall, slender, pretty girl whose photographs probably did her an
injustice, Mary late in the 1850's met and married James T. Cobb,
the handsome and cultured Dartmouth College graduate then
teaching in Salt Lake City. Cobb too came from well-known Mormon stock: his mother was Augusta Adams Cobb, and his sister
was Charlotte Cobb. "After graduating at college in the East," the
New York *Herald* related, "he came West for the avowed purpose
of reclaiming his mother and sister, but, under the influence of his
mother, he himself became a Mormon."[108]

James and Mary seemed perfectly matched, and in the early
1860's the couple had a daughter, Luella.[109] In one way at least
Mary resembled Augusta and Charlotte. "Accustomed to the best
and latest modes in fashion," she possessed, according to one
authority, "rare taste in dress."[110]

For this and other reasons Augusta grew apprehensive about
Mary's position in the celestial kingdom. "The old Cobb conceived for her daughter-in-law the high ambition of a union with
Brigham," Judge Joseph C. Hemmingway of Salt Lake City later
informed the *Herald*, "and actually had her own son divorced so
that his wife might become the concubine of President Young.
Brigham's youngest child is the issue of this immoral trans-
action."[111] James, however, refused to pine. He remarried and had
nine more children.[112]

51. ANN ELIZA WEBB

Renowned because she sued Young for divorce, Ann Eliza, the daughter of Chauncey G. Webb, Joseph Smith's grammar teacher in Kirtland, was born in Nauvoo on September 13, 1844. In 1846 Chauncey embraced polygamy and two years after that moved his family to Utah. In all he married five times.

Ann Eliza grew into a lovely woman. She was "tall and slender, with a remarkably sweet face, features regular and soft, eyes dark blue, hair very dark brown and thrown loosely behind after the fashion of the school miss of fifteen." On April 10, 1863, she married James L. Dee, a plasterer who neglected and mistreated her. Before divorcing him, she bore two children.

As Ann Eliza told it, Young's courtship of her hardly befit a prophet. One Sunday morning in the summer of 1867 Young, his brother, Joseph, and George Q. Cannon attended services near Webb's farm in Little Cottonwood. Afterward Young strolled home with Ann Eliza, asking along the way if she had received any proposals since her divorce. She said she had but had rejected them. Young advised her to marry not a man she loved but one she could respect and from whom she could receive counsel.

Following the afternoon service Young spoke to Chauncey for two hours. He said he had watched Ann Eliza blossom from infancy into womanhood, described his love for her, and urged her parents to help him win her. Young supposedly promised Webb a fine house and Ann Eliza over a thousand dollars a year in pocket money if the match was consummated. Informed of the proposal, the girl became hysterical. "Oh! the horrible hours that I spent crying and moaning no tongue can picture," she told the New York *Herald*. But when her brother fell into financial difficulties with Young and faced excommunication, she yielded. On April 7, 1868, in the Salt Lake City Endowment House she was sealed to Young. The bride was twenty-three, the groom sixty-seven.

Then, in 1873, charging neglect, cruelty, and desertion, Ann Eliza sued the prophet for divorce. She left Utah, published her memoirs, and spent much of her time lecturing against the church.[113] Like Mary Ann Turley and Mary Jane Bigelow, she found life with Young intolerable.

52. ELIZABETH JONES, the widow of
Captain Dan Jones

Derisively dubbed the "Welsh Queen" by her enemies, Elizabeth, the daughter of Thomas and Elizabeth Jones of Cleddy, South Wales, was born on April 5, 1813, and married Captain Dan Jones, Joseph Smith's close friend and shipmaster, in December 1849. Out of respect for Captain Jones, who led the church's Welsh mission from 1852 to 1855 and died in 1862, Young was sealed to Elizabeth, then fifty-six, for time on July 3, 1869.[114]

53. LYDIA FARNSWORTH

Lydia was born on February 5, 1808, in Dorset, Vermont, and was sealed to Young on May 8, 1870, at the age of sixty-two.[115]

The dates of Young's sealings to his remaining wives are uncertain. These women are listed in the order they were probably married to him.

54. NANCY CHAMBERLAIN

In her book, *Wife No. 19*, Ann Eliza Young spoke of Nancy Chamberlain, "a very old, half-crazed woman, known, I fancy, to every Mormon in the Territory, who solemnly declares that she was sealed to Brigham in Nauvoo, and that she had the promise of being promoted to the place of first wife. She lived in his family for a long time, but she grew old, and infirm, and useless, and he turned her out of the house some years ago; and now she lives as best she may, going about from house to house, and performing light work to pay for her support. She considers it her duty every little while to go and 'free her mind,' as she calls it, to Brigham's wives, telling them that they may usurp her place and defraud her of her rights in this world, but she shall be Brigham's queen in heaven. She is an eccentric old woman, but there is no doubt, I think, about her having been sealed to the Prophet."[116]

55. and 56. TWO UNNAMED SIOUX GIRLS

In 1852 William Hall, who, decades before the Saints admitted it, revealed that Kimball had married Christeen Golden and Young had taken Zina Huntington from Henry Jacobs, reported: "Alliances are forming, and are to be formed, with the Mormons wherever they can be effected. As an aid to this grand design, even Brigham Young was married to two young squaws, the daughters of different Chiefs, at a place near Council Bluffs, called Winter Quarters; and they were 'sealed up' to him, and became his spiritual wives." The weddings took place in mid-January of 1847 during a feast honoring the Sioux. To the delight of the Indians Young dressed his two new brides in large gold chains, elegant slippers, and various ornaments, and proudly showed them off. That day other Mormon leaders married young Indian women.[117]

57. CHARLOTTE COBB, the daughter of Augusta Adams Cobb and later the wife of William S. Godbe

Charlotte, "the belle of Salt Lake City," was unquestionably Young's most beautiful wife. Remy and Brenchley called the girl, an accomplished pianist who sometimes entertained Young's guests,[118] "one of the loveliest persons it has ever been our fortune to see."[119]

Charlotte was born in Boston in either 1836 or 1837,[120] migrated to Nauvoo with her mother in 1843, and went from there to Salt Lake City. Sarah Harris recalled boarding in 1851 with Fanny Young Murray, Young's sister and a plural wife of Joseph

Smith. "I often came in contact with Mrs. Cobb, and her daughter Charlotte, a pretty girl of fourteen, occupying a portion of Mrs. Murray's house, in whom I became interested. I learned long afterward that she had left her husband and family at the East, taking only this child, to join the Mormons. Brigham had brought her into his harem, and at this very time she was his wife.

"As her daughter grew to womanhood, her beauty appealed to Brother Brigham's eyes, and he desired to take her also. She was, with many other young girls, made to believe the hideous doctrine that the older the man they married, the greater would be their glory in the world to come. There was no one to prevent the sacrilege, and she was sealed to him, entering as his wife, his ever-increasing family. An event so common as this—that mother and daughter were wives of the same man—caused not a ripple of excitement or remark, even, in the Mormon community."[121]

Charlotte married twice more. For some reason Young permitted her to become the fourth wife of William S. Godbe, the prominent Salt Lake City druggist who apostatized in 1869. She subsequently divorced him and married an extremely wealthy Salt Lake City man twenty years her junior.

Throughout the years Charlotte wondered about her family in the East. In 1900 she went to Boston, rang the doorbell of a cousin, and identified herself. As she slammed the door in Charlotte's face, the cousin excitedly exclaimed: "We wrote you off the family tree fifty years ago! Goodbye!"[122]

58. MOTHER WESTERN

In December 1852 Mrs. Benjamin Ferris, whose husband was the new territorial secretary, talked to Aunty Shearer, the plural wife of Joseph Smith that historians have overlooked, "about an old lady by the name of Western—commonly known as 'Mother Western'—one of Brigham's wives. I was marveling why she should marry in her old age, especially as fiftieth or sixtieth wife, when my oracle said 'she was only sealed for the sake of salvation.' She further informed me that Brigham had more wives in

this way than anybody knew of—that he did not even know himself, the sealing to him being considered a more certain guarantee
for salvation, because he was the reigning prophet, and was sure
to remain faithful."[123]

59. MISS WATT

Many visitors to Utah discussed George D. Watt, the church
stenographer, who migrated to Utah with his half sister. Young
saw the girl, fell in love with her, and married her, but a few
weeks later, discovering she was carrying Watt's child, he annulled
this marriage and sealed her to Watt. Loba was referring to this
episode when in 1858 he told *The New York Times*: "I have
known another in incestuous intercourse with his own sister, and
then witnessed Brigham taking this woman as his wife when she
was about to become a mother."[124]

60. MARGARET G——

In 1857 Samuel Hawthornthwaite, a Mormon elder for eight
years, described how "Margaret G——, a young lady well
known to the Saints in Manchester, was decoyed to America by
Elder Moses Martin. He disgraced her on the way. When they had
been in Salt Lake city a few months, Martin 'turned her up.' She
was then joined to the Prophet's establishment, where she spent
another short honey-moon. Elder James Ferguson was the next to
marry her, 'but,' to use his own words, (for it was he who gave me
the information,) 'I found that I had more on my hands than I
could well manage, so I 'turned her up.' But how have they disposed of her, after they have all had her? Thus: A young man by
the name of John Cook had paid his address to Margaret while she
was in England, before Martin decoyed her to America; but finding himself 'diddled' by the Yankee out of his fair one, he made up
his mind to forget her and woo another. He did so, and was married to a young lady in England. In a year or two after he emi-

grated with his wife and family to Salt Lake, where he at present resides. Margaret at this juncture was 'out of place,'—in want of a husband, and depending upon Brigham to find her one. (That's law in Utah.) No sooner had John settled himself in the Valley, than Brigham had a revelation, telling him all about John's courtship with Margaret in England. John received 'counsel' to take Margaret and make her his wife; he did not like it, for she had now grown into a little withered old woman, and nothing like what she was; but it was of no use to demur against the counsel of the Prophet, for his arguments were so conclusive on the subject: 'You courted her in England before she came here,' said Brigham, 'and if she was good enough for you to pay your addresses to then, she is good enough for you to marry now; so take her to yourself.' John took counsel, however, much against his will; he built her a mud hut, in which she resides, and the last I heard of her was, that she was working in the fields, like an old hack, thoroughly 'used up.' "[125]

61. ELENOR J. MCCOMB, the wife of Hector McLean and the plural wife of Parley P. Pratt

Elenor, who deserted McLean to become Pratt's twelfth wife, was born in Wheeling, Virginia, on December 29, 1817. Captain Ginn called her "tall," "handsome," the "queenly looking Mrs. McLean," and "one of Brigham's concubines." He noted that after McLean murdered Pratt in Arkansas, "Mrs. McLean continued with the train to Salt Lake City, where she made her home with Brigham Young and his numerous other concubines in the Lion Mansion, and where she was frequently pointed out to me by Mormons on the street during my sojourn in the city of the saints."[126] Elenor later taught school and lived in a one-story adobe house built on Pratt's land. She died on October 24, 1874.[127]

62. TALULA GIBSON, the daughter of Walter
Murray Gibson and later the wife of Fred H.
Hayselden

None of Young's wives lived more adventurously than Talula
—and none exploited the usually perceptive Mormon prophet as
she did. Incontestable evidence ties Young to Talula. In 1860
Burton observed: "Captain Gibson, a well-known name for 'personal initiative' in the Eastern Main, where he was seized by the
Dutch of Java, lately became a convert to Mormonism, married
his daughter to Mr. Brigham Young, and in sundry lectures delivered in the Tabernacle, advised the establishment of a stake of
Zion in the 'islands of the seas,' which signified, I suppose, his
intention that the Netherlanders should 'smell H–ll.' "[128] And in
the 1860 census Young, a notoriously poor speller, listed as his
wife seventeen-year-old "Toledah Gibson" of Georgia.[129]

Walter Murray Gibson was, as Burton indicated, from first to
last a man of the world. He was born at sea to English emigrants
bound for the United States and grew up in Georgia. After his
wife's death in the early 1850's left him with three small children
to rear, he moved to Sumatra in the Dutch East Indies, where he
bought forty square miles of land, which he intended to turn into
an American colony. The Dutch convicted him of high treason
and threw him into solitary confinement. Seventeen months later,
aided by the prettiest native girl on the island, he disguised himself
as a Dutch officer and escaped.[130]

In the fall of 1859 Gibson went to Utah and proposed to
Young the creation of a Mormon state in the Pacific. Elated,
Young personally baptized Gibson on January 15, 1860, allowed
him to preach in Salt Lake City, and sent him on a tour of the
Eastern United States.[131]

In November 1860, after marrying Talula, Young authorized
Gibson to start a Mormon colony in Japan and even allowed his
newest bride to accompany her father, although Gibson's two sons
remained in Salt Lake City.[132] But Gibson dreamed other dreams.
Instead of heading for Japan, he and Talula steered toward
the Sandwich Islands, now Hawaii, landing on July 4, 1861.

There he displayed to the illiterate natives the impressive-looking parchment Young had given him, stalked about like an emperor, forced the natives to enter his home on all fours, placed *The Book of Mormon* in a hollow stone and warned that touching it meant instant death, sold church offices for as low as fifty cents and as high as $150, and registered all church property in his own name. Gibson soon became rich enough to buy half of the island of Lanai and employ a private army.

Hearing rumors of strange goings on, Young sent some investigating elders to Hawaii in 1864. Far from denying his exploits, Gibson bragged about them and proudly exhibited his parchment from Young, now embellished with seals and ribbons. In October 1865 at the General Church Conference in Salt Lake City, Gibson was excommunicated.[133]

Undaunted, Gibson retained his holdings on Lanai, entered the Hawaiian legislature, and eventually became Prime Minister of the islands. In 1887 a revolution forced Gibson, Talula, and Talula's second husband, Fred H. Hayselden, to flee to San Francisco, where the captain died penniless the next year.[134] But Talula remained to recall gleefully how she and her father had outmaneuvered the supposedly infallible Mormon prophet.

63. to 65. SUSAN TAFFINDOR; MINNA A. COOK; and ELIZA Y. YOUNG

In the 1860 census Young listed these three Englishwomen as his wives. At the time Susan was sixteen years old,[135] Minna was thirty-seven,[136] and Eliza was nineteen.[137]

66. MRS. HAMPTON, the wife of Mr. Cole

Several visitors to Utah repeated the complicated story of Mrs. Hampton, a tall, dark-haired woman with round features and large, lustrous eyes. When a young girl, she married a Mr. Hampton, had six children, and became a Mormon. Her husband died and the Saints left Nauvoo, but Mrs. Hampton remained, married a Gentile named Cole, and bore a daughter, Vilate. Four years later Cole decided to pan for gold in California, and Young sent for Mrs. Hampton and was sealed to her for time. Cole, meanwhile, enlisted in the army and in 1863 was sent to Salt Lake City, where he saw Vilate, now a beautiful young lady. He hoped to take her away from Utah before she entered polygamy. About then Mrs. Hampton refused to be sealed to Young for eternity, left him in a huff, and moved into her son's home in Ogden.[138]

67. MRS. LEWIS

Ann Eliza Young wrote at length about young Thomas Lewis, who lived with his widowed mother in Sanpete County. Lewis flirted with a girl desired by a Bishop Snow, was beaten, and later disappeared. "But a still greater marvel is that the mother of Bishop Snow's poor victim still retains her faith in Mormonism, and since the cruel and disgraceful tragedy which deprived her of her son, has been sealed to Brigham Young as one of his wives. It was not pity that moved him to marry her, nor a desire to comfort her and lighten her burdens; but it was because he saw by doing that he could advance his own interests. Mrs. Lewis is never mentioned among his wives, yet he was sealed to her about two years after his marriage to me." According to Ann Eliza, Young courted Mrs. Lewis to get her property in Provo, which he needed for a factory. Before their wedding he promised to end her loneliness and care for her forever, but after it he shipped her off to Forest Farm and never visited her.[139]

68. and 69. ELIZA BABCOCK and ELIZABETH ROBISON

In his book, *Pioneers and Prominent Men of Utah*, published in 1913, Frank Esshom called these girls wives of Young. Eliza's parents, Adolphus Babcock and Jerusha Jane Rowley, came to

Utah in 1847.[140] Elizabeth's mother and father, Peter Robison and Mary Ashley, migrated to Utah in 1850. Their daughter was born on April 29, 1850, and lived in Fillmore.[141]

70. SARAH ANN MCDONALD

Esshom twice listed Sarah as Brigham Young's wife,[142] but he also called her the wife of Brigham J. Young.[143] Sarah was born on either March 3, 1855, or March 3, 1856, to William McDonald and Seriah Shirts and was married to Brigham J. Young on April 11, 1875. William McDonald had assisted in building the Nauvoo temple and helped Young establish agricultural settlements in Utah. To please her father the prophet may have taken the girl for eternity but given her to Brigham J. Young for time.

Several other women claimed they were wives of Young but undoubtedly were not. In 1855, for example, someone calling herself Sarah Young lectured and wrote to newspapers about her escape from Utah. "One morning after Young left my bed," she declared, "I discovered under the pillow a paper, of which I have a copy. It is a secret plot, contrived to overthrow this Government." Sarah wanted "to warn my female friends to beware of the false prophets who are daily sent out from the Great Salt Lake City to deceive people."[144] She was an obvious fraud.

Still, Young married all kinds of women. His wives included the earthy Eliza Burgess and the refined Harriet Barney, old ladies like Cynthia Porter Weston and Mother Western and adolescents like Talula Gibson, Clara Decker, and Lucy Bigelow, illiterates and maniacs such as Nancy Chamberlain, Clara Chase Ross, and Olive Grey Frost and intellectuals such as Harriet Cook and Eliza R. Snow, the devout Zina Huntington and the mocking Amelia Folsom, the unattractive Lucy Decker and the ravishingly beautiful Charlotte Cobb. Like Amelia, some of Young's wives were forced into polygamy by ambitious parents. But most of them, including Zina, Elenor McLean, Eliza Snow, and Augusta Cobb, were enticed into it by promises of heavenly rewards. A few, like

Talula and Ann Eliza, disregarded the next world and used their positions to enrich themselves in this one.

Young too thought about this existence. Although he always said he followed Joseph Smith in all things, he viewed women far differently than Smith did. Young admired pretty girls, but Smith worshipped them and considered his hours with them as perhaps the most satisfying of his life. Young cared nothing for the approbation of others and everything for his own purposes and desires. Smith, on the other hand, cherished praise. Tender or ardent words conquered and disarmed him and, as at Carthage, led him to trust false friends. Cold and calculating, Young seldom forgot who he was and what he wanted. Only someone as cunning as Walter Murray Gibson or with Amelia's indomitable will could beat Young at this game he played so well: salvation.[145]

But Young, Smith, and Parley Pratt were alike in one way. Each violated what he claimed to hold dear. As the revelation on celestial marriage explained: "If any man espouse a virgin, and desire to espouse another, and the first give her consent, and if he espouse the second, and they are virgins, and have vowed to no other man, then he is justified; he cannot commit adultery. . . . and if he have ten virgins given unto him by this law, he cannot commit adultery, for they belong to him."[146]

Important Saints, however, took not "virgins" but mothers "vowed" to other men. Pratt ran off with Elenor McLean, Young with Augusta Adams. Asked by the New York *World* whether she had divorced McLean before marrying Pratt, Elenor answered: "No, the sectarian priests have no power from God to marry; and, as a so-called marriage ceremony performed by them is no marriage at all, no divorce was needed. The priesthood with its powers and privileges, can be found nowhere upon the face of the earth but in Utah. . . . I regard the law of celestial marriage, or, as the 'Gentiles' term it, polygamy, as the keystone of our religion. That is where in we differ from the sects of the world. They hope for salvation in a heaven where husbands and wives shall be utter strangers to each other; we expect to reach a heaven where we shall rear families, the same as we do here. We could not do this unless we had a revelation authorizing celestial marriage; and we could not be saved in the celestial kingdom without obeying this revelation. It is the great distinctive feature of our religion, and by it must our religion stand or fall."[147]

But Young, who constantly swore he would kill the man who touched any of his wives, stole women from Mormon husbands, something justified by neither the Bible nor Smith's revelation. Zina Huntington, Lucy Decker, and Mary Van Cott were wives of Saints and mothers before Young annexed them to his kingdom. On this "great distinctive feature of our religion" Mormon polygamy must, in the light of history, "stand or fall."

XI

"Love We Regard as a False Sentiment"

I

PERHAPS EPITOMIZING THE VIRTUES AND FAULTS of the members of his sex, Young wooed and managed women with varying success. He often bragged about his love for women in general but rarely discussed a specific wife or child, undoubtedly because the size of his family precluded his knowing and loving its members equally. Silence masked his favoritism.

Because Young won such beautiful and accomplished girls as Charlotte Cobb, Amelia Folsom, Harriet Barney, Emmeline Free, and Mary Van Cott, his contemporaries invariably concluded that he got every woman he went after. Most people forgot—or never knew—that several girls refused to marry him.

In Nauvoo Young encountered three rebuffs. Martha Brotherton's affidavit, published in papers throughout the country in 1842, described in humiliating detail his advances and her rejection of him, and Catherine Lewis's memoirs told how she repeatedly refused to marry Young, Kimball, or any other Mormon apostle. But when Young, like David after King Saul's death, decided to take his predecessor's widows, he let the biggest prize get away. He easily won Louisa Beaman, Olive Frost, Maria Lawrence, Zina Huntington, Eliza Snow, Emily Partridge, and Rhoda Richards but failed with Smith's first and most important wife, Emma, the mother of Joseph's four sons. In 1870 a Mormon elder recalled how Young had wooed "the masculine Emma Hale" in Nauvoo, an episode still discussed in Salt Lake City. The feminine, gentle, clinging Eliza and the worshipful Emily were no match for Young, but Emma, with strength of character, an iron will, and an intense dislike for polygamy, was different. "Undoubtedly Brigham would have taken Emma Hale as well," the elder speculated, "but the first wife of the Prophet hated Brigham Young even more than she despised her husband, and so the celestial queenship of the church fell upon Eliza R. Snow."[1]

Few events in Mormon history proved more important than Emma's rejection of Young. Had the couple married, Smith's sons eventually would have led the Utah church and the many dissenters who apostatized with them after Young took over would have remained loyal Saints. Plural marriage, which Emma loathed because it had deprived her of her husband's affection, might conceivably have died out during Young's lifetime, and the Saints would have returned to Independence, Missouri, their Zion, which in a court battle fell to the Smith family. As if intentionally adding to the injuries of Young and his church, Emma, whose mourning period for Smith was remarkably brief, shed her widow's weeds and in 1847 married the dashing unbeliever Major Lewis Bidamon. Emma allowed the ceremony to be performed by a preacher of the Methodist Episcopal church.[2]

After Young's death, a Mormon woman told *The New York Times* another story of failure. "In 1859 a younger sister of mine visited us. She lived in Chicago. She is married now, and has the distinction of having refused the hand and harem of Brigham Young. He met her at our house, and only three days afterward asked her to become his wife—his twelfth I think. She refused the honor with considerable indignation, and was in such terror lest Brigham should seize and force her to marry him that she asked permission of a party of tourists, who were on their way east after a trip overland to California, to accompany them back, which she did the very next day. The Mormons had everything their own way in those days, and I often tremble to think what might have

befallen the girl in thus defying the head of the Church. I believe if
it had been John D. Lee, or Orson Pratt, or Bishop Hyde, instead
of Brigham, my sister would never have left Utah. And I think
now that it was more consideration for us than any scruples he
had that made Brigham submit to defeat so calmly."[3]

More famous was the affair of Selima Ursenbach, the beautiful
Swiss convert who reached Utah in 1862. An accomplished musician and singer and the sister of Octave Ursenbach, the designer
of the huge organ in the Salt Lake City Tabernacle, she was appalled by Young's proposal and returned home.[4]

Equally notorious was Young's courtship of the noted Gentile
actress, Julia Dean Hayne, who reportedly refused him on the
spot. Undaunted, Young named his sleigh for her. One evening, so
the story went, Kimball, infuriated by the scandal, assembled his
huge family, knelt, and began praying for Young. Suddenly he
sprang to his feet and exclaimed: "I can't pray for him, but he
needs it badly enough, for the greater the strumpet the more
Brother Brigham is after her."[5]

II

YOUNG RAN HIS LARGE FAMILY extremely efficiently. The President's block, a self-sufficient community of twenty acres in downtown Salt Lake City, was enclosed within a ten-foot wall and
guarded by an armed sentry in a box before the main gate, over
which rested a huge stone eagle. It contained the church tithing
office, the *Deseret News* office, a white schoolhouse with green
blinds, a cattle yard and barn, and carpenter's, shoemaker's, and
blacksmith's shops. Laid out by Young's adopted son, William C.
Staines, the grounds held plum, pear, peach, apricot, apple, and
walnut trees and strawberry and grape vines that each year bore
prize-winning fruit. Also within the compound was Young's large,
airy office, complete with maps, scales for weighing gold dust,
account books, desks, and armchairs. On its walls rested photos of
favored Saints and Gentiles and a lithograph of *Sunlight and Shad-
ows* by the great landscape painter and Western explorer, Albert
Bierstadt.[6]

Young's office and a hallway connected the Beehive and Lion

Houses, the buildings in which most of his wives lived. The Beehive, the smaller of the two, was named for the honeybee, Deseret's symbol, and bore a beehive on its dome. It was built in
1854 and designed by Young and Truman O. Angell, whose sister, Mary Ann Angell, ran it before moving to the nearby White
House in 1860. Lucy Decker then became its mistress. Young
gave her title to it on condition she never mortgage it or return it
to him, no matter how desperate his financial condition, a promise
she kept. Young's servant girls and workmen also lived in the
Beehive, a square building with white pillars reaching to its second
story; thick-plastered adobe brick walls calcimined pale yellow;
huge windows; green shutters; a big, solid oak front door; and a
silver doorknob. Its bedrooms and two parlors were spacious and
beautiful. In the downstairs parlor Young usually breakfasted and
entertained important visitors. His bedroom, light and airy with
simple, well-built furniture, was also on the first floor.[7]

The Lion House, built by Angell in 1856, was one of Utah's
finest edifices, taking its name from the effigy of the crouching
lion—emblematic of the Lion of the Lord—upon the roof over
the main entrance. The building was finished in cream plaster and
had white woodwork and green shutters.[8]

Through the center of each of the Lion House's three floors ran
a long hallway, off which were rooms. The upper floor contained
twenty neat, clean bedrooms for Young's childless and older
wives; the main floor held a parlor and rooms for the wives with
small children; the basement had a dining room, butteries, a
kitchen, and a laundry.[9]

Even Amelia's room was plainly furnished. It contained a
French provincial bed, several chairs, a dressing area, a mirror,
and a bureau. An ingrain carpet softened the floor. Only the count-
less bottles of sweet-smelling colognes and perfumes hinted at the
elegance of the room's occupant.

The Lion House's parlor was far more elaborate. Its carpet was
a richly patterned velvet tapestry, its furniture was made of the
best rosewood available, and its curtains were lace and damask.
An expensive piano filled one side of the room, and a large table
with books, a lamp, photograph albums, and vases of flowers occupied the center. Two fine kerosene chandeliers—gas was un-

known in Utah—hung from the ceiling. Everything but the flowers came from outside the territory.[10]

Anyone used to less routine would probably have found life in Young's household like an extended prison sentence. The members of the family rose early in the morning, cleaned their rooms, and assembled in the parlor for prayers. Then they gathered for breakfast around two long tables that ran the length of the dining room. For Young, who often took the meal alone or with a favorite wife, this usually meant huge gobs of cornmeal mush swimming in milk, hot doughnuts and syrup, codfish gravy, squabs, and strawberries, all of which he devoured in record time. The prophet bragged that he could "live on as cheap and as plain food as can any man in Israel."[11]

While Young took care of personal or church business, each wife performed her allotted tasks. Eliza Snow meditated and composed the poems that Saints cherished and memorized. Zina nursed the sick. Amelia puttered with her perfume bottles and clothes, practiced the piano, and sang. And Twiss supervised the Lion House's kitchen. Everyone worked, noted William Hepworth Dixon. "Lucy and Emiline, sometimes called the lights of Brigham's harem, are said to be prodigies of skill in the embroidery of flowers. Some of Emiline's needlework is certainly fine, and Susan's potted peaches are beyond compare."[12]

The entire family gathered for supper, Young sitting at the head of one table. Then at seven o'clock the tinkle of a bell summoned everyone to the parlor for evening prayers, during which Eliza Snow occupied the honored place on Young's right that Emma Smith had refused. Sometimes the prophet's brothers, Joseph and Lorenzo, attended this phase of the day's activities, which began when Young announced: "Come now, let us have prayers." All knelt and listened attentively as Young simply, directly, and briefly blessed "the poor, the needy, the sick and the afflicted, the widow and the fatherless, that He might be a stay and a staff to the aged and a guide to the youth." On Sundays the girls of the family then clustered around the piano and sang. Young ended the festivities by bouncing a small child on his knee and entertaining it with odd noises. The wives and children retired to their rooms, and Young either visited a fortunate woman or returned to his office.[13]

Several wives lived outside the Lion and Beehive Houses. Augusta and Charlotte Cobb occupied a spacious cottage nearby,[14] and for years Susan Snively resided at Forest Farm. Because Young constantly traveled about the territory, he assigned Eliza Burgess to Provo and Lucy Bigelow to St. George in southern Utah.[15] As he frequently bragged, he was never far from home.

Even excluding these women, Young maintained a huge household in Salt Lake City. In the 1850 census, which did not accurately reflect the size of his family because the Mormons still denied they practiced polygamy and Young claimed only one wife, Mary Ann Angell, he listed fifteen people. Ten years later the number jumped to eighty-five, and in 1870, by which time Young's children were marrying and his wives were dying, it fell to fifty-four. In size only Kimball's household, seventy people in 1860, approached Young's.[16]

Having such a large family was easy compared with governing it. "If the Lord gives you a wife, take care of her," Young advised. "Never quarrel. Dogs, pigs and devils quarrel. If you want to control your families, show them a good example, and tell them what to do, and then let them do as they have a mind to."[17]

Fanny Young Murray disclosed another of Young's secrets. "My brother's family is the best regulated in Zion. He will not listen to any complaints, and it is an established rule that any dissatisfied ones can withdraw from the family circle if they wish. So great is the honor of being sealed to him in this world and the next, that no one ever leaves. No grievances reach his ear, and outside harmony prevails."[18]

III

IN 1869, WHILE DESCRIBING to the New York *World* the responsibilities of Mormon women, Zina Huntington inadvertently revealed how lonely and unhappy she and Young's other wives were. "It is the duty of a first wife to regard her husband not with a selfish devotion that would claim the whole of his society, time, and attention," she noted, "but rather as owing attentions to other women also, which they have a right to expect. She finds before she has been many years the head of a polygamous household that she must regard her husband with indifference, and with no other

feeling than that of reverence, for love we regard as a false sentiment; a feeling which should have no existence in polygamy. The
marriages which we read of in the Old Testament were not love
matches, as, for instance, the marriage of Isaac to Rebekah, of
Jacob to Leah; and we believe in the good old custom by which
marriages should be arranged by the parents of the young people."

Zina further reflected her experiences in Young's house. "I
think that much of the unhappiness found in polygamous families
is due to the women themselves. They expect too much attention
from the husband, and because they do not get it, or see a little
attention bestowed upon one of the other wives, they become sul-
len and morose, and permit their ill-temper to finally find vent.
Then perhaps they think they must have fine dresses and fashion-
able hats from the dress-maker and milliner, instead of making
those articles themselves; and because the means of the husband
will not permit it, they are ready to quarrel with him about it.
When one wife has anything new and pretty, all the other women
think they must have something new and pretty too, and petty
jealousies are in this way constantly arising, which serve to make
their lives miserable. Then it is, in a measure, also, the fault of the
husband, for he should learn to control his own household, and
rule it in order."[19]

In that same issue the *World* carried accounts of quarrels between Young's wives, but such episodes received scant notice until
1875, when Ann Eliza's book, *Wife No. 19*, appeared. Like the
World six years before, Ann Eliza attributed much of the discord
in the Lion House to Amelia Folsom. As Ann Eliza told it, no one
escaped Amelia's venomous attacks. One day, for example,
Young escorted both Amelia and Emmeline to a dance, not realizing his dilemma until arriving there. With whom should he dance
first? Young thought it over and finally walked up to Emmeline
and ordered gruffly: "Come along and dance." Without offering
her his arm he pranced onto the floor, leaving her to follow. They
danced silently for a while, then the prophet hastily led his partner
to her seat. As the next number began, Young turned quickly to
Amelia, gave her his arm, and said: *"Now* I will dance with my
wife."[20]

Amelia especially despised Mary Van Cott Cobb and Ann
Eliza, both of whom Young married after her. Once, as Ann Eliza

and a friend strolled toward Young's garden, Amelia preceded them. Reaching the garden gate, Amelia passed through it, slammed it shut, and shouted to Ann Eliza: "There, madam! I'd like to see you get in now." Several minutes later she began scolding the gardener, who afterward told Ann Eliza: "But ain't she a master hand to scold, though? Why you'd ought to hear her give it to me sometimes. I'm pretty well used to it, and don't mind very much. It's some consolation to think that Brother Brigham gets it worse than I do, and when he's round, I'm safe."

Amelia once caught Young and Mary in the family store selecting some household furnishings. In white heat she elbowed a path between them, stormed into Young's waiting carriage, and ordered the driver to take her home. When the coachman hesitated, Amelia shouted, "Home, I say," and left Mary and Young to ponder and to walk.[21]

More impersonal was another kind of rivalry. According to a story that circulated in Salt Lake City, Young often placed a chalk mark on the door of the wife he intended to visit that night, and sometimes, it was said, a woman slipped quietly from her room, erased the chalk on another door, and marked her own.[22]

IV

Kimball is usually credited with sixty-five children, Lee with sixty-four, and Young with fifty-six,[23] but none of these men knew how many they had. In 1872, for example, Young admitted to fifty-eight.[24] Nor are Young's census declarations helpful, for he failed to distinguish between his children and the many needy youngsters he took into his home and reared. Young and Kimball produced most of their children in the late 1840's and early 1850's, while both were still vigorous but were shielded from Gentile persecution by Utah's remoteness. In 1850 rumor gave Kimball eighteen children not yet old enough to work, and Young bragged he had fourteen boys under seven years of age.[25]

Even Mormons joked about the day Young met a fourteen-year-old boy on the street. "You're a fine looking young man," he remarked, patting the lad on the shoulder. "Whose boy are you?" "Brigham Young's," the youngster answered.[26]

Fortunately, however, Young had something few other Mormon fathers possessed: sufficient wealth to care for his children. "It may or may not have occurred to those who read about the polygamy of the Mormons," observed the New York *Tribune* in 1870, "that a plurality of wives is a luxury in which only an unusually rich man can afford to indulge. For instance, Brigham Young took his whole family, spouses and pledges and all, to the circus the other day, and the tickets cost him $75."[27]

Marrying off fifty-six offspring might overwhelm most men, but Young was far from ordinary. During a Utah stay Alexander K. McClure, the editor of the Philadelphia *Times*, shrewdly noted how Young sealed his children to members of the territory's most influential families. "By this system he is directly related to every family of importance in Zion, and his power is perpetuated."[28]

As might be expected, Young's children varied greatly in size, shape, and ability. Joseph Angell Young, his eldest son by Mary Ann Angell, proved a great disappointment. "Brigham Young's own son, Joseph, may be seen, almost any day, rolling through the streets of Salt Lake City as drunk as a pig," Hawthornthwaite commented in 1857, "cursing and swearing in such a manner as would disgrace the lowest haunts of Gentile England. One day he rode up to Mr. Hill's door in Salt Lake City, and presented a pistol at his head, saying at the same time, 'If you don't hold your tongue, you bl——dy old b–gg–r, I'll blow your d—d brains out, that I will!' At the same time he could not stand on his feet through the effects of a bottle of whiskey which he had by his side."

In the mid-1850's Joseph obeyed a call to preach the gospel in England. "Elder Kelly and myself commenced a grammar-class almost entirely on his account," Hawthornthwaite explained. "He attended once or twice, and that was all; at last he said to me, 'Brother Hawthornthwaite, this grammar's too dry for me; I want something with fun in it. So I'll go and see sister ———.' He spent most of his time in England at the theatre, the opera, or among the lasses."[29]

Tall and stout like his father, Joseph married three times. His first wife, Mary Ann Ayers, was, related a reporter for the New York *World*, "what the boys would call a 'gay girl,' and emphatically a Mormon girl of the period." Her love of liquor matched his.[30] Returning from England, Joseph was sealed to Thalia

Grant, Jedediah Grant's lovely young niece. She opposed the marriage but was given no alternative.[31]

Then in the mid-1860's Joseph was sealed to Clara Stenhouse, whose father subsequently apostatized and wrote an exposure of Mormonism. Clara induced Joseph to abandon his other wives and live only with her, but the match was unhappy nonetheless. Both husband and wife had violent tempers, and their public squabbles shocked and amused the people of Salt Lake City.[32]

Joseph lost the girl he desired most, Sarah Alexander, "the handsomest woman that ever walked in Utah." Sarah was a Mormon but laughed at its rituals. In the fall of 1863 she made her debut in the Salt Lake City theater and immediately became the rage of the territory. A half-dozen prominent elders went wild over her. One even carried her off to his home, but an appeal to Young by her father saved her. The prophet then took Sarah into his house and after a time decided to give her to Joseph. The girl heard of the plan, fled to San Francisco with a group headed by Lisle Lester, the lecturess, and joined a theatrical troupe. Joseph and three friends followed her, but Sarah noticed their arrival in a newspaper and told her employer she was afraid to appear. Warned by the entire company to leave San Francisco, Joseph speedily complied.[33]

Young's most famous child, Brigham, Jr., was Joseph's full brother. Five feet ten inches tall and stout, with a ruddy complexion, a round, full face, large, clear, penetrating eyes, and a head slightly bald on top, he sported closely cropped whiskers that made him seem more the country gentleman than the religious leader. But his faith in Mormonism was deep and undying.[34]

Brigham, Jr., married three times while his father was alive and six times in all. His third wife, Elizabeth Fenton of Philadelphia, was visiting Salt Lake City when young Brigham saw her. But Lizzie was so bright and pretty she captivated the prophet too. Consequently the father courted her in the forenoon, the son in the afternoon. Lizzie finally chose the son, who left his other wives for her.[35]

Far more level-headed than his impetuous brother, Brigham, Jr., often shielded Joseph from serious trouble. One evening in the fall of 1858 the two men demanded payment from Gilbert and Gerrish, the Salt Lake City merchants, for a partial shipment of lumber. When Albert Gilbert refused to pay until the entire load was delivered, the drunken Joseph cursed him and was thrown out of the store. Vowing to kill Gilbert, Joseph mounted his horse, drew and cocked his revolver, and was prepared to ride into the store when his brother grabbed the reins and led him home.[36]

John W. Young, the third son of Young and Mary Ann Angell, was the prophet's ablest child. A railroad builder and business-man, he was medium in height, was rather stout and had a florid complexion, light hazel eyes, and dark brown hair. A heavy mus-tache hid his mouth. One of Young's favorites, he had been born while mobs attacked Nauvoo.[37]

Before Young's death John wed four times. He met his third wife, Elizabeth Canfield, the cousin of his first, in Philadelphia, courted, converted, and married her, and brought her to Utah. To her cousin's horror Libby induced John to live only with her. Pointing to John and Brigham, Jr., the people of Salt Lake City whispered that Philadelphia girls seemed to have the knack of making monogamists out of Mormons and that one was all any man could handle.[38]

Facing the unenviable task of marrying off many daughters, Young gave pairs to each of four men. Among the girls thus disposed of was the fair, petite, and blue-eyed Alice, his eldest daughter by Mary Ann Angell. In the early 1850's Alice fell in love with the Gentile army lieutenant, John Tobin, but the prophet drove him away and sent Alice's brother, Joseph, and some Danites to ambush him. Tobin was shot in the head and blinded in one eye, but he made it to California. Alice then turned to a young Saint named William Wright, whom the prophet de-spised and sent to the Sandwich Islands for four years. Alice prom-ised to wait for Wright, but she soon yielded and became Claw-son's third wife.[39] Clawson later added a fourth bride, Emily Young, the daughter of Emily Partridge.[40]

Alice, a talented actress and the mother of four children, was found dead in bed on December 2, 1874. A bottle of poison lay beside her. Rumor had it that the burdens of polygamy had over-whelmed her.[41]

Alice's full sister, Luna, also experienced heartache. A "bright and beautiful blonde, self-willed and gay as a bird," she seemed imperial in looks and manner. Her father adored this wayward child more than any of his fifty-five others and proudly awarded her to George W. Thatcher. Soon, however, Thatcher desired Fanny Young, the prophet's daughter by Lucy Decker. Luna loved her husband dearly and begged him not to marry again. Young, who usually pushed such matches, was also infuriated by this affront to his favorite and ordered Thatcher to Europe for four years. More alarmed by this than by the thought of sharing her husband with another woman, Luna fell gravely ill and persuaded her father to erase Thatcher's name from the list of missionaries. Young finally allowed the second marriage.[42]

Nor was this all. Mary Eliza Young, Clara Chase Ross's child, and Caroline Young, another daughter of Emily Partridge, both married Mark Croxall, the Salt Lake City telegraph operator.[43] But Charles Decker created the most confusion. "Put a bandage around your head," one reporter suggested, "and consider the following:—Brigham Young married two sisters of Charlie Decker, and Decker married two daughters of Brigham, by other women. All have children. Now, the offspring of Clara Decker Young and Lucy Decker Young are the cousins of Charlie Decker's children. But the latter are grandchildren of the former's father, and consequently nephews and nieces of their own cousins. But the nephews of a cousin—blood relationship holding—are second cousins; hence Decker's children must hold that relationship toward each other. Decker's wives are half-sisters to the children of their own sisters-in-law, they are sisters-in-law to their father, and aunts to their own half-sisters! Now, if the relationship were half blood throughout, the canons of descent—at least in Indiana—would exclude them; but as it doubles on both sides, they would probably be included. Hence the two Mrs. Deckers are (in law) their own aunts, while Clara D. and Lucy D. Young are legal grandmothers to their nieces, and the two sets of children are respectively cousins, aunts and nieces, and the Lord knows what besides."[44]

V

ZINA YOUNG, the tall, slim, attractive daughter of Young and Zina Huntington, proved that happiness and heartache coexisted in a large family. Born in 1850, Zina had an extremely happy childhood. "My father's family lived in a world of their own, there being ten girls with not more than four years' difference in their ages. Our father affectionately called us his 'big ten,' and nowhere on the earth could be found a happier, merrier set of children. We attended school and were instructed in music and dancing on our premises."[45]

On Sunday evenings after prayers these girls were allowed to entertain beaus in the Lion House's parlor. One Sunday the couples in the room, desiring more privacy, turned down the coal-oil lamp on the center table and barricaded it with books until its light barely emerged. For a time all went well. Then the door slowly opened and Young entered holding a candle. He surveyed the room, walked to the table, removed the books one by one, and finally turned to the group and remarked: "The girls will go upstairs to their rooms, and I will say good night to the young men."[46]

Like her half sister, Alice, Zina became an actress. For a time Thomas B.H. Stenhouse, Clara Stenhouse's father, wooed her. The courtship dragged on endlessly and Stenhouse's first wife, Fanny, finally told Young the couple ought to marry. Young said he was willing, but since girls could have but one husband he would be fair and consult Zina. "If Zina has really changed her mind," he added, "I have plenty of other daughters, and they have all got to be married, let him take one of them—if one won't another will!"[47]

Then Joseph Young treacherously soured his half sister on Stenhouse. When Joseph asked for Clara's hand, Stenhouse agreed on condition that Joseph help him win Zina. Joseph consented but for some reason later told Zina that Stenhouse abused his first wife. Zina broke the engagement and became the second wife of Thomas Williams, the ticket seller in the Salt Lake City theater.[48]

The decision ushered in tragedy. Williams's first wife deeply resented Zina and even refused to sit in the same room with her. One day at Zina's table Williams collapsed and died. Exercising her right, the first wife brought the body to her house and prepared it for burial, but she forbade Zina from riding in the funeral carriage with her.[49] For daughter Zina as for her mother, life proved burdensome.

But to Young and other devout Saints another kind of misfortune transcended these episodes. A Mormon who married a Gentile surrendered his place in the celestial kingdom and disgraced his family forever. Since the day the California Gold Rush brought non-Mormons into Salt Lake City, Young feared his children would run off with them. As trails and rails stretched towards Utah, this fear mounted.

During the 1860's the worst often happened. John Taylor's eldest daughter married an army officer and went to California. The eldest girl of William Kimball, Heber's first son, eloped with a Californian and moved to the East. And Orson Hyde's eldest daughter married a Jew named Ellis and fled to California.

Under great family pressure, Ezra Taft Benson allowed his daughter, Emma, to marry a Nevada Gentile named Roberts. Benson opposed the match, but the girl's mother and brother insisted they would rather see her an apostate than the fifth or sixth wife of a Mormon bishop. Benson finally yielded.[50]

Another episode directly affected Young's family. As a child, the eldest daughter of Orson Spencer, the president of the church's European mission and the former editor of the *Millennial Star*, had played with the prophet's daughters, but when she began associating with Gentiles Young ordered her ostracized. Because of her beauty and talent, she was chosen to portray the Goddess of Liberty on the Fourth of July, but Young saw her name on the program and had her replaced. Her closest friends, the children of President Daniel Wells, snubbed her. One day as she and two other girls sat in a parlor with some Gentile boys, a rock crashed through the window and hit one of the girls in the forehead. Spencer's daughter finally eloped with a Gentile and moved to Nevada.[51]

Orson Pratt's children also disappointed their father. In the mid-1860's Orson Pratt, Jr., a talented musician, announced he would not preach a false religion, refused a mission, and was excommunicated. Several years later at the Salt Lake City skating pond Zina Pratt met and fell in love with a Gentile named Frank McGovern. They arranged to be married secretly by a federal judge, but on the appointed evening the police heard about it and informed Pratt. Two constables held McGovern while the usually meek apostle beat and kicked him into submission. Ordered to leave town within twenty-four hours, the boy took the stagecoach for Wyoming the next morning. More bitterly opposed to polygamy than ever, Zina, meanwhile, returned to her father's home.[52]

After that Young told his children to stay away from the skating pond, but when he turned his back two of his daughters disobeyed him. Louisa Young, then fifteen, was short and stout but very pretty, like her mother, Emmeline Free. Her father adored her almost as much as he loved Luna and affectionately dubbed her "Punk." Nabby Young, Clara Decker's child, was seventeen and also stout but taller than her half sister and the town's best skater. Both were adroit flirts and any fine day might be seen promenading, fashionably attired, on Main Street, casting sly glances at the clerks—Jew, Gentile, and Saint—standing in the doorways admiring them. The two girls loved the skating pond, where Mormon and non-Mormon mixed promiscuously, and whenever Young left town they ignored his edict, donned their skates, and, escorted by male friends, flew swiftly over the ice. Asked if she would again defy her father, Punk responded: "I am going to if I can, though pa thinks it's perfectly awful for us girls to go on the ice and skate. I don't see what makes him think so; for my part, I like it first-rate, although I got bumped pretty hard while learning."[53] Even a father with fifty-six children could not help spoiling a daughter like Punk.

Nabby and Punk flirted whenever and wherever possible. At the Salt Lake City theater the *World*'s correspondent saw them coquetting with some young men many rows away. "Opera glasses were used on both sides, smiles and winks were exchanged, and all went as lively as a marriage bell until Brigham appeared in the opposite box, when festivities were suspended until a more favorable opportunity."[54]

Such things were nothing compared with the blow Dora Young, Lucy Bigelow's daughter, dealt her father. In an Episcopal ceremony Dora married Morley Dunford, a Gentile. Following Mormon doctrine, Young refused to recognize the marriage.[55]

To his everlasting credit the prophet took into his family young Mormons without parents or in need of certain kinds of training. One of these was Sarah Alexander, the beautiful actress who subsequently rejected Joseph A. Young and fled to California. Sarah was a soubrette, especially good in light vaudeville parts and already a favorite in 1865, when the great actress, Julia Dean Hayne, came to town. Julia's leading man, George Waldron, fell hopelessly in love with Sarah and proposed. Sarah loved him but referred him to her guardian. "Mr. Waldron," Young said when told the story, "you are a very good actor. You can play Hamlet well, and Julius Caesar to a charm, but you can't play Alexander." Waldron was so stunned that he gave up Sarah, who in fury called Young an old fool.[56]

Jealously guarding his actresses, Young for years refused to let Gentiles enter the stock company of his theater. His most popular actress was Annie Adams, revered by the Saints as their "Valley Flower." Reared on her father's farm in Utah, Annie wiled away her summers herding cows and her winters irregularly attending school, where she learned to read and write a little. One evening when she was about fifteen her father took her to Young's theater, and the smoldering embers of genius immediately fanned into flame. She was sure she could act and pestered her father until he talked to the prophet, who agreed to board, clothe, and educate her for three years in return for her acting services. At first she was crude. But Julia Dean Hayne arrived, immediately recognized Annie's innate talents, and tutored her. Annie was soon the company's leading lady. Rounds of applause always greeted her, and she was an even greater favorite with Gentiles than with Saints. Twice the Gentile merchants and federal officers of Salt Lake City held benefits for her and showered her with gifts. Deeply resentful, Young warned Annie to cease seeing these men. Finally, on August 15, 1869, in Clay County, Missouri, where her father had sent her to get her away from Gentiles, she married the recently divorced non-Mormon, James Kiskadden. The Saints, who still adored their Valley Flower, were shocked. They praised her acting but decried her wandering from the fold. Then in 1872 Annie returned to Salt Lake City and gave birth to a daughter, who, when she starred in New York at the turn of the century as the original Peter Pan, adopted her mother's maiden name and called herself simply Maude Adams.[57]

XII

"*The Blood That Stains the Walls of Carthage Jail*"

Look AROUND YOU if you want to know what kind of people
we are," Young instructed William Hepworth Dixon in
1866. "Nineteen years ago this valley was a desert, growing
nothing but the wild sage and dwarf sunflower; we who came
to it brought nothing with us but a few oxen and waggons, and
a bag of seeds and roots; the people who came after us, many
of them weavers and artisans, brought nothing, not a cent, not
even skill and usage of the soil; and when you look from this
balcony you can see what we have made of it."[1] The industry of
the Saints amazed the indefatigible railroad builder and general,
Grenville M. Dodge, who noted that from land "hardly green
enough for a grasshopper to live on" the Mormons got bountiful
harvests.

Unfortunately, Dodge added, the Saints paid a high price for
these accomplishments. Even women, "the Lord's hand laying
heavily upon them," labored for hours at the spinning wheel or in
the field. "They are bearing a cross for their views that is beyond
anything I ever expected to see."[2]

If Young touched the desert and made it bloom, he also made
Salt Lake City one of the West's great centers. Accustomed to the

filth of Eastern communities, Ludlow noted with wonder that even small children dared not discard anything in the city's streets. The water supply, running along a ditch near the gutter, was spotless.[3]

In 1867 Young added to the city's attractions with the most famous building finished during his lifetime, the new Tabernacle. Two hundred and fifty feet long, one hundred and fifty feet wide, and over sixty feet high, it contained at one end a pulpit and a huge organ. Its interior, pulpit and all, was white pine. Long uncushioned benches, curved in the seat and back for comfort, accommodated fifteen thousand persons.[4] The building is still used.

II

BY THE END OF THE MORMON WAR Young gathered about him the advisers who, with slight exceptions, served him until his death. Kimball, his closest and oldest friend, was a striking figure. Erect, portly, full-chested, and powerfully built, the six-foot, two hundred-pound Saint looked every inch the former blacksmith. "Everything about him spoke of rude animal vigor, . . ." Ludlow commented. "His bright black eyes were small and twinkling; his well proportioned nose regular, but coarse. His cheeks encroached on the orbital cavities above them, and in common with his whole face were puffy and blonde, with a glaze of sunburn from apostolic summer tours. His lips were very full, and the expression of the whole mouth lickerish as Falstaff's; his chin was double and shiny, from the twin effect of good living and close shaving."[5]

Kimball's platform manner shocked most observers. Beginning a speech, he rose on tiptoe and frantically waved his arms to emphasize some things, then descended to stress others. He reminded Burton of Johann Tetzel, the friar whose hawking of indulgences precipitated Martin Luther's revolt in 1517.[6] Bowles noticed that Kimball "in church and theater keeps the cold from his bare head and the divine afflatus in by throwing a red bandanna handkerchief over it."[7]

Wells, "a lantern-jawed, long-faced, raw-boned, shambling-gaited man," completed the First Presidency. He was six feet tall, but unlike Kimball did not seem that height. "His forehead is somewhat retreating," the New York *Herald* reported, "his nose is large and the massive jaw and formidable teeth seen at times through his gash-like mouth are those of a man of rude, sudden action, not a man of thought." A long, grizzled goatee finished the face. First seeing him, Fanny Stenhouse mistook him for the carpenter.[8]

Three apostles stood out. George Smith, who joined the First Presidency after Kimball's death in 1868, was "a huge, burly man, with a Friar Tuck joviality of paunch and visage, and a roll in his bright eye which, in some odd, undefined sort of way, suggested cakes and ale. He talked well," the British politician, Justin McCarthy, remembered, "in a deep rolling voice, and with a dash of humor in his words and tone—he it was who irreverently but accurately likened the Tabernacle to a land turtle."[9] Orson Pratt, small, thin, and meek, had been a Saint since the 1830's, but by 1860 he and Young barely spoke, for the prophet distrusted the apostle's intellectualism and remembered that in 1842 Pratt had sided with his wife, Sarah, now an apostate, when she had accused Joseph Smith of attempted seduction. To rid himself of this pest Young sent him on one distant mission after another.[10] Young also disliked John Taylor, whom Mrs. Ferris called "a heavy, dark-colored, beetle-browed man." In 1856 United States Army Sergeant Barnard W. Gammon, a resident in Taylor's home for several months, swore in New York Supreme Court that he heard Young call Taylor a "G–d d—d son of a bitch, and he wished he was rotten in hell."[11] The appetites of prophets and apostles seemed all too human.

Several other leading Saints held unenviable reputations. "Lorenzo D. Young, Brigham's brother, is a finished scamp," one Saint informed *The New York Times*. "To collect a debt from him is about impossible. . . . Ezra T. Benson and Lorenzo Snow are of the Lorenzo Young stamp, shrewd traders and consummate rogues. Lorenzo Snow conceived the magnificent idea of establishing a 'Scientific Institute and Library.' A fine building was put up on credit; the library was furnished in the same manner. As soon as all was in running order, Brother Snow moved into the house, and has since claimed it, and all that was contributed towards the glorious project."[12]

III

"The world elsewhere may be sought in vain for a despotism so relentless and pitiless as is Mormonism, . . ." Alexander K. Mc-Clure, the editor of the Philadelphia *Times*, wrote from Salt Lake City in 1867. "There are churches wherein infallibility is accorded to the head, or limited power of an absolute character conceded, but in none could any spiritual potentate rise up, as did Brigham on Sunday last, before 2,500 people, and prescribe their world actions, their ordinary daily dealings, with the penalty of eternal damnation proclaimed for disobedience."[13]

In 1865 Albert D. Richardson composed for the New York *Tribune* the best description of Young ever written. Nearly six feet tall, the prophet grew heavier every year almost against his will and now weighed two hundred pounds. But he remained "wonderfully well-preserved for a man who has passed his sixty-fourth birthday. His face is fresh and unwrinkled, his step agile and elastic. I can hardly detect a single gray hair in his curling auburn locks, or the whiskers of the same hue, which in smooth, crescent line fringe his cheek and chin. Is Brigham Young indeed a new Ponce de Leon, who has discovered in Polygamy the fountain of Perpetual Youth?

"His eyes are grayish blue. They do not impress me as frank and open, but have a secretive expression. He has an eagle nose and a mouth that shuts like a vice, indicating tremendous firmness. His manner is dignified—agreeable and affable rather than cordial; and he carries the unmistakable air of one having authority. Ordinarily cold in conversation, he has little ebullitions of earnestness in which he speaks right at people, using his dexter fore-finger with great force to point a moral. . . . Yet those who hold Brigham Young a cheap charlatan, are wilder if possible than the Saints who receive him as an angel of light, or those Gentiles who denounce him as a goblin damned. A most striking embodiment of the One Man Power, he holds a hundred thousand people in the hollow of his hand. Gathered from every nation, always poor, usually ignorant, sometimes vicious, he has molded them into an industrious, productive, honest and homogeneous community. He has grown very rich; the Gentiles charge him with extortion among his own people. He certainly owns much of the desirable property in Utah. But his adherents as a class have vastly improved their condition by coming here. I believe all admit that his large commercial dealings are characterized by integrity; and that he possesses great kindness of heart. He is a man of brains, quick intuitions, good judgment and untiring industry. He would doubtless have achieved great success in politics, trade, manufacturing, or almost any other walk of life."[14]

Some other writers were hardly this generous. McCarthy termed Young "the oddest, most whimsical figure I had ever seen off the boards of an English country theatre." At their meeting the prophet wore a swallow-tailed coat that nearly swept the floor, a collar reaching to his ears, and "natty little boots of the shiniest polished leather."[15] In 1869 the New York *World*'s correspondent found Young "stout and portly, looking very much as a London alderman is supposed to after a life spent in eating roast-beef dinners and indulging in champagne suppers."[16]

Like Kimball, Young had idiosyncracies. Neuralgia forced him to wear his hat in his office and while preaching. The prophet's speeches, moreover, resembled those of no other clergyman. He usually ignored the Bible, filling his sermons instead with hints on stock raising and fence building, tales of Mormon sufferings, advice to the lovelorn, and anecdotes.[17]

Still, Young's platform manner was sometimes impressive. "He spoke in a cool, deliberate manner and very slowly," noted a reporter for the New York *Herald* in 1858. "His articulation was very distinct; every syllable could be heard. His gesticulations were not elaborate or constant, but strong and impressive. His style of elocution was not so winning as commanding, though he by no means lacks suavity. . . . He uses whatever word comes first to express his idea, so his language is quite original and his expressions frequently very telling. His language does not flow along like a torrent, but is strong, harsh and commanding. . . . He could not minister to a graceful and accomplished society, but he is a man preeminently qualified to rule a mountain people with a rod of iron and a gloved hand."[18]

"When he speaks," another newspaperman observed, "the words seem to be calmly weighed by the brain, clipped by the teeth, and finally squeezed through the left half of the almost locked-up lips." In the early 1860's Frank Fuller, the new Utah secretary, immeasurably improved Young's diction and that of several of his wives and some of the apostles. An excellent dentist, Fuller inserted into these apostolic mouths handsome sets of false teeth.[19]

Young's speech reflected his New England background and meager education. Possessing what Burton called "a mind uncorrupted by books," the prophet continually mispronounced "impetus." "Provincialisms of his Vermont boyhood and his Western manhood still cling to him," Richardson keenly observed. "He says 'leetle,' 'beyend' and 'disremember.' An irrepressible conflict between his nominatives and verbs now and then crops out in expressions like 'they was.' "[20]

Young was popular with his people, partially because they feared him but also because he showed he was interested in them. Accompanied by a couple of wives and several apostles, he frequently visited every settlement in the territory. He spoke often and made Mormonism personal and attractive. "Is it any wonder," asked the New York *Herald*, "that this man is regarded by his followers as the anointed of the Lord, their sovereign ruler, guide and friend?"[21] "He treats the brethren with warmth," Richardson added, "throwing his arm caressingly about them and asking carefully after the wives and babies."[22]

McCarthy talked to one workingman who tearfully recalled Young's concern for him. The man had been ill for some time, and on the first day he reappeared on the street Young happened to drive by. "He stopped his carriage, sir, called me over to him, addressed me by name, shook hands with me, asked me how I was getting on, and said he was glad to see me out again." The Saint was as proud of this as a French private might have been had Napoleon recognized him and called him by name.[23]

To the dismay of Gentiles, who continually complained because Utah had no public schools and because the few church schools in the territory were inadequate, Young disliked education and feared educated men. The prophet believed diseases were demonic possessions curable only by exorcism, said he had not allowed a doctor into his house for forty years, and insisted Salt Lake City had no illness until doctors, too lazy to work like others, arrived and made people ill so they might make a living treating them.[24]

One day William E. Waters, an army officer, heard Young boast publicly about a Lutheran minister an angel had visited and ordered to convert to Mormonism. The next day Young privately told Waters that the clergyman had never done a day's manual labor, "but when he came here we put him to work as we do everybody." "The fact of this man being educated was not a source of congratulation to Brigham," Waters commented, "but his complete infatuation and submission were the great things."[25]

In planning Utah's economy Young, showing great wisdom, gave equal attention to agriculture, mining, manufacturing, transportation, and marketing. He wanted his people to be frugal, quiet, and industrious and feared that undue emphasis upon mining would ruin all this and bring huge numbers of Gentiles into the territory. Young repeatedly argued that the world already possessed more precious metal than it needed, that it cost twenty dollars in expenses to take one dollar in gold or silver out of the ground, and that the country, despite the many mines opened up, was poorer in the 1860's than it had been in the 1840's.[26]

Striving for self-sufficiency, Young continually urged his Saints to grow or manufacture something new. One year he introduced honeybees, the next sweet potatoes, the third tobacco, the fourth the manufacture of cast iron.[27]

Everyone worked, and no one was paid for his services to the church. Prophets, presidents, bishops, and elders sold ribbons, grew cabbages, built mills, cut timber, herded cattle, and drove trains. Dixon once bumped into an old man carrying a small basket covered with a snow-white napkin. He later learned the man taking a basket of peaches to market was Joseph Young, Brigham's elder brother and the president of the Council of Seventies. George Smith and Orson Hyde farmed and operated mills, Orson Pratt taught mathematics, Woodruff bred animals, George Q. Cannon printed and edited the *Deseret News*, and Kimball ran linseed oil and carding mills.[28]

Young too engaged in several economic pursuits. A superb farmer and herder, he won prizes at the annual Deseret fairs of the late 1850's and early 1860's for the second best apples, the second best pecks of silver and red onions, the best drumhead cabbage, the best bunches of grapes, the best tomatoes, the best blood beets, the best peppers, the best pigs, the best brood mare, the best yearling colt, and the best Devon bull. In the female competition his wives captured many honors.[29]

Each year Young's dairy in Hampton, Utah, produced over 150 tons of the world's best cheese. And between Mendon and Logan the prophet owned one of the territory's finest ranches, ten thousand acres of very good land on which six hundred head of choice cattle and hundreds of sheep grazed.[30]

Young's factories were everywhere. On City Creek he ran a carding factory and a grist mill, in Salt Lake City a large wagon and repair shop, at the mouth of Parley's Canyon cotton and woolen factories, and in St. George leather tanneries, a shop manufacturing saddles and harnesses, and a shoe factory employing a dozen men.[31] "His fortunes," Burton shrewdly observed, "were principally made in business: like the late Imam of Muscat, he is the chief merchant as well as the high-priest. He sends long trains of wagons freighted with various goods to the Eastern States and supplies caravans and settlements with grains and provisions. From the lumber which he sold to the Federal troops for hutting themselves at Camp Floyd, he is supposed to have netted not less than $200,000."[32]

Within months of his migration to Utah a thousand dollars in debt,[33] Young by his own admission was rich. "Before I had been one year in this place," he bragged in 1850, "the wealthiest man who came from the mines, Father Rhodes, with seventeen thousand dollars could not buy the possessions I had made in one year!"[34] During the 1860's the prophet's personal income averaged $32,000 a year,[35] and in the 1870 census he declared personal property worth $102,000 and real estate valued at $1,010,600.[36]

IV

CONSIDERING THEMSELVES OUTCASTS in the land of the free and the home of the brave, the Mormons, while calling a portion of the United States their Zion and praising the federal Constitution as

Rejecting
MANY American
VAlues

divine, retaliated by rejecting many things dear to America: its marriage system, its appointed and elected officials, its reverence for free enterprise and an unplanned economy, its stress on the worth of the individual, its democratic traditions. Quite naturally, the Saints distrusted those people who had laughed at them and supported their enemies. They remembered that in Ohio, Missouri, and Illinois law men had foreclosed their mortgages and shot and jailed them but had watched as mobs killed their prophet, burned their homes, and forced them to flee. Equating Gentile laws and Gentile government with oppression, the Mormons substituted for something Gentile something Mormon.

All the while Young proclaimed his people's innocence. "Persecution is our portion," he informed Dixon, forgetting that the Saints had often been as guilty as their opponents. "If we are right the world will be against us; but the world will not prevail against the elect of God."[37]

Consciously or unconsciously, Gentile visitors to Utah retaliated by denouncing the Mormons as foreigners who cared nothing for America and its traditions. Even the usually reliable Burton, relying on outlandish figures, reported in 1860 that European Saints now outnumbered Americans, most of whom had apostatized, by ten to one.[38] "Those here," Dodge joined in, "are the lowest foreigners and their lot is better than it was in Old England."[39] "A very large majority of the Mormon people," McClure agreed, "are the rescued serfs of the Old World—not so perhaps in name in most cases, but in fact. They are ignorant, superstitious, fanatical, and ready victims for a new doctrine that promises to bring them into immediate communion with God."[40]

One group of foreigners the Mormons themselves detested. In 1860 George Smith, recalling the recent conflict, still railed at the "wretched Irishmen and Dutchmen sent from the East to try whether the Mormons would receive Federal officers."[41] Orson Hyde also condemned "the flood poured in upon us—merchants, gamblers, whoremasters, thieves, murderers, false writers, drunkards, and, to cap the climax, a drunken, debauched judiciary, with plenty of bayonets to enforce their decree."[42]

If financing the Utah expedition strained the federal treasury, the move to Provo and the march back to Salt Lake City practically bankrupted the Saints. Hard money disappeared from circulation. The Mormons organized the Deseret Currency Association, with Young as president and Wells as treasurer, and printed on tissue paper over $100,000 in shinplasters, each hundred dollars of which could be redeemed for a dollar in livestock. Noted the New York *Tribune*'s correspondent after the return: "I have not seen a piece of silver since I have been in the city."[43]

In other ways the Saints adjusted swiftly. "It is interesting to watch the rapidity with which this City is now improving in every respect," *The New York Times*'s reporter wrote in mid-August. "One can hardly realize that six weeks ago it was entirely deserted; that all these stores, now thronged with customers, were closed, and that all these dwellings were fastened up, with doors nailed and windows boarded."[44]

But the return ushered in the strangest period of Young's life. For the next two years he disappeared from sight. In August 1858 he announced that God had commanded him to remain silent for a season and stopped attending services. Confided one of his wives to the New York *Herald*: "Brigham will not preach again so long as you have a Gentile shorthand reporter here to take down his discourses."[45]

When Young picnicked, he kept the place and time secret. "It is said," Burton observed in 1860, "that Mr. Brigham Young, despite his powerful will and high moral courage, does not show the remarkable personal intrepidity of Mr. Joseph Smith: his followers deny this, but it rests on the best and fairest Gentile evidence. He has guards at his gates, and he never appears in public unattended by friends and followers, who are of course armed."[46]

V

THE YEAR FOLLOWING THE MORMON WAR matched the Reformation in violence and bloodshed. When Buchanan reappointed most of the Gentiles who held office in 1857, the Saints tried to discredit them. They also released a damaging letter the new territorial Chief Justice, Delena R. Eckels, had sent to an officer at Camp Floyd. "I have not yet procured you a bedfellow for the coming winter," Eckels apologized. "I have spoken to one woman

and she says if her husband is agreed to it she would like to go but
not until she is freed from her present *interesting* condition. She
says she has a sister who is the 2nd wife of an old *Cap* and she has
one child and wants to leave him and she will send and inquire if
she will cook and wash for you. I think she will do—I told her
sister to let me know. I think also that if she does not succeed in
that *quarter* I will in some other—hold *on a little*."[47] Eckels "was
engaged here," John Taylor charged, "in the very honorable occupation of pimp for some army officers."[48]

The arrival in Salt Lake City of the anti-Mormon Kirk Anderson, formerly of the St. Louis *Missouri Republican*, further vexed
the Saints. Late in 1858 Anderson began publishing the Salt Lake
Valley Tan, a four-page weekly named for a poor grade of Utah
whiskey.

To the present-day reader the *Valley Tan*, like the Nauvoo
Expositor, whose suppression by the Saints led to the murder of
Joseph Smith, seems mild and no more hostile to Mormonism than
other Gentile newspapers of that day, but in 1858 as in 1844 the
Saints brooked no criticism. They became incensed when the *Val-
ley Tan* played up such things as the murder and hasty burial by a
Mormon policeman of a deaf and dumb boy carrying fifty-five
dollars in gold.[49]

Young publicly ignored the paper, but he privately denounced
it as a "filthy, miserable little sheet." "Mobocracy and Murder are
in their (Burr, Hurt, Craig, Dotson, Kirk Anderson & Co.) hearts,
but so long as they keep hands off we expect to let them live."
Aided by Associate Supreme Court Justices Charles E. Sinclair
and John Cradlebaugh, this "clan" and its flunkies were "striving
and doing all in their power to stir up strife through the courts."
Franklin McNeill, falsely imprisoned during the recent war, was
suing Young, Wells, Robert T. Burton, Jesse C. Little, and several
other Saints for $25,000. Burr was seeking $3,000 from Young,
Feramorz Little, Brigham Young, Jr., Clawson, William Kimball,
and Rockwood for stealing government property, and Thomas
Williams wanted $5,000 for the loss of his library. Finally W.M.F.
Magraw was after Feramorz Little for defaulting on a note given
for some mules. "What else they are bringing we do not know,"
Young complained, "but doubtless sufficient to keep the Court

from engaging in any legitimate business." The following month Young angrily declared: "To destroy their Press, or cowhide Kirk Anderson, the Judge or any of the clique, although they richly deserve it, would be salvation to them. They are rampant for martyrdom, but no one considers them worthy of notice."[50]

In 1859 the battle continued. Expecting to catch something that might lead to Sinclair's impeachment, Young sent stenographers to take down every word uttered in the judge's courtroom. And eight hundred Saints petitioned to replace Morrell, the hated Gentile postmaster of Salt Lake City, with Joseph Smith's one-time secretary, William Clayton. These petitions were forwarded to Kane, Young's Washington lobbyist.[51] Retaliating, Cradlebaugh and Forney traveled about the territory investigating and publicizing the Mountain Meadows massacre and other crimes.[52]

This sorry spectacle dismayed *The New York Times*. "The whole thing—the whole machinery of justice we have established in Utah—is an absurd farce; and we all know it," the paper argued. "We know perfectly well that no sincere Mormon will administer our laws, and we know, also that there is no sincere Mormon who does not feel it to be his duty to obstruct their execution and bring them into contempt. We have no right to place United States Judges in such a ridiculous position as that in which those whom we have sent to Mormondom are placed, and we have no right to place either our Governors or the troops in the position of being obliged to protect themselves from odium at the expense of their duty. If we cannot govern Utah in the regular and constitutional way, it would be far better to let it alone."[53]

In one respect, however, the 1859 struggle differed from the 1857. "In the midst of all these commotions," the New York *Tribune* pointed out, "we hear little or nothing of Brigham Young. He seems quite to have withdrawn himself from the public eye, thinking it best perhaps at this time to devote himself exclusively to his own private affairs, and making the necessary provision for his numerous wives and children."[54]

But Young remained active behind the scene. "It is believed by Mormons, as well as Gentiles," Burton reported, "that Mr. Brigham Young has, in the States, newspaper spies and influential political friends, who are attached to him, not only by the ties of business and the natural respect for a wealthy man, but by the strong bond of a regular stipend. And such is their reliance upon dodgery—which, if it really exists, is by no means honorable to the public morality of the Gentiles—that they deride the idea of a combined movement from Washington ever being made against them."[55] Young used the tithe well.

Then on Sunday, July 10, 1859, the most famous visitor yet to reach Salt Lake City stepped off the stagecoach, onto Temple Street, and into this violent scene. One of the century's two greatest journalists—James Gordon Bennett was the other—Horace Greeley, whose New York *Tribune* was, with the possible exception of Bennett's New York *Herald*, the most widely read and respected paper in the West, stayed in town a week and was honored at a reception attended by almost every important Saint.

In Salt Lake City Greeley got the first interview the Mormon prophet ever gave, "Two Hours with Brigham Young," which papers throughout the world published. In it Young scoffed at stories of Danites, reaffirmed his belief in a devil who constantly battled God, and explained such Mormon ideas as the gathering. A faulty memory undoubtedly was the reason Young estimated his fortune at $250,000 and his wives at fifteen.[56]

In Utah Greeley investigated the stories of Mormon atrocities. "Do I, then," he asked, "discredit the tales of Mormon outrage and crime—of the murder of the Parishes, the Mountain Meadows massacre, &c., &c.,—where with the general ear has recently been shocked? No, I do not. Some of these may have been fabricated by Gentile malice—others are doubtless exaggerated—but there is some basis of truth for the current Gentile conviction that *Mormons have robbed, maimed, and even killed persons in this Territory, under circumstances which should subject the perpetrators to condign punishment, but that Mormon witnesses, grand jurors, petit jurors and magistrates determinedly screen the guilty. I deeply regret the necessity of believing this; but the facts are incontestable.*"[57]

As Greeley headed for California, more murders rocked Utah. On August 10, 1859, Charles M. Drown sued Hickman for $480 and won the case. Ten days later he and his chief witness and neighbor, Josiah Arnold, came to Salt Lake City on business. By doing so Drown signed his own death warrant. About ten o'clock that night Hickman and eight or ten friends went to the house in which Drown and Arnold were staying and ordered them to come out. When they refused, Hickman smashed down the front and rear doors and shot his two enemies. The next morning Drown died. "After committing this bold and dreadful murder," *The New York Times* reported, "the party mounted their horses and rode around town unmolested."[58]

That same month tragedy befell McNeill as he walked along Main Street, Salt Lake City's busiest thoroughfare. About ten o'clock on the night before his $25,000 suit against Young was to be tried three men approached him. One placed a gun against McNeill's side and fired. The victim hovered between life and death for a day, during which he accused Lot Huntington, the Danite, of shooting him, and then died. Huntington was picked up, questioned by federal authorities, and released.[59]

Infuriated, *The Times* considered such outrages unparalleled "by anything to be found within the jurisdiction of any civilized government on the globe. In saying this, we have Algeria, the Punjab and the Caucasus directly before our mind's eye. We take into account the turbulence of the Kabyles, the restless activity of the Nena Sahib, the ferocity of the Sikhs, and the cut-throat propensities of the Circassian mountaineers. And yet we assert that the United States possesses inhabited territory, occupied by a competent force of its troops, within a month's march of a frontier inclosing thirty millions of law-abiding citizens, which, for disorder, insecurity, bloodshed, contempt for the law and its officers, beats anything of the kind which either France, England or Russia can produce."[60]

More violence occurred on Christmas Day of 1859. Before hundreds of Saints, Hickman and Huntington quarreled and exchanged over forty shots. Huntington suffered only a slight leg wound, but Hickman was hit in the groin and had to be carried home. At first he seemed to be dying, but he recovered and by March was again serving Young.[61]

The prophet, meanwhile, bested one Gentile official. On July 9, 1859, Marshal Peter K. Dotson raided a room over the Deseret store, arrested Young's secretary for counterfeiting, and confiscated the Deseret Currency Association's plates. Young sued, and on September 8, 1860, was awarded $1,668 for damages to the plates and $648.66 in court costs. To pay the fine Dotson's house was given to Young. Elias Smith, the judge in the case, also edited the *Deseret News* at the time and was an adviser of Young.[62]

Then in May 1860 the government, burdened by expenses, partially closed Camp Floyd and removed over half of its troops. Completely failing to bring order to Utah, the army brought instead federal funds and prosperity. "Many persons who, two years ago, did not possess the first half of an animal," the New York *Tribune* related, "now boast of ox teams and mule teams; while the numerous Mormon belles and dames literally revel in calicoes and crinolines—all these furnished, too, through the overflowing generosity of the good old uncle." During the occupation prices jumped sharply: flour fifty per cent and wheat, butter, eggs, potatoes, and hay 250 to 300 per cent each. Bidding farewell to the army, Kimball muttered: "You have blessed us, though you did not mean to do it."[63]

Ending his self-imposed confinement, Young now attended his first dance since 1858.[64] It had taken two years, but he had whipped the United States.

VI

"VERILY," COMMENTED *The New York Times*'s Utah correspondent in June 1860, borrowing one of Young's favorite phrases, "the Mormons are 'some pumpkins.'" Now discussing an anti-polygamy bill, an overland mail act, and Pacific railroad and telegraph legislation, Congress was unusually concerned with Utah.[65]

In February 1861 the telegraph proved the most important project. Still smarting because his church had lost $200,000 when the government abruptly cancelled the Express Company's contract in 1857, Young agreed to string one thousand miles of wire from Fort Laramie to Salt Lake City and to California for $175 a mile. To his delight the line to Utah was finished on October 17, 1861, and the one to the Pacific the following week. Young then organized the Deseret Telegraph Company, which eventually connected every Mormon settlement to the Beehive House.[66]

Mark Twain later vouched for Young's integrity in the operation by telling of a Mr. Street, the holder of a contract to string several hundred miles of wire in the mountains. He sublet the most difficult portions to Saints, but they found the job too difficult and abandoned it. In desperation Street complained to Young, who examined the papers and said: "Mr. Street, this is all perfectly plain. These contracts are strictly and legally drawn, and are duly signed and certified. These men manifestly entered into them with their eyes open. I can see no fault or flaw anywhere." Young then called the subcontractors to his office and ordered them to carry out the contract "to the letter . . . if it makes paupers of you!" They never again complained.[67]

In dealings with the prophet, members of some minority groups seldom fared this well. Young especially hated Jews. "I would rather undertake to convert five thousand Lamanites," he announced, "than to convert one of those poor miserable creatures whose fathers killed the Savior, and who say, 'Amen to the deed,' to this day. Yea, I would rather undertake to convert the devil himself, if it were possible."[68]

Jews, in turn, laughed at Mormonism. At Joseph Smith's order Orson Hyde had sought converts in Jerusalem in 1841 but had returned home in failure. Jews ridiculed what they believed to be Mormon perversions of the Old Testament: the revival of polygamy; the supposed restoration of Hebraic ways through revelations received by latter-day prophets; the adoption—Jews called it robbery—of the chosen-people doctrine; and the stress on Zion, the homeland—not Palestine but Independence, Missouri—to which all true believers would migrate.

Salt Lake City's few Jews considered Mormonism a vulgar and impious parody of ancient and revered customs and joked that Abraham, the first polygamist, ought, like his Mormon counterparts, to have been hung for his hideous crimes. "If the ancient Hebrews were as wicked as the Latter-day Saints," scoffed one Utah Jew, "I am sorry the Philistines did not clean them out."[69]

In Mormon belief Negroes were the lowest of all humans. In 1833 the Kirtland *Evening and Morning Star*, citing a revelation received by Smith in December 1830, expressed "our intention not only to stop free people of color from emigrating to this state, but to prevent them from being admitted as members of the church."[70]

Like many defenders of slavery, Young considered Negroes the children of Canaan, who in the Bible had been made a "servant of servants" to his brothers. "The negro is damned," Young preached in 1855, "and is to serve his master till God chooses to remove the curse. . . . These are my views—and, consequently, the views of all the saints—on abolitionism."[71]

VII

THE MORMON OPINION of the American Civil War, which broke out in 1861, reflected this bias and the church's desire for seclusion. Throughout the 1850's slavery and polygamy were America's most pressing political problems and were especially difficult for Democrats like Buchanan, who denied Congress's right to regulate territorial institutions. These men were at wit's end to figure out how they could advocate the use of force in Utah and still deny the government's right to legislate on slavery in Kansas.[72]

To Young's delight the war led to the removal from Utah of the remaining federal troops. Before leaving, the army sold its fort and buildings, fired its remaining shells, burst and buried its mortars, and burned its powder and 25,000 rifles. But after the troops were gone, the Saints dug up everything they could salvage and carted it to foundries to be remolded.[73]

As the Saints saw it, the conflict fulfilled the message received by Joseph Smith during the tariff squabble of 1832 between South Carolina and President Andrew Jackson. This revelation spoke of trouble "that will shortly come to pass, beginning at the rebellion of South Carolina, which will eventually terminate in the death and misery of many souls; And the time will come that war will be poured out upon all nations, beginning at this place. For behold, the Southern States will call on other nations, even the nation of Great Britain, as it is called, and they shall also call upon other nations, in order to defend themselves against other nations; and then war shall be poured out upon all nations." Exhumed from Smith's papers in 1851, this prophecy was applied a decade later to the Civil War.[74] Enterprising Saints might also have cited

Smith's unpublished prediction of May 1843: "You will see the Constitution of the United States almost destroyed. It will hang as it were by a thread and the thread as of the finest silk fibre."[75]

Far more specific than either of these revelations was Kimball's completely ignored but nonetheless remarkable statement in June 1858: "And there is old Buch—d——n him—*he* put his foot in it; but he'll never do it again. I prophesy that there will be peace during the remainder of his Administration but after him will come such a time as we have never yet seen, and I know it and intend to prepare for it, laying up stores in the mountains to be ready for that evil time."[76]

For Abraham Lincoln, who had been elected President of the United States in 1860 on a Republican platform that again called slavery and polygamy the "twin relics of barbarism," the Saints had only scorn. "Our present President, what is his strength?" derided Young shortly after Lincoln's inauguration. "It is like a rope of sand, or like a rope made of water; he is as weak as water. What can he do? Very little. . . . Of late, at times, I have almost wished that I had been born in a foreign nation."[77] Lincoln's Secretary of State, William H. Seward, had not wit enough, Young added, "to find his way across the little city of Washington."[78] The prophet would talk differently at the end of the decade, when Seward visited Salt Lake City.

VIII

ASKED AFTER THE WAR why the Mormons had favored "the late Southern rebels" instead of the North, Brigham Young, Jr., indignantly replied: "*We did not sympathize with the rebellion,* but, on the contrary, earnestly and persistently refused all overtures made us. There is a little bit of history connected with this affair which perhaps you are not aware of. Emissaries were sent to us time after time to urge us to lend a helping hand; inducement was piled upon inducement, and finally, as the last grand *bait,* they offered to admit us as a State, with all the rights and privileges thereof, and with the question of polygamy untouched, and to remain untouched, provided we would make a diversion in their favor. Even this we resented. The only semblance of disloyalty I ever heard was on occasions when the Southern army gained some important victory. Then I heard it remarked, as though in wonderment, that the weaker party was gaining ground. It is true, we had many Southerners among us, but our sympathies were ever with the Government. We had suffered far more at the hands of the Southerners than we ever did at the hands of the Northerners, for it was the former that compelled us to leave Missouri. The United States Government never called upon us for troops, but they did call upon us for money, and our quota of $40,000 was promptly planked down; far more so than was that of some of the States."[79]

But even as the young man spoke, two of his father's wives—both interviewed by the New York *World*—inadvertently contradicted him. Elenor McLean linked the war to the death of Parley Pratt, who was murdered because of his love for her, and said with satisfaction: "His death has been fully avenged upon the nation which has permitted the blood of the Prophets to be spilt without punishing the murderers."[80]

Zina Huntington also showed bitterness. "The Lord has revealed it to the 'Prophet Joseph' that the nations should be broken up and destroyed. The prophecy concerning the war between the North and the South is only partially fulfilled, and it will break out afresh; the next time in the North as well as the South, and result in the destruction of the nation." The reporter questioned this view, but Zina was adamant. "We firmly believe here that such will be the case. We expect some day to return to Jackson County, in Missouri, whence we were forcibly expelled, and occupy again our property and our Zion. That can only be, however, when the people of the United States are weakened by strife and slaughter." Zina said the Saints loved the federal Constitution, "but the government has been in the hands of very bad men, who use the power to their own advantage. The unprovoked murder of the Prophet Joseph and his brother Hiram has yet to be atoned for; the slaughter during the rebellion was but a partial atonement." Both Democrats and Republicans were evil. "They all believe in oppressing and persecuting the Saints; but they will be punished some day."[81]

Eliza Snow agreed. After William Cullen Bryant wrote the patriotic "Our Country's Call," Eliza countered late in 1861 with a poem about the Union that the correspondent of *The New York Times* called "a fair index of the views of the more orthodox Mormons on the present National civil struggle."

> Its fate is fixed—its destiny
> Is sealed—its end is sure to come;
> Why use the wealth of poesy
> To urge a nation to its doom?
> . . . It must be so, to avenge the blood
> That stains the walls of Carthage jail.[82]

At a church conference in 1863 Young joined in by calling the conflict "a visitation from heaven because they have killed the prophet of God, Joseph Smith, Jr."[83] His wartime statements, however, proved to be as far-fetched as Zina's postwar prophecies. In 1861 he predicted that to get husbands thousands of "widows and forlorn damsels" from both the North and the South would convert to Mormonism and enter polygamy.[84] On October 6, 1863, Young ignored Lincoln's recent Emancipation Proclamation and insisted that the Negro "will continue to be the servant of servants, as the Lord has decreed, until the curse is removed. Will the present struggle free the slave? No; but they are now wasting away the black race by thousands."[85] About then Young told Ludlow that both sides would be forced to "come out here to our ark of refuge. . . . You'll all be out here before long. Your Union's gone forever. Fighting only makes matters worse. When your country has become a desolation, we, the saints whom you cast out, will forget all your sins against us, and give you a home."[86] Finally, in the summer of 1864 Young ordered the Saints in several cities to store grain for seven more years of war. Both combatants, he predicted, would look to Utah for food.[87] Nine months later the conflict ended.

Even the scholarly Orson Pratt uttered wild statements. In 1863 he spoke of a speedy return to Jackson County. Once there he intended to inform the Gentiles "that there was stone to quarry and choice timbers to hew for the temple, and when they went and quarried stone and hewed the timbers and built the City of Zion, then he would think of receiving them into the company of the Saints."[88]

IX

YOUNG DESPISED LINCOLN but still hoped to get from him the Utah governorship. In April 1861 the prophet asked Hooper, the territorial Congressional delegate, to try for other appointments: Joseph A. Young, William Clayton, and John T. Caine as secretaries; Burton and Henry Lawrence, the wealthy Salt Lake City merchant and brother of Maria and Sarah Lawrence, two of Joseph Smith's widows, as marshals; Woodruff as postmaster of Salt Lake City; Hosea Stout and Seth Blair as Supreme Court Justices; and Elias Smith as Chief Justice. "Failing in any or all of the above, do the best you can, only we would thank you to keep away from here so miserable a curse as is Morrell, for any position or place within our borders."[89]

Lincoln ignored these suggestions, appointing instead the worst governor ever fobbed off on the Saints. John W. Dawson, the former editor of the Fort Wayne *Times*, arrived in Salt Lake City on December 7, 1861, and left twenty-three days later. In the city he made improper advances towards his housekeeper, grew ill with fear lest the offended girl's relatives seek revenge, made his will, and through his physician repeatedly tried to bribe the girl into silence. After fearfully remaining in his room for ten days, he decided to flee from Utah. About a dozen miles outside of Salt Lake City he was overtaken by some Saints, beaten, and robbed.[90]

At this point Young decided to reestablish the State of Deseret. In January 1862 the Mormon leaders convened, drew up a constitution, and nominated Young for governor and Kimball for lieutenant governor. On March 3 Utah's voters overwhelmingly approved the convention's work. Each year for the next eight years the Deseret legislature met, adopted the territorial laws as its own, petitioned Congress for admission to the Union, designated two men for United States Senators—usually Hooper and Cannon—and adjourned. Congress ignored these requests.[91]

"We meet here in our second Annual Legislature," Young greeted the Deseret governing body in 1863, "and I do not care whether you pass any laws this Session or not, but I do not wish you to lose one inch of ground you have gained in your organization, but hold fast to it, for this is the Kingdom of God, and we are the friends of God, and you will find that much will grow out of this organization. . . . We are called the State Legislature, but when the time comes, we shall be called the Kingdom of God. Our government is going to pieces, and it will be like water that is spilt upon the ground that cannot be gathered. . . . For the time will come when we will give laws to the nations of the earth. Joseph Smith organized this government before, in Nauvoo, and he said if we do our duty we shall prevail over our enemies. We should get things ready, and when the time comes, we shall let the water on to the wheel and start the machine in motion."[92]

As if three governments—the church, territorial, and Deseret— were inadequate, Lincoln added a fourth in November 1862. To guard the mail and telegraph routes he sent troops to Utah. Over-looking the Salt Lake Valley the soldiers erected a camp they named for Stephen A. Douglas, who had died in June 1861. Once Smith's ally, Douglas, because he had denounced Mormonism in 1857 as a "loathsome ulcer," died without a friend in Utah. Not a flag was lowered to half-mast, no one expressed regrets, and no tears were shed.[93] Now soldiers occupying a fort honoring this hated man zeroed their weapons in on the Lion House.

And the new army commander, Colonel Patrick Edward Con-nor, detested Mormonism. Arriving in Utah, he later informed General Dodge, he found "the community almost exclusively members of the Mormon Church, bitter and unrelenting in their hostility to the Government. . . . The so-termed sermons delivered in their Tabernacles, Bowerys and Ward meetings, were models of obscenity and treason. . . . The Church leaders at every opportu-nity repeated the assertion that this war was a Kilkenny cat affair, so far as they were concerned: that they did not care which side got whipped. In either event the war would continue until the North and South were completely exhausted, and then they (the Mormons) would return to Jackson Co., Mo., and control the destiny of the United States." The Saints, ignorant "foreigners" of "the lower classes of Europe, men and women who know nothing about the American Government or its institutions," believed every story the prophet told them. Young, moreover, goaded the Indians into battling the army. Once when fifty Utes attacked six soldiers, 150 Mormons gathered and looked on from nearby roofs, but they refused to aid the white men. And during a skirmish at the Bear River, Connor had captured arms Young had given the Indians.[94]

The troops created other problems for Young. At the Salt Lake City theater Dixon saw a play in which a father warned his daughter about flirting with military sparks. At that the young ladies in the audience "crackled off into girlish laughter." Young roared too, but he later said of the soldiers: "They cause us trouble; they intrude into our affairs, and even into our families; we cannot stand such things; and when they are guilty we make them bite the dust." The prophet quickly added: "I never had any trouble of this sort in my family."[95]

In 1864 Young complained to Secretary of War Edwin M. Stanton about Connor, whose men had dug up half of Utah searching for gold. In getting supplies Connor had shown extravagance and stupidity. He had refused one bid of eight dollars for a hundred pounds of flour and accepted another of fifteen and had paid thirty-five dollars a ton for hay worth twenty. Connor was "so ignorant and oppressive that even the privates despise him." His troops "go so far as to hurrah for Jef. Davis, and indulge in other secession acts and proclivities, but perhaps that is all right in their cases."[96]

Twenty years after leaving Utah, Connor still detested Young. "Bill Hickman told me a half hour after it occurred," he revealed in 1886, "that Brigham had promised him a thousand dollars if he would send a ball through my brain and lay the murder to the Indians. I don't believe that those men were butchers by nature," Connor said of the Danites; "they were fanatics in their belief that they could not be saved if they would not obey any order of the prophet, right or wrong."[97]

One wartime skirmish with the Federals ended in a Mormon victory. In July 1862 the Republicans passed the Morrill Bill outlawing not polygamy but bigamy and limiting to $50,000 the amount of property, excluding houses of worship, the church could hold. On March 10, 1863, after openly violating the law by marrying Amelia Folsom, Young was arrested, but a friendly judge freed him[98]

In Washington on June 6, 1863, Stenhouse asked what Lincoln

proposed to do about the Mormons. "Stenhouse," the President replied, "when I was a boy on the farm in Illinois there was a great deal of timber on the farm which we had to clear away. Occasionally we would come to a log which had fallen down. It was too hard to split, too wet to burn and too heavy to move, so we plowed around it. That's what I intend to do with the Mormons. You go back and tell Brigham Young that if he will let me alone I will let him alone."[99]

To compensate for the loss of Confederate cotton during the war Young ordered Saints to southern Utah, the Mormon "Dixie." Attending one conference at which 250 people, chiefly heads of families, were called to grow cotton, the correspondent of *The Times* observed: "It was amusing to witness the countenances of the congregation during the reading of the list. 'Is it I?' 'Is it I?' could be plainly read on many a one."[100]

In all, however, the war years were among Young's happiest. At conference after conference he allowed his people an extra "hosanna," blessing them in the future. With bared heads the congregation stood and shouted "Hosanna, hosanna, hosanna, to God and the Lamb, to God and the Lamb, to God and the Lamb; amen, amen, amen." At the beginning of each word or phrase every Saint raised his right hand and at each accented word or syllable energetically brought it down on the left.[101] The Great Basin rocked with God's blessing.

If Young could arbitrarily send hundreds of unwilling families to years of privation and toil in the desert, he could also show compassion. Hiram S. Rumfield, the Assistant Treasurer of the Overland Mail Company, recalled viewing from Young's balcony the parade of July 24, 1862, celebrating the entrance of the pioneers into the region. The heat was unbearable, and Young instructed a man with water and a cup to accompany each squad of twenty or thirty children. When Young spied one squad without water, he excused himself, left the governor and other officials, and went below, returning only after correcting things.[102]

XIII

"His Day Is Over"

I

Utah's borders encased Young's world. The prophet
constantly traveled about the territory fostering Mormonism and welcoming newcomers, but never left it after 1848.
Within this self-imposed prison he relied on advisers as ill-
informed as he for news of the outside world. Young even failed
to place the name when introduced to one distinguished Easterner.
"Is this the justly celebrated Ralph Waldo Emerson?" apologized
his secretary. "I have read a great many of your books."[1]

Never acknowledging a Gentile virtue or a Mormon vice, the
prophet seldom related Mormon history as it happened. Such
things as the Kirtland bank fiasco, blood atonement, the Mountain
Meadows massacre, the crimes of the Danites, his immense
wealth, the size of his harem, and the frivolous way he took
women from their husbands or assigned young girls to his favorites entered his brain and emerged from his lips as squashed, mis-
shapen, and unreal concoctions, which his followers eagerly
grasped as God's truth. Only a great leader, and even Young's
enemies called him that, made Mormonism survive. But most Gentiles questioned his honesty and motives.

Just after the conclusion of the Civil War, a famous politician and three outstanding journalists came to Salt Lake City, interviewed Young, and went away shaking their heads in doubt. Colfax, Richardson, Bowles, and William Bross, the lieutenant governor of Illinois and editor of the Chicago *Tribune*, formed the most celebrated party yet to visit Utah. Their dispatches, eagerly gobbled up by readers, were published throughout the world.

Colfax's presence raised an etiquette problem. The president of the church never called on anyone. The Speaker of the United States House of Representatives, on the other hand, called only on the President of the United States. Colfax refused to make the first move. The prophet graciously yielded and with nine subordinates visited Colfax for two hours. "He is a very hale and hearty looking man," Bowles observed after the meeting, "young for 64, with a light grey eye, cold and uncertain, a mouth and chin betraying a great and determined will—handsome perhaps as to presence and features, but repellent in atmosphere and without magnetism. In conversation he is cool and quiet in manner, but courteous, and at the last affected frankness and freedom, if he felt it not. To his followers, I observed he was master of that profound art of eastern politicans, which consists in putting the arm affectionately around them, and tenderly inquiring for health of selves and families; and when his eye did sparkle and his lips soften, it was with most cheering, though not warming effect—it was pleasant but did not meet you." Kimball's "free and coarse speech" made him, Bowles added, Young's "most notorious" associate. "But the strength of most of the party seemed to be in narrowness, bigotry, obstinacy. They look as if they had lived on the same farm as their fathers and grand-fathers, and made no improvements; gone to the same church, and sat in the same pew, without cushions; borrowed the same weekly newspaper for 40 years; drove all their children to the West or the cities; and if they went to agricultural fairs, insisted on having their premiums in pure coin."[2]

Returning Young's courtesy three days later, the Gentiles engaged him in the first debate of its kind in Utah. Opening things, the prophet defended polygamy. "Abuses of it sometimes occur which it is difficult to prevent," he conceded. "But we can point to the highest morality. We have not a house of prositution. I don't believe you can find four illegitimate children in the Territory. You all think Plurality cannot last. Now tell us frankly how you expect it to be done away." "Well," Colfax retorted, "we expect you to have a new revelation prohibiting it." "We should not be sorry for that," Young answered, partially drowned out by Gentile laughter. "If God ever so directs we shall be glad to dispense with it." The prophet admitted *The Book of Mormon* did not sanction polygamy, not a cardinal Mormon doctrine but a privilege and duty under special commandment of God, but quickly added that the Bible justified it. If, he suggested, the Saints abandoned celestial marriage, the government would soon force them to give up *The Book of Mormon* and eventually their religion itself. Shaking his head in disbelief, Colfax responded that polygamy would have to go before Utah entered the Union.

Turning to recent American history, Young called slavery a divine institution and opposed hanging the leaders of the rebellion but said if he had been President in 1861, when two Confederate commissioners to England were captured, he would have speedily put them "where they never would peep." The remark shocked Bowles. "He uttered this sentiment with such a wicked working of the lower jaw and lip, and such an almost demon spirit in his whole face, that, quite disposed to be incredulous on those matters, I could not help thinking of the Mountain Meadows massacre, of Danites and Avenging Angels, and their reported achievements." Such atrocities in mind, Bowles politely refused an invitation to Rockwell's home for a bowlful of Utah's best strawberries and cream.[3]

The next day the guests attended a service at the Bowery, where Young, wearing a "solemn black" suit, explained church doctrine. The address, Bowles and Richardson noted, "lacked logic, lacked effect, lacked wholly magnetism or impressiveness. It was a curious medley of scriptural exposition, exhortation, bold and bare statement, coarse denunciation and vulgar allusions, cheap rant and cant." Young reaffirmed the Mormon belief in the Bible, said God had created Jesus "by the only process known to nature— just as men now create children," cited history to prove that Martin Luther and the Church of England had sanctioned polygamy, and declared that a dissatisfied English husband could still auction off his wife for a pot of beer or a shilling and take another girl. Young attributed Utah's troubles to "a few miserable, stinking lawyers who open offices on Whiskey-street and for $5 will prove that black is white!"[4]

The guests soon departed for California, but in October on the way home Richardson revisited Utah. This time he observed nothing conciliatory. "I have heard sermons here so disloyal," he informed his readers, "that they brought the blood to my cheeks." In one speech George Smith damned the United States and *"hoped to see the day when it would sink to hell."* That Sunday Kimball was even worse: "Colfax told us that they had wiped out one National cancer, and were now about to remove the other; that we should not be permitted to stay here more than three years longer." "This was a deliberate, unmitigated falsehood," fumed Richardson. "Mr. Colfax never said anything of the kind; but such statements serve to embitter the people, who receive as Gospel truth whatever their leaders tell them." A "large man, with an oily sensual face, and a bald head, which he protects by wearing his hat on nearly all occasions," Kimball was "one-third Aminidab Sleek, one-third John C. Calhoun (in disloyalty, not ability), and one-third circus-clown."

In his speech Kimball gave his interpretation of the War. *"The Abolitionists of the North stole the niggers and caused it all. The nigger was well off and happy. How do you know this, Brother Heber? Why God bless your soul, I used to live in the South, and I know! Now they have set the nigger free; and a beautiful thing they have done for him, haven't they? . . . They threatened to come here and destroy us. Let them come. I am the boy that will resist them. . . . Are the Governors our masters? No, sir, not for ME; they are our servants. We have our Apostolic Government. Brigham Young is our leader, our President, our Governor. I am Lieutenant Governor."*

Kimball also described the curative powers of the priesthood. *"Many was healed by touching the hem of my garments."* Two dying women miraculously recovered as soon as he baptized them.

In Utah, Richardson reported, jury trials were farcical, for Mormons never convicted a fellow Saint. The territory had no free schools, and Young controlled its few inadequate newspapers. At least four federal officials were polygamists who obeyed only Young: Stenhouse, now the postmaster of Salt Lake City; Jesse C. Little, the Assessor of Internal Revenue; Burton, the Collector of Internal Revenue; and Hosea Stout, the United States District Attorney. Almost daily, Richardson noted, the Mormon-dominated Nauvoo Legion paraded through Salt Lake City's streets. "I am fully persuaded that Young desires a show of collision—a little bloodshed. If some hot-headed officer of the Government could be irritated into the use of force, and kill half a dozen Mormons it would strengthen Brigham immeasurably, and do more to enthuse his present followers, and procure new converts all over the world than years of patient labor. The Church would live and thrive for half a century on a little martyrdom like this. After careful observation and reflection this is to me the only plausible theory of Brigham's conduct."[5]

I I

THE SOLDIERS FROM CAMP DOUGLAS and the war veterans who moved to Salt Lake City shared none of Richardson's apprehensions about the Legion. They laughed heartily when a pompous colonel rode by wearing the brass buttons of a brigadier, when a captain commanded his men to "stack bayonets," and when a column presented arms instead of looking to the right as it marched past Young's home.[6] Even the Legion's new drillmaster, an anti-American British general named Ross, could not whip it into an effective military force.[7]

Brigadier General Connor snickered too. After the war, he and his paper, the *Daily Union Vedette*, proved as troublesome to Young as during it. "There is not another community on the Continent," Young railed late in 1865, "which would have submitted for a week to the abuse to be heaped upon them that has now for years been systematically leveled at us by his organ, published until within a few weeks, at Camp Douglas under his immediate auspices and inspiration. Ingenuity is tortured to fill its columns with the vilest and most atrocious falsehoods respecting this community. Every day does this foul stream of slander and abuse roll forth, blackening and defaming every prominent citizen in the Territory." Connor must be removed.[8]

Hearing the Committee on Territories of the federal House of Representatives had asked Connor and Norman McLeod, the Congregationalist army chaplain, for information, Young grew apoplectic. "They had better send for Nero to give testimony against the Christians, and for Herod to ask him about the character of John the Baptist and whether Jesus is the Christ. This would be in keeping with what they wish to do for us."[9]

Realizing Young's worst fears, the Committee's report of July 1866 read as if Connor had written it. It noted that federal laws were "openly and defiantly" violated in Utah and praised the army for protecting lives and property.[10]

Still, Young found something cheerful in the army's proximity. "We would like you to find out, if you can, from the War Department what they will give for contracts another year for the troops in this vicinity, . . ." he wrote Hooper. "If you can secure the contract, and secure it in the name of Eldredge & Clawson, they will underbid Gilbert and also Barrow any way. They can do it cheaper and will do it cheaper; and if you cannot get it for Eldredge & Clawson, you might work it into the hands of Ben Holladay and Halsey."[11]

III

ONE HISTORIAN HAS RECENTLY ARGUED that Mormon history shows the tenacity of the Saints, who, despite several migrations, held on to such notions as collectivism and authoritarianism.[12] This cleverly argued thesis is an exaggeration, for Young changed Joseph Smith's Mormonism by opening polygamy to all Saints and by blowing up into a scheme for world conquest the outline for the Kingdom of God.

Like his predecessor, however, Young hated Gentiles. Even the army could not stop atrocities. One day in the mid-1860's Hickman, angered because a favorite wife had been refused credit, beat and dragged down a flight of stairs Fay Kimball, a clerk for Bell and Livingston, the merchants. Kimball was bedridden for several months and then left Utah. His uncle, the senior partner of

Kimball and Lawrence, complained to Young about the attack but, leaving the prophet's office, bumped into Hickman, who asked: "Well, what did you make of it?"[13]

On April 2, 1866, came the murder of S. Newton Brassfield for an unspeakable crime: marrying in a civil ceremony the plural wife of a Saint on a mission to Europe. Several days after the wedding, Brassfield was shot in the back a few steps from his hotel. He died within an hour.[14]

Recognizing only Mormon marriages, Young, who had taken Augusta Cobb, Zina Huntington, Lucy Decker, and Mary Van Cott from their husbands, publicly justified the murder. "Suppose," he asked, "a man should enter your house and decoy away from you a wife of yours, what would you do under the circumstances? I would lay judgment to the line and righteousness to the plummet, so help me God. . . . Were I absent from my home, I would rejoice to know that I had friends there to protect and guard the virtue of my household, and I would thank God for such friends."[15]

General William T. Sherman, the army commander in the West, disagreed. Hearing of the crime, he vowed to protect all citizens "regardless of religious faith. . . . Those murderers must be punished," he warned Young, "and if your people resort to measures of intimidation those must cease."[16]

The Mormons soon answered Sherman. Despite threats, John King Robinson, the thirty-one-year-old former army surgeon, had remained on a parcel of unoccupied land claimed by the church. Then at midnight on October 11, 1866, between twenty and thirty disguised men burned down his bowling alley. On the twentieth, under advice of counsel, Robinson visited the home of Salt Lake City's mayor and gave notice he intended to hold the city responsible for the damage. The incensed mayor ordered Robinson out of the house.

The next night a stranger came to Robinson's door, woke him up, and told him a mule had fallen on and broken his brother's leg. The man urged the doctor to help. Robinson hurriedly dressed and left. About seventy yards from his front porch he was hit over the head twice and shot through the brain. Witnesses saw three men running from the scene. The chief of police learned of the murder almost immediately, but he was not interested and went to bed. The mayor was told of the crime at ten o'clock the next morning.[17]

At the federal government's request ex-Governor John B. Weller of California investigated the incident. His report shocked even a community accustomed to the shedding of innocent blood. He noted that it took three days for the chief of police to reach the murder scene, blamed the atrocity on the Mormon church, and insisted there would have been no indifference had Robinson been a Saint.

Desiring the Mormon version of the crime, a New York *Evening Post* reporter visited Young, who, as often during the past twenty years, had recently created an atmosphere for violence by vowing from the pulpit to allot claim jumpers "a claim six feet by two, which they can hold till the resurrection day!" Young told the correspondent that some wretch had undoubtedly been paid ten dollars to kill Robinson, one of the worst men he ever knew. "He was sarsy and impudent," Young charged, "and pushed himself forward, right against *us*." Young had expected Robinson to "die in the ditch, like a dog, as he'd ha' done, if he'd gone on." Instead of burning Robinson's bowling alley at night, the mob should have "gone through" it in daylight. "I'd have gutted it at noon; torn it down and destroyed it in the light of day, so that every man might see me." Turning to a favorite subject, Young called Utah's federal judges "a set of prejudiced scoundrels" and warned "they'd better be careful, or they'd have to get out of this place. Yes, I'll put them out myself, pretty soon; send 'em home by a short cut." Utah's Gentiles were "lazy, good-for-nothing fortune-hunters" and were trying to drown the city in bars and houses of prostitution and drag it down to the level of the "so-called civilized cities, like Denver, San Francisco, or New York," but Young promised that "these bad men haven't seen anything like the worst yet, if they persist in their course."[18]

Coupled with Young's interview, the Robinson murder, which was never solved, chilled Gentile spines. In fear McLeod moved to Camp Douglas. Connor too was shocked. "I have not dared to go on the streets of Salt Lake after dark since the assassination of Dr. Robinson," he wrote General Dodge early in 1867, "except when accompanied by a number of friends. . . . Unless some change takes place I shall leave my property, $35,000 worth, and start for California in the spring."[19]

IV

LIFE IN UTAH was not always morbid. Besides women and danc-ing, Young loved the theater, first becoming interested in it in the mid-1850's, when Phil Margetts, a British convert, formed the Mechanics Dramatic Association and invited the prophet to a per-formance. The next evening Young and Kimball brought all their wives and children.[20]

In 1861 Young broke ground for a new Salt Lake City theater, employing about two hundred men on the project, his private enterprise. At one Sunday service he asked twenty-five masons to work on the building, promising that once it was finished he would put all energy into the great Salt Lake City temple. He agreed to pay the masons in admission tickets. The congregation unani-mously approved his request.[21]

The theater, the finest in the West, opened on December 24, 1862. It was 144 feet long, eighty feet wide, forty-six feet high, and sat eighteen hundred people. Young occasionally occupied a rocking chair in the middle of the parquet, but he usually sat in one of two private boxes. The scenery, costumes, and supporting players were Utah products; the stars were Gentiles from traveling companies.[22]

Because coins were scarce, the Saints bartered for tickets. "If they want to go to the theater," one visitor observed, "they take along a couple of dozen eggs, a pumpkin, peck of apples or any 'plunder' they may have, to trade for a ticket." "Chickens are taken at the box-office of Brigham Young's theater," the New York *Tribune* explained, "and change is appropriately made with eggs." "All go," Dodge related, "young and old, big and small, babies and all."[23] But as much as they loved the theater, loyal Saints whispered for years that Young had built it with money that should have gone into the temple, which he never completed.[24]

Shocked by several of the plays performed, Young issued in 1865 a manifesto that called recreation the purpose of the theater, instructed actors to use proper language and gestures, and forbade oaths and expressions like "I swear" and "by heavens." Forgetting how his speeches incited violence, he also prohibited representations of villainy and murder. Accordingly, in 1869 Young closed a bloody production of *Oliver Twist* after one performance.[25]

In that same year Lydia Thompson, whose statuesque British Blondes were internationally notorious for the lewd cancan they performed in abbreviated costumes and for their bawdy exchanges with the males in their audience, exclaimed to a reporter: "I want to go to Utah! I want to go to Utah!" Then second thoughts hit. "I wonder if Mr. Young would let us perform in his theater. I believe he insists upon long petticoats, and you know we could not dance in them."[26]

V

THE THEATER GAVE WAY to more serious matters. As early as 1852 Young and the Utah legislature had urged that Congress sponsor a railroad to the Pacific. The next year, repeating his prediction that rails would join the territory to the East by 1861, the prophet pointed out that the road would enable "our brethren from abroad to come out here without walking, as many are now compelled to do."[27]

"Friend Douglas," Young wrote the chairman of the Senate Committee on Territories in 1854. "What are you going to do about a Railroad to the Pacific? Will you advocate the Route by the Box Elder Pass in the Black Hills, Bridger's Pass in the Rocky Mountains, Timpanogos or Provo Canyon, &c., as the best line for the first Railway to be built from the Missouri to the Pacific, or what do you think of it? You need not be shy in expressing your views on this subject, for rest assured that whatever route that Road takes it will be the very best one for the interests of Utah, and precisely where we had rather have it."[28] The following year John M. Bernhisel, Utah's Congressional delegate, suggested to Douglas a line from Fort Riley, Kansas, to Bridger's Pass and Salt Lake City. He argued that it would enable the military to control the West.[29]

In 1862, after Congress passed the Pacific Railroad Act, Young personally hawked shares of the Union Pacific Railroad Company, which planned to build west from the Missouri River. Sure the project would make Utah the commercial center of the United States, he himself bought five thousand shares, becoming the firm's fourth largest shareholder and a member of its board of directors.[30]

When the Union Pacific began preliminary surveys, Young, whose son, Joseph, was in charge of the crews in Utah, bragged that the China trade would soon cross the territory. One road across the continent today would, he predicted, show the need for two tomorrow.[31]

After the Civil War, the work went fast. "Hurry up," Young urged in 1867 as the track stretched through Nebraska and into Wyoming, "hasten the work! We want to hear the iron horse puffing down this valley. What for? To bring our brethren and sisters here."[32]

Then, late in August, two famous Civil War generals rode into the Great Basin on railroad business. Grenville Dodge, Council Bluffs' great citizen-soldier, was now the chief engineer of the Union Pacific, and John A. Rawlins was Ulysses S. Grant's chief of staff. "The Mormons give us great attention," Dodge reported to his wife. "Brigham Young at the head, and was very talkative. His wife, Amelia Folsom of the Bluffs, was with him." Young and Dodge discussed the Central Pacific Railroad, building east from Sacramento toward the Union Pacific, and a grading contract for the Saints.[33]

One seemingly insignificant incident marred the return trip east. "The day before we left Salt Lake," Dodge recorded, "Brigham Young and the apostles started north on the same route for their yearly conference tour. They moved very slowly and at every settlement and town in the valley all the people turned out with bands and flags and gave Brigham and his party a great reception. We generally followed into the same towns a few hours later and although we had a long train with 200 soldiers and with General Rawlins, General Grant's distinguished chief, there was no reception given, no flags came out and it caused Rawlins to think that there was not much patriotism or love of the Government in the valley but I told him that that was not so that it was simply because these people were mostly foreigners and knew nothing about our Government and no one else except those connected with the Mormon Church."[34] The prophet would pay dearly for this affront.

In 1868 Young came to terms with both transcontinental railroads. In May he agreed to grade, bridge, and tunnel for the Union Pacific the route from Echo Canyon to Salt Lake City, about 150 miles, for $2,125,000 and in September consented to build two hundred miles for the Central Pacific for about four million dollars. To the Saints these contracts seemed a godsend, obviating the necessity of importing to Utah thousands of Gentile laborers and providing jobs at two dollars a day for five to seven thousand men idled by a disastrous invasion of huge grasshoppers.[35]

But Sidney Dillon, the president of the Union Pacific, was not so sure the contracts came from heaven. He believed Young had bribed Thomas C. Durant, the road's vice-president, and Silas S. Seymour and Samuel B. Reed, two engineers. "When you see any of them," Dillon instructed Dodge, "if you work it right you can find out all about it. Make them all believe that we are glad. I would give almost anything to know if it is so. It would be a good point. Be sure you speak of it."[36]

In a broadside "To the Brethren Working on My Railroad Contract," Young showed that practical matters sometimes overshadowed religion. "It is my wish and counsel to all the brethren who are working on my contract," he advised in September 1868, "to push the work ahead with all possible dispatch during the fine weather as we cannot count on its long continuance and for this reason I deem it advisable for none of you to leave your work to attend Conference, but wait until next April, when we can meet and enjoy ourselves with the satisfaction of knowing we have finished this work appointed to us in the providence of God. Therefore brethren work at it, until the job is completed and you shall have the prayers and blessing of Your brother in the Gospel, Brigham Young." In red ink at the left Young's secretary added: "besides getting your money."[37]

As the rival roads approached Utah, Young insisted they build into Salt Lake City, now a bustling community of twenty thousand people. Instead, Dodge recommended a line around the northern end of the lake. Forty miles shorter than the route Young favored, it contained "*fine water*, fine grass, considerable timber on mountain sides and at the base, fine farming lands in valleys." The southern passage, Dodge informed General Sherman, "could never be adopted on sound principle." Sherman liked the choice for another reason. The "good people" who would eventually occupy the land along Dodge's route would "make a colony that will trouble our friend Brigham about as the old Connecticut onion patches troubled the Knickerbockers of New York." Polygamy would soon die.[38]

The decision infuriated Young. He called Dodge to his office and announced that God wanted the road to enter Salt Lake City. The country through which Dodge wanted to build would, he added, give the company less business. Unless Dodge yielded, the Saints would stop building and leave the Union Pacific where it was. After arguing back and forth, Dodge remembered, "he finally became really angry, and with expressions of extreme displeasure soon put an end to the interview."

The next Sunday, August 16, 1868, at services attended by Reed, Seymour, Dodge, and Dodge's wife and daughter, Young renewed the attack. "He had a good command of the English language," Dodge related, "although he did not use very pure English and his manners were very aggressive and I could see that it was for the benefit of his people, especially as he had always told them up to this time that the railroad would go through Salt Lake City and on the south end of the lake. . . . At any rate he alarmed my people very much and they were very anxious for me to get out of Salt Lake, but it did not alarm me any." When the Central Pacific also decided to build around the northern end of the lake, Young relented and escorted Dodge's wife and daughter to the Lion House for a visit with his children.[39]

As the Union Pacific crossed the plains and mountains, towns arose at each temporary terminus. Some soon dried up and perished, but Corinne, about eighty miles from Salt Lake City on the Bear River near the northern end of the lake, prospered. As rough and quarrelsome as an unlicked cub, it was, unlike nearby Ogden, Gentile-dominated.

Fearing his enemies would control the transcontinental's junction point, Young in a meeting in Ogden on January 1, 1869, ordered the brethren there to sell him all available land for fifty dollars an acre. With fifteen thousand dollars furnished by Young and ten thousand from Hooper, the church purchased five hundred acres of land, much of it worth three times what Young paid for it. The two companies then accepted Young's offer to make Ogden their terminus.[40]

Still Corinne prospered. For years Gentiles told how Young in frustration rode to the river bank opposite Corinne, lifted his hands skyward, and called down a curse on the town. The prophet predicted Corinne would soon wither away, but it continued to grow. Young forbade his people to trade at Corinne, but they ignored him and his thunderbolts of wrath fell harmlessly into the Bear Valley. The happy Gentiles of Corinne bragged that they had faced the dragon and that "his eyes are made of glass, and his tail is filled with sofa-springs."[41]

As the Union Pacific neared completion, stealing became widespread. "I know of hundreds of faults and frauds, . . ." one engineer confided to Dodge's friends. "I know of Brigham Young shipping new wagons (under pretense of work on grade) which he hauled to Salt Lake and sold—the report of it being made and squashed."[42]

Wracked by inefficiency, the finished roads could not pay Young. The Central Pacific owed him a million dollars, the Union Pacific a million and a quarter. The Central Pacific finally paid him $800,000, and in September 1869 Young settled with the Union Pacific for $600,000 in iron and rolling stock. In all, however, Young made only about $88,000 in profit on the Union Pacific contracts.[43]

With this equipment the Saints started the Utah Central Railroad to connect Salt Lake City with Ogden and the transcontinental. Young was president of the line, William Jennings vice-president, Joseph A. Young general superintendent, John W. Young secretary, and Wells treasurer. But Young's settlement failed to benefit the Saints who had worked on his contracts. They were paid, if at all, in Utah Central bonds, which sold at first for about thirty-five cents on the dollar. Most of the bonds eventually went back to Young, who accepted them for tithing at eighty cents on the dollar. Those who had left their farms and workshops to build the Union Pacific ended up penniless.[44]

All this made financing the Utah Central difficult. Men willing to accept payment in company stock took grading contracts, and laborers agreed to wait for their pay until the road was solvent. Happily, on January 10, 1870, the line, crossing some of the territory's most fertile land, was finished. The last spike, made of Utah iron, bore on top a beehive and the inscription "Holiness to the Lord: Utah Central Railroad." A few minutes past two P.M., as fifteen thousand guests looked on, Young sledge-hammered it home. Then came a salute by thirty-seven guns, one for each mile of road. Three Mormon bands and one from Camp Douglas entertained, and Young, Taylor, and Jennings spoke. That evening a ball was held in the Salt Lake City theater.[45] The city of the Saints was joined to the outside world.

V I

GENTILES POURED INTO UTAH on every train, but Young joked that "his was a damn poor religion if it wouldn't stand one railroad."[46] The year following the completion of the line saw more distinguished visitors in the Territory than ever before. The summer of 1869 brought Senator Lyman Trumbull and Governor Richard J. Oglesby of Illinois. Then came Benjamin F. Wade, the former president of the United States Senate, General Philip Sheridan, and Senator Roscoe Conkling of New York. Seward arrived and chatted about his house in Auburn, New York, which Young had helped build. And General Tom Thumb, the age's greatest attraction, packed Young's theater.[47]

In October the most celebrated party returned. But Colfax, now the Vice-President of the United States, Bowles, and Bross—Richardson had been murdered in New York during a lovers' quarrel —still resented the remarks Young had made that April about President Grant and Colfax. "Who goes to the White House in these days?" Young had inquired. "A gambler and a drunkard. And the Vice-President is the same. And no man can get either office unless he is a gambler and a drunkard or a thief. And who goes to Congress? You may hunt clear through the Senate and House, and if you can find any men that are not liars, thieves, whoremongers, gamblers, and drunkards. I tell you they are mighty few, for no other kind of men can get in there."[48]

In the first public arraignment of polygamy ever delivered in Utah, Colfax conceded the Saints could worship God as they pleased but pointed out that *The Book of Mormon* scolded David and Solomon for having "many wives and concubines." When Colfax recalled Young's insult, a Gentile who swore he heard the statement fought with and knocked down a Saint who said the prophet never uttered it and was arrested, fined fifty dollars, and jailed overnight by a Mormon magistrate.

Following Colfax's talk and one by Bross, Orrin Porter Rockwell struggled to the front of the audience. "I've heard the great men speak," he shouted, "and I know I can make a speech too. I know every one of you, and I'm going to show you up. . . . I'm going to tell, I'm going to tell. I never killed anybody that didn't want to be killed! I never murdered anybody that didn't want to be murdered!" He promised to write a book about his exploits.[49]

Soon thereafter, the greatest showman on earth arrived. "Barnum," Young asked, "what will you give to exhibit me in New York and the Eastern cities?" "Well, Mr. President," Phineas T. Barnum replied, "I'll give you half the receipts, which I will guarantee shall be $200,000 per year, for I consider you the best show in America."[50]

VII

SALT LAKE CITY CHANGED CONSIDERABLY between Bowles's visits. "The new tabernacle, like an immense, long wooden bowl, bottom-side-up, rises in the center of the city—an offense to the eye, but a wonderful receptacle for the multitude." The increase in population, Bowles added, meant more farms and cottages in the outer areas, and several elegant homes had been built. But the most important change was not physical. The railroad had destroyed the city's trade monopoly with the outlying regions. Camp Douglas, Corinne, or any other hostile community might now be supplied from the outside by rail. No longer, as in the 1857 war, could an army be starved. "The old sources of prosperity are clearly gone," Bowles shrewdly observed; "the wise of the Mormon leaders see the fact and are reaching out for new ones; but they do not generally understand the price they must pay for them."[51] Unable to cope with new ideas, Young ignored Bowles's warning.

A high army officer put it even more succinctly. "We used to have some anxiety about Utah," he observed to the New York *Herald*. "That is over. In forty-eight hours we can pour in all the troops wanted. There need be no more uneasiness about the rebellion of Brigham Young. His day is over."[52]

Other things were also different. Jennings, the rich Salt Lake City merchant, noted how the railroad brought to Utah "higher civilization and education." Before it arrived, "Boys eighteen or twenty years old, sons of Brigham Young and other dignitaries, satisfied their highest ambition when they would ride about the town on horseback, dressed fantastically, with beaten leggings, Spanish spurs, soft slouch hat with fur twisted around it and hanging down like a coon's tail. A Bowie-knife would be stuck in their legging, and they would race about the place shouting and halloaing as they went. They were in no way above the cow-boy of to-day and played the part of a Mexican or Spanish rough."[53]

Like a ceremony in the Endowment House, the driving home of the transcontinental's final spike sealed the Saints to the country from which they had fled. "When I crossed the Plains with my family," George Smith noted, "it took me 105 days from the Missouri River to this point; now it hardly requires the same number of hours."[54]

Mormon immigration was dramatically affected. Putting the cost of traveling from Great Britain and Scandinavia to Utah at £100 a family, Brigham Young, Jr., estimated in October 1869 that the church used to spend $500,000 annually for five hundred fully provisioned wagons, each drawn by eight oxen, to transport converts from the Missouri to the Great Basin. "The journey then generally took three months; now it is accomplished in fifty hours."[55]

If the railroad came in, it also went out. Dodge described how one of Young's daughters tried in October 1868 to reach the

Union Pacific's track and the East. "I was taking Miss Young along for the purpose of visiting one of the bishops, her people asking me to do so. When we reached the bishop, I supposed Miss Young would stop there. I was away from my train all day and when I returned at night, I found her still with the train working her way east, evidently trying to get out of Utah. I knew it would not do for me to aid her in escaping and told her that she would have to return to the bishop's house. She protested very strongly and I greatly sympathized with her. I learned that they were trying to induce her to be sealed to one of the bishops as a plural wife, but I told her frankly that I could not help her escape from the territory but that I would write to Brigham Young about the matter, which I did. I wrote a very strong letter giving him all the facts in the matter. He stopped the marriage, I think, more from the fact that I did not propose to make any publicity of the matter unless the girl was forced to accept their bishop, but if she did, the story had become so well known among my party that it would be impossible to keep it a secret."[56]

VIII

YOUNG VIEWED THE RAILROAD with mixed feelings, welcoming the opportunity to gather his people but fearing Gentile goods, styles, and ideas. At the First Presidency's insistence Eliza Snow directed the establishment of units of the Women's Relief Society, whose principal task was to stifle interest in Eastern extravagances. For girls, several of the prophet's daughters, led by Emily Clawson, Dora and Phoebe Young, and Caroline Croxkall, formed branches of the Retrenchment Society, whose resolutions denounced dragging skirts as a waste of material, called short ones "disgusting," ridiculed the Grecian Bend as "a burlesque on the natural beauty and dignity of the human female form," and praised homemade clothes.[57]

"Ladies," Young told a church conference, "do not be extravagant. If we ask you to make your dresses a little shorter, do not cut them so short that you expose the top of your stockings. Dress neatly and in a comely way, and in a manner that will be considered strictly chaste. . . . We are going to cut off the foolish trade we have indulged in and maintain ourselves in every necessity of life."[58]

Young helped ladies, and they helped him. In 1870 the church-dominated territorial legislature enfranchised women, and in return Eliza Snow, Harriet Cook, and Zina Huntington sponsored meetings defending polygamy. "I would observe that General Washington is a member of this Church and Kingdom," Sarah M. Kimball, who in Nauvoo had rejected Joseph Smith's marriage proposal with the comment that he teach polygamy to someone else, informed one such gathering. "I was present when Judge Adams of Springfield was baptized for Washington."[59]

For men, Young organized in December 1867 the School of the Prophets, named for the body Smith had started in 1833. The nine hundred members of its Salt Lake City branch tried to limit outside influence and keep wages low so that local products might compete with imported goods.[60]

Young loved to brag about Mormon self-sufficiency. He once pointed to a chandelier in his theater and asked Ludlow its cost and place of manufacture. Ludlow guessed Young had probably paid a thousand dollars for it in New York. "Capital," shouted the prophet. "*I* made it myself. That circle is a *cart-wheel*, the wheel of one of our common ox-carts. I had it washed, and gilded it with my own hands. It hangs by a pair of ox-chains, which I also gilded; and the gilt ornaments of the candlesticks were all cut after patterns out of sheet tin."[61]

In 1867 Young ordered a boycott of Gentile establishments. "We trust," Orson Pratt advised, "that the Saints in that mountain Territory have goodness and virtue sufficient to follow out strictly the 'let alone policy,' that the merchandise of these unscrupulous hell-hounds may rot in their foul holds, or seek a market in some other quarter of the globe. To trade with these miscreants, is to trade with the devil; and he that trades with the devil, is sure to sell his soul."[62]

In justification of this policy Young continually cited Smith's warning to him in July 1833: "Never spend another day to build up a Gentile city, but spend your days, dollars, and dimes for the up-building of the Zion of God upon the earth, to promote peace and righteousness and to prepare for the coming of the Son and

Man, and he that does not abide this law will suffer loss." Saints should trade with Saints even if it cost more to do so. "You may answer that is none of my d—d business," Young warned. "Perhaps it is none, just now, but the time will come soon when it will be my business to testify respecting this people, and I pledge you that those who disobey this command shall *not* enter into the straight gate." Looking over the audience, McClure, who heard the speech, "saw poor infatuated Mormons shudder at this terrible anathema from what they supposed to be an inspired oracle of God, and the fear of his malediction is one of the strongest elements of cohesiveness with the deluded masses of his followers."[63]

In October 1868 Young announced the formation of Zion's Co-operative Mercantile Institution, which would be owned and operated by church members. The firm would provide a wholesale outlet for the entire city and retail branches for each ward. "We came to this valley to establish the Kingdom of God," Young said, "and it is not right that some of us should grow rich by trading, while the majority of us remain poor. It is time to give the people of God the profits upon the business they create—to give each Saint all that he consumes at the lowest cost price."[64]

Of Salt Lake City's important Mormon merchants only the four Walker brothers, whose store was worth half a million dollars, refused to join the cooperative and display its square sign, the all-seeing eye of Jehovah in the center and the words "Holiness to the Lord" on top and "Zion's Co-operative Mercantile Institution" on the bottom. Boldly expanding their store into the finest in the territory, the brothers drastically cut their prices and made Young swallow his boast that he would buy their store for a song. By 1873 they had, according to one observer, a hundred thousand customers and took in six million dollars a year. Their stock sold for a hundred dollars a share and paid a twenty per cent dividend.[65] But in the heat of the struggle the Mormons sang:

> "Brigham Young may I go buy?"
> "Yes, my son and daughter.
> You can buy from the good
> Co-op, but don't go near the Walker."[66]

Stirring up memories of the Kirtland fiasco of 1837, the church also entered the banking business, taking over Hooper and Eldredge's small establishment, which it renamed the Bank of Deseret. The firm eventually became the leading financial institution in the territory, but in the beginning Young's greediness almost doomed it, for whenever the church needed money he dunned to death rich Saints. Knowing that a wealthy man who refused to give lost his standing in the church, prosperous Mormons often hid their wealth in the Gentile First National Bank.[67]

IX

TO STIFLE THE MORMON DESIRE for outside goods Young enforced Joseph Smith's revelation, "The Word of Wisdom," which counseled Saints to abstain from tobacco, alcohol, and hot drinks, to use wine only "to offer up your Sacraments before Him," and to eat meat only in winter. Young once described the circumstances under which Smith received the revelation. In Kirtland in August 1833 Smith, to teach his people "the great work they were called to accomplish," founded the original School of the Prophets. "The brethren came to that place for hundreds of miles to attend school in a little room no larger than eleven by fourteen. When they assembled together in this room after breakfast, the first they did was to light their pipes, and, while smoking, talk about the great things of the kingdom, and spit all over the room, and as soon as the pipe was out of their mouths a large chew of tobacco would be taken. Often when the Prophet entered the room to give the school instructions he would find himself in a cloud of tobacco smoke. This, and the complaints of his wife at having to clean so filthy a floor, made the Prophet think upon the matter, and he inquired of the Lord relating to the conduct of the Elders in using tobacco, and the revelation known as the Word of Wisdom was the result of his inquiry."[68]

For decades the Saints ignored the Word. Young admitted buying in 1837 "a fine tavern establishment, which was situated in Auburn, directly across the street from the gate of the Penitentiary, which property I still own."[69]

In Nauvoo the Mormons drank heavily. As a merchant's account book shows, Hiram Kimball, Sarah's husband, ran up sizable bills for rum, whiskey, brandy, and wine, and Hyrum Smith bought three quarts of brandy within two months.[70] Theodore Turley, whose daughter married and then deserted Young, repeatedly advertised his brewery in the local papers,[71] and in December 1843 the Mormon-controlled City Council authorized Joseph Smith to sell liquor in his hotel.[72]

In Utah the church dominated the liquor trade. In 1856 Caleb Green freighted six tons of tobacco, rum, whiskey, brandy, tea, and coffee across the plains for Young,[73] and two years later *The New York Times* reported that the "principal drinking-saloon and gambling-room are in Salt Lake House, a building under the control of the Church and the immediate superintendency of Heber C. Kimball."[74] On January 2, 1860, Young's secretary noted: "William C. Staines presented the President with a bottle of black currant wine of his own making."[75]

Young tried his best to rid himself of rival brewers. In the summer of 1861 he sent Salt Lake City's two chief distillers on missions to the Uintah Valley and closed their factories.[76] Then at Cottonwood in 1867 he denounced another brewer, William Howard, who fearlessly rose and called Young a liar. The prophet had Howard ejected from the meeting and told the congregation to tear down Howard's home and factory, but the worshippers ignored him.[77]

Facing the loss of its remaining specie if the Saints bought Eastern tobacco and liquor, both of which were better than Utah products, the church revived the Word in 1867. To those who said they would perish without tobacco and liquor, Young answered: "Then die, and die in the faith, instead of living and breaking the requests of heaven."[78]

Saints who covered the Tabernacle floor with tobacco juice also irked Young. "I want to say to the doorkeeper that when you see gentlemen who cannot omit chewing and spitting while in this house, request them to leave; and if such persons refuse to leave, and continue their spitting, just take them and lead them out carefully and kindly. We do not want to have the house thus defiled. It is an imposition for gentlemen to spit tobacco juice around, or to leave their quids of tobacco on the floor; they dirty the house, and if a lady happens to besmear the bottom of her dress, which can hardly be avoided, it is highly offensive. We therefore request all gentlemen attending Conference to omit tobacco chewing while here."[79]

In his own house Young strictly enforced the Word, serving only milk and water at meals.[80] Knowing the Mormon attitude toward tobacco, six Gentile cadets at West Point in 1872 cornered Young's recently appointed son, Willard, shoved a plug in his mouth, and commanded him to chew or die. He yielded but vowed to fight a dozen cadets if they tried to make him do it again.[81]

XIV

⎍⎍⎍⎍⎍

Who Speaks for God?

I

B
Y 1870 THREE MORMON CHURCHES asserted they held the
priesthood. In 1856 two disappointed converts disposed
of Strang, the leader of the first great splinter group, but other
men chosen by God soon replaced him. One of them was Joseph
Smith III, the son of the first Mormon prophet.

Despite their fierce battles, these warring Mormon factions had
a great deal in common. Young, Joseph Smith III, Strang, and the
rest considered Joseph Smith, Jr., a prophet of the Lord, and *The
Book of Mormon* divine. Each man, however, said he led the holy
priesthood, insisted he alone talked to God, called himself Smith's
successor, and denounced his rivals as agents of Satan.

Mentally if not physically, the Mormon prophets came in one
size and shape, and power struggles revolved about such minor
questions as who had begun polygamy and the Mormon attitude
toward mining. The dissenters revolted against Brigham Young,
not Joseph Smith, Jr., against the *Deseret News* and the *Millennial
Star,* not *The Book of Mormon,* against Eliza Snow's poetry, not
Smith's revelations.

After the first prophet's death, Strang became Young's principal rival, setting up his kingdom on Beaver Island in Lake Michigan and crowning himself King Strang in July 1850. George J. Adams later testified that while portraying St. Paul during the coronation he wore the stage costume in which he once played Richard III.

Like Smith, Young, and the other prophets, Strang possessed boundless ambition. Elected to the Michigan legislature in 1852, he concocted a scheme to create within the state a Mormon territory he would rule. The plan got nowhere. Then, promising to destroy the Brighamites, he asked Secretary of the Interior Robert McClelland, a native of Michigan, to appoint him governor of Utah. Strang's dreams ended with his life on July 9, 1856, after two followers shot him. He was buried in an unmarked grave.[1]

Soon another rival threatened Young. Vowing to establish his own Kingdom of God, Joseph Morris stressed the imminence of Christ's reappearance on earth, called Young a charlatan, and promised to lead an army that would, in turn, conquer Utah, the United States, and the world. As often as twice a day he spoke to God. He preserved over three hundred of the revelations he received between 1860 and 1862 and did not even bother to write down many others.

On the bottom lands of the Weber River, about forty miles from Salt Lake City, Morris and five hundred converts built a colony. They lived in brush huts, held all property in common, did almost no work, and simply waited for Christ to arrive. Their food supply dwindled rapidly.[2]

As Sumner Howard, the United States District Attorney for Utah, later observed, the deaths of Morris and three of his followers equaled the Mountain Meadows massacre in brutality. In 1863 Young sent a posse under Sheriff Robert T. Burton to break up the colony and, according to Howard, kill Morris. Although the sheriff found a peaceful scene at the river, he immediately set up his three cannons and opened fire on the dissenters, killing several of them. The Morrisites briefly withstood the siege but then ceased all resistance, stacked their arms, and allowed Burton to enter their camp. Still on horseback, Burton called Morris out and fired point-blank four times. Morris fell dead at Burton's feet. The sheriff next turned on John Banks, Morris's first counselor, wounding him slightly in the neck. When Mrs. John Bowman shouted "This is cold-blooded murder," Burton shot her dead too. A second woman called it "another Mountain Meadows massacre," and Burton added her to his list. Dr. Jeter Clinton, the Mormon police justice and coroner of Salt Lake City, subsequently finished Banks off by inserting a surgeon's knife into the neck wound, twisting it, and unjointing the neck. The bodies of Morris and Banks were brought to Salt Lake City, kept in City Hall until midnight, and then secretly buried. "Now this is not conjecture nor speculation, . . ." Howard informed the United States Attorney General. "I have taken the evidence of at least six witnesses as to the killing of Morris and the two women by Burton and established the fact, beyond a doubt, that it was done in the manner above stated after the surrender." These crimes were "committed *by the direct order* of Brigham Young."

In 1877 a Grand Jury of fifteen men, only two of whom were Saints, indicted Burton and Clinton for these murders. But, Howard explained, Burton's appearance before a United States Commissioner brought chaos. "The room was immediately filled with Mormon policemen, (all Danites and several of them murderers whose crimes are being inquired into by the Grand Jury)." Halfway through the proceedings Wells "rushed into the room in great excitement, and with threats and menaces informed me that 'these investigations and arrests of their best men must stop or I would see trouble. That the Mormon people were excited and that I would bring on a crisis quicker than I wished or contemplated.' I kept as quiet as possible in order to avoid an inevitable outbreak. The Commissioner granted a motion for a continuance and allowed Burton to go on $10,000 bail."[3] Like his predecessors, Howard accomplished nothing, for a jury of Saints and Gentiles acquitted Burton.[4]

If gossip is to be believed, the episode brought Young and Burton closer together. In 1869 the New York *World*'s Utah correspondent reported: "A rumor prevails at present in Salt Lake City, which I have heard repeated by several persons, that the present leader of the Danites is Robert Burton, Sheriff of Salt Lake County and Major-General of the Nauvoo Legion, who murdered the Morrisite prophet, his first counselor, and a Morrisite woman in cold blood, and who is now on a mission to New

York. I give this, however, as mere rumor, not knowing personally the truth of the story."[5]

I I

THE SMITH FAMILY was a far graver threat to Young than either
Strang or Morris. Until the day he died Young could not forgive
Emma Smith for rejecting him after her husband's death, for marrying instead the dashing Gentile, Major Lewis Bidamon, and for
remaining in Nauvoo as a saloonkeeper.[6]

Forever after the rejected suitor lashed out at the plural wife he
lost. Emma was, Young informed a reporter in 1866, "the damndest liar that ever lived." Several times she had attempted to poison
Joseph, who barely escaped.[7]

Young also reminded his followers that Emma had tried to
destroy the revelation on celestial marriage. After getting it from
God, Smith gave it to Bishop Newel K. Whitney. Hearing about it,
Emma nagged her husband ceaselessly. "Joseph," she stormed,
"you promised me that revelation, and if you are a man of your
word you will give it to me." But as soon as she put her hands on
it, she thrust it into the fireplace, held a candle to it, and watched
it turn to ashes. Luckily, however, Whitney had kept a copy. "She
thought that was the end of it," Young scoffed, "and she will be
damned as sure as she is a living woman. Joseph used to say that
he would have her hereafter, if he had to go to hell for her, and he
will have to go to hell for her as sure as he ever gets her."[8]

Refusing to believe Joseph had sanctioned polygamy, some
Saints had rallied about Granville Hedrick, who in the 1850's led
a small colony in Illinois. In what is now an exceedingly rare
pamphlet Hedrick called plural marriage "a soul sickening doctrine to any man who wishes to keep the commandments of God,
and revere the wholesome laws of the land—who respects himself,
his family, his neighbors; that man or woman who is purely chaste
in Jesus Christ will abhor such a doctrine, with all their soul, and
keep as distant from it as they would from death."[9]

Soon a vastly more attractive figure assumed command of the
movement. On April 6, 1860, thirty years to the day after his
father established the Mormon church, Joseph Smith III became

in Amboy, Illinois, the prophet, seer, and revelator of what became the Reorganized Church of Jesus Christ of Latter-day Saints. Holding "in entire abhorrence" Young's pronouncements, Smith declared: "I have been told that my father promulgated these same doctrines—the doctrines of Young. This I never did believe, and I never can believe it, for the doctrines were not promulgated by divine authority; and I believe that my father was a good man, and no good man could have promulgated such odious doctrines."[10]

Except for polygamy, the Josephites, or Reorganites, closely resembled the Brighamites they so detested. In varying degrees, both leaders conversed with heavenly beings, received revelations, spoke in tongues, miraculously healed the sick, and cast out devils. Each led a church that had a prophet and twelve apostles. Most important of all, each claimed the priesthood. The Josephites differed only in leadership and their belief in monogamy.[11]

Fighting a rear guard action against the Smith family, Young banned in 1865 the book, *Biographical Sketches of Joseph Smith the Prophet,* by Lucy Smith, the mother of the first prophet, and assailed Orson Pratt for originally publishing it. For years the Josephites told how Young prowled about every settlement in Utah and tossed into the fire every copy of the work he found, explaining that it contained "more lies than Lucifer ever told." The book, a disjointed, uncritical account unworthy of the notoriety it received, was far too favorable to Emma.[12]

In 1869 came a confrontation. Alexander Hale Smith and David Hyrum Smith, young Joseph's brothers, arrived in Salt Lake City seeking converts. David's attitude toward the Utah church especially hurt Young, who recalled that shortly before being murdered on June 27, 1844, Joseph Smith, Jr., had prophesied that "the man was not born who was to lead this people, but of Emma Smith should be born a son who would succeed in the Presidency after a season of disturbance." David's birthday was November 17, 1844.[13]

The brothers visited and quarreled with Young, who called their mother a liar and a thief and refused to let them speak in the Tabernacle, forcing them instead to hold Sunday services in the smaller Independence Hall, which Gentiles used. At the meeting in Young's office Eliza Snow and Zina Huntington testified they had been sealed to Joseph in Nauvoo, but the boys refused to believe them.[14]

Asked about the incident by the New York *Tribune*, Young scoffed that Alexander publicly denied his father had been a polygamist but privately had broken down and admitted Emma had "told him all about it. O, they are weak babies," Young mocked, "unworthy of their illustrious father, and vainly striving to tear down what he built up. . . . I have a great affection for them, nevertheless, and would gladly extend to them the honors and privileges of the church. But I am sorry to say they have had bad training, and have not wisdom to discern the right for themselves."[15]

III

No COINCIDENCE BROUGHT DAVID AND ALEXANDER to Salt Lake City with the opening of the railroad, for many outsiders—and outside ideas—rode the rails into Utah. Of these notions few had greater appeal than nationalism. In an age marked by the unification of Germany and Italy, the consolidation of British North America into the Dominion of Canada, and the Northern triumph in the American Civil War, nationalism also rocked the Utah church.

Those converts who followed Young's advice and migrated to the New World found the Great Basin no melting pot. In Utah Young, desiring his people to be Mormons, not Americans, constantly denounced the United States. Consequently the Europeans who gathered in the West remained Europeans. A Welsh Saint considered himself a Welshman, and an English Mormon remained an Englishman.

By 1869 this anti-Americanism turned against its creator, and the Saints split into national factions. For years the Americans who had controlled the church since its founding had been growing weaker. As the New York *Sun* pointed out in 1868, "The additions to the Mormon Church are drawn mainly from the Old World, as but few Americans are now converted to that belief." About then Young himself acknowledged that three out of every four American Saints had apostatized. George Smith said it was five out of six.[16]

To retain power Young constructed what proved to be a shaky coalition. His chief advisers were Puritans with a severe, uncompromising religious outlook. They came from New England, Ohio, and New York and included Kimball, George Smith, and Rockwell. Young also appealed to, but distrusted, the Southerners and frontiersmen who had converted in Missouri and Illinois. Imbued with courage and with the instincts of American enterprise, but with none of the culture of the age, these men, epitomized by Lee, were cunning but crude.

Young also allied with two groups of Europeans. The Scots were important in influence and place. Some became bishops and Young's clerks. George D. Watt became the church stenographer. The Scandinavians were innumerable. Sober, industrious, frugal, and submissive, they settled the frontier and believed every word Young uttered. Almost every leading Saint had several Danish, Swedish, or Norwegian wives.

But members of two other nationalities revolted against Young. Welsh converts were religious, but they disliked the prophet's temporal rule. Most numerous of all were the English. Cut off, with the exception of John Taylor, from high church offices, they despised Young.[17]

The story of Sarah Elizabeth Carmichael, next to Eliza Snow the most talented Mormon poetess, illustrated Young's dictatorial methods. Sarah was reared in Utah, but, unlike Eliza, she was more Grecian than Hebraic. Eliza wrote solely about the Saints. Sarah glorified no sect or people, only God's great world. Gentile in mind and transcendental in spirit, she studied not *The Book of Mormon* and Smith's revelations but Emerson's essays. Eliza recognized her talents and praised her in the *Deseret News*, but Young banned her works. Then a California firm published a volume of her poems, and when Richardson came to Salt Lake City with Colfax, he read them and praised Sarah to Eastern readers. She became so well known in the Gentile world that Young finally offered to help her, but the proud girl refused.[18]

Such narrowness helped bring on a revolt that briefly exceeded in importance the Josephite movement. In 1869 in their *Utah*

Magazine three prominent English Saints, William S. Godbe, Elias L.T. Harrison, and Edward Tullidge, urged that Utah's mines be developed, but they stressed that Saints, not outsiders, should work them. They boldly assailed Young, declaring that "the Priesthood is not intended by God to do our thinking."

The Protestants, or Godbeites, were charged with heresy and summoned before a church high council. At the trial they asked George Q. Cannon whether "it was apostasy to differ honestly with the measures of the President." "A man may be honest even in hell," Cannon answered. "You may as well ask the question," Wells interjected, "whether a man has the right to differ honestly with the Almighty." "During the above trial," Harrison noted, "remarks were made by various speakers, comparing us to every foul apostate—the Laws, the Higbees and Fosters, and every debauchee, drunkard, whoremonger and gambler—that ever left the Church for his own iniquitous purposes." Only one council member, Eli B. Kelsey, defended the Godbeites, and he was excommunicated with them.[19]

For a selfish reason Young feared the rebels. Harrison had argued that supply and demand, not the School of the Prophets, should determine wages. At the time Young employed many men on his railroad contracts. Higher salaries would empty his pocketbook.[20]

After their excommunication, the dissenters formed the Church of Zion. Like the Brighamites and the Josephites, they accepted the divinity of Joseph Smith. But they denounced Young's dictatorial rule, desired to divorce church and state, and wanted greater freedom for the individual. They would end Young's practice of sending enemies on missions to get rid of them, limit the tithe to a tenth of a man's profits rather than a tenth of his income, take control of church funds from Young and give it to a board of trustees and auditors, and allow each merchant to trade with whomever he pleased.[21] Tullidge best summarized their views: "While I applaud Brigham Young as a man with the character and capacity of a great empire founder, I desire to see the republican genius of America supreme in Utah, and not Brigham Young and his iron 'kingdom of God.' "[22]

The revolt cut deeply into Young's empire, for although its

leaders represented groups that had been denied power they were all well known in Utah. Each, for example, was the president of a quorum, or division, of the Council of Seventies, the organization that directed the church's missionaries. Small and dark, with an exceptionally high forehead and curly hair, Godbe had been born in London on June 26, 1833, and was Salt Lake City's leading druggist. He was worth a quarter of a million dollars and had seventeen children. His fourth wife, Charlotte Cobb, was, like her mother, sealed to Young for eternity. Harrison, often called the "Martin Luther of Mormonism," was also small and had black hair and eyes, a bilious temperament, and a full quota of nervous electricity. Although an architect—he designed the interior of Young's Salt Lake City theater—he possessed great literary ability and was a fluent and accomplished speaker. His only wife died during his trial before the high council.[23]

If Young admired Godbe and Harrison, he deeply loved two other apostates. Kelsey, formerly an editor of the *Millennial Star*, was the prophet's adopted son, and the two men were often seen together. Kelsey's mother, Mary Oldfield, was one of Young's plural wives.[24]

The deepest blow was the desertion of Henry W. Lawrence, the wealthy thirty-four-year-old partner of Kimball and Lawrence, the mercantile firm, and the brother of Maria and Sarah Lawrence, both of whom married Joseph Smith in Nauvoo. Following Smith's death, Sarah had wed Kimball and Maria was sealed to Young. Shaken by Lawrence's decision to leave the church, Young, who never visited an inferior, drove to the apostate's house and spent two fruitless hours urging him to reconsider.[25]

Two Godbeites became, next to Young and Smith, the most famous of all Saints. Thomas B. H. Stenhouse and his first wife, Fanny, despised Young, who for years had kept them on one trying mission after another. "I lived, sir," Stenhouse informed the editor of the New York *World*, "one whole year in Williamsburg, without a chair to sit on, a bed to lie on, or a table to eat from, and when I went on the editorial staff of the *Mormon*, in New York City, I received the munificent sum of $4 per week, with which I was to keep a wife, four children, pay house rent, ferriage, coal, light, and clothes. I lived, sir, bravely and never stole from anybody, and my salary augmented till it reached $12 a week! I did all that for Mormonism and never murmured."[26]

Fanny later described her reception in Salt Lake City after decades of toil abroad. She and her husband moved into a new house but could not afford furniture. Then Young asked Fanny to sew a bonnet for Emmeline Free. The prophet was so pleased with the finished product that he ordered one for each of his wives. Fanny would now be able to buy furnishings. Assisted by two girls, each of whom she paid six dollars a week plus board, she went to work, finished the job, sent Young a bill for $275, and began selecting furniture. But instead of paying her, Young credited that amount to the Stenhouses' tithing account.[27]

The final break came in 1869, when Young wanted to transfer Stenhouse's paper, the Salt Lake *Telegraph*, to Ogden. Stenhouse refused to go and joined the Godbeites.[28] On the day Stenhouse was excommunicated Fanny told her son-in-law, Joseph Young: "Joseph, your father is a tyrant, he cares nothing for the poor, and cares for naught but his own selfish purposes."[29]

Godbe, Kelsey, and Lawrence were known and respected in Utah, but the Stenhouses soon attained world-wide reputations. Fanny's autobiography, issued under such titles as *Exposé of Polygamy in Utah, "Tell It All,"* and *An Englishwoman Among the Mormons,* was circulated throughout Europe and North America. And Stenhouse's *The Rocky Mountain Saints,* which appeared in 1873, was at once the most scholarly and best written of the many books by Mormon apostates. If nothing else, the Godbeites produced two of the age's three—the other is Burton's *City of the Saints*—most famous accounts of Mormonism.

IV

YOUNG'S MORMONISM DIFFERED from Joseph Smith, Jr.'s, in many ways. For one, Smith's church rested upon spiritualism, or communications with beings in another world. Up to 1844 revelations from God, manifestations in tongues, signs from heaven, conversations with angels, battles with the devil, and miraculous healings of the sick and wounded were common.

Spiritualism led to enormous church successes in England and

Wales. Within six months in Herefordshire and its surrounding counties Woodruff converted nearly two thousand people, mostly Methodists, and turned forty-nine Methodist ministers into Mormon elders. At times he baptized so many people that it seemed as if entire villages entered the river for the ceremony. Soon the Mormon church had five hundred branches in Britain.

The Saints also pointed with pride to the achievements of Elder Thomas Smith. Everywhere the devil's spirits assaulted him, but "Rough Tom" was mighty in asking them questions, forcing them to answer, and casting them out. One Sunday in Bath, England, as Tom preached on salvation for dead sinners, an evil spirit occupied the body of a youth and began to terrorize the unbelievers in the audience. "Gentiles," Tom shouted, "don't be afraid. It's only the devil." Desiring to exorcise the spirit, Tom and several assistants rushed over to the lad, but Satan fought back. Without touching the ground the boy glided under the seats, like a bird escaping pursuit, and then ran up the wall, like a cat. Several elders pulled him down by the leg, and Tom got rid of the spirit. As late as 1870 the Saints who witnessed this demonstration of Mormon power still talked about it.

Claims of miraculous healings also won many converts. During one cholera epidemic elders laid hands on thousands of ill persons. Mormon men generally possessed the power to heal, women the gift to be healed.

Much of this ended with Young, who turned Mormonism away from spiritualism and consequently lost for the church much of its overseas influence. In 1853 there were 31,000 British Saints, in 1870 about 10,000. Even accounting for migrations to Utah, the drop was astounding. For spiritualism Young substituted iron rule, priestly bondage, and materialism. Far more than Joseph Smith, often ridiculed as money mad, he stressed the attainment of wealth as the greatest manifestation of God's favor.[30] In effect, Young, the New England Puritan, offered for Smith's spiritualism the Calvinistic doctrine of the "calling," which emphasized the religious dignity of man's labor and the Lord's approval of riches.

Driven at first by nationalism and the desire to trade with Gentiles, Godbe and Harrison, preaching a return to Smith's ways, soon adopted spiritualism as their cardinal tenet. At a meeting attended by seven hundred followers—and a New York *Herald* reporter—they described the strong impressions of inspiration they had received in the spring of 1868. These impressions had increased in clarity and intensity until that fall, when the two men began getting messages from heaven. One afternoon they heard the familiar voice of Kimball, who had died that June. Kimball sounded exactly as he had on earth. "Now, brother Elias," he asked after telling them to create a new Mormonism, "do you understand that? If you don't, don't say you do." Kimball introduced them to Joseph Smith, to whom Harrison and Godbe spoke night after night. Much wiser than he had once been, Smith now admitted that on earth he was but a child with remarkable powers he had failed to understand or develop. "I was like Solomon," he explained. "I said and did many very wise things, and some very foolish ones." Smith told Godbe to forget *The Book of Mormon*, "for you shall write a better Book of Mormon." With it Godbe would build a powerful church.

"I knew that another voice was the voice of Jesus," Harrison confessed, "else man knows nothing. The voice was soft, melodious, measured and dignified, and when He spoke there came into my heart such a precious revelation of His nature as I shall never forget to my dying day."

The Godbeites allowed the *Herald* to publish two revelations from the Apostle James, one from Smith, and one from Jesus. "Dear, dear brothers, be comforted," James said. "Consider that we have come to lead you to the truth, and have appointed you to this great work. Do your duty; 'think twice before you speak once;' be patient, be merciful, be prayerful, and all obstacles shall be removed and the light will come with full effulgence. God bless you both."

Smith spoke of the "great and numerous" obstacles confronting the Godbeites but predicted that "in spite of all these you will be triumphant, triumphant!" From "the highest authority" he brought word to " 'Go and redeem Zion; go and feed the people with the rich ripe corn in the Kernel instead of the husks with which they have been so long fed.' Remember this and reflect upon it, and thousands upon thousands will support you and greet you with songs of joy at your entrance to the immortal world for the work you have accomplished for suffering humanity."

The revelation from Jesus was the most potent of all. "I am sent to you as a comforter. Your thoughts have gone forth to the angelic world and have been made known to the controlling powers, and thus you hear the thoughts that I give suppression to telling you that you are treading in the right path, that your mission is important, and that you will live to see the results of this great work. You will not suffer as I suffered, for you have too many powers, too many influences assisting you. You are not working alone. You are working with a force behind you impelling you to free the children of Zion. . . . I am called back to my Father's mansion; but I shall send forth forces to assist you in this work—the work of Him who died to save humanity."[31]

Greatly impressed by all this was Andrew Jackson Davis, the foremost spiritualist of the age. In 1870 he estimated to the New York *World* that between two and three million Americans were spiritualists. The movement had ripped apart the Universalists, the Shakers, and the Quakers. "And now," he said, "Spiritualism has got in Mormondom, and threatens to split it in pieces. The Protestant movement in the Mormon Church is solely attributable to communications received through mediums developed in their midst. It is a very powerful movement, too. You see the Mormon Spiritualists are saying: 'The communications to Joseph Smith or to Brigham Young are no more than the communications to others. They are not infallible.' The consequence is the Mormon Church is being split in twain."[32]

But the *New York Tribune* predicted Young would soon present his own revelations. "In the business of religious thaumaturgy, these veterans of the old school are not likely to be surpassed." Unfortunately, the paper added, Godbe's communications were "in the sloppy and silly style which heavenly messages to the 'Spiritualists' have rendered familiar. . . . The painful part of the matter is that those who are struggling to free themselves from one form of delusion should lapse so easily into another." Noting the size of Godbe's audience, the paper concluded: "Any crafty knave who pleases to start a sect may be sure of followers."[33]

Instead of revelations, Young's subordinates countered with their usual weapons: distortions of Mormon history, cries of persecution, and warnings of Satan at work. The Godbeites were comparable to the Laws, who had opposed Joseph Smith in 1844, the *Utah Magazine* to the Nauvoo *Expositor*. But, boasted the *Deseret News*, Salt Lake City had no Carthage twenty miles away from which mobs could come and kill Young. In line with Young's pronouncement that any revelation not received by him was from the devil, Pratt and Bishop Edwin D. Woolley accused Godbe of falling for the deceptions of Satan, who used ventriloquism to sound like Kimball, Smith, James, and Jesus. The devil would overcome and control in both this world and the next anyone who followed Godbe.[34]

Fighting back, Godbe went to Washington in the winter of 1869–70 and was introduced to Grant by Colfax. As a result of these talks, Grant sent to Utah troops under General Philip Sheridan. Godbe also conferred with Representative Shelby M. Cullom of Illinois, the author of a bill giving federal judges jurisdiction over polygamy cases and declaring plural cohabitation, not just polygamy, a misdemeanor. Godbe recommended so many changes in it that Cullom shouted: "My God, Mr. Godbe, you would strike out all the points of my bill!" The measure passed the House, but friends of the Saints killed it in the Senate.[35]

Godbe even sued the prophet. In 1865, while building a canal from Cottonwood Canyon to Salt Lake City, Young, the church's trustee-in-trust, borrowed $10,020.27 from the druggist. He repaid five thousand dollars, but Godbe demanded the rest and in 1870 won a suit for it.[36]

Young retaliated every way he could. Harrison designed no more church buildings, and the Salt Lake City police arrested and beat up a prominent Godbeite, Joseph Silver.[37] One night four men attacked Fanny and Thomas Stenhouse and covered them with garbage.[38]

Years later Godbe described how in 1870 the Mormon leaders had joked that "In ninety days there wouldn't be a grease spot left of me." To drive him out of business the church started the Lion Drug Store, and loyal Saints refused to pay him the $100,000 they owed him. "In a year or so after being cut off from the Church, instead of being worth at least one hundred thousand dollars which I should have been worth I found myself owing that much and paying interest at the rate of a thousand dollars a month."

Young had vowed to wrap Utah within a wall no Gentile could penetrate. He had, Godbe concluded, succeeded.[39]

But Godbeism perished as much from inertia as from strangulation. Languishing into oblivion, the Protestants set up no church hierarchy and produced no second *Book of Mormon.* Charlotte Cobb left her impoverished husband for a younger, wealthier man, and Jesus, James, Joseph, and Heber suddenly stopped conversing with the apostates. In ability and magnetism Godbe proved no Brigham Young or Joseph Smith, Jr.—or, for that matter, no Joseph Smith III.

XV

Red Cloud and
Blackstone's *Commentaries*

I

"IT IS EASY TO LAUGH AT MORMONISM," the New York *World* observed in 1873, "but not easy to account for it." In the United States alone the church had grown remarkably rapidly. In 1850 it had sixteen branches and 10,880 members; in 1870, 171 branches and 87,838 members.[1]

Despite such progress, Young was fearful. He continually sent Eliza Snow, the Sweet Songstress of Zion, around the territory preaching the glories of the old ways. "She trotted out Abraham, Jacob, David and Solomon," one listener remembered, "all men approved of God, she said, and whose polygamous children became the ancestors of Israel." "We must occupy the land," Eliza warned. "We must keep out the Gentile. We must give him no place for the sole of his foot. Women only fulfill their end when they bear many children," the childless bride of both Young and Joseph Smith proclaimed. "Children are the great asset of the Church. It is the prophecy of the scripture that 'in Zion the streets shall be full of boys and girls playing.' "[2]

In analyzing Young's motives for retaining celestial marriage, F.T. Ferris, the Gentile business manager of the Salt Lake *Daily*

Tribune, pinpointed another fundamental difference between the first and second Mormon prophets. "Brigham Young did not become a polygamist, nor do I believe that he enforced polygamy on his subjects simply for the indulgence of the animal passions. It was different with Joseph Smith, who was a man who could not control his passions, and who practiced polygamy even before he received the revelation making it the bounden duty of all good Mormons. In fact, the belief is common among the more intelligent Mormons that Joseph's carnal passions were the cause of the revelation. With Brigham it is different. With him, it is a matter of statesmanship. He is a shrewd man rather than a fanatic, and looks upon the building up of a power in the territory rather than to the indulgence of his passions. . . . He, I believe, clings to polygamy, first, because he thinks it will more rapidly build up the Mormon state, and, second, because its practice tends to isolate those who practice it from the outer world, keeps them together, and thereby renders his power more secure and stable than if the polygamic institution did not exist."[3]

If during this decade Young worried about the safety of his religion, he was also concerned about himself. He never forgot that his predecessor was the only American religious leader to be assassinated. "When he rides out into the country," one visitor noted, "he has an escort of from seventy-five to one hundred and fifty armed men, as motley and dirty a company as was ever raised since the days of Falstaff!"[4]

II

IN HIS OFFICE Young hung a picture of Andrew Johnson. "We like Johnson because while he was President he sent us fair officers," the prophet explained, "and if one didn't do right he immediately cut off his head and sent him home."[5]

Johnson's successor, however, hated the Saints. Grant never forgave Young for calling Congress and the President "liars, thieves, whoremongers, gamblers, and drunkards."[6]

In November 1869 Brigham Young, Jr., compounded the injury. "Undoubtedly Grant has great abilities as a commander in the field," he informed the Philadelphia *Morning Post,* "but his political abilities, we think, consist simply in knowing how to hold his tongue." And Congress contained the most "dissipated set of men anywhere."[7]

Already bristling with anger, Grant was spurred further forward by the sermon he heard on April 24, 1870, at the Metropolitan Methodist Church in Washington, to which he belonged. That day the Reverend Doctor J.P. Newman attacked plural marriage. Orson Pratt immediately defended the institution, and for the next two months, in long letters to the New York *Herald*, the two men argued the subject.[8]

Then in August a debate took place in Salt Lake City. For three days Pratt and Newman discussed every aspect of plural marriage. Answering the usual Mormon defenses of it, Newman pointed out that marriage, as established by God in the time of man's innocence in the Garden of Eden, was monogamous, that polygamy violated this original institution and was another name for adultery, and that nothing in the Bible, correctly interpreted, sanctioned plural marriage but numerous sections condemned it. He also disputed the Mormon assertion that prostitution flourished under monogamy.[9]

Another of Grant's advisers joined in. Still angry because in 1867 he had been ignored in Utah communities that had given Young a hero's reception, Secretary of War John A. Rawlins filled the President's head with stories of traitorous Saints and of federal officials who neglected their duties.[10]

As a result of all this, Grant appointed to territorial offices three men the Saints detested. Colonel George R. Maxwell, who had lost a leg in battle the day before the Civil War ended, became the Assistant District Attorney. Robert N. Baskin, the thin, red-headed young man who sought to avenge the murder of his client and close friend, John K. Robinson, and reputedly drafted the Cullom Bill in his office in downtown Salt Lake City, became the District Attorney. And James B. McKean, the wiry, balding New Yorker, became the Chief Justice.[11]

In the summer and early fall of 1871 a series of indictments rocked Utah. A Grand Jury, one of whose members was Harrison, charged Henry Lawrence and George Q. Cannon with violating the territorial statute prohibiting lewd and lascivious cohabitation,[12] and warrants were issued for Hickman, George Grant, Rockwell, William Kimball, Wells, Stout, and others for assisting in several killings committed during the Mormon war of 1857. Rumor had it that Hickman had turned state's evidence and confessed to these and other murders.[13] Even Orson Hyde was implicated. After a six-mile chase, he eluded a posse and headed for Arizona and New Mexico.[14] Rockwell too fled and hid out in the desert until April 1872, when he again popped up in Salt Lake City.[15]

Then, on October 2, 1871, Young was arrested for lewd and lascivious cohabitation with sixteen of his wives, a charge the government expected to prove by bringing into court his children by these women. Although the marshal allowed the prophet to remain at home, Brigham Young, Jr., at the church conference on October 5, denounced the federal appointees as tools of the devil and called down on them heaven's curse. "Trust to God," he advised his people, "keep your powder dry, and don't fail to have on hand a good supply of fixed ammunition." Loud cheers greeted his remarks.[16]

Even before these arrests many Saints blamed a rival church for their troubles. Grant, Newman, Colfax, and McKean were Methodists who had seen the Mormons make enormous gains among their fellow churchmen. In England even Methodist clergymen had turned from John Wesley to Joseph Smith.[17] As David Brinton, a Mormon missionary in England, confided to the *World*: "Some members of the Established Church of England come over to us, but the bulk of our converts come from the Methodists and other dissenting sects."[18]

"The people of the United States are not opposed to Polygamy, and Mormon persecution has not been from this cause," Young joined in. "The bitterest trials of the Church were passed through before Polygamy was proclaimed or practiced. That is not the basis of persecution. It lies deeper. . . . It is priestcraft and religious jealousy and intolerance. The Mormons have the key to eternal life; the latest and most complete revelation from God. They are a chosen people set aside to the great work of regeneration, and Satan and his emissaries are opposed to that work. Who murdered Joseph and Hyrum Smith twenty-five years ago? Nobody but leading members of what are called *orthodox* churches. The Baptists, Methodists and Presbyterian preachers disguised themselves, entered the jail at Carthage, and committed murder in the name of their religion. There is no disputing this fact. Every person engaged in that nefarious business is known to us. The party was led on by a Baptist minister, and there were in it members in good standing in the Methodist and Presbyterian churches. The Mormons were a peaceful, law-abiding people, as they are now, and they did not practice polygamy then, because the revelation had not been given them."[19] Again Young confused fact with fiction.

In an interview with the New York *Herald* shortly after his arrest Young was even more specific. Exasperated because their recent Utah drive failed to convert a single Saint, the Methodists, through Grant, proposed to destroy Young in three stages. First, they would try him for lewd and lascivious cohabitation. Failing in that, they would arrest him for violating the anti-bigamy act of 1862. Finally, they would attempt to convict him for the murders committed by such outlaws as Hickman, with whom Young had recently quarreled. Grant was, the prophet laughed, thoughtful to begin this gently. Young would go to court and trust the American people to see to it that justice was done. Fortunately, the United States Supreme Court, which might eventually judge the case, contained eminent jurists, not bigoted hacks.[20]

Young's decision to appear in court came after long discussions with his counselors. During these talks John Taylor, a tall, good-looking, gray-haired man who had been wounded in the attack that had killed Joseph Smith, advised Young to take his chances in the open air rather than in a Gentile prison. Three other Saints —George Smith, grossly overweight, good-humored, and weak, but next to Young the highest man in the church; Orson Pratt, venerable and Mosaic-looking, with a flaming beard and large, introspective eyes; and Joseph Young, Brigham's brother, the president of the powerful Council of Seventies, and the possessor of a low forehead and a lean face with a mouth like Lincoln's— also urged that Young resist. Baked dry in the furnace of old Mormon dangers, which they now recounted with gusto and pride, they warned that the Saints would revolt rather than see

Young jailed. They wanted to cut the irrigation ditches, burn everything in Utah, and take their herds and all they could carry to Mexico. Like an old lion, Young, persecuted at the age of seventy by the country whose telegraph he had strung and whose transcontinental railway he had built, pointed out that he had been promised protection and a fair hearing. "So was Joseph!" Taylor snapped. "I saw the safe treatment they gave him in jail!" Young thought for a minute and then answered: "God is in the courts as well as in battles and marches. There will be no resistance. I shall obey the summons." Shortly after, accompanied by Hooper, Wells, Cannon, Smith, and nine attorneys, he halted his buggy before the little old squalid stone stable holding the federal court—the church, which owned the building, had thrown the court out of its regular meeting place—climbed the creaky outside stairs, and entered the hayloft now used as a courtroom. Feeble from diarrhea, Young, wrapped in shawls, a large overcoat, and a wool comforter, rested on his cane as he pleaded not guilty and posted $5,000 bail. He then returned home.[21]

Soon Young heard that Hickman had implicated him in several murders. He panicked and fled. Fortunately for him, however, the sympathetic George C. Bates now replaced Baskin. "The counsel of Brigham Young, indicted for murder and lewd and lascivious cohabitation, have proposed to me, that he is perfectly willing to come in at once, surrender himself, and give bail in the sum of $200,000," Bates informed his superiors. "His counsel also state that Young left, not to avoid trial, but to escape confinement in the garrison here and for fear of his life."[22]

Early in 1872 Young submitted to arrest for murder, but Salt Lake City had no federal jail and McKean allowed him to return home. But in April the United States Supreme Court declared illegal the special Gentile juries McKean had impaneled to get his indictments and freed Young and the other accused Saints.[23]

A reporter who visited Young about this time was shocked by his poor posture and "his hair frosted by many winters. . . . His troubles of last year are telling fearfully upon him, and unless his enemies relent and give him and his church some peace, it is evident that he will be moved hence ere long."[24]

Like the 1857 conflict, the 1871 battle changed nothing. To the

Attorney General, McKean argued that he had treated the Saints humanely. "I permitted Brigham Young, though indicted for murder, to occupy his own house, and take exercise in his own carriage, surrounded by his friends, and but nominally in the custody of the Marshal. I permitted Mayor Wells, also indicted for murder, to go on bail. Hawkins, convicted of adultery, might have been sentenced to imprisonment for twenty years; but I sentenced him for only three years, the shortest term allowed by the law, and at the same time informed him, that so soon as his conduct and the public good should warrant it, I would recommend his pardon."

The Saints, on the other hand, ceaselessly harassed McKean. One day during the trials the door of the hayloft suddenly flew open, and twenty to thirty armed men dashed inside the courtroom. "They stood for some minutes in a menacing and insulting group near the middle of the room, but as they seemed not to be noticed, they gradually took seats. They were of the organization known as 'Danites.'" Several times these sinister men returned to the hayloft, but they failed to intimidate McKean.

Trying another tack, Clawson, the adjutant general of the Nauvoo Legion, bought one thousand muskets and bayonets from the federal government and distributed them to his troops. For days thereafter armed Legionnaires marched about the streets of Salt Lake City. Two companies of soldiers finally moved into the city, and the next morning not a Mormon was visible. Prominent Saints, insisting they had no intention of resisting authority, now pleaded for quarter. Throughout all this McKean calmly held court.[25]

Grant too remained anti-Mormon. Hearing that Hooper had appointed Young's son to the United States Military Academy at West Point, the President asserted that if "I had known of Hooper's intention, I certainly would have asked the Attorney General whether I had the power under the law to prevent the appointment and if he advised affirmatively I would have settled the matter there and then."[26]

And from his Pennsylvania farm a voice out of the past volunteered to help the government convict Young. His proposal was ignored, so Sidney Rigdon offered instead to save the Utah church for a hundred thousand dollars in gold. Young read the letter, and, recalling that Rigdon had been president of the Kirtland bank, drawled: "I wonder if Sidney wouldn't take one hundred thousand dollars in greenbacks?"[27]

III

MEETING CRISIS WITH ACTION, the Saints revived the State of Deseret. On March 18, 1872, Utah's voters ratified by 25,324 to 368 a new constitution for Deseret and again selected men to get the state into the Union. The New York *Tribune* was shocked. "To throw the political and judicial machinery of Utah (or Deseret) into the hands of the Mormon leaders," it warned, "would be to give a hierarchy of morbid fanatics powers which would drive from the country every 'Gentile' person, and build up in the basin of Great Salt Lake an impregnable State, intolerant of all non-Mormon influences, governed by a hierarchy hostile to ordinary immigration, and infested with a secret system of priestly espionage which is at variance with the spirit of our institutions."[28]

John H. Beadle, the Gentile journalist who was helping Hickman write his memoirs, agreed, and noted that John Jacques, the associate editor of the *Deseret News,* had recently written: "It is not consistent that the people of God should submit to man-made governments. There is but one true and perfect government—the one organized by God; a government by prophets, apostles, priests, teachers, and evangelists; the order of the original Church, of *all* Churches acknowledged by God."

Utah elections were a farce, Beadle explained, for each ballot was numbered and the voter's name was entered in a book opposite this number. Young's men could tell at a glance how everyone voted. Recalling the notorious New York City corruption ring, Beadle asked: "Don't that beat Tweed and Sweeny ten to one?"

If Deseret became a state, Beadle continued, Young would be elected governor, George Smith would be lieutenant governor, and Wells would head the Supreme Court. "What chance would a man like me have for justice with Mormon Danites as constables to arrest, and Mormon Elders as Magistrates to bind over; a Mormon Bishop as Circuit Judge to try, and a Mormon Supreme

Court High Council to appeal to,—presided over by High Chief Justice, President, Lieut. Gen. Daniel H. Wells—a cruel and remorseless bigot who knows as much of law outside of Mormonism as Red Cloud does of *Blackstone's Commentaries*?"[29]

Even now the Saints had their own judicial system. A Mormon took his grievances not to the District Court run by one of the three Supreme Court judges but to his bishop's court and, if necessary, to the stake high council and the church First Presidency. Meanwhile, the Probate Court judges chosen for each county by the Mormon-dominated Utah legislature saw to it that grand juries never indicted Saints. The District Court clerk, a Gentile, and the Probate judge, a polygamist, each placed one hundred names on the list from which grand and petit jurors for the county were selected. The judge nominated one hundred Saints, the clerk one hundred Gentiles. Utah grand juries had fifteen men, with twelve votes needed to indict. During Young's lifetime only two juries with twelve Gentiles were drawn.[30]

As it was, the Utah legislature was the only one in America whose members worshipped before one altar. The chair in each house recognized not "the gentleman from Salt Lake City" or "the distinguished Representative from Provo" but Brother Young, Brother Pratt, or Brother Cannon. Early in 1872 the legislature even voted over $6,000 to Pratt, the Speaker of the House, for translating *The Book of Mormon* into the Deseret Alphabet, which Young devised to draw his people closer together. The Gentile governor vetoed the bill.[31]

To a man the Saints opposed Grant in 1872, supporting instead Greeley, the Democratic presidential nominee, who had reportedly agreed to accept a polygamist as Utah's Congressional delegate. Grant won, but Young, forever grateful, hung Greeley's photo on his office wall alongside pictures of Joseph and Hyrum Smith.[32]

Then in April 1873 Young partially retired. He left the presidency of both Zion's Co-operative Mercantile Institution and the Deseret National Bank and resigned as the church's trustee-in-trust. For the New York *Herald* he summarized "the results of my labors for the last twenty-six years": "the peopling of this Territory by the Latter-day Saints of about one hundred thousand souls, the founding of over two hundred cities, towns and villages inhabited by our people, which extend to Idaho in the north, Wyoming in the east, Nevada in the west, and Arizona in the south, and the establishment of schools, factories, mills and other institutions calculated to benefit and improve our community."[33]

Four months later Ann Eliza, asking for alimony of a thousand dollars a month, $20,000 for her lawyers, and $200,000 in property, sued Young for divorce. The case dragged on until in February 1875 Ann Eliza was awarded alimony of five hundred dollars a month, attorney's fees of three thousand, and back alimony of ninety-five hundred dollars. When Young refused to pay, McKean found him in contempt of court, fined him twenty-five dollars, and sentenced him to one day in jail. Young was allowed to go home, eat dinner, and say good-bye to his family. He took bedding and other comforts, entered his waiting carriage, and with his physician, his second counselor, and a servant was driven to jail by a deputy marshal. A week later Grant removed McKean from office.[34]

The matter ended on April 27, 1877. A judge voided Young's marriage to Ann Eliza and made him pay only court costs.[35]

The following month Young called his marriage to the girl "a foolish thing. It was a thing that I allowed her parents to persuade me into. I did it for her good." The prophet then told a story far different from the one Ann Eliza told. Shortly after Ann Eliza's first husband "had sense enough to run away from her," Young asked her parents why she did not marry again. "You ain't waiting for me to ask her, are you?" he quickly added. "I didn't mean anything by it," Young explained to a reporter, "but Webb and his wife caught at the straw, and never let up on me till I married her. They importuned me; said Ann Eliza must have a solid man to lean on or she would go to ruin, and then, like a fool, I married her. Why, I, an old man, didn't want anything of Ann Eliza, any more than I did from the Sultan of Turkey. She was an elephant, silly, vain, and unfaithful. I gave her that white cottage you see down there on the corner, but she acted very badly. She even drove her own mother away, so as to keep the company of different men. One man, who was afterward baptized into our church, made oath that he had done wrong with Ann Eliza many times."[36] Even a prophet found God's commandment to take many wives a trial.

IV

DURING THE 1870's some people blamed Young for almost everything. In 1874 an eighty-year-old woman in the Stockton, England, almshouse accused him of marrying her in 1820 and deserting her fourteen years and nine children later.[37]

Federal matters fared no better. "We would like to see Sheridan and 10,000 troops in Utah," Young confessed in 1873. "They would put money into our pockets, as Uncle Sam's soldiers have always done; and then, Phil Sheridan is a jolly good fellow, and would be heartily welcome. What we object to are judges who might betray their office, and special legislation depriving our citizens of their rights."[38]

The war against the Gentiles also continued. Early in 1875 the Reverend Duncan J. McMillan moved to Mount Pleasant in the Sanpete Valley. Although all of the town's 1,346 inhabitants were Saints, he built a schoolhouse and a church. In July Young, Cannon, Wells, Hyde, and several other church leaders arrived. "There is a mischievous stranger, a Presbyterian minister in this valley," the prophet warned two thousand Saints from throughout the region. "He has no business here. The Lord has given to me these valleys, and to those whom I choose to have occupy them; this Presbyterian minister has no business here. The Saints do not know how vile a character this man has. In the best society in the United States, not one child in ten can identify his father. Mistresses are luxuries which are conceded to all orthodox ministers. One prominent clergyman keeps twenty-eight mistresses, and though I don't know this minister who has come here, he is one of the same stripe. I am informed that Saints have gone to hear this man preach, and have sent their daughters to his school. The next thing you will know he will send sorrow and distress to the hearts of the mothers of these girls. . . . You must not be deceived by the fact that this man seems a gentleman and a moral man; there is just where the danger lies. He is a wolf in sheep's clothing. What would you do were a wolf to enter the field where your sheep are?

Why, you would shoot him down. Kill him on the spot. Inasmuch as souls are more precious than sheep, it becomes you to be correspondingly more diligent in ridding yourselves of this intruder. I need not tell the Saints how this is to be done. They know well enough. . . . You must obey me the same as though Jehovah had spoken," he asserted with uplifted hands; "for my voice is the voice of Jehovah."

The next night a mob stoned McMillan's home, and the evening after that the minister scared off a man attempting to enter the house. Still later McMillan escaped ambush by taking a different road. His school was soon empty.[39]

Despite his supposed retirement, Young also attended to economic affairs. Flushed with pride because Zion's Co-operative Mercantile Institution paid a fifteen per cent dividend in the first six months of 1872,[40] he revived in 1874 Joseph Smith's United Order of Enoch. Those selected to enter the order surrendered their worldly goods, which according to Mormon doctrine had merely been loaned to them by God, and drew everything they needed from a general fund. In St. George, 350 miles south of Salt Lake City, Young began the plan with thirty families.[41]

"This is all that is now needed to bring in the latter-day glory," he told these pioneers; "this is what is to make us a united and prosperous people; whoever holds back is withholding himself from the privileges of the Church, and he will continue to fall away little by little until he becomes utterly lost. You will not lose anything by giving up control of your property and labor—all you really want will be supplied as before without any care on your part; there will be still larger production by systematized labor, and what is produced will be of better quality than anything you now have. There will be no poor, no rich, or rather all will be rich, and you will see such a progress under the blessing of heaven as has never yet been vouchsafed to any people."[42]

In a touching oration Young connected the Order with his most cherished dream. "If we put our property into the hands of those capable of managing it it will realize more; a united effort is more successful than individual effort. We can then extend our settlement, branch out in every direction. The whole Christian world is already astonished and frightened at our growth; but all the powers of earth and hell cannot stop it. They would have served you and me as they did Hiram and Joseph, if they had had the power, but we are in God's hands, and He says, so far, but no farther. We are His; we have no toil on this earth except to establish the kingdom of God. My dear brethren and sisters, I delight to speak of this beautiful holy order of Heaven."⁴³

Then in October 1875 Grant came west. Young met him at Ogden and escorted him to Salt Lake City. Cheering crowds along the route greatly impressed the President, who, according to Mormon legend, admitted his advisers had deceived him about the disloyalty of the Saints.⁴⁴

Equally satisfying were Young's talks with the Yale University paleontologist, Othniel C. Marsh, soon to add to his fame by coining the word "dinosaur." In a public discussion years before some Englishmen had bested their Mormon opponents by citing numerous scientific blunders in *The Book of Mormon*, including the statement that horses arrived in America with man. Everyone knew, the Gentiles insisted, that around A.D. 1500 Spaniards had brought horses to the New World. Yet the Book of Ether tells of the Jaredites, who in the period following the destruction of the tower of Babel built eight watertight barges that could float any side up and had holes on both top and bottom so those inside could always get air. The Jaredites loaded these vessels with provisions and set sail. Driven across the ocean by a strong wind, they reached America in 344 days. Within sixty-two years they possessed wealth and, according to *The Book of Mormon*, "all manner" of fruits, grains, cattle, oxen, and sheep. "And they also had horses, and asses, and there were elephants, and cureloms and cumoms; all of which were useful unto man, and more especially the elephants and cureloms and cumoms."

The story seemed incredible. In 1841, however, an archaeologist, Doctor P.W. Lund, discovered the fossil bones of a prehistoric horse in a cave in Brazil. Thirty years later Marsh began exploring the portions of Wyoming and Utah Territories that once contained lakes. Young greeted him warmly, spoke to him several times, and helped him in numerous ways. In 1872 John W. Young loaned the scientists a steamer, enabling them to examine the shores of the Great Salt Lake.

These kindnesses paid huge dividends. Mired in a mile of mud and sand in what had once been a lake, Marsh found the bones of an ancient horse, a scrawny little beast scarcely the size of a fox. Its skull was proportionately shorter than a modern horse's, and the orbit of its eye was different. The four toes on each of its forefeet and the three on each of its hind feet all reached the ground. Marsh called the animal an Orohippus.

Overjoyed, Young told Marsh that if for no other reason than that he knew horses existed in prehistoric America Joseph Smith was divinely inspired.[45] But he neglected to mention that these specimens roamed the West fifty million years ago and were extinct long before the Jaredites sailed to America in 2500 B.C.

V

IN 1871 CANNON SAID that Young was "as likely to live twenty years yet as almost any man of my acquaintance." The prophet's family had always enjoyed long life. His grandmother had reached ninety-eight, his sister one hundred. His father had died at eighty, but only after fleeing from Missouri and losing the desire to live. Several of Young's brothers and cousins were already eighty. "Besides this inherited longevity, he has the prayers of the thousands of his people here in the mountain regions, from Idaho to Arizona, and scattered all over the world, that God will preserve his life."[46]

Young was, nevertheless, often ill during the 1870's. Finding the Salt Lake Valley air too sharp for his lungs, he built a home in St. George and wintered there with his favorite nurses, Amelia Folsom and Lucy Bigelow. Mormons joked that Young was just well enough to sit up in bed and be married now and then.[47]

As pictured by one observer, Young's party on its way south resembled a safari. Smith occupied the first wagon, and Brigham, Jr., "a man of about thirty, short, enormously wide, with a jovial face," the second. The third held Lucy and several "stout, romping children." Young, "shapeless and wide," and Amelia, elegantly dressed, brought up the rear. A magnificent otter-skin robe covered their knees, and in Amelia's lap Young had placed a large, red apple. He had spent a few days in this town, but upon leaving he said to no one in particular: "I am much obliged to you, friends, for your hospitality. I wish you all good-day." With that, "a couple of solemn-looking mules" pulled his carriage forward.[48]

Young also owned a beautiful and spacious home in Provo that Eliza Burgess ran and in 1873 started building Gardo House, a magnificent four-story home in downtown Salt Lake City. Called by the New York *Tribune* "one of the most gorgeous and costly residences anywhere between sunrise and sunset," Gardo House was to have thirty-six rooms and 150 windows. It was nicknamed "Amelia's Palace."[49]

Unfortunately these years depleted the ranks of Young's loved ones. His daughter, Alice, died in 1874, and his son Joseph, George Smith, and Emmeline Free all died in 1875. Of the old Mormon leaders only Young, Hyde, Taylor, Pratt, and Woodruff were left. The spirit world was filling fast.

VI

DURING YOUNG'S FINAL YEARS echoes of the bloody past haunted him. In 1875 John D. Lee was tried for the Mountain Meadows massacre but was freed after a Mormon jury failed to reach a verdict. The next year Lee was tried again, and this time the church for some reason decided not to interfere. Lee was convicted of murder in the first degree and sentenced to be shot at the scene of the crime.

Awaiting execution, the condemned man, a trusted Saint for over thirty years, dictated his autobiography, which, with lurid drawings, was published in dozens of editions throughout the remainder of the century. During the winter of 1842–3, Lee recalled, Joseph Smith selected forty bodyguards. Lee was the seventh man chosen. "My station as a guard was at the Prophet's mansion, during his life, and after his death my post was changed to the residence of Brigham Young, he being the acknowledged successor of the Prophet. From the time I was appointed until we started across the plains, when at home I stood guard every night, and much of the time on the road, one-half of the night at a time, in rain, hail, snow, wind, and cold, to nourish, protect and guard, and give strength to the man that has proven to be the most treacherous, ungrateful villain on earth. In return for all of my faithfulness and fidelity to him and the cause that he taught, he has wantonly sacrificed me, in a dastardly and treacherous manner."[50]

On the morning of the execution the ever-present New York *Herald* correspondent asked Lee if he was "very bitter against Brigham Young." "Yes," Lee answered. "He has sacrificed me through his lust for power, after all I have done for him and the Mormon Church."[50]

For decades Brigham Young, Jr., and other Saints had blamed the massacre on Indians.[52] Now, in an astounding about-face, the church hung it all on Lee, a lover of books, the one-time Nauvoo librarian, the husband of nineteen wives, five of whom remained faithful to him, the father of fifty children, the grandfather of about as many, and the great-grandfather of five. Hearing about the condemned man's unpublished memoirs, Young telegraphed the *Herald*: "If Lee has made a statement in his confession implicating me . . . it is utterly false. My course of life is too well known by thousands of honorable men for them to believe for one moment such an accusation."[53] A month later in a long interview with the *Herald* Young defied "the world to prove that the heads of the Church had anything to do with the Mountain Meadows massacre."[54]

Moments before dying, Lee requested "my boys not to seek revenge for my killing, but to leave vengeance to God."[55] These words failed to comfort Young, then wintering in plush comfort in St. George. In June, starting toward Salt Lake City through territory containing Lee's many friends, the prophet recalled the vow of the dead man's sons to avenge their father's betrayal. "I caught a glimpse of him as he was now passing," one tenderfoot recorded. "He went fully armed and protected like some European monarch in danger of assault from disaffected subjects." Thirty braves in war paint preceded Young's stagecoach, and thirty armed white men followed it. Guards on horseback protected the flanks.[56]

Shortly after Young reached Salt Lake City, two of Lee's sons sneaked into the Beehive House and entered the prophet's bedroom. Luckily they were detected and escorted out of town. After that Young always kept a trusted Saint at his elbow.[57]

Hickman too troubled Young. Frequently accused of crimes but never convicted, the partially bald, burly Danite had once practiced law—and violence—but now herded cattle. Like other Western killers, he exaggerated his exploits. In 1869 he claimed he had killed four hundred men, and his autobiography, published in 1872 as *Brigham's Destroying Angel*, recounted the bloodiest of these episodes. Then in the summer of 1877 he told the New York *Herald* about several murders Young had ordered him to commit. Asked about the confession, Young denied all. "I never spoke with Bill Hickman but once in my life; that was here in Salt Lake City. One day some stock was being driven in, and I walked out and down the street to look at them in the corral. While I was waiting alone Hickman came up and began to speak to me. I wouldn't have anything particular to say to him, so I just turned him off by asking him about his family."

This falsehood—through the years Hickman had often visited Young's office[58] and was once appointed sheriff, prosecuting attorney, assessor, and tax collector of Green River County by Young[59]—infuriated Hickman. "He didn't know me, didn't he? The d—— old ———— —— — ————! He didn't know me when he gave me my second wife in the Endowment House! He didn't know me when he authorized Orson Hyde to seal my third wife to me at Council Bluffs! He didn't know me—and oh, no, of course he didn't speak to me when seven other wives were sealed to me at Salt Lake City! He didn't speak to me when I made him a present of two of the finest horses he ever had! When he got me to herd his cattle on my ranch, ten miles south of here, in 1850, he didn't speak to me then! He himself twice published the fact that I saved his life; on that occasion he did not speak to me! He is the damndest liar, the most ungrateful villain, and the cruelest tyrant I ever knew. . . . He always had his select men to do what is called 'dirty work.' These men were of nerve and brain, whom he could absolutely rely on. The killings I have told you of were invariably done by Brigham Young's express command."[60]

Inspired by these interviews, the *Herald* began publishing anti-Mormon articles. One issue brought the story of a murder, the next a conversation with an apostate, the third a long history of Young's misdeeds. Ann Eliza's mother, Eliza J. Webb, an acquaintance of the prophet for forty years, talked about "the terrible order of the Danites," whose members "were ready to strike at anybody at the lifting of Brigham Young's finger, even at such a signal as the scratching of his nose." The next day Sarah Pratt described Joseph Smith's seduction attempts in Nauvoo and Young's consequent hatred of her.

The inevitable occurred on the evening of May 26, 1877. A man behind a tree fired into the carriage carrying Jerome B. Stillson, the *Herald* reporter. Five days later the same man tried again. He entered Stillson's hotel room, plunged a knife into the correspondent's left breast, and shouted: "Take that, you son of a bitch." The force of the blow knocked Stillson over a table, but the reporter sustained only a dented rib. The assailant immediately bolted, "supposing, no doubt, that he had blood-atoned his victim."[61]

The *Herald*, once honored by Joseph Smith because of its friendship for the Saints, thereupon offered a suggestion. "Young now lives in fear of being indicted and tried for murder. He has been for two years or more meditating a new hegira. He took his people to Utah to get out of the reach of the United States, and now finds himself troubled by Gentiles. If he is wise he ought to be meditating, and not only meditating, but preparing for another move into Mexico."[62]

VII

"I FEEL AS YOUNG AS EVER," Young boasted in May 1877. "I am 75, and shall not be here many years more. All I want now is to die and see all my people peaceful, prosperous, and happy."[63]

Realizing that even a prophet must go, Young drew up a will that allotted to each of the mothers of his children twenty-five dollars a month for the remainder of their lives. To his other wives he gave sufficient money "for their comfortable support." Eliza Snow, Twiss, Martha Bowker, Clara Decker, Harriet Cook, Susan Snively, Eliza Burgess, and Margaret Pierce were to share the Lion House, and Amelia Folsom and Mary Ann Angell received Gardo House. Young also made to his family forty-one grants of real property, including one of eighty thousand dollars to Lucy Decker.[64]

The end began at eleven o'clock on Thursday evening, August 23, 1877. After devouring green corn and peaches, Young was seized with an attack of cholera morbus. For almost a week his condition steadily worsened. At ten o'clock in the evening on Tuesday, August 28, as he lay in a kind of stupor, his son, John, whispered: "Do you know me father?" "I should think I ought to," Young snapped. But at four o'clock the next afternoon he died. His last audible words were, according to the *Deseret News,* "Joseph, Joseph, Joseph, Joseph."[65]

Between twelve and fifteen thousand persons attended the funeral in the Tabernacle and listened to eulogies of the prophet by Cannon, Woodruff, and Taylor. Then members of Young's family, representatives of the various orders of the priesthood, and hundreds of Saints accompanied the coffin, a plain redwood box, to the graveyard.[66]

In death as in life Young remained controversial. As the *Deseret News* saw it, the prophet, "having finished his work on earth," had "gone into the spirit world to join with Joseph, Hyrum, Willard, Jedediah, Heber, George A. and other great and glorious servants of the Lord, to continue the great work they all labored for on earth."[67] *The New York Times* disagreed. "Cruel, bloody, and vindictive though this man doubtless was, he must be credited with the possession of abilities of a superior order. He seems to have loved power for its own sake. . . . He is dead. The Mormon State faces now the great problem of its existence. It is difficult to guess what shall be the result of this death. But it does seem that it will be the final blow which shall shatter the monstrous fabric of Mormonism."[68]

An examination of Young's financial accounts ushered in a bitter fight. Young seldom distinguished between his and his church's accounts, and his estate, originally valued at $2,500,000 in real estate, railroad and bank stock, shares in the Z.C.M.I., and other property, was actually worth $999,632.90 less than that. But five of Young's daughters refused to accept these findings. They accused the church of fraud and in 1880 were excommunicated. They included Dora Young Dunford, the daughter of Lucy Bigelow; Vilate Young Decker, whose mother was Miriam Works; Emily Young Clawson, the child of Emily Partridge; and two of

Emmeline Free's daughters, Marinda Hyde Young and, worst of all, Louisa Young Ferguson.[69] No blow would have hurt Young more than Punk's apostasy.

Even more important than this, however, was the selection of the new Mormon prophet. For years Young had expected Brigham, Jr., to succeed him, but scandals hurt the young man. Lee related how the son had been jailed in England. "I have been told that $26,000 were paid from the perpetual emigration fund for his release."[70]

In February 1876 the son's chance for success ended. His daughter, Alice, ran off with a Gentile. After a court battle, Brigham forced the girl to return home with him, but Saints throughout Utah shook their heads in disgust at his inability to control his family.[71]

During his last years Young turned to his most talented son, John, who labored under a different handicap. John had four wives, but he lived only with Libby Canfield. Suddenly, three weeks after his father's death, John was sealed to the buxom seventeen-year-old beauty Luella Cobb, the fourth member of her family to marry a Young. The bride was the daughter of James T. Cobb and Mary Van Cott, the granddaughter of Augusta Cobb, and the niece of Charlotte Cobb.[72]

Shortly after the wedding, following the principle set by Young in 1844, Taylor, the leader of the Twelve, became Young's successor. In Philadelphia, to which she had returned, Libby gloated over her husband's failure. "Don't you imagine he married that girl for love," she informed the New York *Sun*. "No, my husband loves me. It was ambition and in fulfillment of a promise made to his father on his deathbed. His father wished John to succeed to his place in the church, and that he might do so made him promise to become a polygamist. His marriage to Miss Cobb was his first step in the execution of the promise and, as he thought, toward his father's seat. But he has been disappointed. He was not chosen to succeed his father and now he bitterly regrets the step he has taken, and almost every day I receive letters and telegrams from him begging me to return. I treat them with contempt. I will never go back to him. I will be the wife of no man who would give me up and break his vows to me for the sake of power."[73]

VIII

IF RELIGION IS MORE THAN HISTORY, history is more than religion. Religion uses history to ascertain universal truths. To Mormons the exodus to Utah illustrates the determination of God's people to find a Promised Land in the face of Satanic opposition. Utah's prosperity shows God's consideration for His Saints and fulfills the promise of a better life for all believers. And the struggle against the Gentile symbolizes the Saints' determination to survive and live their religion. In this light Young's every move becomes as sacred to his people as Mohammed's is to Moslems and Buddha's to Buddhists.

But history is more than religion, and to accept uncritically the laudatory accounts of Young by historians of his church is to reduce history to mythology. In reality, Young's life was a combination of good and evil. He professed inspiration from Jesus but shunned the Master's fundamental teachings: love for one's enemies, meekness, and the abandonment of material things.

Young left to his followers a mixed legacy. He left a people determined to survive and prosper but one afraid of a monster called Satan and fearful of excommunication and damnation. Like Young, the Saints are a people of limited intellectual interests, a people more concerned with irrigation than with pure mathematics, a people, now as then, involved with their own history and no one else's. Young planted the seeds of this heritage. "There is not a free school in Mormondom," *The New York Times* lamented in 1869. "The result is a general lack of intelligence, except among the leaders, and the intelligence they possess is by no means of the highest order. The newspapers, of which there are several, are very guarded, and give the most meager accounts of everything."[74] For Utah's hundred thousand Saints Young founded one college, the University of Deseret, now the University of Utah, but he saw to it that *The Book of Mormon* was translated into almost every known language.

Young desired unquestioning obedience above all else, and made Utah the thinking man's graveyard. Where another self-proclaimed chosen people stressed education and looked for guidance to the rabbi, or teacher of law, the Saints ridiculed the wise man,

What Young could not understand, he feared. He despised Orson Pratt, the most accomplished, if in many ways the narrowest, Saint of his generation, for Pratt epitomized not the sturdy, indefatigable dirt farmer Young idolized but the absent-minded professor who dressed so shabbily that the prophet twice publicly reprimanded him for his appearance and twice gave him clothes suitable for the Tabernacle. Distrusting Pratt's intellectualism, Young sent him on an endless string of missions.[75]

Young possessed many admirable qualities, but only his wildest adherents considered him a theologian or a deep thinker. Luckily for the Saints, God imbued him with courage, determination, organizational skills, and the capacity to inspire and lead men. Probably no other Mormon could have marched his people to the Rockies, directed the establishment of over 325 Western towns, built railroads, stores, and factories, and brought to Utah tens of thousands of immigrants.

But Young could not do everything, and he was fortunate to have subordinates whose skills complemented his own. Often, however, these were the very men he persecuted. "Of all the Mormon apostles," Edward Tullidge wrote in the New York *World*, "Parley and Orson Pratt stand out incomparably beyond their compeers. They were not so much society-builders as Brigham Young, but they were far more apostolic. Indeed, Brigham has grown out of such men as the Pratts. It is questionable if Brigham has made twenty converts in all his life," Tullidge estimated with some degree of accuracy, although he completely overlooked Young's role in creating the Mormon missionary system in England in 1840. On the other hand, "Orson and Parley Pratt have directly or indirectly converted twenty thousand to Mormonism. Ask the people what brought them into the church, and you would hear from every direction Parley Pratt's 'Voice of Warning,' or 'Orson Pratt's Tracts,' until it would almost seem to you that the Pratts had created the church. Indeed, the best part of Mormon theology has been derived from them, and so it may be said that they also, to a great extent, originated Mormonism."[76]

Unlike the Pratt brothers, Young contributed little to Mormon theology. Polygamy for the masses, his most distinctive innovation, perished with him. By 1877 such marriages, already rare, occurred chiefly in rural areas. "A farmer desires laborers upon whom he can depend," observed one reporter, "and the less the wages he has to pay the better he is satisfied. He seeks wives who can till the soil, and with a half dozen able-bodied women at his command he has a good working force costing nothing but their board and clothes. I know of a farmer who has eight wives; they work in the field just as do the negro women in the south, and the head of the family acts as overseer or superintendent. He is prosperous and presumably happy; whether his wives share his feelings or not I am unable to say. When they quarrel, he administers the soothing cowhide and, if they show discontent and a fondness for freedom and store clothing, the same panacea is found effective. Farmers with four, five, six, or more wives are numerous, and it is among these people that polygamy has its greatest strength. Polygamy in Utah, especially among the rural population, is nothing more nor less than slavery, and its popularity arises almost wholly from its profitableness. It is the system of the south 20 years ago, with more lines of parallel than many of us might suspect."

In Salt Lake City the railroad killed plural marriage. There a Mormon woman heard from outsiders how the world despised her. Peeking into store windows, she saw Eastern finery a husband might be able to give one wife but not two, three, or four. Handsomely dressed Gentile women constantly reminded her of her plight.[77]

Finally, in September 1890, President Wilford Woodruff, Taylor's successor, yielded to the inevitable. He upheld celestial marriage as spiritually ideal but suspended its practice. Two weeks later a church conference ratified his statement. The reward came in 1896. Utah, Young's creation, entered the Union.

"There is no man on earth that has the power to perform a plural marriage," declared President Heber J. Grant, the son of the fiery Jedediah, in 1921. "A so-called plural marriage is adultery before God and the laws of the land."[78] Accepted as equals by their fellow citizens, the Saints no longer found it necessary to flaunt their country's institutions.

Unfortunately even these declarations failed to emancipate women from the bondage in which Smith and Young had placed them. In early Mormonism Smith made woman somewhat akin to man. She shared his baptism, entered the church as an equal, helped him with his assigned tasks, and became his honored partner in the Endowment ceremony. But plural marriage forced her to yield her husband to other women and barred her from heaven if she failed to marry and bear children. She could never hold the priesthood.

To the Mormon assertion that polygamy spawned a higher breed of man, William Hooper Young, the son of Libby Canfield and John W. Young, stood in contradiction. In September 1902 a three-column headline on the front page of the Newark *Evening News* announced his story: "Brigham Young's Grandson Is Wanted for Murder." William had lured Mrs. Anna Pulitzer to his father's apartment in Manhattan, had stabbed her to death, and had disposed of her nude and mutilated body in the meadows separating Newark and Jersey City. He then stuffed her bloodstained clothes into a trunk, which he sent to Chicago. William confessed the crime, was found guilty of murder in the second degree, and was sentenced to life in Sing Sing prison.[79]

With time the Kingdom of God, still revered by orthodox Saints, became less militant, undoubtedly because of Utah's admission to the Union but also because Young's and Smith's predictions proved inaccurate. Significantly, on the day Young died, Henry G. Bywater, a Saint for twenty-eight years, repeated one of them: "We shall some time go back and live peaceably in Jackson County in Missouri, for the Lord has spoken it. But this may not be for many years."[80]

Fate—or Satan—laughed. After a fierce court battle, the Reorganized church occupied Independence, Missouri. The Utah branch suddenly reversed itself, sometimes called Utah as well as Jackson County a Zion, and so completely covered up this once common assertion that in 1957, when the learned Mormon historian, William Mulder, published the story of Scandinavian migrations to Utah, he mistitled the book *Homeward to Zion.* Young Joseph Smith and his successors, not Woodruff and his, peered out onto the world from an office atop Zion.

Nor, as Young and Zina Huntington maintained, did a second Civil War bring the collapse of the United States. Smith had also said that 1866—the year the sixes came together—would find

America swimming in blood[81] and that disaster would again strike the United States about 1890.[82]

Despite all this, Mormonism continues to grow in power and influence, because of superb leadership and bold professions and because neither Gentile nor Saint has studied much of its history. For Young had the courage and audacity to declare himself a prophet in the golden age of American journalism. Greeley, Bennett, Richardson, Bowles, Bross, McClure, and dozens of others left a picture of him that has been ignored to this day. It shows Young to be more than ordinary but less than a god. Bloodthirsty and benevolent, dictatorial and generous, lustful and devout, he survives today in two and a half million Mormon hearts. And, in a world that soon forgets its famous men, he will continue to live as long as the religion he saved endures.

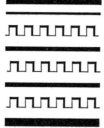

N O T E S

CHAPTER I   *Of Youngs, Kimballs, and Smiths*

1 Albert D. Richardson: *Beyond the Mississippi, From the Great River to the Great Ocean* (Hartford: American Publishing Company; 1867), p. 355.
2 Arthur Conan Doyle: *A Study in Scarlet and The Sign of the Four* (New York: Harper & Brothers; 1904), pp. 101–3.
3 Susa Young Gates and Mabel Young Sanborn: "Brigham Young Genealogy," *Utah Genealogical and Historical Magazine*, XI (January 1920), 21; Mabel Young Sanborn: *The Brigham Young Family*, chart in Genealogy Room, Western Reserve Historical Society, Cleveland.
4 Susa Young Gates: "The Young Family," *Utah Genealogical and Historical Magazine*, I (April 1910), 68; *Latter-day Saints' Millennial Star*, XXV (May 9, 1863), 295 (hereafter cited as *Millennial Star*).
5 M. Hamlin Cannon: "A Pension Office Note on Brigham Young's Father," *American Historical Review*, L (October 1944), 84; Susa Young Gates: "Notes on the Young and Howe Families," *Utah Genealogical and Historical Magazine*, XI (October 1920), 180–6.
6 Mary Van Sickle Wait: *Brigham Young in Cayuga County, 1813–1829* (Ithaca: DeWitt Historical Society of Tompkins Co.; 1964), p. 5.

7 Ibid., p. 36; Gates: "Notes on the Young and Howe Families," 180.

8 Honeoye Falls *Times*, January 26, 1922; *Deseret News*, September 5, 1877; *Millennial Star*, XXV (May 9, 1863), 295–6.

9 *History of Tioga, Chemung, Tompkins, and Schuyler Counties, New York* (Philadelphia: Everts & Ensign; 1879), p. 680; *The New York Times*, October 1, 1877.

10 *Deseret News*, May 11, 1854, and June 8, 1870; *Journal of Discourses*, IV, 312, and XII, 287 (hereafter cited without italics).

11 Wait: *Brigham Young in Cayuga County*, pp. 9–11, 23–4; *Fragments of Experience* (Salt Lake City: Juvenile Instructor Office; 1882), pp. 22–3.

12 *Millennial Star*, XXV (July 4, 1863), 423–4; *Fragments of Experience*, pp. 38–9.

13 Wait: *Brigham Young in Cayuga County*, pp. 38–9; Gates: "Notes on the Young and Howe Families," 182; John H. Beadle, *Western Wilds* (Cincinnati: Jones Brothers; 1877), p. 94.

14 Honeoye Falls *Times*, January 26, 1922, and February 2, 1922.

15 Journal of Discourses, VIII, 37–8, 129, and XII, 95; Honeoye Falls *Times*, January 26, 1922.

16 *Millennial Star*, XXVI (July 23, 1864), 471; Honeoye Falls *Times*, March 30, 1922; Journal of Abraham A. Kimball, p. 15, Utah State Historical Society, Salt Lake City.

17 Lucy Smith: *Biographical Sketches of Joseph Smith, the Prophet, and His Progenitures for Many Generations* (Liverpool: Orson Pratt; 1853), p. 167.

18 George S. Conover and Lewis Cass Aldrich: *History of Ontario County, New York* (Syracuse: D. Mason & Co.; 1893), p. 369; W. H. McIntosh: *History of Ontario Co., New York* (Philadelphia: Everts, Ensign & Everts; 1876), p. 201.

19 Honeoye Falls *Times*, February 2, and 9, 1922; March 30, 1922.

20 *Millennial Star*, XXVI (July 16, 1864), 455; Journal of Discourses, V, 216.

21 Journal of Discourses, XII, 190.

22 *Millennial Star*, XXVI (July 23, 1864), 472, 487; Edward Tullidge: *The Women of Mormondom* (New York: n.p.; 1877), pp. 107–9.

23 *Millennial Star*, XXV (June 6, 1863), 360–1.

24 Ibid.; Smith: *Biographical Sketches of Joseph Smith*, pp. 153, 166–7.

25 See *The New York Times*, May 19, 1858.

26 Honeoye Falls *Times*, February 2, 1922; Orson F. Whitney: *Life of Heber C. Kimball* (Salt Lake City: Kimball Family; 1888), p. 34; *Deseret News*, March 31, 1858, and April 7, 1858.

27 Whitney: *Life of Heber C. Kimball*, pp. 35–6; *Deseret News*, March 31, 1858, and April 7, 1858.

28 Journal of Discourses, IX, 219, and XIII, 211.

29 Rochester *Democrat and Chronicle*, undated clipping, Mormon Collec-

tion, King's Daughters Public Library, Palmyra, New York; Wait: *Brigham Young in Cayuga County*, p. 61.

30 Honeoye Falls *Times*, May 18, 1922; Wayne (New York) *Sentinel*, April 18, 1832, in Dale L. Morgan Collection, Utah State Historical Society, Salt Lake City.

31 *Millennial Star*, XXV (July 11, 1863), 438.

32 *Deseret News*, April 7, 1858; Journal of Discourses, VIII, 15–16.

33 "Three Weeks in Brigham Young's Office," September 10, 1859, Young Papers, Utah State Historical Society, Salt Lake City.

34 *Millennial Star*, XXV (July 11, 1863), 439.

35 Deeds, Liber 28, p. 23, Monroe County Courthouse, Rochester.

36 Deeds, Liber 26, p. 325, and Liber 27, p. 144, ibid.; *Millennial Star*, XXVI (August 20, 1864), 535.

37 *Millennial Star*, XXV (July 11, 1863), 440, and XXVI (August 20, 1864), 535.

CHAPTER II   *"A Child or a Fool Could Have Done It"*

1 J. B. Turner: *Mormonism in All Ages; Or The Rise, Progress, and Causes of Mormonism* (New York: Platt & Peters; 1842), pp. 97–9, 278; R. H. Taneyhill: "The Leatherwood God. An Account of the Appearance and Pretensions of Joseph C. Dylks in Eastern Ohio in 1828," *Ohio Valley Historical Series*, Miscellanies No. 7, part 3 (1870), 13–53.

2 F. L. Stewart: *Exploding the Myth about Joseph Smith, The Mormon Prophet* (New York: House of Stewart; 1967), pp. 9–11; Alice Felt Tyler: *Freedom's Ferment, Phases of American Social History from the Colonial Period to the Outbreak of the Civil War* (New York, Evanston, and London: Harper & Row; 1962), pp. 68, 86.

3 Fawn M. Brodie: *No Man Knows My History, The Life of Joseph Smith, The Mormon Prophet* (New York: Alfred A. Knopf; 1945), pp. 37–40.

4 Brodie: *No Man Knows My History*, pp. 76–9; Stewart: *Exploding the Myth*, pp. 32–3. The summary of *The Book of Mormon* is based on a reading of it.

5 McIntosh: *History of Ontario County*, p. 202.

6 Journal of Discourses, XIII, 77–80; Palmyra *Courier–Journal*, August 10, 1954, clipping in Mormon Collection, King's Daughters Public Library, Palmyra; Pomeroy Tucker: *Origin, Rise, and Progress of Mormonism* (New York: D. Appleton and Company; 1867), pp. 38–9.

7 *Millennial Star*, XIX (August 8, 1857), 497; Journal of Discourses, XII, 70–1, and XIV, 41–2.

8 Journal of Discourses, XVIII, 215; *Seer*, II (January 1854), 205; New York *Herald*, May 6, 1877; *Millennial Star*, XXVI (August 13, 1864), 519–20.

9 *Missouri Intelligencer*, April 13, 1833, in Mormon Collection, Missouri Historical Society, St. Louis. For the opposing view that Mormonism appealed to intellectuals see Stewart: *Exploding the Myth*, pp. 13–15.

10 Washington *Daily Intelligencer*, August 20, 1835, in Morgan Collection; John H. Beadle: *Life in Utah* (Philadelphia: National Publishing Company; 1870), p. 324.

11 Benjamin Brown: *Testimonies to the Truth, A Record of Manifestations of the Power of God, Miraculous and Providential* (Liverpool: S. W. Richards; 1853), *passim.*; I. Woodbridge Riley: *The Founder of Mormonism* (New York: Dodd, Mead & Company; 1902), p. 292.

12 *Deseret News*, May 9, 1855.

13 Fawn Brodie attributes Mormonism's success to these in *No Man Knows My History*, p. 83.

14 New York *Sun*, September 16, 1877.

15 New York *Herald*, February 21, 1858.

16 See New York *World*, November 27, 1870.

17 Journal of Discourses, II, 128; *Deseret News*, May 11, 1854.

18 Marriage Record C, p. 42, Geauga County Courthouse, Chardon, Ohio. The date of this marriage is often erroneously given as February 18, 1834. For Young's comments on Mary Ann see *Millennial Star*, XXV (July 18, 1863), 454.

19 Brodie: *No Man Knows My History*, pp. 128–33.

20 *Millennial Star*, XXV (July 18, 1863), 454–5.

21 Journal of Discourses, IV, 101–5; Eber D. Howe: *Mormonism Unvailed, or, A Faithful Account of That Singular Imposition and Delusion from Its Rise to the Present Time* (Painesville, Ohio: The Author; 1834), pp. 155–6.

22 *Millennial Star*, XXV (July 18, 1863), 455; Journal of Discourses, IX, 88–9.

23 Nauvoo *Times and Seasons*, VI (April 15, 1845), 868–9; *Historical Record*, V (January 1886), 14–15.

24 *Here Is Lake County, Ohio* (Cleveland: Howard Allen; 1964), p. 62; Brodie: *No Man Knows My History*, pp. 179–80; James H. Kennedy: *The Early Days of Mormonism, Palmyra, Kirtland, and Nauvoo* (New York: Charles Scribner's Sons; 1888), p. 171.

25 Whitney: *Life of Kimball*, p. 103.

26 *Millennial Star*, XXV (August 1, 1863), 487.

27 Marriage Record C, pp. 55, 60, 141–4, 215, 230, 235, Geauga County Courthouse.

28 Common Pleas Journal N, p. 304, Geauga County Courthouse; Paines-

ville *Republican*, May 25, 1837; Eber D. Howe: *Autobiography and Recollections of A Pioneer Printer* (Painesville: Telegraph Steam Printing House; 1878), p. 45.

29 Warren (Ohio) *News-Letter*, January 17, 1837, Morgan Collection; Brodie: *No Man Knows My History*, pp. 189, 194–6, 201–2.

30 Painesville *Telegraph*, February 20, 1835; April 17, 1835; and September 20, 1838.

31 Painesville *Republican*, January 19, 1837; *Latter Day Saints' Messenger and Advocate*, III (January 1837), 441–2, and (March 1837), 475–7.

32 Stock Ledger of the Mormon Bank at Kirtland, 1836–1837, pp. 1, 13, 15, 57, 209, 237, Mormon Collection, Chicago Historical Society.

33 Painesville *Telegraph*, January 20, 1837, and February 24, 1837.

34 *The Mormons, or Knavery Exposed* (Philadelphia: E. G. Lee; 1841), p. 14.

35 Kennedy: *Early Days of Mormonism*, p. 171.

36 John A. Clark: *Gleanings by the Way* (Philadelphia: W. J. & J. K. Simon; 1842), p. 334; William Hall: *The Abominations of Mormonism Exposed, Containing Many Facts and Doctrines Concerning That Singular People, during Seven Years Membership with Them; from 1840 to 1847* (Cincinnati: I. Hart; 1852), pp. 19, 130; *Millennial Star*, XXV (August 8, 1863), 503–4.

37 Quincy *Whig*, November 19, 1842, and *Sangamo Journal*, November 11, 1842, Helen and Cecil Snyder Collection, Rare Book Room, New York Public Library. G. B. Frost swore the affidavit.

38 Common Pleas Journal N, pp. 92–399, Geauga County Courthouse.

39 *Millennial Star*, XXV (June 18, 1864), 391–4.

40 Eliza R. Snow: *Biography and Family Record of Lorenzo Snow* (Salt Lake City: Deseret News Company; 1884), pp. 20–4; Lucy Smith: *Biographical Sketches of Joseph Smith*, p. 211.

41 Common Pleas Journal N, p. 290, Geauga County Courthouse. Quoted is Abigail D. Holmes to James J. Strang, Georgetown, Massachusetts, October 6, 1850, Strang Papers, Beinecke Library, Yale University.

42 See Frost's affidavit in *Sangamo Journal*, November 11, 1842, and Quincy *Whig*, November 19, 1842, Snider Collection; Marriage Record C, p. 262, Geauga County Courthouse.

43 *History of Geauga and Lake Counties, Ohio* (Philadelphia: Williams Brothers; 1878), pp. 25, 248.

44 Brigham H. Roberts (ed.): *History of the Church of Jesus Christ of Latter-Day Saints, Period I, History of Joseph Smith, The Prophet, By Himself* (Salt Lake City: Deseret News; 1948), II, 529.

45 Whitney: *Life of Heber C. Kimball*, p. 197.

46 Painesville *Republican*, February 22, 1838.

47 Ibid., February 22, 1838, and March 1, and 15, 1838.

CHAPTER III *The Hand of God*

1 *Millennial Star*, XXV (August 15, 1863), 518–20.
2 Leonard J. Arrington: *Great Basin Kingdom, An Economic History of the Latter-day Saints, 1830–1900* (Lincoln: University of Nebraska Press; 1966), p. 15.
3 T. Earl Pardoe: *Lorin Farr, Pioneer* (Provo: Brigham Young University Press; 1953), p. 50; Journal of Discourses, XVI, 48.
4 *Millennial Star*, XXV (August 22, 1863), 535–6.
5 *Document Containing the Correspondence, Orders, &c. in Relation to the Disturbances with the Mormons; and the Evidence Given before the Hon. Austin A. King, Judge of the Fifth Judicial Circuit of the State of Missouri, at the Court-House in Richmond in A Criminal Court of Inquiry, Begun November 12, 1838, on the Trial of Joseph Smith, Jr., and Others, for High Treason and Other Crimes Against the State* (Fayette, Missouri: Boon's Lick Democrat; 1841), pp. 57–8, 97.
6 Ibid., 114.
7 Ibid., 17, 58.
8 Lu B. Cake: *Peepstone Joe and the Peck Manuscript* (New York: L. B. Cake; 1899), pp. 95–7.
9 "Reminiscences of John Taylor": pp. 17–19, Manuscript in Mormon Collection, Bancroft Library, University of California, Berkeley; *Millennial Star*, XIX (June 20, 1857), 394.
10 John Corrill: *Brief History of the Church of Christ of Latter Day Saints (Commonly Called Mormons); Including An Account of Their Doctrine and Discipline; With the Reasons of the Author for Leaving the Church* (St. Louis: The Author; 1839), pp. 30–2; Oliver B. Huntington Diary, I, 36, Utah State Historical Society; Albert P. Rockwood to Parents, Far West, October 29, 1838, Rockwood Papers, Beinicke Library, Yale University.
11 Kennedy: *Early Days of Mormonism*, pp. 193–4; Jedediah M. Grant: *A Collection of Facts, Relative to the Course Taken by Elder Sidney Rigdon, in the States of Ohio, Missouri, Illinois and Pennsylvania* (Philadelphia: Brown, Bicking & Guilbert; 1844), p. 11.
12 Cake: *Peepstone Joe and the Peck Manuscript*, pp. 97–8.
13 Brodie: *No Man Knows My History*, pp. 225–40; *Millennial Star*, XXV (June 20, 1863), 29.
14 John D. Lee: *Mormonism Unveiled* (St. Louis: Excelsior Publishing Company; 1891), pp. 74–5.
15 Brodie: *No Man Knows My History*, pp. 234–40.
16 *Deseret News*, November 2, 1854; *Historical Record*, VII (January

1888), 712–15; Brigham H. Roberts: *The Missouri Persecutions* (Salt Lake City: George Q. Cannon; 1900), pp. 262–4.

17 *Millennial Star*, XXV (September 6, 1863), 567–8, and (September 12, 1863), 583–5; *Tullidge's Quarterly Magazine*, III (April 1884), 121–2.

18 Robert Bruce Flanders: *Nauvoo, Kingdom on the Mississippi* (Urbana: University of Illinois Press; 1965), p. 23; undated clipping, Folder 11, Thomas L. Kane Papers, Stanford University Library, Palo Alto, California; New York *Herald*, August 3, 1841; Nauvoo *Times and Seasons*, III (October 1, 1842), 936–7.

19 *Tullidge's Quarterly Magazine*, III (April 1884), 123–4.

20 *Millennial Star*, XXV (October 10, 1863), 645–6.

21 *Deseret News*, August 3, 1854.

22 New York *Herald*, May 6, 1877.

23 *Millennial Star*, XXV (October 17, 1863), 663–4, and (November 7, 1863), 711–12; *Deseret News*, March 3, 1858.

24 "Mormonism; or, New Mohammedanism in England and America," *Dublin University Magazine*, XXI (March 1843), 295–6.

25 *Journal of Heber C. Kimball* (Nauvoo: Robinson & Smith; 1840), p. 57; Nauvoo *Times and Seasons*, IV (April 15, 1843), 162; *Deseret News*, March 3, 1858; Journal of Discourses, IV, 34–5; XIII, 211–13; and XIV, 80–1.

26 *Tullidge's Quarterly Magazine*, III (April 1884), 132; Journal of Discourses, XV, 344.

27 Journal of Discourses, III, 368–9, and IV, 2.

28 *Deseret News*, March 10, 1858; Journal of Discourses, III, 229–30.

29 *Deseret News*, March 10, 1858; *Millennial Star*, XXVI (January 30, 1864), 71.

30 Journal of Discourses, XVII, 259.

31 Kennedy: *Early Days of Mormonism*, p. 220; New York *Herald*, June 26, 1841, and May 6, 1842.

32 New York *Herald*, January 18, 1843; Journal of J. M. Sharpe, pp. 34–5, Beinicke Library, Yale University; Charlotte Haven: "A Girl's Letters from Nauvoo," *Overland Monthly*, XVI (December 1890), 623.

33 New York *Herald*, January 18, 1843.

34 Edwin de Leon: *Thirty Years of My Life on Three Continents* (London: Ward and Downey; 1890), I, 57; Henry Adams: "Charles Francis Adams Visits the Mormons in 1844," *Proceedings of the Massachusetts Historical Society*, LXVIII (October 1944–May 1947), 285; New York *Log Cabin*, August 7, 1841.

35 Peoria *Register and Northwestern Gazette*, April 17, 1840, Snider Collection; Quincy *Whig*, October 17, 1840, ibid.

36 Nauvoo *Times and Seasons*, III (October 15, 1842), 955. For Bennett's comment about baptism see *Littel's Living Age*, 2nd Series, VI (July 15, 1854), 106.

37 *Millennial Star*, I (February 1841), 270; Nauvoo *Times and Seasons*, II (January 1, 1841), 264; *Sangamo Journal*, June 10, 1842, Snider Collection; Warsaw *Signal*, February 2, 1842.

38 Quoted in *Sangamo Journal*, July 22, 1842, Snider Collection.

39 Davenport *Gazette*, undated clipping, ibid.

40 Journal of Discourses, III, 120–2.

41 New York *Herald*, May 21, 1842; *Millennial Star*, I (March 1841), 267; Warsaw *Signal*, April 24, 1844.

42 Nauvoo *Times and Seasons*, II (October 15, 1841), 569–70.

43 J. Butterfield to C. B. Penrose, Springfield, Illinois, August 2, 1842, December 17, 1842, and May 25, 1843, Box 25, Letters Received, United States Attorneys, Clerks of Courts and Marshals, Records of the Solicitor of the Treasury, Record Group 206, National Archives.

44 *Deseret News*, July 1, 1874; Brigham H. Roberts: *Plural Marriage, The Mormon Marriage System* (Salt Lake City: Truth Publishing Company; n. d.), p. 15.

45 *Deseret News*, November 23, 1878.

46 For the article see *Latter Day Saints' Messenger and Advocate*, I (August 1835), 163.

47 Nauvoo *Times and Seasons*, I (April 1840), 85.

48 Helen Mar Whitney: *Plural Marriage As Taught By the Prophet Joseph* (Salt Lake City: Juvenile Instructor Office; 1882), pp. 11–12.

49 Udney Hay Jacob (An Israelite and A Shepherd of Israel): *An Extract from A Manuscript Entitled the Peace Maker, or the Doctrines of the Millennium, Being A Treatise on Religion and Jurisprudence, Or A New System of Religion and Politicks* (Nauvoo: J. Smith, Printer; 1842), pp. 2, 36.

50 *Utah Genealogical and Historical Magazine*, XXIX (July 1938), 137; Frank Esshom: *Pioneers and Prominent Men of Utah* (Salt Lake City: Utah Pioneers Book Publishing Company; 1913), p. 956.

51 Brodie: *No Man Knows My History*, pp. 320, 334–7. For Smith's promise see Whitney, *Life of Heber C. Kimball*, p. 339.

52 Eduard Meyer: *Ursprung und Geschichte Der Mormonen* (Halle: Max Niemeyer; 1912), p. 166; *In the Circuit Court of the United States, Western District of Missouri . . . The Reorganized Church of Jesus Christ of Latter Day Saints, Complainant, vs. The Church of Christ at Independence, Missouri . . . Respondents, Complainant's Abstract of Pleading and Evidence* (Lamoni, Iowa: Herald Publishing House and Bindery; 1893), p. 166 (hereafter cited as *Temple Lot Case*).

53 Journal of Discourses, III, 266.

54 New York *Herald*, November 21, 1871; *The New York Times*, March 10, 1879.

55 *Sangamo Journal*, July 22, 1842; New York *Herald*, July 27, 1842.

56 Nauvoo *Times and Seasons*, III (April 15, 1842), 763.

57 John Bowes: *Mormonism Exposed* (London: R. Bulman; 1854), p. 64; Samuel M. Smucker: *The Religious, Social, and Political History of the Mormons* (New York: Miller, Orton & Co.; 1857), p. 381.

58 *Deseret News*, March 17, 1858.

59 De Leon: *Thirty Years of My Life on Three Continents*, I, 55–6, 60.

60 New York *World*, September 4, and 11, 1870. See the New York *Herald*, April 24, 1852, for the dates the Mormons allotted to each dispensation.

61 New York *Herald*, July 21, and 24, 1842; John C. Bennett: *The History of the Saints, or An Exposé of Joe Smith and Mormonism* (Boston: Leland & Whiting; 1842), pp. 236–49.

62 Nauvoo *Times and Seasons*, III (July 1, 1842), 839–42, and (August 1, 1842), 870–2.

63 Document dated July 27, 1842, Nauvoo City, Folder 17, Oliver H. Olney Papers, Beinicke Library, Yale University.

64 Nauvoo *Times and Seasons*, V (April 15, 1844), 504–6.

65 Nauvoo *Neighbor*, March 6, 1844, and July 31, 1844; Newark *Daily Advertiser*, July 5, 1844.

66 *Deseret News*, March 24, 1858; Warsaw *Signal*, June 29, 1844; New York *Herald*, July 8, 1844.

CHAPTER IV   *"I Know the Twelve"*

1 *A Series of Instructions and Remarks by President Young at A Special Council, Tabernacle, March 21, 1858* (n. p.: n. p.; n. d.), pp. 3–4. The only copy of this document is in Beinicke Library, Yale University.

2 Warsaw *Signal*, February 19, 1845; Roberts (ed.): *History of the Church*, VII, 420.

3 Nauvoo *Times and Seasons*, V (July 1, 1844), 568.

4 *Deseret News*, March 24, 1858.

5 *Millennial Star*, XXV (March 21, 1863), 183.

6 Mary Ettie V. Smith: *Mormonism, Its Rise, Progress, and Present Condition* (Hartford: Belknap & Bliss; 1870), pp. 37–9.

7 *Deseret News*, June 25, 1856; Nauvoo *Times and Seasons*, IV (September 15, 1843), 329–30. See *Millennial Star*, V (December 1844), 109, for Woodruff's comments.

8 *Millennial Star*, XXV (March 28, 1863), 200, and (April 4, 1863), 215.

9 Ibid., XXV (April 11, 1863), 231–2; Nauvoo *Times and Seasons*, V (September 2, 1844), 637–8.

10 *Correspondence of Bishop George Miller with the Northern Islander,*

From His First Acquaintance with Mormonism Up to Near the Close of His Life (Burlington, Wisconsin: Wingfield Watson; 1916), p. 23.

11 John Pulsipher Journal, 1837–74, p. 7, Utah State Historical Society; Journal of Discourses, XIII, 181.

12 Nauvoo *Times and Seasons*, V (September 15, 1844), 647–55; (October 1, 1844), 660–7; (October 15, 1844), 685–7.

13 Brigham Young to Brother Rogers, Nauvoo, December 5, 1844, Mormon Collection, Beinecke Library, Yale University.

14 Nauvoo *Times and Seasons*, V (January 1, 1845), 760.

15 *Latter Day Saints' Messenger and Advocate*, I (October 15, 1844), 11–12, and (December 16, 1844), 61.

16 New York *Herald*, November 18, 1844.

17 *Messenger and Advocate of the Church of Christ*, I (April 15, 1845), 172.

18 Charles L. Woodward: *Bibliothica* [sic] *Scallawagiana* (New York: n. p.; 1880), p. 11.

19 James J. Strang Autobiography, Binder One, Strang Papers.

20 Warsaw *Signal*, August 18, 1846; Voree *Herald*, I (April 1846), 3–4.

21 *Gospel Herald*, III (April 27, 1848), 21–3; Joseph Smith to Strang, Nauvoo, June 18, 1844, Binder One, Strang Papers. See the similar postmarks on the following letters: Albert Brown to Amos L. Underwood, Nauvoo, November 11, 1844, Brown Papers, Library of Congress; John E. Forsiguen to Hiram Hunt, Nauvoo, June 12, 1844, Forsiguen Papers, New-York Historical Society.

22 See Dale L. Morgan's discerning remarks in the Calendar to Strang Papers, pp. 21–8, Beinicke Library, Yale University. Many of the reflections in this paragraph are Professor Morgan's. Several are mine.

23 *The Star of the East*, I (November 1846), 12–14.

24 *Missouri Republican*, August 8, 1846, Snider Collection; *Gospel Herald*, II (September 23, 1847), 116; *The Star of the East*, I (November 1846), 17–19.

25 New York *Herald*, January 15, 1870; Nauvoo *Times and Seasons*, V (September 2, 1844), 631.

26 St. Louis *American*, April 1, 1846, Snider Collection; Brodie: *No Man Knows My History*, pp. 362–3.

27 Hall: *Abominations of Mormonism Exposed*, pp. 103–4.

28 *Temple Lot Case*, p. 36.

29 Lee: *Mormonism Unveiled*, p. 161.

30 James M. Monroe Diary, May 29, 1845, pp. 132–3, Beinecke Library, Yale University.

31 William Smith to Jesse C. Little, Nauvoo, August 20, 1845, William Smith Papers, Utah State Historical Society.

32 Warsaw *Signal*, October 29, 1845. For Smith's six wives see *Temple Lot Case*, pp. 380, 384.

33 *Deseret News*, July 22, 1857.

34 *Temple Lot Case*, p. 324.

35 *Millennial Star*, XXVII (February 11, 1865), 83; Journal of Discourses, XIII, 110; *Historical Record*, V (January 1886), 10.

36 Catherine Lewis: *Narrative of Some of the Proceedings of the Mormons; Giving An Account of Their Iniquities, With Particulars Concerning the Training of the Indians by Them, Description of the Mode of the Endowment, Plurality of Wives, &c., &c.* (Lynn, Massachusetts: The Author; 1848), p. 6.

37 Lee, *Mormonism Unveiled*, p. 160.

38 Manuscript Testimony Before High Council at Voree, April 6, 1846, Binder One, Strang Papers; Milo M. Quaife: *The Kingdom of Saint James, A Narrative of the Mormons* (New Haven: Yale University Press; 1930), pp. 28–30. See also Fanny Stenhouse: *"Tell It All," The Story of A Life's Experience in Mormonism* (Hartford: A. D. Worthington & Co.; 1874), pp. 306–7.

39 *Deseret News*, September 2, 1857; New York *Herald*, October 28, 1857.

40 Manuscript Testimony Before High Council at Voree, April 6, 1846, Binder One, Strang Papers.

41 Robert Glass Cleland and Juanita Brooks (eds.): *A Mormon Chronicle, The Diaries of John D. Lee, 1848–1876* (San Marino: Huntington Library; 1955), I, 330.

42 Wilhelm Wyl: *Mormon Portraits, or The Truth About the Mormon Leaders from 1830 to 1886* (Salt Lake City: Tribune Printing and Publishing Company; 1886), p. 52.

43 Brigham Young to James K. Polk, Nauvoo, May 10, 1845, Vol. 81, Polk Papers, Library of Congress; Young to Governor James Fenner of Rhode Island, Nauvoo, April 25, 1845, Mormon Collection, Chicago Historical Society; Young to Governor James McDowell of Virginia, Nauvoo, April 30, 1845, Young Papers, Manuscript Division, New York Public Library; Young to Governor William Owsley of Kentucky, Nauvoo, April 30, 1845, in Salt Lake *Tribune*, April 6, 1962, and *Deseret News and Telegram*, April 6, 1962; New York *Herald*, June 9, 1845.

44 Journal of Discourses, XIII, 110–14.

45 *Millennial Star*, XXIV (October 4, 1862), 630.

46 Unpublished Manuscript of Thomas C. Sharp, p. 24, Sharp Anti-Mormon Papers, Beinicke Library, Yale University.

47 Ibid., pp. 12–13; Warsaw *Signal*, September 17, 1845, Snider Collection; Harold Schindler: *Orrin Porter Rockwell, Man of God, Son of Thunder* (Salt Lake City: University of Utah Press; 1966), p. 145.

48 New York *Herald*, October 1, 1877; Fitz Hugh Ludlow: *The Heart of the Continent* (New York: Hurd and Houghton; 1870), p. 354; Charles Kelly and Hoffman Birney: *Holy Murder, The Story of Porter*

Rockwell (New York: Milton Balch and Company; 1934), *passim*. See also the incisive but bitter account of Rockwell in New York *World*, January 16, 1870.

49 *Millennial Star*, XXXIV (July 2, 1872), 429; Juanita Brooks (ed.): *On the Mormon Frontier, The Diary of Hosea Stout, 1844–1861* (Salt Lake City: University of Utah Press and Utah State Historical Society; 1964), I, 64.

50 Bloomington (Illinois) *Herald*, May 8, 1846, Snider Collection; St. Louis *American*, May 30, 1846, ibid.; Wallace Stegner: *The Gathering of Zion, The Story of the Mormon Trail* (New York, Toronto, London: McGraw-Hill Book Company; 1964), p. 90.

51 *Sangamo Journal*, October 1, 1845, Snider Collection; Young to John J. Hardin, Nauvoo, September 30, 1845, Hardin Papers, Chicago Historical Society; Young to Hardin, W. B. Warren, S. A. Douglas, and J. A. McDougall, Nauvoo, October 1, 1845, ibid.

52 New York *Herald*, October 18, 1845.

53 Lee, *Mormonism Unveiled*, p. 145.

54 Tullidge: *Women of Mormondom*, pp. 418–22.

55 *Historical Record*, VI (May 1887), 235; Smith: *Mormonism, Its Rise, Progress, and Present Condition*, pp. 36–7.

56 *Temple Lot Case*, p. 364.

57 New York *Tribune*, December 16, 1871.

58 Brodie: *No Man Knows My History*, p. 448.

59 Lee: *Mormonism Unveiled*, p. 132.

60 Hall: *Abominations of Mormonism Exposed*, pp. 43–4. See the interview with Zina in New York *World*, November 17, 1869.

61 Lee: *Mormonism Unveiled*, pp. 132, 166–9.

62 Lewis: *Narrative of Some of the Proceedings of the Mormons*, pp. 5–6; Quincy *Whig*, December 22, 1847, Snider Collection.

63 Lewis: *Narrative of Some of the Proceedings of the Mormons*, pp. 5–7, 19.

64 Brodie: *No Man Knows My History*, p. 456.

65 Hall: *Abominations of Mormonism Exposed*, pp. 44–5.

66 Whitney: *Life of Heber C. Kimball*, p. 433. Kimball listed Christeen as a wife in Eighth Census (1860), Utah, Vol. 1, p. 270, Records of the Bureau of Census, Record Group 29, National Archives.

67 *Millennial Star*, VI (July 1, 1845), 22–3.

68 Esshom: *Pioneers and Prominent Men of Utah*, p. 1113.

69 Office of the District Attorney of the United States for Illinois, December 31, 1845, in Reports of the United States District Attorneys, 1845–50, Vol. I, Records of the Solicitor of the Treasury, Record Group 206.

70 Journal of Discourses, XIV, 218–19.

71 Smith: *Mormonism, Its Rise, Progress, and Present Condition*, p. 55; Lee: *Mormonism Unveiled*, p. 175.

72 Journal of Discourses, XV, 165–6.

73 Burlington *Iowa Territorial Gazette and Advertiser*, February 14, 1846; *Millennial Star*, XXXIX (May 14, 1877), 309.

74 Lewis: *Narrative of Some of the Proceedings of the Mormons*, p. 23.

CHAPTER V   *To the White Horse of Safety*

1 Warsaw *Signal*, October 29, 1845.

2 St. Louis *Weekly American*, May 8, 1846, Snider Collection.

3 William J. Petersen: "Mormons on the March," *Palimpsest*, 27 (May 1946), 147; New York *Herald*, February 23, 1846.

4 St. Louis *American*, February 11, 1846, Snider Collection; New York *Herald*, February 23 and 27, 1846.

5 Warsaw *Signal*, February 11, 1846, and March 11, 1846. For the size of the migration see Dexter C. Bloomer: "The Mormons in Iowa," *Annals of Iowa*, 3rd Series, II (January 1897), 590–1.

6 Journal of Discourses, XVII, 7.

7 *Hancock Eagle*, July 10, 1846; Brigham Young to Harriet Cook, March 25, 1846, Young Papers, Utah State Historical Society; J. Keith Melville: "Theory and Practice of Church and State during the Brigham Young Era," *Brigham Young University Studies*, III (Autumn 1960), 40.

8 Genevieve P. Mauck: "Kanesville," *Palimpsest*, XLII (September 1961), 391; Young to Harriet Cook, Council Bluffs, June 23, 1846, Young Papers, Utah State Historical Society.

9 *Hancock Eagle*, June 13, 1846.

10 New York *Herald*, May 23, 1846; *Hancock Eagle*, August 28, 1846.

11 Warsaw *Signal*, January 7, 1846.

12 James J. Strang to Emma Smith, Voree, February 22, 1846, Mormon Collection, Chicago Historical Society.

13 Almon W. Babbitt, John S. Fullmer, and Joseph L. Heywood to Lucy Smith, no date, Binder 2, Strang Papers; Lucy Smith to Babbitt, Heywood, and Fullmer, March 22, 1846, Binder 2, ibid.

14 See the advertisement in Rigdon's *Messenger and Advocate of the Church of Christ*, I (October 15, 1845), 367–8; John C. Bennett to Strang, Cincinnati, March 29, 1846, Binder 5, Strang Papers.

15 Bennett to Strang, June 2, 1846, Binder 2, Strang Papers.

16 Bennett to Strang, March 1846, Binder 2, ibid.

17 Bennett to Strang, Cincinnati, April 2, 1846, Binder 2, ibid.

18 Warsaw *Signal*, August 18, 1846, and November 14, 1846.

19 William Smith to Strang, Knoxville, Illinois, December 14, 1846, Binder 2, Strang Papers.

20 Young to Beloved Brethren, Nauvoo, January 24, 1846, Binder 1, ibid.; Reuben Miller to Strang, Nauvoo, February 15, 1846, Binder 1, ibid.

21 The pamphlet was published in Keokuk, Iowa.

22 Stang to I. A. Hopkins, Burlington, Wisconsin, December 21, 1846, Binder 3, Strang Papers; St. Louis *American*, October 1, 1846, Snider Collection.

23 *Millennial Star*, XXIX (February 16, 1867), 101.

24 Journal of Discourses, V, 231–2.

25 Young to James K. Polk, Mormon Camp near Council Bluffs, August 9, 1846, Vol. 106, Polk Papers, Library of Congress.

26 *Millennial Star*, VIII (November 15, 1846), 117; Thomas B. Stenhouse: *The Rocky Mountain Saints* (London: Ward, Lock and Tyler; 1874), p. 248.

27 Ursulia B. Hascall to Colonel Wilson Andrews, Camp of Israel, September 19, 1846, Mormon Collection, Missouri Historical Society, St. Louis.

28 Melville: "Theory and Practice of Church and State," 41; Ernest Widtsoe Shumway: "Winter Quarters, Nebraska, 1846–1848," *Nebraska History*, XXXV (June 1954), 118; Thomas H. Harvey to William Medill, St. Louis, December 3, 1846, Thomas L. Kane Papers, Stanford University Library.

29 Arthur C. Wakeley: *Omaha, The Gate City, and Douglas County, Nebraska* (Chicago: S. J. Clarke; 1917), I, 52.

30 Lee: *Mormonism Unveiled*, pp. 183, 195–7.

31 Charles Kelly (ed.): *Journals of John D. Lee, 1846–1847 and 1859* (Salt Lake City: Western Publishing Company; 1938), pp. 34, 60–61; Journal History, August 14, 1846, Mormon Church Historian's Office, Salt Lake City; Arrington: *Great Basin Kingdom*, p. 21.

32 *Correspondence of Bishop George Miller with the Northern Islander*, pp. 36–37.

33 Journal of Discourses, VI, 173–4.

34 Wakeley: *Omaha*, I, 52; Omaha *Bee*, January 30, 1887.

35 Harvey to Medill, St. Louis, December 3, 1846, Kane Papers, Stanford University Library.

36 Two-Page Document by Oliver Olney, July 20, 1842, Folder 15 and Four-Page Document, July 22, 1842, Folder 16, Olney Papers.

37 Unpublished Prophecy of Joseph Smith, Related to Edwin and Theodore Turley on or about May 6, 1843, Smith Papers, Utah State Historical Society.

38 Hyrum L. Andrus: "Joseph Smith and the West," *Brigham Young University Studies*, II (Spring–Summer 1960), 136; Klaus Hansen: "The Making of King Strang: A Re-Examination," *Michigan History*, 46 (September 1962), 208; James R. Clark: "The Kingdom of God, The Council of Fifty and the State of Deseret," *Utah Historical Quarterly*, XXVI (April 1958), 137.

39 *Correspondence of Bishop George Miller with the Northern Islander,* p. 20; Hansen: "Making of King Strang," 214–15; Flanders: *Nauvoo,* pp. 294–5.

40 *Millennial Star,* XXV (December 19, 1863), 805.

41 Journal History, December 27 and 29, 1845, and March 27, 1846, Mormon Church Historian's Office; Reva Stanley: *A Biography of Parley P. Pratt, The Archer of Paradise* (Caldwell, Idaho: Caxton Publishers; 1937), p. 187.

42 Dodge Records, VIII, 78, Grenville M. Dodge Papers, Iowa State Department of History and Archives, Des Moines; Milton R. Hunter: *Brigham Young, The Colonizer* (Salt Lake City: *Deseret News*; 1940), pp. 28–9.

43 New York *Tribune,* May 24, 1858; Bernard de Voto: *The Year of Decision, 1846* (Boston: Little, Brown and Company; 1943), p. 237; Young to Colonel Kearney, Captain Clary, or Whomever May Be in Command of Fort Leavenworth, Near Council Bluffs, Omaha Nation, August 10, 1846, Kane Papers, Stanford University Library.

44 Kane to William L. Marcy, Washington, April 30, 1847, Kane Papers, Library of Congress.

45 *Millennial Star,* XII (January 15, 1850), 18; "The Word and Will of the Lord Concerning the Camp of Israel in Their Journeyings to the West," Winter Quarters, January 14, 1847, copy, Mormon Collection, Beinicke Library, Yale University; Stenhouse: *Rocky Mountain Saints,* p. 255.

46 Kelly (ed.): *Journal of John D. Lee,* p. 130.

47 Ibid., pp. 128–9.

48 Clara Decker Young: "A Woman's Experience with the Pioneer Band," p. 4, Manuscript in Bancroft Library, University of California, Berkeley; Howard Egan: *Pioneering the West, 1846 to 1878* (Richmond, Utah: Howard R. Egan Estate; 1917), p. 24.

49 Egan: *Pioneering the West,* pp. 23–4.

50 *Millennial Star,* XII (January 15, 1850), 18.

51 Bernard de Voto: *Across the Wide Missouri* (Boston: Houghton Mifflin Company; 1964), p. 319; *Millennial Star,* XII (January 15, 1850), 18, and (February 1, 1850), 33.

52 *Millennial Star,* XII (March 1, 1850), 66.

53 Ibid., XII (April 1, 1850), 99–100.

54 Hall: *Abominations of Mormonism Exposed,* pp. 64–5, 121–3.

55 John Y. Nelson: *Fifty Years on the Trail* (New York: Frederick Warne & Company; 1889), p. 88.

56 *Millennial Star,* XII (April 15, 1850), 114; (May 1, 1850), 129; (May 15, 1850), 146.

57 Ibid., XII (May 15, 1850), 147; Hunter: *Brigham Young, The Colonizer,* p. 29.

58 *Millennial Star*, XII (June 1, 1850), 163–5.

59 Hunter: *Brigham Young, The Colonizer*, p. 31; *William Clayton's Journal, A Daily Record of the Journey of the Original Company of 'Mormon' Pioneers from Nauvoo, Illinois, to the Valley of the Great Salt Lake* (Salt Lake City: *Deseret News*; 1921), pp. 312–14.

60 Journal of Discourses, XVI, 207.

61 *The New York Times*, August 9, 1880; J. Cecil Alter: *Jim Bridger* (Norman: University of Oklahoma Press; 1962), p. 225.

62 "Reminiscences of John R. Young," *Utah Historical Quarterly*, III (July 1930), 83–4; John Codman: *The Mormon Country, A Summer with the 'Latter-Day' Saints* (New York: United States Publishing Company; 1874), pp. 123–4.

63 New York *Herald*, November 18, 1877; New York *Tribune*, October 27, 1889. For Pratt's remarks see Hunter: *Brigham Young, The Colonizer*, p. 32. Kane wrote Horace Greeley in August 1847: "Take it all in all, the Utah country is a country of sweet grass, heavy timber, clear air, pure water. . . . But they fear it wants rain." Kane Papers, Stanford University Library.

64 *Millennial Star*, XII (June 15, 1850), 180; Whitney: *Life of Heber C. Kimball*, p. 390.

65 Eliza R. Snow: "Sketch of My Life," p. 30, Manuscript in Bancroft Library, University of California, Berkeley.

66 Young to Charles C. Rich and the Presidents and Officers of the Emigrating Company, Pioneer Camp, Valley of the Great Salt Lake, August 2, 1847, Young Papers, Utah State Historical Society.

67 Lorenzo Dow Young Diary, August 26, 1847, Utah State Historical Society; Ray Allen Billington: *The Far Western Frontier, 1830–1860* (New York: Harper & Row; 1956), p. 200.

68 *Historical Record*, V (June 1886), 73–4; Stenhouse: *Rocky Mountain Saints*, pp. 262–4.

69 *Millennial Star*, XXII (December 22, 1860), 802–3.

70 New York *Herald*, March 4, 1848; *Millennial Star*, IX (December 1, 1847), 365.

71 Oliver B. Huntington Diary, May 14, 1848, II, 17, Utah State Historical Society.

72 *Millennial Star*, XXXI (January 9, 1869), 20–1.

73 Shumway: "Winter Quarters," 124–5. See also the following entries in Huntington Diary, II, Utah State Historical Society: June 4, 1848, p. 21; July 20, 1848, p. 33; August 20, 1848, p. 34.

74 Hunter: *Brigham Young, The Colonizer*, pp. 128–9, 132–3, 136.

75 Ibid., pp. 136–8; Billington: *Far Western Frontier*, pp. 201–2.

CHAPTER VI   *Honey in the Carcass of the Dead Lion*

1 Orson Pratt: *The Kingdom of God, Part I, No. 2* (Liverpool: S. W. Richards; October 31, 1848), p. 1.

2 John Taylor: *The Government of God* (Liverpool: S. W. Richards; 1852), pp. 93, 95. See also Pratt: *Kingdom of God, Part I, No. 2*, pp. 1–8.

3 Parley P. Pratt: *Autobiography* (New York: Russell Brothers; 1874), pp. 471–2.

4 Taylor: *Government of God*, pp. 103–4.

5 Orson Pratt: *The Kingdom of God, Part II* (Liverpool: R. James; 1848), p. 1.

6 Orson Pratt: *The Kingdom of God, Part III* (Liverpool: R. James; January 14, 1849), p. 7.

7 Preston Nibley: *Brigham Young, The Man and His Work* (Independence: Zion's Printing & Publishing Company; 1936), p. 418.

8 New York *Tribune*, November 18, 1871.

9 Bill Hickman: *Brigham's Destroying Angel* (Salt Lake City: Shepard Publishing Company; 1904), p. 96.

10 Louis B. Schmidt: "The Miller-Thompson Election Contest," *Iowa Journal of History and Politics*, XII (January 1914), pp. 43–7; *History of Pottawattamie County, Iowa* (Chicago: O. L. Baskin & Co.; 1883), pp. 22–5. Hyde's letter is in Bloomington *Iowa Democratic Enquirer*, August 26, 1848, Snider Collection.

11 Schmidt: "The Miller-Thompson Election Contest," 24–5; Dodge Records, VIII, 75, Dodge Papers.

12 Quoted in Fairfield *Iowa Sentinel*, October 20, 1848, Snider Collection.

13 Keokuk *Dispatch*, November 2, 1848, Snider Collection.

14 Mauck: "Kanesville," 396.

15 New York *Sun*, September 9, 1877.

16 Clarissa Young Spencer with Mabel Harmer: *One Who Was Valiant* (Caldwell, Idaho: Caxton Publishers; 1940), p. 64.

17 *Millennial Star*, XI (August 1, 1849), 227–32; Oliver Jennings Journal, May 16, 1851, pp. 106–7, Beinicke Library, Yale University.

18 New York *Sun*, November 7, 1889; New York *Herald*, November 4, 1871.

19 New York *Tribune*, October 9, 1849.

20 New York *Herald*, August 12, 1860.

21 *Millennial Star*, XI (January 1, 1849), 21–4.

22 "The History and Journal of the Life and Travels of Jesse W. Crosby," *Annals of Wyoming*, II (July 1939), 182.

23 Cleland and Brooks (eds.): *A Mormon Chronicle*, I, 86–9.

24 Ibid., I, 88.

25 Ibid., I, 98–9.

26 Ibid., I, 80; *Deseret News*, December 17, 1856; Stanley S. Ivins: "A Constitution for Utah," *Utah Historical Quarterly*, XXV (April 1957), 95; Leland H. Creer: "The Evolution of Government in Early Utah," *Utah Historical Quarterly*, XXVI (January 1958), 33.

27 Stenhouse: *Rocky Mountain Saints*, p. 269; *The Mormon Conspiracy to Establish An Independent Empire to Be Called the Kingdom of God on Earth, The Conspiracy Exposed by the Writings, Sermons and Legislative Acts of the Prophets and Apostles of the Church* (Salt Lake City: The Tribune Company; 1886?), p. 2; San Francisco *Daily Alta Californian*, September 2, 1851; Milton R. Hunter: "The Mormon Corridor," *Pacific Historical Review*, VIII (June 1939), 182–3.

28 Grant Foreman: *Marcy & the Gold Seekers, The Journal of Captain R. B. Marcy, with An Account of the Gold Rush Over the Southern Route* (Norman: University of Oklahoma Press; 1939), pp. 76–8; Oquawka (Illinois) *Spectator*, October 10, 1849, Snider Collection.

29 Wingfield Watson (ed.): *The Revelations of James J. Strang* (Boyne, Michigan: n. p.; 1885), p. 13; St. Louis *American*, June 17, 1846, Snider Collection; Bloomington (Iowa) *Herald*, June 26, 1846, ibid.

30 Reuben Miller: *James J. Strang Weighed in the Balance of Truth, and Found Wanting. His Claims as First President of the Melchizedek Priesthood Refuted* (Burlington, Wisconsin: n. p.; September 1846), pp. 1–3, 18–20; Young to Jesse C. Little, Winter Quarters, November 15, 1846, Young Papers, Utah State Historical Society.

31 *Gospel Herald*, II (November 25, 1847), 157–8, and (December 2, 1847), 164–5.

32 Minutes of High Council Meeting, October 4, 1846, on Conduct of John C. Bennett, Binder 2, Strang Papers; Bennett to Strang, Plymouth, Massachusetts, December 13, 1849, Binder 5, ibid.

33 Testimony at Trial of William Smith for Adultery, April 23, 1847, Binder 4, ibid.; *Gospel Herald*, III (August 17, 1848), 90–1.

34 George J. Adams to Strang, Baltimore, January 26, 1850, and Boston, January 31, 1850, Binder 5, Strang Papers.

35 *Gospel Herald*, II (February 17, 1848), 234; II (February 24, 1848), 241; IV (June 7, 1849), 52.

36 D. R. Whipple to A. P. Hosmer, Washington, December 28, 1849, Binder 5, Strang Papers.

37 Whipple to Strang, Washington, January 9, 1850, Binder 5, ibid.

38 William Smith and Isaac Sheen to Zachary Taylor, Covington, January 1, 1850, Utah Territorial Papers, Records of the Office of the Secretary of the Interior, Record Group 48, National Archives. See also "Remonstrance of Smith Et Al., of Covington, Kentucky, Against the Admission of Deseret into the Union," 31 Congress, 1 Session, Miscellaneous Document No. 43.

39 Almon W. Babbitt to Stephen A. Douglas, New York, July 18, 1850, Box 1, Douglas Papers, University of Chicago Library; Everett L. Cooley: "Carpetbag Rule—Territorial Government in Utah," *Utah Historical Quarterly*, XXVI (April 1958), 110; *Millennial Star*, XII (November 1, 1850), 330.

40 Strang to Increase M. Van Deusen, December 19, 1849, Binder 3, Strang Papers; Woodward: *Bibliothica* [sic] *Scallawagiana*, p. 46. The full title of Van Deusen's first pamphlet is *A Dialogue between Adam and Eve, the Lord and the Devil, Called the Endowment. As Was Enacted by Twelve or Fifteen Thousand, In Secret, In the Nauvoo Temple, Said to Be Revealed from God As A Reward for Building That Splendid Edifice, and the Express Object for Which It Was Built* (Albany: C. Killmer; 1847), 24 pp.

41 Ann Eliza Young: *Wife No. 19, or The Story of A Life in Bondage* (Hartford: Dustin, Gilman & Company; 1876), pp. 129–31.

42 New York *Tribune*, September 21, 1875; M. Hamlin Cannon: "The English Mormons in America," *American Historical Review*, LVII (July 1952), 897.

43 Hunter: "The Mormon Corridor," 183–200.

44 Stenhouse: *Rocky Mountain Saints*, p. 265; Monmouth (Illinois) *Atlas*, June 9, 1848, Snider Collection.

45 Journal of Discourses, XII, 280.

46 See George Alfred Townsend: *The Mormon Trials at Salt Lake City* (New York: American News Company; 1871), p. 44.

47 *Millennial Star*, XI (February 1, 1849), 39–40; *Littel's Living Age*, XLII (July 22, 1854), 147.

48 Journal of Discourses, IV, 294.

49 *The New York Times*, July 31, 1854, and October 24, 1854; Philadelphia *Morning Post*, November 1, 1869; Springfield (Massachusetts) *Republican*, December 1, 1866.

50 William Mulder: *Homeward to Zion, The Mormon Migration from Scandinavia* (Minneapolis: University of Minnesota Press; 1957), p. 142; Gustive O. Larson: "The Story of the Perpetual Emigrating Fund," *Mississippi Valley Historical Review*, XVIII (September 1931), 185–7; *Millennial Star*, XVIII (January 12, 1856), 26.

51 Arrington: *Great Basin Kingdom*, p. 99; John T. Caine to Albert Cumming, Great Salt Lake City, February 1, 1860, Utah Territorial Papers, General Records of the Department of State, Record Group 59, National Archives; Philadelphia *Morning Post*, October 28, 1869.

52 Springfield *Weekly Republican*, July 22, 1865.

53 New York *Tribune*, July 17, 1867; August 19, 1870; September 2, 1870.

54 William Hepworth Dixon: *New America* (London: Hurst and Blackett; 1867), I, 236.

55 Springfield *Weekly Republican*, December 1, 1866.

56 Cannon: "English Mormons in America," 894–5; Arrington: *Great Basin Kingdom*, pp. 108–112.

57 Nelson Slater (compiler): *Fruits of Mormonism, or A Fair and Candid Statement of Facts Illustrative of Mormon Principles, Mormon Policy, and Mormon Character, By More Than Forty Eye-Witnesses* (Coloma, California: Harmon & Springer; 1851), pp. 1, 3, 30–7; Jacob H. Holeman to Luke Lea, Great Salt Lake City, March 29, 1852, Records of the Bureau of Indian Affairs, Utah Superintendency, Record Group 75, National Archives.

58 Journal of Discourses, IX, 101–2.

59 Ibid., V, 27.

60 Ibid., I, 161.

61 Ibid., IX, 87.

62 New York *Herald*, June 2, 1877; "Laws in Utah," *House of Representatives Reports*, 41 Congress, 2 Session, Report No. 21, Part II, 10–11.

63 New York *Herald*, May 6, 1877; Jules Remy and Julius Brenchley: *A Journey to Great-Salt-Lake City* (London: W. Jeffs; 1861), II, 240–5.

64 *The New York Times*, October 18, 1873.

65 Sarah Hollister Harris: *An Unwritten Chapter of Salt Lake, 1851–1901* (New York: Printed Privately; 1901), pp. 5–6, 13–15, 35–7.

66 Ibid., 39–40.

67 See New York *Herald*, January 10, 1852. Young denied making the statement about Taylor in Journal of Discourses, I, 185.

68 New York *Herald*, February 15, 1852; Journal of Discourses, I, 97.

69 Slater, compiler: *Fruits of Mormonism*, pp. 15–16; William W. Phelps to Kane, Great Salt Lake City, June 25, 1852, Kane Papers, Beinicke Library, Yale University.

70 Hunter: *Brigham Young, The Colonizer, passim.*

71 Juanita Brooks: "Indian Relations on the Mormon Frontier," *Utah Historical Quarterly*, XII (January–April 1944), 1–48; Dixon: *New America*, I, 238.

72 New York *Herald*, September 4, 1860.

73 Ibid., May 22, 1875.

74 Ibid., June 23, 1860.

75 Dixon: *New America*, I, 181–2; *Millennial Star*, II (July 1841), 40.

76 Holeman to Lea, Great Salt Lake City, November 28, 1851, Records of the Bureau of Indian Affairs, Utah Superintendency, Record Group 75.

77 Holeman to Lea, Great Salt Lake City, December 28, 1851, Records of the Bureau of Indian Affairs, Utah Superintendency, ibid.

78 Henry R. Day to Lea, Great Salt Lake City, January 2, 1852, Records of the Bureau of Indian Affairs, Utah Superintendency, ibid.

79 Holeman to Lea, Great Salt Lake City, December 28, 1851, Records of the Bureau of Indian Affairs, Utah Superintendency, ibid.

80 Day to Lea, Washington, June 2, 1852, Records of the Bureau of Indian Affairs, Utah Superintendency, ibid.

CHAPTER VII *The Twin Relic of Barbarism*

1 New York *Herald*, January 9, 1848.
2 Roy F. Nichols: *The Disruption of American Democracy* (New York: Collier Books; 1962), p. 110.
3 *Deseret News*, November 23, 1878. Quoted is Brigham H. Roberts: *The Rise and Fall of Nauvoo* (Salt Lake City: Deseret News; 1900), p. 114. On polygamy in general see Kimball Young: *Isn't One Wife Enough?* (New York: Henry Holt; 1954).
4 New York *Tribune*, November 18, 1871.
5 *Three Nights' Public Discussion between the Revds. C. W. Cleeve, James Robertson, and Philip Cater, And Elder John Taylor of the Church of Jesus Christ of Latter-day Saints at Boulogne-Sur-Mer, France* (Liverpool: John Taylor; 1850). For Taylor's ten wives see *Saintly Falsity, On Questions Affecting Their Fanatical Tenets and Practices* (Salt Lake City: n. p.; 1885), p. 3; JUAB (Private in Israel): *The Gospel Concerning Church & State* (Salt Lake City: n. p.; 1897), p. 27.
6 New York *Herald*, January 10, 1852.
7 *Deseret News Extra*, September 15, 1852.
8 Journal of Discourses, XII, 268.
9 Ibid., III, 96, 368–9; V, 55; VII, 28–9; XV, 242–3.
10 Ibid., VIII, 30.
11 *Deseret News*, October 1, 1856; Journal of Discourses, III, 264–8.
12 New York *World*, September 4, 1870; Journal of Discourses, I, 50.
13 Tullidge: *Women of Mormondom*, p. 196.
14 Journal of Discourses, XII, 268; New York *World*, September 4, 1870.
15 New York *Tribune*, July 21, 1865; Springfield *Weekly Republican*, July 22, 1865.
16 *The New York Times*, May 25, 1857; New York *Tribune*, April 25, 1857.
17 Springfield *Weekly Republican*, July 22, 1865; New York *Tribune*, July 31, 1865.
18 Journal of Discourses, IV, 57.
19 See Charles Marshall: "Characteristics of Mormonism," *Transatlantic Magazine*, IV (August 1871), 172.
20 Stenhouse: *"Tell It All,"* p. 254.
21 Cincinnati *Commercial*, March 11, 1872.
22 New York *Tribune*, November 22, 1871; James Bonwick: *The*

Mormons and the Silver Mines (London: Hodder and Stoughton; 1872), pp. 103–4.

23 New York *Herald*, January 2, 1870.

24 Journal of Discourses, IV, 57.

25 Dixon: *New America*, I, 291–2.

26 Ibid., I, 295–6.

27 Ibid., I, 266–7.

28 *Seer*, I (February 1853), 31–2, and (March 1853), 41.

29 Hamilton (Ohio) *Intelligencer*, September 15, 1859.

30 Richard F. Burton: *The City of the Saints* (New York: Alfred A. Knopf; 1963), p. 481. This edition was edited by Fawn M. Brodie.

31 Remy and Brenchley: *Journey to Great-Salt-Lake City*, II, 250–4.

32 Philadelphia *Morning Post*, November 1, 1869.

33 Journal of Discourses, XVIII, 360–1.

34 Dixon: *New America*, I, 317–18.

35 Marshall: "Characteristics of Mormonism," 172.

36 Stanley S. Ivins: "Notes on Mormon Polygamy," *Western Humanities Review*, X (Summer 1956), 230, 233, 234. A year after this article appeared Thomas F. O'Dea wrote that "something like 8 per cent of the families were plural families." See *The Mormons* (Chicago: University of Chicago Press; 1957), p. 246.

37 Remy and Brenchley: *Journey to Great-Salt-Lake City*, II, 169. For Young's statement see Philadelphia *Morning Post*, November 1, 1869.

38 John Benjamin Franklin: *The Horrors of Mormonism* (London: n. p.; 1858), p. 7.

39 William Chandless: *A Visit to Salt Lake* (London: Smith, Elder and Co.; 1857), pp. 191, 261.

40 Benjamin G. Ferris: *Utah and the Mormons* (New York: Harper & Brothers; 1854), pp. 306–8.

41 New York *World*, November 25, 1869.

42 *The New York Times*, April 17, 1860.

43 Dodge Personal Biography, III, 636–7, Dodge Papers.

44 Richard T. Ely: "Economic Aspects of Mormonism," *Harper's Monthly Magazine*, CVI (April 1903), 667–8.

45 New York *Tribune*, December 9, 1870.

46 Ibid., May 18, 1857.

47 Ivins: "Notes on Mormon Polygamy," 234. On Lyman see Esshom: *Pioneers and Prominent Men of Utah*, p. 1015. On Johnson, New York *Herald*, September 16, 1871.

48 Caleb Green Diary, pp. 40–1, Missouri Historical Society, St. Louis; Stenhouse: *"Tell It All,"* p. 248.

49 *The New York Times*, May 28, 1873.

50 Luman Andros Shurtliff Diary, p. 73, Utah State Historical Society.

51 New York *Herald*, April 16, 1877.

52 New York *World*, November 28, 1869.

53 Remy and Brenchley: *Journey to Great-Salt-Lake City*, II, 60; Grenville M. Dodge to Anne Dodge, Salt Lake City, September 3, 1867, Dodge Records, VI, 705–6, Dodge Papers.

54 Burton: *City of the Saints*, p. 477; *The New York Times*, May 19, 1857.

55 New York *Tribune*, August 30, 1858.

56 New York *Herald*, October 19, 1856. See especially Joseph Troskolawsski to the Editor of the New York *Herald*, Brooklyn, May 19, 1857, in New York *Herald*, May 24, 1857.

57 *The New York Times*, September 11, 1858.

58 *Deseret News*, April 2, 1853.

59 Dixon: *New America*, I, 313–14.

60 Samuel Hawthornthwaite: *Mr. Hawthornthwaite's Adventures Among the Mormons As An Elder during Eight Years* (Manchester: the author; 1857), p. 62.

61 New York *Herald*, May 18, 1877; Esshom: *Pioneers and Prominent Men of Utah*, p. 1113.

62 Hawthornthwaite: *Mr. Hawthornthwaite's Adventures*, pp. 123–6; Esshom: *Pioneers and Prominent Men of Utah*, pp. 1113–14.

63 *The New York Times*, May 1, 1858.

64 Ibid., May 19, and 20, 1856.

65 New York *Tribune*, May 15, 1860; *The New York Times*, April 17, 1860.

66 Fitz Hugh Ludlow: "Among the Mormons," *Atlantic Monthly*, XIII (April 1864), 484.

67 *The New York Times*, February 15, 1852.

68 Ibid., September 21, 1857.

69 New York *Tribune*, August 19, 1869.

70 *The New York Times*, June 7, 1854.

71 Smith: *Mormonism, Its Rise, Progress, and Present Condition*, pp. 315–16.

72 Dixon: *New America*, I, 340.

73 *Deseret News*, July 22, 1857.

74 Journal of Discourses, IX, 37.

75 Ibid., XVII, 159.

76 New York *Tribune*, January 3, 1859.

77 New York *World*, November 25, 1869.

78 Dixon: *New America*, I, 339, 340, 348.

79 Springfield *Weekly Republican*, August 19, 1865.

80 New York *Tribune*, July 10, 1865; Dodge Records, VI, 881–2, Dodge Papers.

81 Samuel Bowles: *Our New West* (Hartford: Hartford Publishing Company; 1869), p. 249.

82 Mrs. Sarah A. Cooke: "Theatrical and Social Affairs in Utah," Salt Lake City, 1884, Mormon Collection, Bancroft Library, University of California, Berkeley.

83 Chandless: *A Visit to Salt Lake*, p. 191. Quoted in Journal of Discourses, VIII, 202.

84 New York *Tribune*, July 8, 1865.

85 New York *Herald*, March 28, 1868.

86 Richardson: *Beyond the Mississippi*, p. 354.

87 Whitney: *Life of Heber C. Kimball*, p. 26; Samuel H. Goodwin: *Mormonism and Masonry* (Washington: Masonic Service Association, 1924), p. 3; William M. Stuart: "Masonic Pioneers: The Land Called Deseret," *The Master Mason*, IV (February 1927), 124.

88 Wyl: *Mormon Portraits*, p. 147.

89 John Hyde, Jr.: *Mormonism, Its Leaders and Designs* (New York: W. P. Fetridge & Company; 1857), pp. 90–100. See also New York *World*, September 4, 1870.

90 *The New York Times*, November 15, and 19, 1889; *The Inside of Mormonism* (Salt Lake City: Utah Americans; 1893), pp. 16–17.

CHAPTER VIII   *"As Firm in His Seat as the Czar of Russia"*

1 New York *World*, November 17, 1869.

2 Henry Steele Commager: *The American Mind* (New Haven: Yale University Press; 1950), p. 186. For the comparison by the Saints of their religion and the Prussian army see New York *World*, November 27, 1870.

3 New York *Sun*, November 7, 1889; Chandless: *A Visit to Salt Lake*, p. 154.

4 *Millennial Star*, XIV (September 4, 1852), 444; William J. Conybeare: *Mormonism* (London: Longman, Brown, Green, and Longmans; 1854), pp. 101–7; Philadelphia *Morning Post*, November 1, 1869.

5 *The New York Times*, December 5, 1859; New York *Tribune*, October 7, 1871.

6 *Millennial Star*, XVI (April 15, 1854), 236.

7 *The New York Times*, March 2, 1858.

8 Chandless: *A Visit to Salt Lake*, p. 178.

9 *The New York Times*, December ?, 1855, clipping in Charles L. Woodward: *The First Half Century of Mormonism* (New York: n. p.; 1880), I, 107, scrapbook in Newspaper Annex, New York Public Library.

10 San Francisco *Daily Times*, May 24, 1869.

11 New York *Herald*, May 29, 1856; Ivins: "A Constitution for Utah," 95.

12 *The Mormon Conspiracy to Establish An Independent Empire to Be Called the Kingdom of God on Earth*, p. 7.

13 Ibid., 9.

14 Nels B. Lundwall (ed.): *Discourses of Master Minds* (Salt Lake City: Deseret News; 194?), p. 6.

15 Journal of Discourses, V, 219.

16 New York *Herald*, November 15, 1857, and July 2, 1858. For Young's denunciation of Bridger see Alter: *Jim Bridger*, p. 236.

17 *The New York Times*, November 12, 1853; Gene Caesar: *King of the Mountain Men, The Life of Jim Bridger* (New York: E. P. Dutton; 1961), pp. 235–7; Hickman: *Brigham's Destroying Angel*, pp. 91–2.

18 New York *Tribune*, January 18, 1858; New York *Herald*, July 2, 1858.

19 *The New York Times*, January 25, 1854; Norman Furniss: *The Mormon Conflict, 1850–1859* (New Haven and London: Yale University Press; 1960), pp. 40–1; Schindler: *Orrin Porter Rockwell*, pp. 206–7.

20 Quoted in *Deseret News*, March 30, 1854.

21 Brigham Young to Stephen A. Douglas, Great Salt Lake City, April 29, 1854, Box 3, Douglas Papers.

22 *The New York Times*, May 18, 1855; New York *Semi-Weekly Tribune*, May 22, 1855, in Scrapbook of Newspaper Clippings Relating to the Mormons, p. 73, Newspaper Annex, New York Public Library.

23 Smith: *Mormonism, Its Rise, Progress, and Present Condition*, p. 318.

24 Burton: *City of the Saints*, p. 268.

25 New York *Tribune*, August 19, 1870.

26 *Deseret News*, October 15, 1853; Journal of Discourses, I, 192–7.

27 S. N. Carvalho: *Incidents of Travel and Adventure in the Far West* (New York: Derby & Jackson; 1857), p. 299; Journal of Discourses, I, 163–8.

28 Hyde: *Mormonism, Its Leaders and Designs*, p. 32; Caleb Green Diary, pp. 23–4, Missouri Historical Society.

29 Carvalho: *Incidents of Travel and Adventure in the Far West*, p. 301.

30 Austin and Alta Fife: *Saints of Sage & Saddle, Folklore Among the Mormons* (Bloomington: Indiana University Press; 1956), p. 156; Nels Anderson: *Desert Saints, The Mormon Frontier in Utah* (Chicago: University of Chicago Press; 1944), pp. 144–5.

31 Carvalho: *Incidents of Travel and Adventure in the Far West*, pp. 188–94.

32 *Millennial Star*, XVI (September 23, 1854), 606–7.

33 Garland Hurt to George W. Manypenny, Salt Lake City, May 2, 1855, Records of the Bureau of Indian Affairs, Utah Superintendency, Record Group 75.

34 *The New York Times*, March 30, 1857; Journal of Discourses, I, 187–8.

35 *The New York Times*, August 30, 1877; Journal of Discourses, II, 311, 322.

36 New York *Tribune*, April 25, 1857.

37 New York *Semi-Weekly Tribune*, October 12, 1858; New York *Tribune*, April 5, 1858.

38 New York *Semi-Weekly Tribune*, October 12, 1858.

39 *Deseret News*, April 16, 1856.

40 New York *Semi-Weekly Tribune*, October 12, 1858.

41 *Congressional Record*, 42 Congress, 2 Session (April 18, 1872), 2546–7; New York *Semi-Weekly Tribune*, October 12, 1858.

42 Chandless: *A Visit to Salt Lake*, p. 145.

43 New York *Semi-Weekly Tribune*, October 12, 1858; *Deseret News*, September 17, 1856.

44 *Deseret News*, March 5, 1853.

45 Ibid.: July 30, 1856.

46 *Utah and the Mormons. Speech of Hon. John Cradlebaugh of Nevada, on the Admission of Utah As A State. Delivered in the House of Representatives, February 7, 1863* (n. p.: n. p.; n. d.), p. 13.

47 Ludlow: "Among the Mormons," 487.

48 Holeman to Luke Lea, Fort Bridger, November 3, 1852, Records of the Bureau of Indian Affairs, Utah Superintendency, Record Group 75.

CHAPTER IX   *Of Danites, Blood Atonement, and War*

1 *Millennial Star*, XVII (December 22, 1855), 813–14; Jay Monaghan: "Handcarts on the Overland Trail," *Nebraska History*, XXX (March 1949), 8.

2 *Millennial Star*, XIX (August 8, 1857), 506–7; Monaghan: "Handcarts on the Overland Trail," 9.

3 *Millennial Star*, XVIII (June 14, 1856), 370.

4 Ibid., XIX (August 8, 1857), 506–7.

5 Ruth A. Gallagher: "The Handcart Expeditions," *Palimpsest*, III (June 1922), 220.

6 *The New York Times*, July 1, 1888.

7 Journal of Discourses, IV, 68; Brigham Young to Erastus Snow, Great Salt Lake City, December 7, 1856, Snow Papers, Utah State Historical Society.

8 Chandless: *A Visit to Salt Lake*, p. 141.

9 Young to Snow, Great Salt Lake City, January 30, 1857, Snow Papers.

10 *The New York Times*, September 21, 1857.

11 Stenhouse: *"Tell It All,"* pp. 313–14; Ann Eliza Young: *Wife No. 19*, pp. 184–6.

12 Gustive O. Larson: "The Mormon Reformation," *Utah Historical Quarterly*, XXVI (January 1958), 47–8, 53–5.

13 New York *Herald*, April 25, 1857; *Deseret News*, January 28, 1857.

14 Young to Snow, Great Salt Lake City, January 30, 1857, Snow Papers; *The New York Times*, September 9, 1877.

15 Lee: *Mormonism Unveiled*, p. 101.

16 *Deseret News*, June 25, 1856.

17 *The Mormon Question, Being A Speech of Vice-President Schuyler Colfax at Salt Lake City* (Salt Lake City: Deseret News Office; 1870), p. 14.

18 *Deseret News*, October 1, 1856.

19 Ibid., February 8, 1857.

20 Joseph F. Smith, Jr.: *Blood Atonement and the Origin of Plural Marriage* (Salt Lake City: Deseret News; 1905), p. 52. This book inadvertently answers those who say the church archives in Salt Lake City contain secret materials. Written by the son of the then prophet of the church to show Joseph Smith was a polygamist, it is based on readily available data. Its author ignored such indispensable sources as manuscripts and Gentile newspapers.

21 Charles W. Penrose: *Blood Atonement, As Taught by Leading Elders of the Church of Jesus Christ of Latter-day Saints* (Salt Lake City: Juvenile Instructor Office; 1884), p. 45.

22 For Douglas's speech see *Deseret News*, September 2, 1857; for Morrill's New York *Tribune*, April 25, 1857. See also *The New York Times*, March 10, 1860.

23 New York *Herald*, October 19, 1856.

24 *Deseret News*, July 15, 1857. Young was paraphrasing the Biblical passage from which the Danites took their name: "Dan shall be a serpent by the way, an adder on the path, that biteth the horse in the heels, so that his rider falleth backward."—Genesis 49:17. The origin of "Shenpip" remains a mystery.

25 Caleb Green Diary, pp. 42–5, Missouri Historical Society.

26 *The New York Times*, May 19, 1858.

27 New York *Herald*, May 4, 1855.

28 Caleb Green Diary, pp. 16–20, Missouri Historical Society.

29 On Twiss's statement see Schindler: *Orrin Porter Rockwell*, p. 239.

30 New York *Herald*, July 26, 1857.

31 *The New York Times*, August 8, 1857.

32 New York *Tribune*, May 19, 1857.

33 *The New York Times*, August 30, 1877; Catharine V. Waite: *The Mormon Prophet and His Harem* (Cambridge: Riverside Press; 1866), pp. 24–5.

34 New York *Herald*, October 19, 1856.

35 Ibid., March 29, 1857.

36 New York *Tribune*, May 21, 1857; "The Utah Expedition," *House of Representatives Executive Documents*, 35 Congress, 1 Session, Document No. 71, 120–1.

37 Remy and Brenchley: *Journey to Great-Salt-Lake City*, I, 469–70.

38 *Millennial Star*, XIX (May 23, 1857), 324–7; New York *Tribune*, April 13, 1857.

39 *Millennial Star*, XIX (May 23, 1857), 328–33.

40 *Deseret News Weekly*, April 21, 1886.

41 *The New York Times*, May 10, 1857, and May 7, 1858; New York *Tribune*, May 18, 1857.

42 Peter K. Dotson to Jeremiah S. Black, June 22, 1857, Attorney General's Papers, Letters Received, 1853–70, General Records of the Department of Justice, Record Group 60, National Archives; New York *Tribune*, June 8, 1857; New York *Herald*, June 8, 1857; *The New York Times*, May 20, 1857, and June 11, 1857.

43 New York *Herald*, June 6, 1857.

44 New York *Tribune*, August 11, 1858.

45 New York *Tribune*, May 19, 1857; *The New York Times*, May 1, 7, 15, 1858; Schindler: *Orrin Porter Rockwell*, p. 287.

46 *The New York Times*, June 1, 1857; Stanley: *Parley P. Pratt*, p. 305; Esshom: *Pioneers and Prominent Men of Utah*, p. 1114. For a revealing interview with Elenor see New York *World*, November 23, 1869.

47 For the account of Brigham Young, Jr., see Philadelphia *Morning Post*, November 1, 1869. For Lee's version see Beadle: *Western Wilds*, pp. 305–7.

48 *The Mountain Meadows Massacre, With the Life, Confession and Execution of John D. Lee, The Mormon* (Philadelphia: Barclay & Co.; 1877), pp. 1–28.

49 See Juanita Brooks: *The Mountain Meadows Massacre* (Norman: University of Oklahoma Press; 1962), p. 219.

50 New York *Herald*, February 29, 1872.

51 Ibid., April 16, 1877.

52 Ibid., May 6, 1877.

53 Young to Douglas, Great Salt Lake City, April 29, 1854, Box 3, Douglas Papers.

54 Richard D. Poll: "The Mormon Question Enters National Politics, 1850–1856," *Utah Historical Quarterly*, XXV (April 1957), 117–31; New York *Herald*, August 4, 1856.

55 Young to Kane, Great Salt Lake City, January 31, 1857, Kane Papers, Beinicke Library, Yale University.

56 Young to Kane, Great Salt Lake City, January 7, 1857, ibid.

57 See the able discussions in Furniss: *The Mormon Conflict*, pp. 70–3; Arrington: *Great Basin Kingdom*, p. 172.

58 Henry Slicer to James Buchanan, Loch Haven, May 25, 1857, Box

94, Buchanan Papers, Pennsylvania Historical Society, Philadelphia; William Bigler to Buchanan, Pittsburgh, May 25, 1857, Box 94, ibid. Ferris's comments are in *The New York Times*, May 13 and 23, 1857.

59 Nichols: *Disruption of American Democracy*, p. 110.

60 *Deseret News*, September 2, 1857; *The New York Times*, June 23, 1857.

61 *Deseret News*, September 16, 1857.

62 Furniss: *The Mormon Conflict*, p. 94; *The New York Times*, September 21, 1857.

63 New York *Tribune*, August 19, 1857.

64 Leonard J. Arrington: "Mormon Finance and the Utah War," *Utah Historical Quarterly*, XX (July 1952), 220; Nichols: *Disruption of American Democracy*, pp. 109, 111.

65 Journal of Discourses, V, 226–7. See also Arrington: *Great Basin Kingdom*, pp. 169–70, 463.

66 *The Mormon Conspiracy to Establish An Independent Empire to Be Called the Kingdom of God on Earth*, p. 9.

67 *Millennial Star*, XX (January 23, 1858), 54; Salt Lake *Valley Tan*, December 10, 1858.

68 New York *Tribune*, October 14, 1857, and October 13, 1873.

69 Alter: *Jim Bridger*, p. 266.

70 *Millennial Star*, XIX (October 17, 1857), 670.

71 New York *Tribune*, October 28, 1857.

72 *House Executive Document No. 71*, 35 Congress, 1 Session, 34–5.

73 New York *Herald*, November 17, 1857.

74 Brigham Young to Edmund B. Alexander, October 14, and 16, 1857, Box 105, Dodge Papers.

75 New York *Herald*, January 15, 1858.

76 Salt Lake *Valley Tan*, December 17, 1858; New York *Herald*, October 28, 1857.

77 *The New York Times*, November 16, 1889.

78 Journal of Discourses, V, 132–3, and VI, 192.

79 Burton: *City of the Saints*, p. 207.

80 William S. Harney to Buchanan, Fort Leavenworth, November 29, 1856, Box 96, and January 30, 1858, Box 97, Buchanan Papers.

81 Frank A. Golder: "The Purchase of Alaska," *American Historical Review*, XXV (April 1920), 414.

82 New York *Herald*, December 1, 1857.

83 John C. Bennett to Douglas, Polk City, Iowa, January 20, 1858, Box 9, Douglas Papers.

84 James Arlington Bennett to Buchanan, Arlington House, New Utrecht, Long Island, June 4, 1857, Box 94, Buchanan Papers.

85 James Bennett to Buchanan, Arlington House, June 24, 1857, Box

94, ibid.; Buchanan to Bennett, Washington, July 1, 1857, Box 94, ibid.

86 James Bennett to Buchanan, Washington Cemetery, Gravesina, Long Island, April 8, 1858, Box 98, ibid.

87 James C. Van Dyke to Buchanan, Philadelphia, December 9, 1857, Box 96, ibid.

88 Van Dyke to Buchanan, Philadelphia, December 29, 1857, Box 96, ibid.; Kane to Buchanan, Philadelphia, December 31, 1857, Box 96, and January 3, 1858, Box 97, ibid.

89 John I. Ginn: "Mormon and Indian Wars, The Mountain Meadows Massacre, and Other Tragedies and Transactions Incident to the Mormon Rebellion of 1857," pp. 21–3, Unpublished Manuscript, Beinicke Library, Yale University.

90 New York *Herald*, July 2, 1877.

91 New York *Tribune*, October 7, 1871; New York *World*, November 25, 1871.

92 New York *Herald*, January 19, 1858.

93 Hunter: "The Mormon Corridor," 179–200.

94 *The New York Times*, July 14, 1858.

95 Albert Cumming to Lewis Cass, Near Camp Scott, January 24, 1858, Utah Territorial Papers, General Records of the Department of State, Record Group 59.

96 *The New York Times*, April 27, 1858.

97 Ibid., May 15, 1858.

98 New York *Tribune*, March 1, 1858.

99 New York *Herald*, January 12, 1858.

100 Furniss: *The Mormon Conflict*, pp. 178–82; New York *Herald*, May 30, 1858.

101 New York *Herald*, May 30, 1858, and June 13, 1858; New York *Tribune*, June 12, 1858.

102 *A Series of Instructions and Remarks by President Brigham Young at A Special Council, Tabernacle, March 21, 1858*, pp. 3–11.

103 Ibid., 10.

104 Kane Diary, March 28, 1858, Kane Papers, Stanford University Library; New York *Herald*, June 11, 1858.

105 Cumming to Cass, Great Salt Lake City, May 2, 1858, Utah Territorial Papers, General Records of the Department of State, Record Group 59; New York *Herald*, July 2, 1858.

106 Cumming to Cass, Great Salt Lake City, May 2, 1858, Utah Territorial Papers, Records of the Department of State, Record Group 59; Beadle: *Life in Utah*, pp. 190–1.

107 Cumming to James L. Orr, Salt Lake City, May 12, 1858, Box 98, Buchanan Papers; Orr to Buchanan, Washington, June 21, 1858, Box 98, ibid. See also Young to Cumming, Great Salt Lake City, May 8, 1858, Cumming Papers, Duke University Library, Durham.

108 Furniss: *The Mormon Conflict,* pp. 193–203; New York *Herald,* July 15, 1858.

109 New York *Herald,* July 30, 1858; *The New York Times,* July 30, 1858.

110 New York *Herald,* July 30, 1858.

111 *The New York Times,* July 31, 1858.

112 New York *Tribune,* July 30, 1858; *The New York Times,* July 31, 1858.

113 New York *Tribune,* July 1, 1858, and July 27, 1858; New York *World,* February 15, 1885.

114 Philadelphia *Morning Post,* November 1, 1869.

CHAPTER X   *The Seventy Wives of Brigham Young*

1 Lewis: *Narrative of Some of the Proceedings of the Mormons,* pp. 7, 11, 19.

2 Ibid., 7, 11.

3 See the interview with Mrs. Benson in New York *World,* November 25, 1869.

4 Ivins: "Notes on Mormon Polygamy," 230–3.

5 *The New York Times,* May 1, 1858.

6 Ivins: "Notes on Mormon Polygamy," 232.

7 Brodie: *No Man Knows My History,* pp. 434–65.

8 Stenhouse: *"Tell It All,"* p. 253. Consult also Mrs. Benjamin Ferris: "Life Among the Mormons," *Putnam's Monthly,* VI (September 1855), 262.

9 Journal of Discourses, XVI, 166–7.

10 See Harriet Cook's statement in New York *Tribune,* December 16, 1871.

11 For Kimball's forty-five wives see Whitney: *Life of Heber C. Kimball,* pp. 430–6.

12 *The New York Times,* September 21, 1857.

13 Austin and Alta Fife: *Saints of Sage & Saddle,* p. 169.

14 Stenhouse: *"Tell It All,"* pp. 384–5.

15 Quoted in *The New York Times,* June 27, 1857.

16 Hall: *Abominations of Mormonism Exposed,* pp. 44–5; New York *World,* November 28, 1869; Springfield *Weekly Republican,* August 19, 1865.

17 Burton: *City of the Saints,* p. 274.

18 *The New York Times,* September 21, 1857.

19 Irving Wallace: *The Twenty-seventh Wife* (New York: Simon and Schuster; 1961); Stegner: *The Gathering of Zion,* p. 227. The list,

still woefully inadequate, was found in the church genealogical archives and is now in the Utah State Historical Society.

20 New York *Herald*, May 4, 1855; *The New York Times*, May 5, 1855.

21 "Brigham Young and His Women," *Galaxy*, II (December 1, 1866), 671–2.

22 Wilfred H. Munro: "Among the Mormons in the Days of Brigham Young," *Proceedings of the American Antiquarian Society*, New Series, 36 (October 1926), 227.

23 *The New York Times*, September 14, 1857.

24 Journal of Discourses, XIV, 20.

25 Ibid., IV, 56.

26 Dixon: *New America*, I, 298.

27 New York *World*, November 17, 1869.

28 James H. Crockwell: *Pictures and Biographies of Brigham Young and His Wives* (Salt Lake City: James H. Crockwell; n. d.), pp. 14–15.

29 Ibid., 15–17; Waite: *The Mormon Prophet and His Harem*, pp. 191–4; Tullidge: *The Women of Mormondom*, pp. 359–61.

30 Crockwell: *Pictures and Biographies of Brigham Young and His Wives*, pp. 17–18; Waite: *The Mormon Prophet and His Harem*, pp. 194–5.

31 New York *Tribune*, January 9, 1867; New York *Herald*, November 21, 1871.

32 New York *World*, November 17, 1869.

33 New York *Herald*, November 21, 1871.

34 Ibid., May 24, 1857. See also Mrs. Benjamin Ferris: *The Mormons at Home, With Some Incidents of Travel from Missouri to California, 1852–1853* (New York: Dix & Edwards; 1856), pp. 145–7.

35 New York *World*, October 2, 1870.

36 Ibid., November 17, 1869.

37 *The New York Times*, March 10, 1879.

38 New York *Herald*, May 24, 1857.

39 Quincy *Whig*, December 22, 1847, Snider Collection; New York *World*, November 17, 1869.

40 Mary Cable: "She Who Shall Be Nameless," *American Heritage*, XVI (February 1965), 50–4; Quincy *Whig*, December 22, 1847, Snider Collection.

41 Lewis: *Narrative of Some of the Proceedings of the Mormons*, pp. 5–6, 11.

42 Ibid., 12–13.

43 Quincy *Whig*, December 22, 1847, Snider Collection.

44 Cable: "She Who Shall Be Nameless," 55.

45 *Deseret News*, February 10, 1886.

46 Crockwell: *Pictures and Biographies of Brigham Young and His Wives*, pp. 19–20.

47 Ibid., 20–1; Brodie: *No Man Knows My History*, pp. 441–2.

48 New York *World*, November 17, 1869.

49 *Temple Lot Case*, p. 364; Esshom: *Pioneers and Prominent Men of Utah*, p. 1015; Brodie: *No Man Knows My History*, pp. 451–2.

50 Spencer: *One Who Was Valiant*, pp. 60, 73; Waite: *The Mormon Prophet and His Harem*, p. 199.

51 Smith: *Mormonism, Its Rise, Progress, and Present Condition*, pp. 36–7.

52 New York *World*, November 17, 1869; Springfield *Weekly Republican*, March 20, 1869.

53 Lee: *Mormonism Unveiled*, pp. 166–7.

54 New York *World*, November 17, 1869.

55 Crockwell: *Pictures and Biographies of Brigham Young and His Wives*, p. 27; Waite: *The Mormon Prophet and His Harem*, p. 199.

56 Crockwell: *Pictures and Biographies of Brigham Young and His Wives*, pp. 27–8.

57 Stanley S. Ivins's List.

58 Brodie: *No Man Knows My History*, p. 462.

59 Ibid., 443–4; *Utah Genealogical and Historical Magazine*, XVII (October 1926), 260.

60 Esshom: *Pioneers and Prominent Men of Utah*, p. 1267; Crockwell: *Pictures and Biographies of Brigham Young and His Wives*, p. 29.

61 Stenhouse: *"Tell It All,"* p. 279; *The New York Times*, March 10, 1879.

62 Salt Lake *Daily Tribune*, August 4, 1887; Brodie: *No Man Knows My History*, pp. 457–8; Edward W. Tullidge: *History of Salt Lake City* (Salt Lake City: Star Printing Company; 1886), p. 50.

63 New York *Tribune*, December 16, 1871.

64 Stanley S. Ivins's List.

65 Ibid.

66 Ibid.

67 Ibid.

68 *The New York Times*, March 10, 1879.

69 Young listed Cynthia as his wife in Eighth Census (1860), Utah, Vol. I, p. 270, line 3, Records of the Bureau of Census, Record Group 29, National Archives. See also Stanley S. Ivins's List.

70 Stanley S. Ivins's List.

71 Ibid.

72 Ibid.

73 Tullidge: *Women of Mormondom*, pp. 418–22; *Deseret News*, March 16, 1854; Brodie: *No Man Knows My History*, pp. 458–9.

74 Nauvoo *Times and Seasons*, II (April 1, 1841), 374; Crockwell: *Pictures and Biographies of Brigham Young and His Wives*, pp. 32–4.

75 Lee: *Mormonism Unveiled*, p. 132; Brodie: *No Man Knows My History*, pp. 442–3.

76 Hall: *Abominations of Mormonism Exposed*, pp. 43–4; Brodie: *No Man Knows My History*, pp. 442–3.

77 New York *World*, November 17, 1869.

78 Oliver B. Huntington Diary, II, 95, Utah State Historical Society.

79 New York *World*, November 17, 1869.

80 Stanley S. Ivins's List.

81 Ibid.

82 Ibid.

83 Ibid.

84 Esshom: *Pioneers and Prominent Men of Utah*, p. 1218.

85 New York *World*, November 17, 1869.

86 Eliza R. Snow: "Sketch of My Life," pp. 1–6, Bancroft Library, University of California, Berkeley.

87 Ibid., 13, 30–3.

88 New York *World*, October 2, 1870.

89 Spencer: *One Who Was Valiant*, pp. 76–7.

90 New York *World*, October 2, 1870.

91 Crockwell: *Pictures and Biographies of Brigham Young and His Wives*, p. 28; Waite: *The Mormon Prophet and His Harem*, p. 197.

92 Stanley S. Ivins's List.

93 Ibid.

94 Ibid.

95 Crockwell: *Pictures and Biographies of Brigham Young and His Wives*, pp. 31–2.

96 Quoted in *The New York Times*, March 10, 1879.

97 Esshom: *Pioneers and Prominent Men of Utah*, pp. 1021, 1267.

98 New York *Herald*, November 21, 1871.

99 New York *Tribune*, February 22, 1870; Esshom: *Pioneers and Prominent Men of Utah*, p. 983.

100 *The New York Times*, March 10, 1879; Esshom: *Pioneers and Prominent Men of Utah*, pp. 810–11.

101 Waite: *The Mormon Prophet and His Harem*, pp. 197–8; *The New York Times*, March 10, 1879.

102 Unidentified clipping, interview with Amelia Folsom Young, 1894, Young Papers, Utah State Historical Society; New York *World*, November 17, 1869.

103 Unidentified clipping, interview with Amelia Folsom Young, 1894, Young Papers, Utah State Historical Society.

104 New York *World*, November 17, 1869.

105 Eighth Census (1860), Utah, Vol. I, p. 270, line 5, Records of the Bureau of Census, Record Group 29; Esshom: *Pioneers and Prominent Men of Utah*, p. 874.

106 New York *World*, November 17, 1869.

107 Esshom: *Pioneers and Prominent Men of Utah*, p. 1222.

108 New York *Herald*, November 21, 1871.

109 Ibid., September 16, 1877, and December 11, 1877.

110 Fairfax Proudfit Walkup: "The Sunbonnet Woman: Fashions in Utah Pioneer Costume," *Utah Humanities Review*, I (July 1947), 203.

111 New York *Herald*, December 11, 1877.

112 Cable: "She Who Shall Be Nameless," 54–5.

113 New York *Herald*, August 8, 1873; Springfield *Daily Republican*, February 23, 1874.

114 Esshom: *Pioneers and Prominent Men of Utah*, p. 973; Ferris: *Utah and the Mormons*, p. 309; Stanley S. Ivins's List.

115 Stanley S. Ivins's List.

116 Ann Eliza Young: *Wife No. 19*, p. 417.

117 Hall: *Abominations of Mormonism Exposed*, pp. 64–5, 121–3.

118 *The New York Times*, November 12, 1855.

119 Remy and Brenchley: *Journey to Great-Salt-Lake City*, II, 152.

120 Eighth Census (1860), Utah, Vol. I, p. 192, line 39, Records of the Bureau of Census, Record Group 29.

121 Harris: *An Unwritten Chapter of Salt Lake*, p. 38.

122 New York *World*, November 17 and 28, 1869; New York *Tribune*, February 12, 1870; Cable: "She Who Shall Be Nameless," 54.

123 Ferris: *The Mormons at Home*, p. 130; Ferris: "Life Among the Mormons," 264.

124 For Loba's comment see *The New York Times*, May 1, 1858. All of the following repeat this story: Hyde: *Mormonism, Its Leaders and Designs*, pp. 56–7; Remy and Brenchley: *Journey to Great-Salt-Lake City*, II, 139–40; William E. Waters: *Life Among the Mormons* (New York: Moorhead, Simpson & Bond; 1868), pp. 137–8; Bowles: *Our New West*, p. 217; New York *World*, November 28, 1869.

125 Hawthornthwaite: *Mr. Hawthornthwaite's Adventures Among the Mormons*, pp. 57–8.

126 Ginn: "Mormon and Indian Wars," pp. 32, 44, 46.

127 New York *World*, November 23, 1869; Esshom: *Pioneers and Prominent Men of Utah*, pp. 1113–14.

128 Burton: *City of the Saints*, p. 474.

129 Eighth Census (1860), Vol. I, p. 270, line 4, Records of the Bureau of Census, Record Group 29.

130 Ralph S. Kuykendall: *The Hawaii Kingdom, 1854–1874, Twenty Critical Years* (Honolulu: University of Hawaii Press; 1953), pp. 102–4; *The New York Times*, January 24, 1888; Walter Murray Gibson: *The Prisoner of Weltevreden; And A Glance at the East Indian Archipelago* (New York: J. C. Riker; 1855).

131 New York *Herald*, April 12, 1860; *The New York Times*, April 12, 1860, and December 6, 1860. See also Young to William Hooper,

Great Salt Lake City, April 26, 1860, and March 28, 1861, Young Papers, Beinicke Library, Yale University.

132 *History of Brigham Young, 1847–1867* (Berkeley: MassCal Associates; 1966), p. 309.

133 *Fragments of Experience* (Salt Lake City: Juvenile Instructor Office; 1882), pp. 60–75; Wallace Stegner: *Mormon Country* (New York: Duell, Sloan & Pearce; 1942), pp. 129–34; *The New York Times,* November 5, 1865.

134 *The New York Times,* January 24, 1888; Lorrin A. Thurston: *Memoirs of the Hawaiian Revolution* (Honolulu: Advertiser Publishing Company; 1936), pp. 79–80, 279–80.

135 Eighth Census (1860), Utah, Vol. I, p. 268, line 24, Records of the Bureau of Census, Record Group 29.

136 Ibid., p. 269, line 17.

137 Ibid., p. 270, line 13.

138 Springfield *Weekly Republican,* March 20, 1869; New York *Herald,* November 21, 1871; Waite: *The Mormon Prophet and His Harem,* pp. 199–201.

139 Ann Eliza Young: *Wife No. 19,* pp. 280–6.

140 Esshom, *Pioneers and Prominent Men of Utah,* pp. 728, 1267.

141 Ibid., 1138, 1267.

142 Ibid., 1057, 1267.

143 Ibid., 1271.

144 *The New York Times,* January 23, 1855 and February 14, 1855.

145 See New York *World,* October 2, 1870.

146 *Doctrine and Covenants,* Section 132.

147 New York *World,* November 23, 1869.

CHAPTER XI   *"Love We Regard as a False Sentiment"*

1 New York *World,* October 2, 1870.

2 For Emma's wedding to Bidamon see *Saints Herald,* March 14, 1891, clipping in Woodward: *First Half Century of Mormonism,* II, 196, Newspaper Annex, New York Public Library.

3 *The New York Times,* September 9, 1877.

4 Waite: *The Mormon Prophet and His Harem,* pp. 211–14; Beadle: *Western Wilds,* p. 601.

5 Wyl: *Mormon Portraits,* p. 265; Stenhouse: *"Tell It All,"* p. 282.

6 *Deseret News,* May 21, 1856; New York *Tribune,* July 14, 1865.

7 Spencer: *One Who Was Valiant,* pp. 36, 38, 64.

8 New York *World,* November 17, 1869.

9 Spencer: *One Who Was Valiant,* pp. 24–8.

10 New York *World,* November 17, 1869.

11 New York *Herald*, February 4, 1878; New York *Times*, September 14, 1857; Spencer: *One Who Was Valiant*, p. 17.

12 Dixon: *New America*, I, 250.

13 Spencer: *One Who Was Valiant*, pp. 31–2, 76–7; Christopher G. Crary: "Kirtland, Personal and Pioneer Reminiscences," Unpublished Manuscript, pp. 95–6, Western Reserve Historical Society, Cleveland.

14 New York *Tribune*, August 2, 1858.

15 Stenhouse: *"Tell It All,"* p. 278.

16 For Young's family see the following in the Records of the Bureau of Census, Record Group 29: Seventh Census (1850), Utah, Vol. I, p. 150; Eighth Census (1860), Utah, Vol. I, pp. 268–70; Ninth Census (1870), Vol. I, pp. 701–2. For Kimball's see Eighth Census (1860), Utah, Vol. I, pp. 270–2.

17 *Millennial Star*, XXXIII (July 11, 1871), 434.

18 Harris: *An Unwritten Chapter of Salt Lake*, pp. 49–50.

19 New York *World*, November 17, 1869.

20 Ann Eliza Young: *Wife No. 19*, pp. 326–8.

21 Ibid., 461–3.

22 Austin and Alta Fife: *Saints of Sage & Saddle*, pp. 117–18.

23 Ivins: "Notes on Mormon Polygamy," 236.

24 New York *World*, October 6, 1872.

25 Slater: *Fruits of Mormonism*, p. 86.

26 Austin and Alta Fife: *Saints of Sage & Saddle*, p. 168.

27 New York *Tribune*, June 1, 1870.

28 Ibid., July 9, 1867.

29 Hawthornthwaite: *Mr. Hawthornthwaite's Adventures Among the Mormons*, p. 56. On Joseph's drinking see also New York *World*, November 28, 1869, and New York *Herald*, September 9, 1877.

30 New York *World*, November 28, 1869.

31 *The New York Times*, May 20, 1857, and March 10, 1879.

32 New York *World*, November 28, 1869.

33 *The New York Times*, September 9, 1877; New York *World*, November 28, 1869.

34 Philadelphia *Morning Post*, October 28, 1869.

35 *The New York Times*, March 10, 1879.

36 New York *Tribune*, December 16, 1858; *The New York Times*, November 23, 1858.

37 New York *Herald*, August 13, 1873, and August 30, 1877.

38 *The New York Times*, March 10, 1879.

39 New York *World*, November 17, 1869; *The New York Times*, May 20, 1857; Schindler: *Orrin Porter Rockwell*, p. 287.

40 *The New York Times*, March 10, 1879.

41 New York *Herald*, August 30, 1877; *The New York Times*, March 10, 1879.

42 New York *World*, November 25, 1869.

43 Esshom: *Pioneers and Prominent Men of Utah*, pp. 830, 1267; New York *World*, November 17, and 25, 1869.

44 Unidentified clipping in Woodward: *First Half Century of Mormonism*, II, 34, Newspaper Annex, New York Public Library.

45 Augusta Joyce Cocheron: *Representative Women of Deseret* (Salt Lake City: J. C. Graham & Co.; 1884), p. 122.

46 Spencer: *One Who Was Valiant*, pp. 33–4.

47 Stenhouse: *"Tell It All,"* p. 546.

48 New York *World*, November 17, 1869.

49 *The New York Times*, March 10, 1879.

50 New York *World*, November 25, 1869.

51 Ibid., December 5, 1869.

52 Ibid., November 23, 1869.

53 Ibid., November 25, 1869.

54 Ibid., November 28, 1869.

55 *The New York Times*, March 10, 1879.

56 New York *World*, November 28, 1869.

57 For this story see New York *World*, November 28, 1869. For some dates tending to corroborate the *World*'s amazingly accurate report of eighty years before see Percy W. Jenkins: "Kiskadden-Slade, Some Historical Incidents Recalled," *Annals of Wyoming*, 21 (January 1949), 91.

CHAPTER XII   *"The Blood That Stains the Walls of Carthage Jail"*

1 Dixon: *New America*, I, 238–9.

2 Dodge Records, VI, 705–6, 881–2, Dodge Papers.

3 Ludlow: *The Heart of the Continent*, pp. 328–9.

4 Cincinnati *Daily Gazette*, July 10, 1869.

5 Ludlow: *The Heart of the Continent*, pp. 341–2.

6 Burton: *City of the Saints*, pp. 289–90.

7 Springfield *Weekly Republican*, August 19, 1865.

8 New York *Herald*, August 23, 1871; Cincinnati *Commercial*, March 12, 1872; Stenhouse: *"Tell It All,"* p. 245.

9 Justin McCarthy: *Reminiscences* (New York and London: Harper & Brothers; 1899), I, 258.

10 New York *Tribune*, August 12, 1867; New York *Herald*, September 22, 1877.

11 Ferris: *The Mormons at Home*, p. 157; *The New York Times*, June 26, 1856.

12 *The New York Times*, May 19, 1858.

13 New York *Tribune*, July 9, 1867.

14 Ibid., July 21, 1865.

15 McCarthy: *Reminiscences*, I, 258–9.

16 New York *World*, November 28, 1869.

17 New York *Sun*, September 9, 1877; Caleb Green Diary, p. 34, Missouri Historical Society.

18 New York *Herald*, July 30, 1858.

19 New York *Herald*, August 12, 1868; Ludlow: *The Heart of the Continent*, p. 367. Quoted in the *Herald*.

20 Burton: *City of the Saints*, p. 265; New York *Tribune*, July 21, 1865.

21 New York *Herald*, February 23, 1868.

22 New York *Tribune*, July 21, 1865.

23 Justin McCarthy: "Brigham Young," *Galaxy*, IX (February 1870), 183.

24 *Deseret News*, May 14, 1856; John W. Gunnison: *The Mormons, or Latter-Day Saints* (Philadelphia: J. B. Lippincott & Co.; 1852), p. 140; Unidentified clipping, Lee Kohns Memorial Collection, Manuscript Division, New York Public Library.

25 Waters: *Life Among the Mormons*, pp. 174–5.

26 Springfield *Weekly Republican*, August 5, 1865; Arrington: *Great Basin Kingdom*, pp. 201–3, 473–4.

27 *Millennial Star*, XXIV (November 8, 1862), 715.

28 Dixon: *New America*, I, 251–2; *The New York Times*, January 1, 1861; *Deseret News*, May 4, 1864.

29 *Deseret News*, October 12, 1859; October 23, 1861; October 8, 1862.

30 Codman: *Mormon Country*, pp. 13–14.

31 *Deseret News*, March 18, 1863, and August 31, 1864; New York *Semi-Weekly Tribune*, April 1, 1870.

32 Burton: *City of the Saints*, p. 268.

33 See Young's statement in Journal of Discourses, XVI, 10.

34 *Millennial Star*, XIII (January 15, 1851), 18.

35 Leonard J. Arrington: "Taxable Income in Utah," *Utah Historical Quarterly*, XIV (January 1956), 27.

36 Ninth Census (1870), Utah, Vol. I, p. 701, line 1, Records of the Bureau of Census, Record Group 29.

37 Dixon: *New America*, I, 220.

38 Burton: *City of the Saints*, p. 327.

39 Dodge Records, VI, 705–6, 881–2, Dodge Papers.

40 New York *Tribune*, July 9, 1867.

41 Burton: *City of the Saints*, p. 267.

42 Journal of Discourses, VIII, 236.

43 New York *Tribune*, July 19, 1858; *Millennial Star*, XX (July 17, 1858), 461–2. The war cost the federal government at least $500,000. See Leonard J. Arrington: "Mormon Finance and the Utah War," *Utah Historical Quarterly*, XX (July 1952), 221.

44 *The New York Times*, September 11, 1858.

45 New York *Herald*, August 13, 1858.

46 Burton: *City of the Saints*, p. 249.

47 Delena R. Eckels to Lieutenant Bennett, August 12, 1858, Kane Papers, Beinicke Library, Yale University.

48 John Taylor to George Taylor, Great Salt Lake City, January 12, 1859, ibid.

49 Salt Lake *Valley Tan*, December 24, 1858, and January 18, 1859.

50 Young to Horace S. Eldredge, Great Salt Lake City, November 20, 1858, Kane Papers, Beinicke Library, Yale University; Young to George Q. Cannon, Great Salt Lake City, December 24, 1858, ibid.

51 Salt Lake *Valley Tan*, January 25, 1859; William W. Phelps to Kane, Great Salt Lake City, February 10, 1859, Kane Papers.

52 *The New York Times*, May 2, 1859; New York *Tribune*, July 7, 1859.

53 *The New York Times*, April 29, 1859.

54 New York *Tribune*, June 10, 1859.

55 Burton: *City of the Saints*, p. 275.

56 Elias Smith Journal, July 10, 13, and 16, 1859, Utah State Historical Society; Horace Greeley: *An Overland Journey from New York to San Francisco in the Summer of 1859* (New York: C. M. Saxton, Barker & Co.; 1860), pp. 209–16.

57 New York *Tribune*, August 24, 1859.

58 *The New York Times*, September 28, 1859.

59 New York *Tribune*, December 1, 1858; *The New York Times*, September 15, 24, and 28, 1859.

60 *The New York Times*, September 29, 1859.

61 Ibid., February 1, and 15, 1860.

62 Arrington: "Mormon Finances and the Utah War," 234; *The New York Times*, October 10, 1860.

63 New York *Tribune*, May 1, 1860.

64 Elias Smith Journal, February 7, 1860, Utah State Historical Society.

65 *The New York Times*, June 19, 1860.

66 Young to Hooper, Great Salt Lake City, February 7, 1861, Young Papers, Beinicke Library, Yale University; New York *Herald*, January 27, 1861.

67 Mark Twain: *Roughing It* (Hartford: American Publishing Company; 1875), pp. 114–17.

68 Journal of Discourses, II, 143.

69 New York *Tribune*, August 19, 1869.

70 Nauvoo *Times and Seasons*, VI (March 1, 1845), 818; Wallace R. Bennett: "The Negro in Utah," *Utah Law Review*, 3 (Spring 1953), 347.

71 New York *Herald*, May 4, 1855. See Genesis, 9: 25–7.

72 New York *Tribune*, April 5, 1860.

73 *Millennial Star*, XXIII (October 12, 1861), 662–3.

74 Journal of Discourses, VIII, 236; IX, 367; XII, 42.
75 This prophecy, related to Edwin and Theodore Turley, is in the Smith Papers, Utah State Historical Society.
76 *The New York Times*, July 31, 1858.
77 *Deseret News*, May 1, 1861.
78 New York *Herald*, March 27, 1861.
79 Philadelphia *Morning Post*, November 1, 1869.
80 New York *World*, November 23, 1869.
81 Ibid., November 17, 1869.
82 *The New York Times*, January 20, 1862.
83 Ibid., November 8, 1863.
84 Ibid., August 16, 1861.
85 *Millennial Star*, XXV (December 12, 1863), 787.
86 Ludlow: "Among the Mormons," 489.
87 *The New York Times*, July 3, 1864.
88 Alex Badger to Alice E. Clayton, Salt Lake City, January 19, 1863, Badger Papers, Missouri Historical Society, St. Louis. Badger heard and quoted the speech.
89 Young to Hooper, Great Salt Lake City, April 4, 1861, Young Papers, Beinicke Library, Yale University.
90 *The New York Times*, December 28, 1861, and January 27, 1862.
91 Melville: "Theory and Practice of Church and State," 48–50; *Deseret News*, March 19, 1862; *The New York Times*, February 15, 1863.
92 Unidentified clipping, Journal History, January 19, 1863, Mormon Church Historian's Office.
93 *The New York Times*, July 8, 1861, and November 23, 1862.
94 Patrick Edward Connor to Dodge, Denver, April 6, 1865, Dodge Records, V, 373–4, Dodge Papers.
95 Dixon: *New America*, I, 207–8.
96 Young to John F. Kinney, Great Salt Lake City, March 7, 1864, Young Papers, Utah State Historical Society.
97 Wyl: *Mormon Portraits*, pp. 254–5.
98 *Deseret News*, March 11, 1863; New York *Herald*, December 11, 1877.
99 *Millennial Star*, XXV (August 8, 1863), 508; Gustive O. Larson: "Utah and the Civil War," *Utah Historical Quarterly*, 33 (Winter 1965), 66–7.
100 *The New York Times*, September 21 and November 15, 1862.
101 Ibid., November 2, 1862.
102 Hiram S. Rumfield to Frank Rumfield, Salt Lake City, July 27, 1862, Rumfield Papers, Beinicke Library, Yale University.

CHAPTER XIII   *"His Day Is Over"*

1 James B. Thayer: *A Western Journey with Mr. Emerson* (Boston: Little, Brown and Company; 1884), p. 36.

2 Springfield *Weekly Republican*, July 15, 1865; Chicago *Tribune*, July 10, 1865.

3 New York *Tribune*, July 14, 1865; Springfield *Weekly Republican*, July 22 and August 19, 1865.

4 New York *Tribune*, July 31, 1865; Springfield *Weekly Republican*, July 22, 1865.

5 New York *Tribune*, November 10, 1865.

6 New York *Herald*, March 6, 1866.

7 *The New York Times*, November 27, 1865.

8 Young to Hooper, Great Salt Lake City, December 26, 1865, Young Papers, Beinicke Library, Yale University. See, for example, *Daily Union Vedette*, May 4 and 5, 1865.

9 Young to Hooper, Great Salt Lake City, February 21, 1866, Young Papers, Beinicke Library, Yale University.

10 "The Condition of Utah," *House of Representatives Reports*, 39 Congress, 1 Session, Report No. 96.

11 Young to Hooper, Great Salt Lake City, December 5, 1865, Young Papers, Beinicke Library, Yale University.

12 Davis Bitton: "A Re-evaluation of the 'Turner Thesis and Mormon Beginnings,'" *Utah Historical Quarterly*, 34 (Fall 1966), 326–33.

13 New York *World*, December 26, 1869.

14 *The New York Times*, April 27, 1866.

15 Young to Hooper, Great Salt Lake City, April 5, 1866, Young Papers, Beinicke Library, Yale University; *Deseret News*, April 12, 1866.

16 *The New York Times*, May 15, 1866.

17 New York *Tribune*, November 30, 1866.

18 New York *Evening Post*, November 28, 1866.

19 George C. Bates to Benjamin F. Bristow, December 17, 1871, Source-Chronological Files, Utah, Box 681, General Records of the Department of Justice, Record Group 60, National Archives. For McLeod see Springfield *Weekly Republican*, December 1, 1866; for Connor, Connor to Dodge, Stockton, Utah, January 16, 1867, Dodge Records, VI, 829–30, Dodge Papers.

20 Cannon: "English Mormons in America," 908; John S. Lindsay: *The Mormons and the Theatre* (Salt Lake City: Century Printing Co.; 1905), p. 22.

21 *The New York Times*, September 18, 1861.

22 New York *Tribune*, July 10, 1865; *The New York Times*, January 18, 1863.

23 Badger to Alice Clayton, Salt Lake City, January 19, 1863, Badger Papers; New York *Tribune*, February 21, 1870; Dodge to Anne Dodge, Salt Lake City, August 30, 1867, Dodge Records, VI, 696–7, Dodge Papers.

24 New York *World*, November 28, 1869.

25 *The New York Times*, February 26, 1865, and April 7, 1869.

26 New York *Tribune*, December 6, 1869.

27 *Millennial Star*, XXXI (February 27, 1869), 139–42; *Deseret News*, November 24, 1853.

28 Young to Douglas, Great Salt Lake City, April 29, 1854, Box 3, Douglas Papers.

29 John M. Bernhisel to Douglas, Washington, February 2, 1855, Box 4, ibid.

30 *The New York Times*, December 7, 1862. For the Union Pacific's shareholders see Jacob Blickenderfer to Dodge, Salt Lake City, January 31, 1869, Dodge Records, VII, 930–6, Dodge Papers.

31 Dodge Personal Biography, II, 497, ibid.; Henry Kendall: "A Week in 'Great Salt Lake City,' " *Hours at Home*, I (May 1865), 65–6.

32 Journal of Discourses, XII, 54.

33 Dodge to Anne Dodge, Salt Lake City, August 30, 1867, Dodge Records, VI, 696–7, Dodge Papers; Robert West Howard: *The Great Iron Trail, The Story of the First Transcontinental Railroad* (New York: G. P. Putnam's Sons; 1962), pp. 263–4.

34 Dodge Personal Biography, III, 665, Dodge Papers.

35 *Millennial Star*, XXX (September 12, 1868), 588; Arrington: *Great Basin Kingdom*, pp. 261–3.

36 Sidney Dillon to Dodge, New York, June 16, 1868, Dodge Personal Biography, III, 766. Young and Durant were extremely friendly. See Young to Thomas C. Durant, Salt Lake City, April 22, 1868, William West Durant Papers, Library of Congress.

37 This document is in the Mormon Collection of the Chicago Historical Society.

38 Dodge to William T. Sherman, Red Boone Pass, September 6, 1868, Vol. 24, Sherman Papers, Library of Congress; Sherman to Dodge, St. Louis, September 24, 1868, Box 15, Dodge Papers.

39 Dodge Records, I, 519–23, Dodge Papers; Dodge Personal Biography, III, 801–2, ibid. Dodge's account is corroborated in *The New York Times*, August 31, 1868.

40 New York *Tribune*, October 9, 1871; New York *Herald*, April 30, 1872.

41 *The New York Times*, August 25, 1875.

42 S. W. Y. Schimonsky to Webster Snyder, Echo, April 13, 1869, Dodge Records, VII, 1139, Dodge Papers.

43 Arrington: *Great Basin Kingdom*, pp. 265–70; Luther S. Bent to Dodge, New York, September 2, 1869, Dodge Records, VII, 1406,

Dodge Papers; William Jennings: "Carson Valley," p. 9, Manuscript in Bancroft Library, University of California, Berkeley.

44 *The New York Times*, October 3, 1871.

45 Ibid., January 19, 1870.

46 Springfield *Weekly Republican*, November 6, 1869.

47 *The New York Times*, July 14 and 26, 1869; Frederick W. Seward: *Seward at Washington, As Senator and Secretary of State* (New York: Derby and Miller; 1891), p. 410.

48 Salt Lake *Daily Reporter*, April 10, 1869.

49 Springfield *Weekly Republican*, October 16, 1869, and November 6, 1869; Chicago *Tribune*, October 14, 1869.

50 P. T. Barnum: *Struggles and Triumphs; or, Forty Years' Recollections* (Buffalo: Warren, Johnson & Co.; 1872), pp. 849–50.

51 Springfield *Weekly Republican*, November 6, 1869.

52 New York *Herald*, March 25, 1872.

53 William Jennings: "Material Progress in Utah," p. 1, Salt Lake City, 1884, Manuscript in Mormon Collection, Bancroft Library, University of California, Berkeley.

54 *Millennial Star*, XXXI (June 26, 1869), 412.

55 Philadelphia *Morning Post*, October 28, 1869.

56 Dodge Personal Biography, III, 826–7, Dodge Papers.

57 New York *World*, June 30, 1870, and November 14, 1871; Arrington: *Great Basin Kingdom*, pp. 251–4.

58 New York *Herald*, October 25, 1868.

59 Ibid., January 23, 1870.

60 Arrington: *Great Basin Kingdom*, pp. 245–51.

61 Ludlow: *Heart of the Continent*, pp. 370–1.

62 *Millennial Star*, XXIX (February 23, 1867), 124–5.

63 New York *Tribune*, July 9, 1867; Journal of Discourses, XII, 59.

64 *The New York Times*, November 3, 1868; New York *Tribune*, August 19, 1869; Arrington: *Great Basin Kingdom*, pp. 298–9.

65 San Francisco *Daily Times*, May 17, 1869; Springfield *Weekly Republican*, November 6, 1869. The 1873 figures are from Codman: *The Mormon Country*, pp. 201–3.

66 Austin and Alta Fife: *Saints of Sage & Saddle*, p. 97.

67 *The New York Times*, October 31, 1871.

68 Journal of Discourses, XIX, 157–8.

69 *Millennial Star*, XXV (August 1, 1863), 487–8.

70 Nauvoo, Illinois, Account Book Kept by A Merchant, 1839, pp. 98–9, Mormon Collection, University of Chicago Library.

71 Nauvoo *Neighbor*, December 27, 1843, and March 27, 1844.

72 Warsaw *Message*, January 10, 1844.

73 Caleb Green Diary, pp. 8–9, Missouri Historical Society.

74 *The New York Times*, October 13, 1858.

75 "Three Weeks in Brigham Young's Office," January 2, 1860, Young Papers, Utah State Historical Society.
76 *The New York Times*, October 4, 1861; Sacramento *Daily Union*, January 30, 1869.
77 New York *Tribune*, July 29, 1867.
78 Journal of Discourses, XII, 117–18, 156–7; XIV, 20.
79 New York *Herald*, May 13, 1870.
80 New York *World*, November 17, 1869.
81 Cincinnati *Commercial*, March 13, 1872.

CHAPTER XIV   *Who Speaks for God?*

1 *The New York Times*, September 3, 1882; New York *Herald*, July 3, 1856. See also the comments of Dale L. Morgan in the Calendar to the Strang Papers, p. 16, Beinicke Library, Yale University.
2 Cannon: "The English Mormons in America," 903–5.
3 Sumner Howard to Charles Devens, Salt Lake City, July 28, 1877, Source-Chronological Files, Utah, Box 683, General Records of the Department of Justice, Record Group 60, National Archives.
4 Frank J. Cannon and George L. Knapp: *Brigham Young and His Mormon Empire* (New York: Fleming H. Revell; 1913), p. 327.
5 New York *World*, December 26, 1869.
6 Ibid., October 2, 1870.
7 Springfield *Weekly Republican*, December 1, 1866.
8 Journal of Discourses, XVII, 159.
9 Granville Hedrick: *The Spiritual Wife System Proven False and the True Order of Church Discipline* (Bloomington, Illinois: W. E. Footel Power Press; 1856), pp. 25–7.
10 New York *Tribune*, April 14, 1860.
11 New York *World*, November 27, 1870.
12 *Millennial Star*, XXVII (October 21, 1865), 657–63; Joseph Smith and Heman Smith: *History of the Church of Jesus Christ of Latter Day Saints, 1844–1872* (Lamoni, Iowa: Reorganized Church; 1904), III, 502.
13 *The New York Times*, August 1, 1869; Dixon: *New America*, I, 321–3.
14 *The New York Times*, August 31, 1869; New York *World*, November 17, 1869.
15 New York *Tribune*, June 2, 1871.
16 New York *Sun*, August 7, 1868; Bowles: *Our New West*, p. 237.
17 "The Mormons, Who and What They Are," *Phrenological Journal*, 52 (January 1871), 38–45.

18 New York *World*, October 2, 1870. See Sarah E. Carmichael: *Poems* (San Francisco: Towne and Bacon; 1866).

19 *Utah Magazine*, III (October 30, 1869), 406–8, 411–12; Stenhouse: *Rocky Mountain Saints*, pp. 630–1.

20 *The Inside of Mormonism*, pp. 52–5.

21 New York *Tribune*, February 12, 1870; *Utah Magazine*, III (November 27, 1869), 470–3.

22 New York *Herald*, July 26, 1870.

23 Esshom: *Pioneers and Prominent Men of Utah*, p. 891; New York *World*, November 17, 27, and 28, 1869; New York *Tribune*, February 12, 1870.

24 New York *Tribune*, February 12 and 22, 1870.

25 New York *World*, January 2, 1870; New York *Tribune*, December 16, 1871.

26 New York *World*, January 16, 1870.

27 Stenhouse: *"Tell It All,"* pp. 350–1.

28 Fanny Stenhouse: *Exposé of Polygamy in Utah* (New York: American News Company; 1872), pp. 135–41.

29 New York *World*, October 2, 1870.

30 See the comments in New York *World*, October 30, 1870.

31 New York *Herald*, January 15, 1870; New York *World*, November 27, 1870.

32 New York *World*, October 9, 1870.

33 New York *Tribune*, January 27, 1870.

34 New York *Herald*, January 2, 3, and 15, 1870.

35 Tullidge: *History of Salt Lake City*, pp. 468–9; *The New York Times*, February 10, 1890.

36 New York *Herald*, July 31, 1870.

37 Ibid., January 15 and April 22, 1870.

38 Ibid., September 8, 1870.

39 Statement by William Samuel Godbe, pp. 1–6, 19–20, Salt Lake City, September 2, 1884, Mormon Collection, Bancroft Library, University of California, Berkeley.

CHAPTER XV   *Red Cloud and Blackstone's* Commentaries

1 New York *World*, March 31, 1873.

2 George Robert Bird: *Tenderfoot Days in Territorial Utah* (Boston: Gorham Press; 1918), p. 114.

3 New York *World*, November 14, 1871.

4 Kendall: "A Week in 'Great Salt Lake City,'" 65.

5 Cincinnati *Commercial*, March 11, 1872.

6 *The New York Times*, May 21, 1871.

7 Philadelphia *Morning Post*, November 1, 1869.

8 New York *Herald*, April 25, May 30, and July 3, 1870.

9 New York *Tribune*, August 18, 1870; New York *Herald*, August 21 and 23, 1870.

10 Dodge Personal Biography, III, 665, Dodge Papers; New York *Herald*, March 25, 1872.

11 Townsend: *The Mormon Trials at Salt Lake City*, p. 17.

12 New York *Tribune*, October 9, 1871.

13 New York *Herald*, September 6, 1871; New York *Tribune*, November 9 and 29, 1871.

14 New York *Herald*, October 30, 1871.

15 New York *Tribune*, April 20, 1872.

16 *The New York Times*, October 3, 1871; New York *Herald*, October 6 and 7, 1871.

17 New York *World*, July 10, 1870.

18 Ibid., November 4, 1871.

19 New York *Tribune*, June 2, 1871.

20 New York *Herald*, October 4 and 5, 1871.

21 Townsend: *The Mormon Trials at Salt Lake City*, pp. 24–5; New York *Tribune*, October 26 and November 1, 1871; New York *Herald*, October 12, 1871.

22 Bates to United States Attorney General, Salt Lake City, December 7 and 9, 1871, Source-Chronological Files, Utah, Box 681, General Records of the Department of Justice, Record Group 60; New York *Tribune*, November 17, 1871.

23 *Millennial Star*, XXXIV (May 14, 1872), 312; *The New York Times*, January 3, 1872.

24 Cincinnati *Commercial*, March 11, 1872.

25 James B. McKean to George H. Williams, Salt Lake City, November 12, 1873, Source-Chronological Files, Utah, Box 682, General Records of the Department of Justice, Record Group 60.

26 New York *Herald*, June 6, 1871.

27 New York *Tribune*, October 7, 1871; Wyl: *Mormon Portraits*, p. 124.

28 New York *Tribune*, April 30, 1872.

29 *The New York Times*, April 14, 1872.

30 New York *Herald*, June 2, 1877; *The New York Times*, October 18, 1873.

31 *The New York Times*, March 4, 1872.

32 Ibid., April 24, 1874 and May 20, 1877.

33 New York *Herald*, April 10 and 11, 1873.

34 *Millennial Star*, XXXVII (April 6, 1875), 217–18; New York *Herald*, August 8, 1873 and March 22, 1875.

35 *The New York Times*, April 28, 1877.

36 Ibid., May 20, 1877.

37 New York *Herald*, February 7, 1874.

38 Springfield *Weekly Republican*, March 7, 1873.
39 Mulder: *Homeward to Zion*, pp. 278–9; Jennie Anderson Froiseth (ed.): *The Women of Mormondom* (Detroit: C. G. G. Paine; 1872), pp. 382, 414–16.
40 Journal of Discourses, XV, 166.
41 Springfield *Daily Republican*, August 3, 1874; *The New York Times*, March 14, 1874. See also Edward J. Allen: *The Second United Order among the Mormons* (New York: Columbia University Press; 1936).
42 New York *Tribune*, August 14, 1874.
43 New York *Herald*, April 21, 1877.
44 *Millennial Star*, XXXVII (November 1, 1875), 700–1.
45 New York *Tribune*, November 17, 1873 and May 4, 1874. See in *The Book of Mormon*, Ether 2:17–20; 6:7–11, 9:19.
46 New York *Tribune*, November 22, 1871.
47 William Hepworth Dixon: *White Conquest* (London: Chatto and Windus; 1876), I, 206; Salt Lake *Daily Tribune*, February 23, 1952.
48 Charles Marshall: "Salt Lake City and the Valley Settlements," *Fraser's Magazine*, IV (July 1871), 107.
49 *Millennial Star*, XXXV (September 30, 1873), 622–3; New York *Tribune*, October 31, 1873.
50 Lee: *Mormonism Unveiled*, p. 132.
51 New York *Herald*, March 25, 1877.
52 Philadelphia *Morning Post*, November 1, 1869.
53 New York *Herald*, March 22, 23, and 25, 1877; Juanita Brooks: *John Doyle Lee, Zealot—Pioneer Builder—Scapegoat* (Glendale, California: Arthur H. Clark Company; 1962) pp. 378–84.
54 New York *Herald*, May 6, 1877.
55 Ibid., March 25, 1877.
56 Bird: *Tenderfoot Days*, pp. 121–2, 125.
57 New York *Herald*, September 1, 1877.
58 Elias Smith Journal, March 23, 1860, p. 60, Utah State Historical Society.
59 Hunter: *Brigham Young, The Colonizer*, p. 286.
60 New York *Tribune*, December 4, 1869; New York *Herald*, July 2, 1877.
61 New York *Herald*, April 16, 1877, and June 1, 2, 8, and 18, 1877.
62 Ibid., July 31, 1877.
63 *The New York Times*, June 2, 1877.
64 Brigham Young Will, November 14, 1873, Utah State Historical Society; Probate Records, Estates, Vol. H, pp. 1–365, County and City of Salt Lake, County Clerk's Office, Salt Lake City.
65 *Deseret News*, September 5, 1877.
66 *The New York Times*, September 3, 1877.
67 *Deseret News*, September 5, 1877.
68 *The New York Times*, August 30, 1877.

69 Leonard J. Arrington: "The Settlement of the Brigham Young Estate, 1877–1879," *Pacific Historical Review*, XXI (February 1952), 13–14; Salt Lake *Daily Tribune*, June 15, 1879, and May 8, 1880; *The New York Times*, June 16, 1879.

70 Lee: *Mormonism Unveiled*, pp. 162–4.

71 *The New York Times*, February 13, 1876.

72 New York *Tribune*, September 21, 1877; New York *Herald*, September 16 and December 11, 1877.

73 New York *Sun*, October 11, 1877.

74 *The New York Times*, October 23, 1869.

75 New York *Herald*, May 18, 1877.

76 New York *World*, September 25, 1870.

77 *The New York Times*, June 4, 1877.

78 Rochester *Democrat and Chronicle*, August 10, 1927, in Mormon Collection, King's Daughters Public Library, Palmyra, New York.

79 Newark *Evening News*, September 20 and 21, 1902; *The New York Times*, October 18, 1902, and February 10, 1903.

80 New York *World*, August 31, 1877.

81 Journal of Discourses, XIV, 2.

82 *Deseret News Weekly*, April 7, 1886.

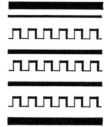

BIBLIOGRAPHY

Manuscripts and Scrapbooks Cited

Alex Badger Papers, Missouri Historical Society, St. Louis.

James Buchanan Papers, Pennsylvania Historical Society, Philadelphia.

Records of the Bureau of Census, Record Group 29, National Archives.

Court of Common Pleas Journal, Geauga County Courthouse, Chardon, Ohio.

Christopher G. Crary Reminiscences, Western Reserve Historical Society, Cleveland, Ohio.

Albert Cumming Papers, Duke University Library, Durham, North Carolina.

Deeds, Monroe County Courthouse, Rochester, New York.

Grenville M. Dodge Papers, Iowa State Department of History and Archives, Des Moines.

Stephen A. Douglas Papers, University of Chicago Library.

William West Durant Papers, Library of Congress.

John I. Ginn Collection, Beinicke Library, Yale University, New Haven, Connecticut.

Caleb Green Diary, Missouri Historical Society, St. Louis.

John J. Hardin Papers, Chicago Historical Society.

Oliver B. Huntington Diary, Utah State Historical Society, Salt Lake City.

Records of the Bureau of Indian Affairs, Record Group 75, National Archives.

Records of the Office of the Secretary of the Interior, Record Group 48, National Archives.

Stanley S. Ivins Papers, Utah State Historical Society, Salt Lake City.

Oliver Jennings Journal, Beinicke Library, Yale University, New Haven, Connecticut.

Journal History, Mormon Church Historian's Office, Salt Lake City, Utah.

General Records of the Department of Justice, Record Group 60, National Archives.

Thomas L. Kane Papers, Beinicke Library, Yale University, New Haven, Connecticut.

Thomas L. Kane Papers, Stanford University Library, Palo Alto, California.

Lee Kohns Memorial Collection, Manuscript Division, New York Public Library.

Marriage Records, Geauga County Courthouse, Chardon, Ohio.

James M. Monroe Diary, Beinicke Library, Yale University, New Haven, Connecticut.

Dale L. Morgan Collection, Utah State Historical Society, Salt Lake City.

Mormon Collection, Bancroft Library, University of California, Berkeley.

Mormon Collection, Beinicke Library, Yale University, New Haven, Connecticut.

Mormon Collection, Chicago Historical Society.

Mormon Collection, King's Daughters Public Library, Palmyra, New York.

Mormon Collection, Missouri Historical Society, St. Louis.

Mormon Collection, University of Chicago Library.

Oliver H. Olney Papers, Beinicke Library, Yale University, New Haven, Connecticut.

James K. Polk Papers, Library of Congress.

Probate Records, County and City of Salt Lake, County Clerk's Office, Salt Lake City, Utah.

John Pulsipher Journal, Utah State Historical Society, Salt Lake City.

Albert P. Rockwood Papers, Beinicke Library, Yale University, New Haven, Connecticut.

Hiram S. Rumfield Papers, Beinicke Library, Yale University, New Haven, Connecticut.

Scrapbook of Newspaper Clippings Relating to the Mormons, Newspaper Annex, New York Public Library.

Thomas C. Sharp Anti-Mormon Papers, Beinicke Library, Yale University, New Haven, Connecticut.

Journal of J. M. Sharpe, Beinicke Library, Yale University, New Haven, Connecticut.

William T. Sherman Papers, Library of Congress.

Luman Andros Shurtliff Diary, Utah State Historical Society, Salt Lake City.

Elias Smith Journal, Utah State Historical Society, Salt Lake City.

Joseph Smith Papers, Utah State Historical Society, Salt Lake City.

William Smith Papers, Utah State Historical Society, Salt Lake City.

Erastus Snow Papers, Utah State Historical Society, Salt Lake City.

Helen and Cecil Snyder Collection, Rare Book Room, New York Public Library.

General Records of the Department of State, Record Group 59, National Archives.

James J. Strang Papers, Beinicke Library, Yale University, New Haven, Connecticut.

Records of the Solicitor of the Treasury, Record Group 206, National Archives.

Charles L. Woodward Papers, Manuscript Division, New York Public Library.

Charles L. Woodward Scrapbooks, Newspaper Annex, New York Public Library.

Brigham Young Papers, Beinicke Library, Yale University, New Haven Connecticut.

Brigham Young Papers, Manuscript Division, New York Public Library.

Brigham Young Papers, Utah State Historical Society, Salt Lake City.

Newspapers Cited

Chicago *Tribune*, 1865–9.

Cincinnati *Commercial*, 1872.

Cincinnati *Daily Gazette*, 1869.

Deseret News, 1850–86.

Deseret News and Telegram, 1962.

Deseret News Weekly, 1886.

Hamilton (Ohio) *Intelligencer*, 1859.

Hancock (Illinois) *Eagle*, 1846.

Honeoye Falls (New York) *Times*, 1922.

Burlington *Iowa Territorial Gazette and Advertiser*, 1846.

Nauvoo (Illinois) *Neighbor*, 1843–4.

Nauvoo *Times and Seasons*, 1840–5.

Newark *Daily Advertiser*, 1844.

Newark *Evening News*, 1902.

New York *Evening Post*, 1866.

New York *Herald*, 1840–80.

New York *Log Cabin*, 1841.

New York *Semi-Weekly Tribune*, 1858, 1870.

New York *Sun*, 1868–89.

The New York Times, 1851–1903.
New York *Tribune*, 1846–89.
New York *World*, 1868–85.
Painesville (Ohio) *Republican*, 1837–8.
Painesville *Telegraph*, 1835–8.
Philadelphia *Morning Post*, 1869.
Sacramento *Daily Union*, 1869.
Salt Lake *Daily Reporter*, 1869.
Salt Lake *Daily Union Vedette*, 1865.
Salt Lake *Tribune*, 1879–87, 1962.
Salt Lake *Valley Tan*, 1858–9.
San Francisco *Daily Alta Californian*, 1851.
San Francisco *Daily Times*, 1869.
Sangamo (Illinois) *Journal*, 1842.
Springfield (Massachusetts) *Republican*, 1866–77.
Springfield *Weekly Republican*, 1865–74.
Warsaw (Illinois) *Message*, 1844.
Warsaw *Signal*, 1841–50.

Public Documents

Document Containing the Correspondence, Orders, &c. in Relation to the Disturbances with the Mormons; and the Evidence Given before the Hon. Austin A. King, Judge of the Fifth Judicial Circuit of the State of Missouri, at the Court-House in Richmond in A Criminal Court of Inquiry, Begun November 12, 1838, on the Trial of Joseph Smith, Jr., and Others, for High Treason and Other Crimes Against the State. Fayette, Missouri: Boon's Lick Democrat; 1841.

In the Circuit Court of the United States, Western District of Missouri . . . The Reorganized Church of Jesus Christ of Latter Day Saints, Complainant, vs. The Church of Christ at Independence, Missouri . . . Respondents, Complainant's Abstract of Pleading and Evidence. Lamoni, Iowa: Herald Publishing House and Bindery; 1893.

U.S. Congress, House of Representatives. *Laws in Utah.* House Report 21, 41 Congress, 2 Session.

U.S. Congress, House of Representatives. *Remonstrance of Smith Et Al., of Covington, Kentucky, Against the Admission of Deseret into the Union.* Miscellaneous Document 43, 31 Congress, 1 Session.

U.S. Congress, House of Representatives. *The Condition of Utah.* House Report 96, 39 Congress, 1 Session.

U.S. Congress, House of Representatives. *The Utah Expedition.* House Document 71, 35 Congress, 1 Session.

Periodicals

Gospel Herald, 1847–8.
Historical Record, 1886–7.
Journal of Discourses, 1854–86.
Latter Day Saints' Messenger and Advocate, 1834–7.
Latter-day Saints' Millennial Star, 1840–1900.
Littel's Living Age, 1854.
Messenger and Advocate of the Church of Christ, 1845.
Seer, 1853.
The Star of the East, 1846.
Tullidge's Quarterly Magazine, 1884.
Utah Genealogical and Historical Magazine, 1910–40.
Utah Historical Quarterly, 1932–68.
Utah Magazine, 1869–70.
Voree Herald, 1846–7.

Articles

Adams, Henry: "Charles Francis Adams Visits the Mormons in 1844," *Proceedings of the Massachusetts Historical Society*, LXVIII (October 1944–May 1947).

Andrus, Hyrum L.: "Joseph Smith and the West," *Brigham Young University Studies*, II (Spring–Summer 1960).

Arrington, Leonard J.: "Mormon Finance and the Utah War," *Utah Historical Quarterly*, XX (July 1952).

———: "Taxable Income in Utah," *Utah Historical Quarterly*, XIV (January 1956).

———: "The Settlement of the Brigham Young Estate, 1877–9," *Pacific Historical Review*, XXI (February 1952).

Bennett, Wallace R.: "The Negro in Utah," *Utah Law Review*, 3 (Spring 1953).

Bitton, Davis: "A Re-evaluation of the 'Turner Thesis and Mormon Beginnings,' " *Utah Historical Quarterly*, 34 (Fall 1966).

Bloomer, Dexter C.: "The Mormons in Iowa," *Annals of Iowa*, 3rd Series, II (January 1897).

"Brigham Young and His Women," *Galaxy*, II (December 1, 1866).

Brooks, Juanita: "Indian Relations on the Mormon Frontier," *Utah Historical Quarterly*, XII (January–April 1944).

Cable, Mary: "She Who Shall Be Nameless," *American Heritage*, XVI (February 1965).

Cannon, M. Hamlin: "A Pension Office Note on Brigham Young's Father," *American Historical Review*, 50 (October 1944).

————: "The English Mormons in America," *American Historical Review*, LVII (July 1952).

Clark, James R.: "The Kingdom of God, The Council of Fifty and the State of Deseret," *Utah Historical Quarterly*, XXVI (April 1958).

Cooley, Everett L.: "Carpetbag Rule—Territorial Government in Utah," *Utah Historical Quarterly*, XXVI (April 1958).

Creer, Leland H.: "The Evolution of Government in Early Utah," *Utah Historical Quarterly*, XXVI (January 1958).

Ely, Richard T.: "Economic Aspects of Mormonism," *Harper's Monthly Magazine*, CVI (April 1903).

Ferris, Mrs. Benjamin G.: "Life Among the Mormons," *Putnam's Monthly*, VI (September 1855).

Gallagher, Ruth A.: "The Handcart Expeditions," *Palimpsest*, III (June 1922).

Gates, Susa Young: "Notes on the Young and Howe Families," *Utah Genealogical and Historical Magazine*, XI (October 1920).

————: "The Young Family," *Utah Genealogical and Historical Magazine*, I (April 1910).

Gates, Susa Young, and Mabel Young Sanborn: "Brigham Young Genealogy," *Utah Genealogical and Historical Magazine*, XI (January 1920).

Golder, Frank A.: "The Purchase of Alaska," *American Historical Review*, XXV (April 1920).

Hansen, Klaus: "The Making of King Strang: A Re-examination," *Michigan History*, 46 (September 1962).

Haven, Charlotte: "A Girl's Letters from Nauvoo," *Overland Monthly*, XVI (December 1890).

Hunter, Milton R.: "The Mormon Corridor," *Pacific Historical Review*, VIII (June 1939).

Ivins, Stanley S.: "A Constitution for Utah," *Utah Historical Quarterly*, XXV (April 1957).

————: "Notes on Mormon Polygamy," *Western Humanities Review*, X (Summer 1956).

Jenkins, Percy W.: "Kiskadden-Slade, Some Historical Incidents Recalled," *Annals of Wyoming*, 21 (January 1949).

Kendall, Henry: "A Week in 'Great Salt Lake City,'" *Hours at Home*, I (May 1865).

Larson, Gustive O.: "The Mormon Reformation," *Utah Historical Quarterly*, XXVI (January 1958).

————: "The Story of the Perpetual Emigrating Fund," *Mississippi Valley Historical Review*, XVIII (September 1931).

————: "Utah and the Civil War," *Utah Historical Quarterly*, 33 (Winter 1965).

Ludlow, Fitz Hugh: "Among the Mormons," *Atlantic Monthly*, XIII (April 1864).

McCarthy, Justin: "Brigham Young," *Galaxy*, IX (February 1870).

Marshall, Charles: "Characteristics of Mormonism," *Transatlantic Magazine*, IV (August 1871).

————: "Salt Lake City and the Valley Settlements," *Fraser's Magazine*, IV (July 1871).

Mauck, Genevieve P.: "Kanesville," *Palimpsest*, XLII (September 1961).

Melville, J. Keith: "Theory and Practice of Church and State during the Brigham Young Era," *Brigham Young University Studies*, III (Autumn 1960).

Monaghan, Jay: "Handcarts on the Overland Trail," *Nebraska History*, XXX (March 1949).

"Mormonism; or, New Mohammedanism in England and America," *Dublin University Magazine*, XXI (March 1843).

Munro, Wilfred H.: "Among the Mormons in the Days of Brigham Young," *Proceedings of the American Antiquarian Society*, New Series, 36 (October 1926).

Petersen, William J.: "Mormons on the March," *Palimpsest*, 27 (May 1946).

Poll, Richard D.: "The Mormon Question Enters National Politics, 1850–1856," *Utah Historical Quarterly*, XXV (April 1957).

"Reminiscences of John R. Young," *Utah Historical Quarterly*, III (July 1930).

Schmidt, Louis B.: "The Miller-Thompson Election Contest," *Iowa Journal of History and Politics*, XII (January 1914).

Shumway, Ernest Widtsoe: "Winter Quarters, Nebraska, 1846–1848," *Nebraska History*, XXXV (June 1954).

Stuart, William M.: "Masonic Pioneers: The Land Called Deseret," *The Master Mason*, IV (February 1927).

Taneyhill, R. H.: "The Leatherwood God. An Account of the Appearance and Pretensions of Joseph C. Dylks in Eastern Ohio in 1828," *Ohio Valley Historical Series*, Miscellanies No. 7, Part 3 (1870).

"The History and Journal of the Life and Travels of Jesse W. Crosby," *Annals of Wyoming*, II (July 1939).

"The Mormons, Who and What They Are," *Phrenological Journal*, 52 (January 1871).

Walkup, Fairfax Proudfit: "The Sunbonnet Woman: Fashions in Utah Pioneer Costume," *Utah Humanities Review*, I (July 1947).

Autobiographies, Memoirs, and Published Collections of Letters and Documents

A Series of Instructions and Remarks by President Young at A Special Council, Tabernacle, March 21, 1858. N.p.: n.p.; n.d.

Barnum, P. T.: *Struggles and Triumphs; or, Forty Years' Recollections.* Buffalo: Warren, Johnson & Co.; 1872.

Bennett, John C.: *The History of the Saints, or An Exposé of Joe Smith and Mormonism.* Boston: Leland & Whiting; 1842.

Bird, George Robert: *Tenderfoot Days in Territorial Utah.* Boston: Gorham Press; 1918.

Bowles, Samuel: *Our New West.* Hartford: Hartford Publishing Company; 1869.

Brooks, Juanita (ed.): *On the Mormon Frontier, The Diary of Hosea Stout, 1844–1861.* 2 vols. Salt Lake City: University of Utah Press and the Utah State Historical Society; 1964.

Cake, Lu B.: *Peepstone Joe and the Peck Manuscript.* New York: L.B. Cake; 1899.

Carvalho, S. N.: *Incidents of Travel and Adventure in the Far West.* New York: Derby & Jackson; 1857.

Chandless, William: *A Visit to Salt Lake.* London: Smith, Elder and Co.; 1857.

William Clayton's Journal, A Daily Record of the Journey of the Original Company of 'Mormon' Pioneers from Nauvoo, Illinois, to the Valley of the Great Salt Lake. Salt Lake City: Deseret News; 1921.

Cleland, Robert Glass, and Juanita Brooks (eds.): *A Mormon Chronicle, The Diaries of John D. Lee, 1848–1876.* 2 vols. San Marino: Huntington Library; 1955.

Codman, John: *The Mormon Country, A Summer with the 'Latter-Day' Saints.* New York: United States Publishing Company; 1874.

Correspondence of Bishop George Miller with the Northern Islander, From His First Acquaintance with Mormonism Up to Near the Close of His Life. Burlington, Wisconsin: Wingfield Watson; 1916.

Corrill, John: *Brief History of the Church of Christ of Latter Day Saints (Commonly Called Mormons); Including An Account of Their Doctrine and Discipline; With the Reasons of the Author for Leaving the Church.* St. Louis: The Author; 1839.

De Leon, Edwin: *Thirty Years of My Life on Three Continents.* 2 vols. London: Ward and Downey; 1890.

Dixon, William Hepworth: *New America.* 2 vols. London: Hurst and Blackett; 1867.

————: *White Conquest.* 2 vols. London: Chatto and Windus; 1876.

Egan, Howard: *Pioneering the West, 1846 to 1878.* Richmond, Utah: Howard R. Egan Estate; 1917.

Esshom, Frank: *Pioneers and Prominent Men of Utah*. Salt Lake City: Utah Pioneers Book Publishing Company; 1913.

Ferris, Mrs. Benjamin: *The Mormons at Home, With Some Incidents of Travel from Missouri to California, 1852–1853*. New York: Dix & Edwards; 1856.

Ferris, Benjamin G.: *Utah and the Mormons*. New York: Harper & Brothers; 1854.

Fragments of Experience. Salt Lake City: Juvenile Instructor Office; 1882.

Franklin, John Benjamin: *The Horrors of Mormonism*. London: n.p.; 1858.

Gibson, Walter Murray: *The Prisoner of Weltevreden; and A Glance at the East Indian Archipelago*. New York: J. C. Riker; 1855.

Greeley, Horace: *An Overland Journey from New York to San Francisco in the Summer of 1859*. New York: C. M. Saxton, Barker & Co.; 1860.

Gunnison, John W.: *The Mormons, or Latter-Day Saints*. Philadelphia: J. B. Lippincott & Co.; 1852.

Hall, William: *The Abominations of Mormonism Exposed, Containing Many Facts and Doctrines Concerning That Singular People during Seven Years Membership with Them; from 1840 to 1847*. Cincinnati: I. Hart; 1852.

Harris, Sarah Hollister: *An Unwritten Chapter of Salt Lake, 1851–1901*. New York: Printed Privately; 1901.

Hawthornthwaite, Samuel: *Mr. Hawthornthwaite's Adventures Among the Mormons As An Elder during Eight Years*. Manchester: The Author; 1857.

Hickman, Bill: *Brigham's Destroying Angel*. Salt Lake City: Shepard Publishing Company; 1904.

Howe, Eber D.: *Autobiography and Recollections of A Pioneer Printer*. Painesville: Telegraph Steam Printing House; 1878.

Hyde, John, Jr.: *Mormonism, Its Leaders and Designs*. New York: W.P. Fetridge & Company; 1857.

Journal of Heber C. Kimball. Nauvoo: Robinson & Smith; 1840.

Kelly, Charles (ed.): *Journals of John D. Lee, 1846–1847 and 1859*. Salt Lake City: Western Publishing Company; 1938.

Lee, John D.: *Mormonism Unveiled*. St. Louis: Excelsior Publishing Company; 1891.

Lewis, Catherine: *Narrative of Some of the Proceedings of the Mormons; Giving An Account of Their Iniquities, With Particulars Concerning the Training of the Indians by Them, Description of the Mode of the Endowment, Plurality of Wives, &c., &c.* Lynn, Massachusetts: The Author; 1848.

Ludlow, Fitz Hugh: *The Heart of the Continent*. New York: Hurd and Houghton; 1870.

Lundwall, Nels B. (ed.): *Discourses of Master Minds*. Salt Lake City: Deseret News; 194?.

Nelson, John Y.: *Fifty Years on the Trail*. New York: Frederick Warne & Company; 1889.

Pratt, Parley P.: *Autobiography*. New York: Russell Brothers; 1874.

Remy, Jules, and Julius Brenchley: *A Journey to Great-Salt-Lake City*. 2 vols. London: W. Jeffs; 1861.

Richardson, Albert D.: *Beyond the Mississippi, From the Great River to the Great Ocean*. Hartford: American Publishing Company; 1867.

Roberts, Brigham H. (ed.): *History of the Church of Jesus Christ of Latter-Day Saints*. 7 vols. Salt Lake City: Deseret News; 1948.

Sanborn, Mabel Young: *The Brigham Young Family*. N.p.: n.p.; n.d.

Slater, Nelson (compiler): *Fruits of Mormonism, or A Fair and Candid Statement of Facts Illustrative of Mormon Principles, Mormon Policy, and Mormon Character, By More Than Forty Eye-Witnesses*. Coloma, California: Harmon & Springer; 1851.

Smith, Mary Ettie V.: *Mormonism, Its Rise, Progress, and Present Condition*. Hartford: Belknap & Bliss; 1870.

Stegner, Wallace: *The Gathering of Zion, The Story of the Mormon Trail*. New York, Toronto, London: McGraw-Hill Book Company; 1964.

Stenhouse, Fanny: *Exposé of Polygamy in Utah*. New York: American News Company; 1872.

————: *"Tell It All," The Story of A Life's Experience in Mormonism*. Hartford: A. D. Worthington & Co.; 1874.

Thayer, James B.: *A Western Journey with Mr. Emerson*. Boston: Little, Brown and Company; 1884.

The Mormon Question, Being A Speech of Vice-President Schuyler Colfax at Salt Lake City. Salt Lake City: Deseret News Office; 1870.

The Mountain Meadows Massacre, With the Life, Confession and Execution of John D. Lee, The Mormon. Philadelphia: Barclay & Co.; 1877.

Townsend, George Alfred: *The Mormon Trials at Salt Lake City*. New York: American News Company; 1871.

Utah and the Mormons. Speech of Hon. John Cradlebaugh of Nevada, on the Admission of Utah As A State. Delivered in the House of Representatives, February 7, 1863. N.p.: n.p.; n.d.

Watson, Wingfield (ed.): *The Revelations of James J. Strang*. Boyne, Michigan: n.p.; 1885.

Woodward, Charles L.: *Bibliothica* [sic] *Scallawagiana*. New York: n.p.; 1880.

Young, Ann Eliza: *Wife No. 19, or the Story of A Life in Bondage*. Hartford: Dustin, Gilman & Company; 1876.

Monographs, Biographies, and Novels

Allen, Edward J.: *The Second United Order among the Mormons.* New York: Columbia University Press; 1936.

Alter, J. Cecil: *Jim Bridger.* Norman: University of Oklahoma Press; 1962.

Anderson, Nels: *Desert Saints, The Mormon Frontier in Utah.* Chicago: University of Chicago Press; 1944.

Arrington, Leonard J.: *Great Basin Kingdom, An Economic History of the Latter-day Saints, 1830–1900.* Lincoln: University of Nebraska Press; 1966.

Beadle, John H.: *Life in Utah.* Philadelphia: National Publishing Company; 1870.

————: *Western Wilds.* Cincinnati: Jones Brothers; 1877.

Billington, Ray Allen: *The Far Western Frontier, 1830–1860.* New York: Harper & Row; 1956.

Bonwick, James: *The Mormons and the Silver Mines.* London: Hodder and Stoughton; 1872.

Bowes, John: *Mormonism Exposed.* London: R. Bulman; 1854.

Brodie, Fawn M.: *No Man Knows My History, The Life of Joseph Smith, The Mormon Prophet.* New York: Alfred A. Knopf; 1945.

Brooks, Juanita: *John Doyle Lee, Zealot—Pioneer Builder—Scapegoat.* Glendale, California: Arthur H. Clark; 1962.

————: *The Mountain Meadows Massacre.* Norman: University of Oklahoma Press; 1962.

Brown, Benjamin: *Testimonies to the Truth, A Record of Manifestations of the Power of God, Miraculous and Providential.* Liverpool: S. W. Richards; 1853.

Burton, Richard F.: *The City of the Saints.* New York: Alfred A. Knopf; 1963.

Caesar, Gene: *King of the Mountain Men, The Life of Jim Bridger.* New York: E. P. Dutton; 1961.

Cannon, Frank J., and George L. Knapp: *Brigham Young and His Mormon Empire.* New York: Fleming H. Revell; 1913.

Carmichael, Sarah E.: *Poems.* San Francisco: Towne and Bacon; 1866.

Clark, John A.: *Gleanings by the Way.* Philadelphia: W.J. & J.K. Simon; 1842.

Cocheron, Augusta Joyce: *Representative Women of Deseret.* Salt Lake City: J.C. Graham & Co.; 1884.

Commager, Henry Steele: *The American Mind.* New Haven: Yale University Press; 1950.

Conover, George S., and Lewis Cass Aldrich: *History of Ontario County, New York.* Syracuse: D. Mason & Co.; 1893.

Conybeare, William J.: *Mormonism.* London: Longman, Brown, Green, and Longmans; 1854.

Crockwell, James H.: *Pictures and Biographies of Brigham Young and His Wives*. Salt Lake City: James H. Crockwell; n.d.

De Voto, Bernard: *Across the Wide Missouri*. Boston: Houghton Mifflin Company; 1964.

———: *The Year of Decision, 1846*. Boston: Little, Brown and Company; 1943.

Doyle, Arthur Conan: *A Study in Scarlet and The Sign of the Four*. New York: Harper & Brothers; 1904.

Fife, Austin and Alta: *Saints of Sage & Saddle, Folklore Among the Mormons*. Bloomington: Indiana University Press; 1956.

Flanders, Robert Bruce: *Nauvoo, Kingdom on the Mississippi*. Urbana: University of Illinois Press; 1965.

Foreman, Grant: *Marcy & the Gold Seekers, The Journal of Captain R. B. Marcy, with An Account of the Gold Rush Over the Southern Route*. Norman: University of Oklahoma Press; 1939.

Froiseth, Jennie Anderson (ed.): *The Women of Mormondom*. Detroit: C.G.G. Paine; 1872.

Furniss, Norman: *The Mormon Conflict, 1850–1859*. New Haven and London: Yale University Press; 1960.

Goodwin, Samuel H.: *Mormonism and Masonry*. Washington: Masonic Service Association; 1924.

Grant, Jedediah M.: *A Collection of Facts, Relative to the Course Taken by Elder Sidney Rigdon, in the States of Ohio, Missouri, Illinois and Pennsylvania*. Philadelphia: Brown, Bicking & Guilbert; 1844.

Hedrick, Granville: *The Spiritual Wife System Proven False and the True Order of Church Discipline*. Bloomington, Illinois: W. E. Footel Power Press; 1856.

Here is Lake County, Ohio. Cleveland: Howard Allen; 1964.

History of Geauga and Lake Counties, Ohio. Philadelphia: Williams Brothers; 1878.

History of Pottawattamie County, Iowa. Chicago: O.L. Baskin & Co.; 1883.

History of Tioga, Chemung, Tompkins, and Schuyler Counties, New York. Philadelphia: Everts & Ensign; 1879.

Howard, Robert West: *The Great Iron Trail, The Story of the First Transcontinental Railroad*. New York: G.P. Putnam's Sons; 1962.

Howe, Eber D.: *Mormonism Unvailed, or, A Faithful Account of That Singular Imposition and Delusion from Its Rise to the Present Time*. Painesville, Ohio: The Author; 1834.

Hunter, Milton R.: *Brigham Young, The Colonizer*. Salt Lake City: Deseret News; 1940.

Jacob, Udney Hay (An Israelite and A Shepherd of Israel): *An Extract from A Manuscript Entitled the Peace Maker, or the Doctrines of the Millennium, Being A Treatise on Religion and Jurisprudence, Or A New System of Religion and Politicks*. Nauvoo: J. Smith, Printer; 1842.

JUAB (Private in Israel): *The Gospel Concerning Church & State*. Salt Lake City: n.p.; 1897.

Kelly, Charles, and Hoffman Birney: *Holy Murder, The Story of Porter Rockwell*. New York: Milton Balch and Company; 1934.

Kennedy, James H.: *The Early Days of Mormonism, Palmyra, Kirtland, and Nauvoo*. New York: Charles Scribner's Sons; 1888.

Kuykendall, Ralph S.: *The Hawaii Kingdom, 1854–1874, Twenty Critical Years*. Honolulu: University of Hawaii Press; 1953.

Lindsay, John S.: *The Mormons and the Theatre*. Salt Lake City: Century Printing Co.; 1905.

McCarthy, Justin: *Reminiscences*. 2 vols. New York and London: Harper & Brothers; 1899.

McIntosh, W. H.: *History of Ontario Co., New York*. Philadelphia: Everts, Ensign & Everts; 1876.

Meyer, Eduard: *Ursprung und Geschichte der Mormonen*. Halle: Max Niemeyer; 1912.

Miller, Reuben: *James J. Strang Weighed in the Balance of Truth, and Found Wanting. His Claims as First President of the Melchizedek Priesthood Refuted*. Burlington, Wisconsin: n.p.; September 1846.

Mulder, William: *Homeward to Zion, The Mormon Migration from Scandinavia*. Minneapolis: University of Minnesota Press; 1957.

Nibley, Preston: *Brigham Young, The Man and His Work*. Independence: Zion's Printing & Publishing Company; 1936.

Nichols, Roy F.: *The Disruption of American Democracy*. New York: Collier Books; 1962.

O'Dea, Thomas F.: *The Mormons*. Chicago: University of Chicago Press; 1957.

Pardoe, T. Earl: *Lorin Farr, Pioneer*. Provo: Brigham Young University Press; 1953.

Penrose, Charles W.: *Blood Atonement, As Taught by Leading Elders of the Church of Jesus Christ of Latter-day Saints*. Salt Lake City: Juvenile Instructor Office; 1884.

Pratt, Orson: *The Kingdom of God, Part I, No. 2*. Liverpool: S.W. Richards; October 31, 1848.

———: *The Kingdom of God, Part II*. Liverpool: R. James; 1848.

———: *The Kingdom of God, Part III*. Liverpool: R. James; January 14, 1849.

Quaife, Milo M.: *The Kingdom of Saint James, A Narrative of the Mormons*. New Haven: Yale University Press; 1930.

Riley, I. Woodbridge: *The Founder of Mormonism*. New York: Dodd, Mead & Company; 1902.

Roberts, Brigham H.: *Plural Marriage, The Mormon Marriage System*. Salt Lake City: Truth Publishing Company; n.d.

———: *The Missouri Persecutions*. Salt Lake City: George Q. Cannon; 1900.

————: *The Rise and Fall of Nauvoo.* Salt Lake City: Deseret News; 1900.

Saintly Falsity, On Questions Affecting Their Fanatical Tenets and Practices. Salt Lake City: n.p.; 1885.

Schindler, Harold: *Orrin Porter Rockwell, Man of God, Son of Thunder.* Salt Lake City: University of Utah Press; 1966.

Seward, Frederick W.: *Seward at Washington, As Senator and Secretary of State.* New York: Derby and Miller; 1891.

Smith, Joseph, and Heman Smith: *History of the Church of Jesus Christ of Latter Day Saints.* 4 vols. Lamoni, Iowa: Reorganized Church; 1897–1908.

Smith, Joseph F., Jr.: *Blood Atonement and the Origin of Plural Marriage.* Salt Lake City: Deseret News; 1905.

Smith, Lucy: *Biographical Sketches of Joseph Smith, the Prophet, and His Progenitures for Many Generations.* Liverpool: Orson Pratt; 1853.

Smucker, Samuel M.: *The Religious, Social, and Political History of the Mormons.* New York: Miller, Orton & Co.; 1857.

Snow, Eliza R.: *Biography and Family Record of Lorenzo Snow.* Salt Lake City: Deseret News Company; 1884.

Spencer, Clarissa Young, with Mabel Harmer: *One Who Was Valiant.* Caldwell, Idaho: Caxton Publishers; 1940.

Stanley, Reva: *A Biography of Parley P. Pratt, The Archer of Paradise.* Caldwell, Idaho: Caxton Publishers; 1937.

Stegner, Wallace: *Mormon Country.* New York: Duell, Sloan & Pearce; 1942.

Stenhouse, Thomas B.: *The Rocky Mountain Saints.* London: Ward, Lock and Tyler; 1874.

Stewart, F. L.: *Exploding the Myth about Joseph Smith, The Mormon Prophet.* New York: House of Stewart; 1967.

Taylor, John: *The Government of God.* Liverpool: S.W. Richards; 1852.

The Inside of Mormonism. Salt Lake City: Utah Americans; 1893.

The Mormon Conspiracy to Establish An Independent Empire to Be Called the Kingdom of God on Earth. The Conspiracy Exposed by the Writings, Sermons and Legislative Acts of the Prophets and Apostles of the Church. Salt Lake City: The Tribune Company; 1886?.

The Mormons, or Knavery Exposed. Philadelphia: E. G. Lee; 1841.

Three Nights' Public Discussion between the Revds. C. W. Cleeve, James Robertson, and Philip Cater, and Elder John Taylor of the Church of Jesus Christ of Latter-day Saints at Boulogne-Sur-Mer, France. Liverpool: John Taylor; 1850.

Thurston, Lorrin A.: *Memoirs of the Hawaiian Revolution.* Honolulu: Advertiser Publishing Company; 1936.

Tucker, Pomeroy: *Origin, Rise, and Progress of Mormonism.* New York: D. Appleton and Company; 1867.

Tullidge, Edward W.: *History of Salt Lake City.* Salt Lake City: Star Printing Company; 1886.

————: *The Women of Mormondom.* New York: n.p.; 1877.

Turner, J. B.: *Mormonism in All Ages; Or The Rise, Progress, and Causes of Mormonism.* New York: Platt & Peters; 1842.

Twain, Mark: *Roughing It.* Hartford: American Publishing Company; 1875.

Tyler, Alice Felt: *Freedom's Ferment, Phases of American Social History from the Colonial Period to the Outbreak of the Civil War.* New York, Evanston, and London: Harper & Row; 1962.

Van Deusen, Maria and Increase M.: *A Dialogue between Adam and Eve, the Lord and the Devil, Called the Endowment. As Was Enacted by Twelve or Fifteen Thousand, In Secret, In the Nauvoo Temple, Said to Be Revealed from God As A Reward for Building That Splendid Edifice, and the Express Object for Which It Was Built.* Albany: C. Killmer; 1847.

Wait, Mary Van Sickle: *Brigham Young in Cayuga County, 1813–1829.* Ithaca: DeWitt Historical Society of Tompkins Co.; 1964.

Waite, Catharine V.: *The Mormon Prophet and His Harem.* Cambridge: Riverside Press; 1866.

Wakeley, Arthur C.: *Omaha, The Gate City, and Douglas County, Nebraska.* Chicago: S.J. Clarke; 1917.

Wallace, Irving: *The Twenty-seventh Wife.* New York: Simon and Schuster; 1961.

Waters, William E.: *Life Among the Mormons.* New York: Moorhead, Simpson & Bond; 1868.

Werner, M. R.: *Brigham Young.* New York: Harcourt, Brace and Company; 1925.

Whitney, Helen Mar: *Plural Marriage As Taught By the Prophet Joseph.* Salt Lake City: Juvenile Instructor Office; 1882.

Whitney, Orson F.: *Life of Heber C. Kimball.* Salt Lake City: Kimball Family; 1888.

Wyl, Wilhelm: *Mormon Portraits, or The Truth About the Mormon Leaders from 1830 to 1886.* Salt Lake City: Tribune Printing and Publishing Company; 1886.

Young, Kimball: *Isn't One Wife Enough?* New York: Henry Holt; 1954.

Bibliography

INDEX

A NOTE ABOUT THE AUTHOR

Stanley P. Hirshson was born in 1928 in Brooklyn, New York. He received his B.A. degree from Rutgers University and his M.A. and Ph.D. from Columbia. Since 1963 he has taught at Queens College of the City University of New York, where he is now Professor of History.

In 1962–3 he received a fellowship from the American Council of Learned Societies and in 1966–7 held a Guggenheim Grant. He is the author of *Farewell to the Bloody Shirt* (1962) and *Grenville M. Dodge* (1967).

A NOTE ON THE TYPE

The text of this book was set on the Linotype in a face called Times Roman, designed by Stanley Morison for *The Times* (London) and first introduced by that newspaper in 1932.

Among typographers and designers of the twentieth century, Stanley Morison has been a strong forming influence, as typographical adviser to the English Monotype Corporation, as a director of two distinguished English publishing houses, and as a writer of sensibility, erudition, and keen practical sense.